Marianne Sawicki

The Gospel in History

Portrait of a Teaching Church: The Origins of Christian Education

Paulist Press
New York/Mahwah

The Publisher gratefully acknowledges excerpts reprinted from M. L. W. Laistner: *Christianity and Pagan Culture in the Later Roman Empire.* Copyright 1951 by Cornell University. Used by permission of the publisher, Cornell University Press.

Excerpts from *The Nicene and Post-Nicene Fathers (VII)*, Wm. B. Eerdmans Publishing Co. Used by permission.

Excerpts from *The Age of Faith* by Will Durant, copyright © 1950, 1977 are reprinted by permission of Simon & Schuster, Inc.

Library of Congress Cataloging-in-Publication Data

Sawicki, Marianne.
    The gospel in history : portrait of a teaching church : the origins of Christian education / Marianne Sawicki.
       p.   cm.
    Includes bibliographies and index.
    ISBN 0-8091-2954-X (pbk.) : $14.95
    1. Church history.   2. Church—Teaching office—History.
3. Christian education—History.   I. Title.
BR148.S34   1988
270—dc19

Published by Paulist Press
997 Macarthur Boulevard
Mahwah, N.J. 07430

Printed and bound in the United States of America

Contents

In memory of
Mary B. Keelan Nelson
and
Alexandra Teodorowicz-Sawicka

Foreword

Would it be ungracious of me to begin by saying that Professor Marianne Sawicki is sneaky? Suggesting that the author is somehow underhanded or devious seems to be a lapse of etiquette if not actual slander. The publisher invited me to write this Foreword; now to begin this way makes it sound as if I have just entered a house and immediately criticized those who host me. Yet it should be clear in a moment that in this case the concept of sneakiness is designed to turn to author Sawicki's advantage.

My specific charge is that she is a smuggler. Now, there is smuggling and then there is smuggling. If one brings illegal goods into a country, that is reprehensible and dangerous. Yet if one brings a birthday present to a party, a present drably wrapped, and then opens it only to reveal a splendid gift, such smuggling is honorable, even delightful. Professor Sawicki has done that kind of smuggling, and her sneakiness should merit praise.

Her package, under whatever label, suggests "A History of Christian Education." The reference to "Teaching" in the very subtitle could lead us or mislead us into thinking that's all this book is. Now, histories of Christianity are needed, are conceivably interesting, could perform a good service. But the genre as such, like the package described above, is usually seen as drab because it is drab. Some specialists must read such histories, and some authors are gifted enough to transcend the limits of conventional expectation about such books. But, as someone who has long known he ought to know something about the subject and who has sampled the occasional examples of such histories, I have to admit to acute cases of boredom, profound experiences of ennui.

What Sawicki has done in a book that suggests such a history of Christian education is to smuggle in a history of the whole church. But to speak in those terms may also sound alienating to many potential readers. Perhaps they were conditioned back in high school to despise history. Names, dates, incidents kept flying past one as a teacher droned on about them, or lay inertly on a page while comic books or exciting science texts waited for attention. The past was past, was even dead, a loss, a burden, a set of bad examples and, once again, boring.

1

History, church history, does not have to be boring. It is a story about people like ourselves who, though they lived in other times and other places, have something to tell us. They are like us, that is, in that they were people who had to make sense of a world in which hate and betrayal and death were as common as love and trust and life. These people also can quicken us because they are unlike us. Someone has said that "the past is a foreign country; they do things differently there." But in their very differences they can tantalize us to think about who we are, what our times mean, and how we can help shape a future. Sawicki knows enough about the "likenesses" and the "unlikenesses" to win and keep holding attention.

A general history of the church rarely satisfies unless we bring some question to it, unless the author has some special angle on events of the past, some extraordinary interest in telling a story. We would not ordinarily like to be stopped in the street by someone who is senile, deep into anecdotage, who would regale us with rambling and unconnected stories about their past. We might in charity be kind enough to listen for a moment, but would then hurry on because we have our own lives to live. Not all stories affect us directly.

What if someone comes along and says, "We are beginning to fall in love. But first I better tell you who I am, and what to expect of me, because I. . . . " We are ready to give that person our hours and our attention. Or: "All these years you thought we were your blood parents. But now we are going to tell you that you were adopted, and when you hear the story of your real parents, we think you will both love us more and understand yourself better. Here is how it all came about. . . . " And we would be glued in attention. Sawicki convinces us that the story of the Christian church is such a story, one that tells us by whom we are loved, who our parent is, all about the family to which we belong. She gets and holds our attention.

I implied a moment ago that history in general may not move us the way history with a special angle does. This book makes that clear once again. Instead of being a church history without a point, it is pointed about seeing the Christian movement as "a teaching church." I suppose you could pull at almost any strand of Christian history and find something of interest. To take a wild example: picture the history of the church from the viewpoint of roofing technology. Why might we find rockhewn catacomb roofs sheltering a few early Christians, or the roofs of caves covering Ethiopian Copts in their desert environs? What does it tell us about some people of the past if we see a cathedral roof or a humble thatch over a chapel? We could learn much about Christian history through a well-told story of Christian music, or art, or worship, or ideals of parenting, or health care.

Here the subject is teaching. In my first reading of the first two chapters I did not think the book would live up to its billing. In those chapters the author had to tell us what story meant, what symbols are; she had to clear up some misconceptions and make clear how she was going to use terms. From those early chapters we learn what the footnotes keep revealing: that she is uncommonly well read in the technical literature, so well read that she is allowed to speak in simpler language than some of that literature permits itself to use. Once we know what to expect, Sawicki keeps offering the unexpected.

I didn't expect, for example, to start thinking about fourth century figures like John Chrysostom sounding "almost modern" about behavior modification, or perhaps getting my attention as Chrysostom tells parents why and how to keep their children from X-rated entertainment. I would not have expected to take lessons from Cyril, from popes of long ago, from the Catholic reformers as well as the Protestant. (Let me hasten to say that some of the lessons are negative, not positive.)

I did expect, though maybe not all readers might, to find her saying that there were no good old days, no Golden Ages, when the church found it easy to teach. Anyone who looks out at small, apathetic adult education classes, inattentive confirmands, unruly and distracted Sunday school students, is tempted to think that it must have been nice to be a teacher in a teaching church back then, before television and the lures of the weekend and public education and the disintegration of the family. Here we learn that there were always apathetic and distracted people. Yet the church found ways to teach. It had to. Without teaching there would have been no church into our own time.

The author ends her story abruptly in the nineteenth century. There was no need for her to give us a moving picture of all centuries; instead she chose the snapshot method for a half dozen of them. That left out the twentieth century. It may be unnecessary for that story to be told in a book like this. Parts of the story may be familiar. Others are hard to gather, to formulate, to tell. Most of all, as a little conclusion suggests, our generation is "making" that history. This book helps us know who we in this generation are and hints at what we might do about a plot as old as the Bible, which is an unfinished book in whose plot we are. This is, then, our story, to be put to work in our lives in the years ahead.

Martin E. Marty
The University of Chicago

Chapter One

Introduction

Gospel means "good news": the glad tidings of the wonderful things that God has done for us in and through Jesus Christ. The gospel narratives are stories about God's works. Gospel *is* history, but it also *has* a history of its own. As the gospel story was resounding through the last twenty centuries of human history, it was fashioning a church in every era and every culture it touched. The churches which arose to hear and repeat the gospel became a part of the gospel's own story and, eventually, a part of the gospel itself.

That's where this book comes in. The book you are holding is one which aims to tell *the story of* the story that made us who we are.

A great deal of this book consists in historical narrative, that is, church history—a kind of biography of the church. But this book is also a *portrait* of the church. The narrative lines come together into a theological sketch of what the church truly is as it receives and replicates the gospel's message. To draw such a portrait is to discern the identity of the church. We do this with brushstrokes of several kinds. Historically, we look for certain features that always are present in every era of the church's life. (The activity of teaching will be one of the most important of these features.) Theologically, we examine the way in which these features mesh with one another and with the past, in hopes of discovering the outlines of the future church that we must build. Portraiture of the teaching church depicts not only what the church has been, but also what it will become as God's reign draws ever nearer.[1]

Therefore, this book is a work of theory as much as of history. The theory makes it possible to uncover the history, but the history in its turn provides the basis for theory. The gospel's story is not yet completed. Moreover, in this book we can tell only *a part of* that part of the story that already has happened. We will focus only on Western civilization, and particularly North America, while keeping in mind that ours is only a part of the history of the gospel.

Many other writers have told parts of this story before. They have told it from the particular vantage points where they found themselves, within or without the church. There have been histories of the church, and of the priesthood, and of the mass, and of religious life. There have been histories of education and of spirituality and of women and of ministry itself.

But this book's distinctive angle on the gospel story's story is one that has been less common. The focus here will be on the telling of the story itself. How did the gospel get itself told and retold in successive generations? How did that telling transform the quality of human living for the ordinary people? Who were the people who became tellers of the gospel story—or ministers of the word—and why? What means did they devise to carry out this ministry?

Insofar as it is possible, this book seeks to follow the "low road" of the gospel's travel from mouth to mouth, heart to heart, among ordinary Christians. The writings of learned scholars and the achievements of ecclesiastical administrators are regarded as secondary to this grass-roots communications process. It is hoped that "ordinary" Christians today will benefit from this recovery of their heritage.

THE GOSPEL, GOD'S WORD

To track the gospel through the last twenty centuries, we first need a good idea of the kind of phenomenon or event which we will be looking for. The gospel is good news, a story, a message. That is to say, it is an effective communication. It is a message that has an impact, and interestingly, part of its impact is that it gets itself repeated. It "snowballs." Human being is a being-together, a "we," which means it is a continuous activity of communication. As an infectious story, the gospel message penetrates human being by changing the deepest structures of human living, so that human existence, and human being itself, are never the same again. This takes place in certain highly distinctive ways. Certain human activities need to be coordinated so that the way is open for God's transforming grace to act through the communication of this gospel message.

The style of investigation which will be employed in this book may be termed phenomenological. Phenomenology is a kind of description and analysis which focuses upon the impact which realities have upon human consciousness. The method is "subjective" in the literal sense of the term: its starting point is the human subject. Subjectivity is the quality of human beings which distinguishes them from things. We *know* things; they don't know us. In knowing, we also know that we know. In knowing, we come into possession of ourselves as knowers.

What is interesting about all of this is that it takes place among persons, as well as between individual persons and things. *Inter*subjectivity is the quality of being human together in some sort of group, and knowing that the group itself also has being—a being different from the being of things, and also different from the individual subjectivities who enact the group.

Communication, and in particular the telling of stories, is what sustains both subjectivity and intersubjectivity. It is what creates and maintains both the personal being of persons and the social being of groups. The "phenomena" in which this creation and maintenance occur are the events which make up the field which phenomenology studies.[2]

Yet we regard the gospel as God's word, God's communication. It is a supremely powerful revelation of God's loving intention toward human beings. Paradoxically, the power of God's word is also its weakness. God's word needs help: God's word needs ministers. This need will become apparent if one reflects on the fact that the terms "word of God" and "revelation" usually refer to three different realities: a book, a person, and a process.

The book which we call the word of God is the Bible, an ancient text compiled by two related religious communities. This book did not reach the form in which Christians cherish it today until sometime in the third century of the common era. It is really a book of books, and each book records something of a relationship, an experience with God by people who stand in our past. The authors who wrote down the Bible's books, most of them anonymously, evidently thought that they had received something so special and precious in their relations with God that it must be handed down to future generations. Their gratitude and reverence for the gift of contact with God—even when that contact seemed to have a distincly negative flavor—made them want to preserve it in some way.

Many of the Bible's books record contact with God through historical events; subsequent reflection upon the events discerned in them a pattern of God's care for the people. In other books, this contact—which we call "revelation"—seems to have been conveyed in an experience of outrage at the dissonance between evil encountered in the world and the inherent goodness of the creator. Sometimes God's presence and action seemed localized in a place, like a mountain or the Temple, or in the Law, or in the whole people of Israel, or in the person of Jesus, or in the evangelizing activities of Christian missionaries. Each of these was a window onto the provident goodness of God, which was without limit.

In time, a curious thing happened to this book that told about occasions of God's presence and action in the human world. It, too, became one of the locations in the world where God's nearness and power could be especially felt. It came to be regarded as "the word of God," a very special communication from God.

Today this book is treasured by Christians because we find in it a means of contact and communication with the person whom one of the biblical authors calls "the word of God," Jesus Christ. The author of the Gospel of John writes, "In the beginning was the word, and the word was with God, and the word was God." This eternal reality is God personally addressing creation and creation's masterpiece, human beings, with a message of love which expresses absolutely all that God is and wants. God's Word holds back nothing of God. In the cries of the baby from Bethlehem's manger, in the tales of the rabbi on Galilee's hillside, in the screams of the convict at Calvary's gallows, we hear it pronouncing God's longing for a human response. Jesus is God's word taking flesh in an invitation which cannot escape our notice.

But Jesus is also our answer to God's invitation. Jesus is the human word of acceptance of everything that God is and wants. His life is the "Paschal Mystery": the prime pattern of the divine call and the human response, inseparably joined. To pray "in the name of Jesus" means to enter into the back-and-forth exchange, the rhythm of relationship with God, that made up the inner core of the human being of Jesus. The gospel message is "good news" because it tells us that we are welcomed into that relationship between Jesus and the One whom he calls Father. We are at home there: it is the place where we belong, and have belonged since before we even came into existence.

The concept "God's word," then, points both to the Bible and to Jesus Christ. But there is also a third meaning to the term. That antique book, and that historical individual who lived and died twenty centuries ago, do indeed present communication from God to human beings; but such communication is not confined to them. We think of God's Word also as a process which continues every day in every human life. For a communication to be successful, it must be received. God said everything there was to say in Jesus; but God's communication cannot be completed until the last human being in history has responded to God's invitation. In this sense, the Bible is still becoming the word of God for each person who picks it up and receives its message. The Dogmatic Constitution on Divine Revelation of the Second Vatican Council notes that:

> . . . there is a growth in the understanding of the realities and the words which have been handed down. This happens through the contemplation and study made by believers, who treasure these things in their hearts (cf. Lk 2:19, 51), through the intimate understanding of spiritual things they experience, and through the preaching of those who have received through episcopal succession the sure gift of truth. For, as the centuries succeed

one another, the church constantly moves forward toward the fullness of divine truth until the words of God reach their complete fulfillment in it.[3]

Jesus became God's effective word as he humanly came to know and respond in love to his Father and drew others to follow. The notion that Jesus "became" God's son is known technically as "ascending christology" or "christology from below." Such christology is thinking that starts out with the experience of Jesus as a human being, and goes on to investigate what there is about Jesus that is unlike other human beings. This approach is characteristic of the older parts of the Christian scriptures (e.g., the story of Jesus's baptism in Mk 1:9–11). The Acts of the Apostles also attributes this kind of understanding both to Peter and to Paul. For example, "God has made both Lord and Messiah this Jesus whom you crucified." (Acts 2: 36; see also Acts 10:34–43 and Acts 13:23–33.) Christ's response to God's invitation is still being added on to, as Paul tells us (Rom 8:19–23).

The strength of God's Word—book, person, process—is that it is gentle, persuasive, and respectful of the characteristics of human nature. God's word, then, is needful of help, that is, of helpers. The ministry of the word ministers *to God's word*, by helping it take flesh, happen, live, and become effective. The ministry of the word ministers *to people* when it *ad*ministers or applies God's good news to their circumstances and particular needs.

THE CHURCH

When God's Word is effective, it becomes a part of the ongoing flow of communications through which people participate in human society and find their place in it. The process by which individuals become members of a society is called socialization.[4] "In the beginning was the word," the Gospel of John tells us, and the same may also be said of human life. The gift of a name is the first gift which parents give to the newborn child. With that name, and with the whole stream of messages that are continually showered on the infant, comes the gift of a unique identity. Personal being within the human community arises as a response to, an acceptance of, the communications which the child receives. The quality and tenor of those first world-establishing communications affects the individual being of the person, who enters human society through them.

The reality of society itself is sustained through continuous traffic in communications. Individuals are linked in society by means of the sending and receiving of messages. The same is true of the church, which is also a society of individuals—a society linked by means of the gospel message. Postponing for the moment any attempt to define the church theologically, we can understand a great deal about the human reality of the church if we take a look at its relationship to the dynamic reality of the gospel story.

First, the church is the *result* or outcome of the telling of the gospel story in our history. We could say that the church is simply the collection of all those people who have heard and accepted the good news of the gospel. But it would be more accurate to say that the church is a particular way of being human together, a way that is made possible by the recognition that the deepest meaning of human existence is to love and be loved by God. The church *is* a particular way of being together *because* its members are those who have accepted the gospel. But this way of looking at the church highlights the fact that the quality of our being-together depends on the quality of the meanings which we share. Those who have received their names and their personal identities from the gospel story have the assurance that God intends to provide all the goods and all the meaning that are necessary for human life. This effectively frees them from the need to struggle for material security and peace of mind by competing with other people. Christians often think of the church, then, as the hearer of God's word.

Second, the church is the *agent* of the gospel. It tells or proclaims the gospel story to the world. The activities which are identifed as ministries of the word are activities of the church itself, done by church members on behalf of the church rather than in their own name. These activities include evangelization, catechesis, preaching, liturgical and paraliturgical celebrations of the word, theological writing and teaching, religious journalism in both broadcast and print media, Bible study, and other forms of religious education.[5] Christians who participate in these activities are called ministers of God's word. They see themselves working for the church, in the service of the gospel but also in the service of other men, women, and children. The church itself is not an individual, personal subject and so it cannot literally act; rather, it is *en*acted, as a mode of being-human, in the actions of Christians who act in its behalf. Yet metaphorically, we do think of the church as the announcer of God's word as well as the hearer of God's word.

Third, the church is the *medium* through which the gospel message travels to people in lands and times that are far distant from those in which Jesus and the biblical books appeared. The media in which God's communication of overwhelming love and longing for humanity first reached men, women, and children were common ones: the sound waves, the air, the languages in which the biblical stories first were told; the papyrus or parchment and ink used to write them down; the face, voice, hands, and gestures of Jesus of Nazareth and of the men and women who followed him. All these were perishable, of course. The church renewed and renews the materials which have physically carried the gospel to present-day people. The biblical books have been lovingly recopied and translated; today one can even find them encoded on microfilm and stored in computer files, as well as in printed form and in the memories of people who have learned parts of the scriptures by heart. Moveover, since the historic body of Jesus is gone from this world, the church itself is the body of Jesus Christ in which God's reconciling word continues to address the world. Each day it renews his sacramental presence in the eucharistic celebration. Materially, mystically, and sacramentally, then, the church is the channel or carrier of God's word.

Fourth, the church itself embodies the *message* of the gospel. If the church is a way of being-human-together, its very existence is a guarantee of the possibility of what the gospel promises. The circularity of this thought is owing to the fact that the gospel story is a peculiarly self-replicating story, from a communications point of view. Aspects of the church's concrete existence stand as a guarantee of the gospel's promises. In particular, it is the intrinsic universality of the church which embodies the gospel promise. The gospel's offer of salvation, conveyed through the church, is for everyone; nationality, sex, race, age, culture, and historical era cannot limit the offer. The gospel purports to be a universal offer, open to all, and the church is (at its best) a universal community making no distinction by race or sex or class. The gospel asserts the providence of the Father, and the ecclesial community provides for the material welfare of its needy members. The medium is the message; the parish is the curriculum. Even before it speaks a single word of sermon or catechesis, the church community already has delivered its version of the gospel message by being what it is.[6]

SYMBOL

As effect, agent, medium, and message of the gospel, the church is said theologically also to be its symbol, the symbol of God's reconciling love. The realm of the symbol is the realm of human communication. Symbol is an ancient word and a useful one. Today it is used to denote various realities, by everyone from mathematicians to artists to educators to philosophers. For theologians, the word symbol still carries the ancient Greek meaning, *symbolon:* to draw or throw or hurl together. (Interestingly, the etymological opposite would be the word for devil, *diabolos*, literally the slanderer or liar, the one who hurls across a false charge and thereby causes division.)

Theologically, the pulling-together of the symbol implies a sharing of being among the elements that are pulled together. Their connection is not artificial or superficial; but rather it is a deep and necessary relation of things among which there is really only an apparent and/or a logical distinction. The reality of God's self-gift makes itself present and effective in material things which it causes to be there by an inner, formal, performative causality. God does not merely "use" Jesus or the church or the sacraments to communicate to us something that is really extrinsic to God's own being. Rather, Jesus, the church, and the sacraments are symbols because they are (in different degrees, to be sure!) expressions of God's own self as it is reaching out toward us. God's touch upon us through these symbols is an inner touch—from within God to within our own selves. The coming-together which symbol facilitates is to be distinguished from any extrinsic bumping of two independent realities, like billiard balls colliding on a pool table.[7]

So, for instance, the ancient creeds of the churches were called "symbols." They were statements which pulled together the various intrinsically related but apparently distinct elements of faith. These statements also pulled together the individual believers and individual local churches into one church, unified by virtue of its unanimous belief, and identifiable by the symbol, or creed, which all members professed. The symbol, in pulling together the faith, allowed the church to express itself, and be, as what it was. It made the truth effective.

In theology, the term symbol usually is used in cases where what is being pulled together are, on the one hand, a transcendent spiritual reality, and on the other hand, one or more concrete, tangible, expressions or realizations of that reality. In this sense of the word symbol, I can say that my body is the symbol of me. When I stand before a class of students on any particular Tuesday morning, what they see is really me, of course. I do my best to express to them what is in my heart, using the language and gestures, the anecdotes and examples, available to a 37-year-old woman in our culture. I am really there and available to them—but everyone recognizes that what they see is not all of me there is. I transcend that moment. Besides being a teacher, I am also other things: a wife, a writer, an amateur athlete. Besides what I am on that morning, I am also my past and my future. Yet the only way I have of being available to the students is in the particular circumstances of that morning. In fact, I myself have to use the same route of access to myself: through my body, my symbol. My body *is* me; it is not *all* of me, but it is the only route of access to me and it is the only means I have of expressing, and thereby becoming, myself.

It is in this sense that we say Jesus Christ, God's Word, is God's symbol. Like my body, the historical human body of Jesus probably could not express all of the Father's love on any one given morning of his life. But unlike my body, Jesus' body has now completed all the mornings of its human life. As a risen glorified body, it is now the completely adequate symbol to make available to us the transcendent reality of the Father's love and longing for us. My symbol—my body, face, hands, and heart—is a relatively effective communicator. Jesus Christ is a superbly effective communicator, but his communication still resembles that of which even I am capable in one very important respect: it is symbolic.

Symbol pulls together the transcendent and the concrete. It literally makes present: it makes the present. This is what is meant by the efficacy, the effectiveness, of symbol. As the transcendent is brought to bear upon the concrete situation, the concrete situation is quite likely to undergo transformation. In simplest terms, a symbol is a point or location in material reality where a person becomes present, active, and available for the sake of relationship with another person.[8] I would identify this as the first or simplest level of symbolic efficacy.

Once personal presence is achieved, we can detect a second level of symbolic efficacy. On a Tuesday morning, as I stand before my theology class after having established the rapport of personal availability between the students and myself, I use my symbol—my voice, gestures, face—to introduce and bring into play the stories of the Christian tradition which form the subject matter of our study. For example, I may discuss Jesus' story of the Prodigal Father (Lk 15:11–32). This story, too, is an effective symbol. It not only effects an entry of an expression of God's personal love into the present (for those students who are listening!), but it also begins to subtly change the present structures of social reality for them. In other words, the symbol first spans space to let an absent God be present; it then spans time to let a promised future eschatological reconciliation play a role in reality definitions in the here-and-now. The class discussion may help students to see that Jesus' story of the Father's foolish investment of love in a seemingly worthless offspring also "fits" their own situations in interesting ways. The insights that may arise will be factors in students' subsequent decisions.

To identify this second level of symbolic function, we may say that a symbol is the persuasive projection of an ideal vision of future relationship upon present reality, in such a way that points of incongruity are noticed, and an impulse is generated toward bringing the present into line with the projected future.[9] It may easily be seen that both of these modalities of symbolic function identify processes that are entirely human and natural. These are not specifically religious phenomena. All persons express themselves symbolically. Social or political action is possible only because we are able to imagine a future different from the present and then work to achieve it. But both sorts of symbolic efficacy must enter into theological discussion, because God works within human structures as far as is possible. In other words, a good deal of theological work can and must be done before the theologian gets to the point where he or she resorts to supernatural explanations.

UNDERSTANDING THROUGH SYMBOL

To grasp the history of the gospel, one must trace through human history the ways in which the gospel effected a personal presence and availability of God, and also effected the transformation of human society. The gospel, being a story or message, is accomplishing these things symbolically. That is to say, it has worked the way symbols always work. There is no magic; grace works with nature. The symbolic transformation of human existence, which still continues, is the most substantial, solid, real sort of transformation one could possibly attribute to the gospel.

This story of the gospel's on-going symbolic transformation of human being could not have been told in such terms before the present century. The communications revolution of our times has focused attention on the nature of mass and interpersonal communications. The advertising and public-relations industries are founded on the conviction that the symbol, the image, the story, are the most powerful and effective elements in the modern world. Medieval theologians were stumped when called upon to provide an explanation for how the sacraments worked: in precisely what sense are they "signs that bring about what they signify"? In the thirteenth century, they called that a mystery. To us, it is a commonplace, even a nuisance. Symbolic efficacy is very well understood today and is manipulated for profit and political power. Coercion through story and symbol is so common that western populations today have built up resistance to it. This jaded distrust of communications is a new threat which the gospel must overcome in our century. Nevertheless, modern familiarity with the ways messages work upon people allows us a hitherto unavailable perspective upon the history of the gospel's pulling-together of the church. We call this perspective "critical."

A critical historian tries to take into account both the factors that account for her own viewpoint, and the differences in the viewpoints of others. The human community has grown wiser in its understanding of symbol over the centuries, and it is now possible to identify certain distinct stages in the church's characteristic way of relating to its foundational symbols. As the human community has matured in its grasp of symbol, so each individual child must in turn retrace the developmental journey anew. Each child moves through a series of developmental steps as she or he grows in the possibility of religious understanding. As modern psychological studies indicate, young minds not only constantly increase their store of facts, they also become more adept at handling those facts and more sophisticated in the meanings which they can derive from them.

To round out this chapter's discussion of the symbolic functioning of the gospel, through the church, to transform the human world, it remains now to sketch out how the understanding of symbol develops. [11]

Early in life—that is to say, early in the life of a child, and early in the life of a culture—the mind's relation to its religious symbols is best described as literal and concrete. A child of about seven years has developed the remarkable human ability to entertain a mental conception inwardly representing things and actions which are not physically present. He or she can imaginatively manipulate the idea of apples and oranges (for example, by adding or subtracting them) just as if the fruits were there upon the table before him or her and could be touched with the hands and moved around. Thinking at this age is a matter of mental handling, and the seven-year-old's wondrous achievement is to do with the mind what younger children can do only with their hands. This ability is needed throughout life: adults continue to think by mentally handling absent objects.

(For an illustration, the reader is invited to look inward to examine her or his own mental processes. Think for a moment of preparing dinner tonight for family or friends with the help of a ten-year-old child. You and she might first talk over and plan together what you are going to do. If you two discover that some special ingredient must be purchased, the child would be able to understand and follow your instructions to proceed to the corner grocery store and get what is needed. Both child and adult think the same way when planning a task which involves work upon material elements.)

This concrete, literal style of thinking is characteristic of children not only in the kitchen, but in all areas of their understanding, including the religious. Adults, too, often use a concrete style of thinking about religious matters. Children and adults who are thinking concretely will hear and appropriate a religious symbol such as the statement, "God raised Jesus from the dead," in a concrete and literal way. For them, it will evoke a mental picture of Jesus lying dead in a tomb and then sitting up and breathing again. A mental picture like this probably forms the foundation of Christian faith even for the most theologically sophisticated believer. In chapter 4, we shall examine the process by which the first generation of

Christian writers filled in concrete details to support the resurrection faith of their communities; hence the details of eating and touching the risen Jesus, which characterize the Easter appearance stories, and the mention of shroud and linen face cloth in John's Gospel. This attention to material detail will be seen to be in tension with both Jesus' and Paul's attempts to discourage material curiosity about the resurrection and to focus attention upon the dimension of relationship.

Similarly, the symbol of the Eucharist will be understood by the concrete thinker as the real, physical body and blood of the human being Jesus of Nazareth. Of course, that is exactly what the consecrated bread and wine *are* for Christian faith, although the meaning of this symbol does reach far beyond the human and divine availability of Jesus on the altar and in the tabernacle. It is easy to see how concrete, literal understanding of this symbol supports pious practices such as visiting the Blessed Sacrament in the tabernacle, or exposing the eucharistic species for special veneration. In the middle ages, some people had such a literal understanding of the physical presence of Jesus in the Eucharist that they were disappointed not to be able to see his face or form when they looked at the consecrated host; they thought their faith must not be strong enough. Even today, some adults are afraid to chew the consecrated bread when they receive Communion, lest they hurt or dishonor the body of Christ which they understand themselves to be literally eating. Yet, notwithstanding these misconceptions, the child's concrete and literal appreciation of the reality of Jesus' availability in the eucharistic bread and wine—the *real presence*—remains the foundation of orthodox adult faith, even when other perspectives enrich it in maturity.

When young people have the advantage of stimulating education and contact with adult reasoning, they typically develop a new capacity of thought about the time they enter high school. The adolescent not only thinks about things, he or she thinks about statements. By tenth grade, young people are beginning to reason abstractly and in terms of relations. Long able to add and subtract, multiply and divide those absent apples and oranges, teenagers become able to manipulate relationships among quantities without knowing specifically what the quantities are. Algebra and geometry come within the range of their understanding. Not discrete tangible things, but grandly abstract constellations of relation, can now be manipulated mentally.

The adolescent's new need to belong to a group is part of this new cognitive threshold which is being crossed. Relationships among people become even more absorbing than relations among numbers, shapes, and equations. The dawning capacity for abstract understanding brings with it a dedication to ideals and to principles, which can make the adolescent a difficult person for family members to live with. Yet adolescent idealism is also a great natural resource for renewal within the family and for society at large.

(It is easy to suggest an example of abstract or formal reasoning, which is a new achievement for the teenager but an everyday tool of adult thought. Think for a moment of talking over an issue such as world hunger with some teenagers in your own home or at church meeting. *Concrete* understanding will come into play as you all feel some compassion for those who are suffering from hunger; even small children can mentally represent the concrete reality of hunger to themselves. *Abstract, formal* understanding will take over as both you and the young people grasp that all the world's people are in some way related to one another. With typical idealism and fervor, your young conversation partners may want to "do something" to call attention to a situation of injustice—and coincidentally to allow themselves to feel involved in an important work deserving of community recognition. You and they will be able to conceive of and to plan complex agenda of community action and consciousness-raising. But it would not be surprising if instead the teenagers sized up the issue in terms of what "we," i.e., the United States, ought to do to keep "them," i.e., hungry nations, from envying our plenty and moving to take it away from us. Both responses exhibit the presence of abstract thought.)

The ability to think abstractly and in terms of relationships is an achievement which the young person will use throughout life in all areas of endeavor. Conventional expressions of belief and of religious practice usually have this kind of understanding behind them. Resurrection belief, the belief that "God has raised Jesus from the dead," takes on a new level of symbolic function for the mind which is capable of conventional as well as of literal understanding. The teenager or adult who is capable of abstract relational thought understands the resurrection symbol in terms of the once-dead-but-now-living Jesus, who continues to call Christians to reconciliation with the Father and who continues to be present and active within the Christian community itself. The concrete mental picture of Jesus sitting up in the tomb on Easter morning may very well remain; however, overlaid upon that picture is the certitude that the possibility of relationship with Jesus in community has been reopened despite his death. Conventional Easter faith focuses not on the details of how a dead body can breathe again, but rather upon the encounter with a living Jesus by and in a Christian community.

Similarly, the eucharistic symbol presents a relational reality to the mind which is equipped with conventional understanding and which can understand in an abstract and relational way: the Eucharistic body of Christ makes one body out of all the people in the church. The symbol "body of Christ" is both the community and the eucharistic species. Such an understanding undoubtedly underlies the theology of the fathers of the Second Vatican Council, whose documents so strongly emphasize the church's nature as People of God.[11]

It is important to note here that both styles of thinking—concrete understanding and conventional understanding—are really mental manipulations of symbol. We might say that the efficacy of symbol, that is, its power to illuminate and transform human existence, is at work through the mental grasp of religious realities which both varieties of understanding permit human consciousness to have. These modalities of understanding might be termed "hands-on" understandings, because the mind is taking hold of the religious symbols and running with them. But there are at least two other varieties of human understanding, in which the human grasp of the symbol is loosened and the symbol in turn grasps human understanding itself. These ways of understanding occur more rarely, and they are more difficult to describe.

Some young people cross another threshold of cognitive development during their college years; others reach this point later in life, or not at all. The experience of leaving home, leaving one's own social group, and discovering that there are other worlds of value and meaning can bring about a kind of estrangement from the symbols which had permitted a rich understanding of life within a conventional faith stance. At first, it may seem that all values are relative and that arbitrary choice is the only foundation for meaning in a world where diverse meanings and values compete for one's allegiance. Cognitionally, the person is thinking not just about things, not just about thoughts, but about subjectivity itself. (Subjectivity, it will be recalled, is the philosophical term which refers to the structures of knowing and meaning which are intrinsic to the human mind itself.) For the first time, the person is noticing the important role which the mind always plays in constructing the reality which hitherto had been accepted without question. It takes a while for the mind to become comfortable with its realization that "objective" reality cannot be known without the constitutive participation of the knower's own subjectivity in the act of knowing. The world, although it is real, is very really "my" world and no one else's. The mind becomes aware of how it knows; it recognizes that knowing is affected by the knower's position in society, needs, desires, historical era, and so forth. Such a mind is said to be capable of critical thought.

(Perhaps the best example of critical thinking is the work of the modern historians, who keep in mind the fact that both their own understanding, and that of their sources, is filtered through some particular viewpoint based upon participation in some particular society. Another example would be the approach to the gospel's history which this book is trying to suggest right now: an awareness that different people of different ages and times have different capacities for understanding the Christian symbols which all hold in common.)

Critical thought is a natural development in the maturing human being, and in fact it is a necessary step on the way to an even more complex level of understanding. Nevertheless, this kind of thinking is quite rough on faith. For many people, it comes as a moment of purgation, of purification, for conventional belief. Critical faith can look like no faith at all, so radically does it sometimes disengage the mind from conventional religious symbols. The mind which has learned to think critically is impatient with symbols. It wants to get behind them or under them; it wants to translate them into logical statements or into ethical commands. Where concrete and conventional understanding were two ways of grasping or holding onto religious symbols, critical understanding lets go of the symbol, sets it down, and tries to dissect it. Who does this? Some college students, some older people in mid-life crisis, . . . and all of the greatest theologians of the twentieth century. (In fact, contemporary theology differs most from traditional theology in that today's theologians investigate the cognitive preconditions of the symbolic realities which yesterday's theologians propounded.)

Critical understanding might go after Resurrection belief in the following manner. "God raised Jesus from the dead" cannot literally mean that Jesus sat up in the tomb as if he were waking up from sleep to start another day in his life. This was going to be a new life, a life so new that our human experience gives us no examples or models with which we can compare it. The model of waking from sleep is inadequate, because it can give the impression that risen life was just "business as usual" for Jesus. The Easter experience, as it is reflected in the gospels, seems not to have been that of breathing again, a mere resuscitation. The Easter experience is described in the gospel record as being different things to different people. For Peter, it was the experience of meeting a living Jesus who still called him to great things, after having deserted Jesus and known him to be dead. For Jesus, it was an experience of reconciliation with the Father, after having felt abandoned on the cross by the Abba in whom he had placed his trust. For the community of Jesus' disciples, it was an experience of being regathered and sent out on mission by the Spirit, after having run away when Jesus was arrested. Critical understanding asks hard questions of the biblical evidence. It factors into faith an awareness that the faith of others has shaped the stories which they preserved in the Christian scripture.

Critical understanding wants to translate and get beyond symbols, and so it is uncomfortable with liturgical celebration. On the one hand, critical faith is (often painfully) aware of the similarities between the Eucharist and other ritual acts in other religions. Anyone who studies other cultures soon finds instances of "pagan" ceremonies in which eating is understood both to lead to participation in the life of a god, and to bind a community together. On the other hand, the Christian who is thinking critically discerns the ethical imperative expressed in the eucharistic meal. Those who break bread together must live in peace, and those who have plenty must share with sisters and brothers in need. This critical stance toward ritual is not uncommon among young adults. It explains why many cease participating in Sunday services and find sacraments meaningless. But such a lapse in practice does not mean that faith is gone; faith is regrouping and refining itself, in preparation for growth into another stage of understanding.

Later in life, and not often before the age of thirty, critical understanding may become critical of itself to the extent that it recognizes that its project of dissecting symbols has failed. The religious symbols are seen to retain a tantalizing depth of meaning even when one has pared away their surface similarities with "pagan" rites, even when one has boiled them down to distill ethical imperatives. One hungers for that elusive meaning, and senses that it can come only as gift, and not as achievement. The critical Christian may have the experience that one cannot sustain activism for justice without being personally sustained by the Eucharist. He or she may have discovered that one cannot hang on to the reconciliation, conversion, and sense of mission made available in Easter faith, without being embraced by the risen body of the Lord like the women at the empty tomb. A new relationship with symbol dawns for such a person, and a new mode of understanding becomes possible: conjunctive understanding, conjunctive faith. This understanding has passed through the desert of criticism, and returned home again to its own tradition. This time, however, the mind understands not by handling or manipulating the symbols, but rather by letting them grasp it.

Conjunctive faith appreciates the radical surprise of the Resurrection experience as a hope humbly received.[12] It sees the Eucharist transubstantiating the existences of individual lives by conforming them to the pattern of the Paschal Mystery, Jesus' obedient response to the Father. Symbol is understood to be the vehicle of such transformation. Little can be said about that kind of understanding in a book such as this one. Our goals are set one notch lower, at the level of critical thought. Yet I hope that conjunctive understanding would draw closer for any reader who attempted to work through the critical understanding that is suggested in this book.

This introductory chapter has set the stage for our survey of the history of the gospel's transformation of human existence. We have defined some important terms: the gospel, the church, and symbol. We have also examined different varieties of understanding in which the mind grasps, or is grasped by, the symbol. These levels of understanding emerge in sequence in the maturing individual. In our Christian history, we will see that different historical eras tended to adopt one or another characteristic style of understanding, according to the general level of the culture of the times. This historical survey is going to demand critical understanding from the reader—because it is the story *of* a story, seeking to understand religious understanding itself. The next chapter will discuss symbolic transformation, and then we will be in a position to begin our historical survey in the beginning, with Jesus Christ God's Word.

Notes for Chapter One

1. "Portraiture" as an aspect of the theological task is proposed by Edward Farley in *Ecclesial Reflection: An Anatomy of Theological Method* (Philadelphia: Fortress, 1982).

2. The phenomenological tradition in philosophy and in sociology is grand and complex. Among its masters is Edward Farley, who is Professor of Theology at Vanderbilt Divinity School. My view of the gospel at work in the church, and particularly my discussion in the first two chapters of this book, are greatly indebted to Professor Farley's phenomenology of ecclesial transformation. Readers who wish to pursue this approach are encouraged to study Farley's two volumes *Ecclesial Man: A Social Phenomenology of Faith and Reality* (Philadelphia: Fortress, 1975) and *Ecclesial Reflection*.

3. *Dei Verbum* No. 8. See also the discussion in chapter 3 of the National Catechetical Directory, *Sharing the Light of Faith* (Washington: U.S. Catholic Conference, 1979) concerning revelation. The document speaks, e.g. in No. 50, of revelation along with other "manifestations" and "communications"—which it calls "modes by which God continues to make himself known and share himself with human beings through his presence in the church and the world."

4. An intriguing introduction to this phenomenon is presented by Peter L. Berger and Thomas Luckmann in *The Social Construction of Reality: A Treatise in the Sociology of Knowledge* (Garden City, N.Y.: Doubleday & Co., 1966), especially chapter 3, "Society as Subjective Reality." Socialization theory has been useful to educators, and particularly to religious educators. See, for example, Berard L. Marthaler's essay, "Socialization as a Model for Catechetics," in *Foundations of Religious Ed-*

ucation, edited by Padraic O'Hare (New York: Paulist Press, 1978). For
an excellent summary of socialization theory, and of the contributions of
theorists who have adapted it within the field of religious education, see
chapter 6 of *Christian Religious Education: Sharing Our Story and Vision,*
by Thomas H. Groome (San Francisco: Harper & Row, 1980). Groome's
work itself also highlights the central role of communication in building
both the church and the world.

5. Both the General Catechetical Directory, No. 17, and the National Catechetical Directory (Washington: U.S. Catholic Conference,
1971), No. 31, give non-exclusive lists of the forms of the ministry of the
word: evangelization, catechesis, liturgy, and theology. These documents
can be studied with profit by anyone who seeks to understand the development of Roman Catholic Church policy and theory concerning the ministry of teaching in the era following the Second Vatican Council. For a
more comprehensive view, see the articles and documents collected in
Sourcebook for Modern Catechetics, edited by Michael Warren (Winona,
Minn.: Christian Brothers Publications, 1983).

6. Pope Paul VI's Apostolic Exhortation *Evangelii Nuntiandi* (Washington: U.S. Catholic Conference, 1976) treats the church as effect, agent,
medium, and message of the gospel, though it does not use these terms.

7. This is the understanding of symbol that underlies Karl Rahner's
theology of the "Realsymbol." Rahner never systematized this theology,
but the ideas are introduced in an essay entitled "Zur Theologie des Symbols" in his *Schriften zur Theologie* vol. 4, pp. 275–311 (Einsiedeln: Ben-
ziger, 1960). Unfortunately, the English translation is unintelligible in
Theological Investigations vol. 4, pp. 221–52 (Baltimore: Helicon, 1966).

8. This seems to be the understanding of symbol underlying the
thought of Edward Schillebeeckx in his earlier works, for example, in
Christ the Sacrament of the Encounter With God, and in *The Eucharist*
(New York: Sheed and Ward, 1968). Traces of it also are to be found in his
mature christology in *Jesus: An Experiment in Christology* (New York:
Seabury Press, 1979) and *Christ: The Experience of Jesus as Lord* (New
York: Seabury Press, 1980). The whole world, human being, and most especially the humanity of Jesus Christ all function in this way for Schillebeeckx. They are material realities which are media of personal
communication from God. This amounts to a sublime sacramental vision:
all creation is transparent to the loving outreach of the Creator. I have discussed Rahner's and Schillebeeckx's theologies of symbol at greater depth
in my doctoral dissertation, *Aesthetic Catechetics: An Approach Via the
Effective Symbol as Described by Schillebeeckx, Rahner, and Heidegger*
(Ann Arbor, Mich.: University Microfilms, 1984).

9. This conception of symbol, too, comes from Edward Schille-

beeckx, but it is presented only in his later work where he takes into account the dynamics of human social transformation. The phenomenon of changing being by changing meaning, which was noted in *The Eucharist*, is further explored in *God the Future of Man* (New York: Sheed and Ward, 1968) and *The Understanding of Faith* (New York: Seabury Press, 1974), until in *Christ* Schillebeeckx has developed what amounts to an alternative model of symbolic function. One might characterize the older view, that symbol is the medium of personal presence, as a static view, and the later view, that symbol is the principle of empowerment for change, as a dynamic view. They would correspond to two themes of the Gospels portraits of Jesus: his experience of God as "Abba," and his feeling driven by the Spirit to do the deeds that constituted the out-breaking of the Reign of God.

10. The following discussion is based upon the work of James Fowler, presented in *Stages of Faith: The Psychology of Human Development and the Quest for Meaning* (San Francisco: Harper & Row, 1976). Both Fowler's and my discussions draw on the work of Jean Piaget and Erik Erikson as well. A good introduction to the "genetic epistemology" of Piaget may be found in *Six Psychological Studies*, by Jean Piaget (New York: Random House, 1967). Readable works by Erik Erikson include *Childhood and Society*, second edition (New York: W.W. Norton & Company, 1963) and *Identity and the Life Cycle* in *Psychological Issues* (New York: International Universities Press, 1959). To Erikson belongs the distinction of having invented the phrase "identity crisis."

11. See, for example, chapter 2, "The People of God," of the Second Vatican Council's Dogmatic Constitution on the Church, *Lumen Gentium*.

12. I take the name "conjunctive" from James Fowler, who calls the fifth stage of faith "conjunctive faith." Following Fowler, I note also that Paul Ricoeur, the great phenomenologist of religion, has given us the term "second naivete" to describe the person's relationship to her or his religious tradition at this stage. See *The Symbolism of Evil*, by Paul Ricoeur (New York: Harper & Row, 1967), and especially the last chapter, "The Symbol Gives Rise to Thought." Ricoeur mentions the "desert of criticism," through which one passes into more adequate understanding.

Chapter Two

Ecclesial Transformation

In telling the story of how the story of God's act in Jesus has transformed human existence, it is our purpose to emphasize the human side of both stories. Symbol is a human phenomenon, a natural part of human communication and one which is becoming better understood in the twentieth century than ever before. Scholars today have available a wealth of factual information about the events of Christian history: information which may be termed *objective* by virtue of the rigorous scientific historical inquiry upon which it rests. At the same time, there is also a better understanding of the part which Christian *subjectivity* plays in the church's appropriation of those facts and their significance. When today one undertakes a critical investigation of the gospel's story, one keeps in sight above all the interrelationship of these two aspects of human being: our situation within a real, solid world, and the fact that our very participation in that world has a good deal to do with its reality.

Our option for a critical investigation of the symbolic processes by which the gospel has been transforming history is an option at the same time to emphasize the human side of the picture. Nevertheless, a note of theological balance must be sounded at the outset. The transformation of human existence—which is to say, redemption—is thoroughly a work of God. Human beings do not lift themselves into heaven by their own bootstraps. It is God's grace, God's absolutely free and surprising gift of meaning, which makes Christian redeemed existence possible. God's Spirit, the Spirit of Jesus, saturates all of the human processes to be investigated in this book, including the apparently natural growth of human understanding of symbol which was described in the last chapter. But God works through human processes. It is God who gives the meaning, which human beings apprehend in a great variety of ways. Grace penetrates nature in the subtlest, gentlest manner conceivable.

In investigating human redemption insofar as it is a phenomenon of human communication, one must not for a moment forget that it is at the same time God's work, and is therefore a mystery that can never be explained away. On the contrary: one honors the depth of the mystery by reserving the term for that to which it most properly refers: God's approach to humanity from out of the depth of humanity itself. We do not call every little puzzle or peculiarity of symbolic interaction a mystery. We seek human explanations for those phenomena which can have them; and when the last word that can be said about them has been said, God's own mystery will stand forth in the silence.

WHAT JESUS STARTED

What is being attempted, then, is to understand in twentieth-century terms the phenomenon which Jesus of Nazareth set in motion and which his Spirit maintains. Jesus came preaching the eruption of God's Reign into his own society. This concept, the Reign of God, was the centerpiece of his message. It was not an easy concept for him to communicate, or for his followers to understand. A generation after Jesus, those who called themselves Christian were no longer preaching God's Reign exactly as Jesus had done. Paul, for example, says that the content of his own preaching is "that Christ died for our sins in accordance with the Scriptures, that he was buried and, in accordance with the Scriptures, rose on the third day" (1 Cor 15:3–4). What did Jesus mean by "the Reign of God," and why did the first generation of preachers see a need to revise the content of his proclamation when they themselves undertook to pass on the gospel message? Our historical investigation of the gospel's story must start with this question in the next two chapters.

Jesus surely understood himself to be someone who had a significant part to play in the opening up of God's Reign within human society. But just as surely, Jesus' death raised questions about his significance and about the validity of his message.

The New Testament presents a record of some of the ways in which the first generations of Christians began to face and to answer those questions. Their formulations of faith in Jesus show that they were trying to correlate the undeniable fact of Jesus' disappointing death with another fact, one which was just as real and undeniable to them: Jesus was alive in the community and was still calling them to follow him to reconciliation with the Father. Jesus' new, post-death presence was indeed more powerful than had been his presence with them before he went to Jerusalem and Calvary. They felt this presence as a pouring out of Jesus' power into themselves. They were transformed: they were a church. And this church, this sphere of influence of Jesus' Spirit in the world, was growing. When they told the story of Jesus, they found that his Spirit flowed out to the story's hearers, changed their existence, changed them into tellers of the story.

Some of their memories of these early events are recorded in the book of the Acts of the Apostles. If we examine the logic of these early sermons, we can see how the Christians were making sense out of the apparent disappointment of their hopes for God's Reign which was occasioned by Jesus' untimely death. The following remarks are attributed to Peter in Acts 2: 22–24, 36:

> Men of Israel hear these words. Jesus the Nazarene was a man commended to you by God with mighty works, wonders, and signs, which God did through him in your midst, as you yourselves know. This man, given up by the set plan and foreknowledge of God, you killed, using lawless people to crucify him. But God raised him up, releasing him from the pangs of death, because it was impossible for him to be held by it. . . . Therefore let all the house of Israel know for certain that God has made him both Lord and Christ, this Jesus whom you crucified.[1]

There is a similar summary of Peter's gospel in another speech recorded in Acts 10:36–43:

> You know the word which God sent to the Israelites, proclaiming peace through Jesus Christ—who is Lord of all!—what took place all over Judea, beginning in Galilee after the baptism which John preached: how God anointed Jesus of Nazareth with the Holy Spirit and power; how he went about doing good and healing all those oppressed by the devil, for God was with him. We are witnesses to all the things he did, both in the country of the Jews and in Jerusalem. They put him to death by hanging him on a tree. This one God raised on the third day and let him become visible, not to all the people, but to witnesses chosen by God in advance, to us who ate and drank with him after he rose from the dead. He commanded us to preach to the people and testify that he is the one designated by God as judge of the living and the dead. To this one all the prophets bear witness, that everyone who believes in him receives forgiveness of sins through his name.

These early renditions of the gospel message, God's good news, recount the story of Jesus' life, death, and resurrection. They affirm the unique significance of Jesus within a plan of God for the reconciliation of human beings to God. Jesus is "Lord," "Christ," "a man commended to you by God," "anointed . . . with the Holy Spirit and power," "the one designated by God," "judge of the living and the dead." Interestingly, Peter's gospel does not assert that Jesus is God. The divinity of Jesus does not seem to have occurred to anyone yet, at this early stage of the church's life. Perhaps Paul's speech in Acts 13 comes closest to asserting divine sonship for Jesus, although it identifies God's fathering of Jesus with the Resurrection:

> We are preaching the good news to you that what God promised our ancestors God has brought to fulfillment for us, their children, by raising up Jesus, as it is written in the second psalm, "You are my son; today I have begotten you." . . . Then let it be known to you, my brothers and sisters, that through this one forgiveness of sins is being proclaimed to you. . . . (Acts 13:32–33, 38)

FIRST FRUITS OF THE GOSPEL

Clearly, the message in these early sermons is *Jesus*—what he did, what God did through him, what God did to him, and what the telling of these things means: forgiveness of sins. The telling of these things, the telling of the gospel story, has various consequences according to the book of Acts. For example, Peter and the other followers of Jesus have to spend a night in jail (Acts 4:3) for teaching and healing in the power of Jesus' name. More importantly, the community that tells and hears the gospel leads a common life which Acts depicts as rather unusual. Chapter 2, verses 42–47 and 4:32–35 give us a perhaps idealized picture of the lifestyle which the gospel seemed to make possible:

> They devoted themselves to the teaching of the apostles and to the partnership, to the breaking of the bread and to the prayers. Fear came upon every soul, and many wonders and signs were done through the apostles. All who believed were together and had all things in common; they would sell their property and possessions and distribute them to all according to each one's need. And day by day they devoted themselves to meeting together in the temple area and to breaking bread in their homes. They shared food in gladness and simplicity of heart, praising God and enjoying favor with all the people. And day by day the Lord added to their number those who were being saved. . . .

> The multitude of believers were of one heart and one soul, and no one claimed that any of one's possessions was one's own, but they had everything in common. With great power the apostles gave their testimony to the resurrection of the Lord Jesus, and great grace was upon them all. There was no needy person among them, for those who owned lands or houses would sell them, bring the proceeds of the sale, and place them at the feet of the apostles, and they were distributed to each according to need.

The cooperative, mutually supportive spirit of the community is presented by the author of Acts as one of the signs and wonders which accompany the proclamation of the gospel. The forgiveness of sins seems to be experienced not so much as a future benefit between individuals and God, but as a present condition facilitating brotherly-sisterly care among the members of the community.

It is this aspect of the gospel which is to be the focus of this book. The circumstances of the Christians' common life would count as evidence of the effectiveness of the telling of the gospel. As we trace the telling of the gospel through the twenty centuries of the church's life, we will be tracing the history of a transforming force which influences communities of people according to the particular circumstances provided by their times and their culture. We will be looking for indications that social relationships, family and political structures, are being modified by the telling of the gospel.

The question of the what and the how of the transformation of human existence gives us the lens through which we are going to scrutinize the history of the church, and particularly the history of the ministry of the word. Other sorts of lenses could be used, and indeed have been used, to study the same material. For example, many church historians have employed the question of leadership or of authority as their tool for analysis of the church's past and its ongoing life. When the leadership question has been used as the lens for observing the church's present and past ministry, it has brought into focus a view of the church as having a threefold mission: to teach, to govern, and to sanctify. The church is seen to be carrying on for Jesus in his threefold office of prophet, king, and priest.

There is much to be said in favor of this traditional observation about the church. For example, Jesus did indeed understand himself to be a prophetic teacher. But the lens of leadership has also distorted our view of the Jesus whom the gospels present to us. That Jesus was not a king. He did not govern. He was not a priest, but a layman. His "law" and his "sacrifice" were so different from any others that one can use the terms only metaphorically when describing what Jesus did. Law and sacrifice for him meant having his heart set so entirely upon the Father that all else paled to insignificance. The mundane particularity of the many laws and many sacrifices of his day was exactly what Jesus wanted to sweep aside in the simplicity and unity of his one gesture of submission to the Father, receptivity to the Father's will.

THE TROUBLE WITH HUMAN BEING

It seems impossible to avoid distortion entirely, no matter what lens is used. Any instrument of observation introduces its own sort of bias into the picture which it produces. Life in the twentieth-century communications culture has sensitized us to the impossibility of absolute objectivity in any human viewpoint. Nevertheless, one can try for relative objectivity by seeking, insofar as one is able, to allow the object of study to speak on its own terms. The Gospels provide reliable historical information about Jesus, but they do so from various standpoints more or less removed from the situation in which Jesus lived. The historical facts filter down to us through several layers of interpretation by the different ecclesial communities of the first century. The portrait, or portraits, of Jesus in the New Testament are collages made up of materials that come from Jesus himself, along with materials that originate in communities which experience the risen Lord living in their midst. People in those communities turned that experience into the stories of Resurrection which have allowed subsequent generations to glimpse the risen Lord.

The Gospels witness to a Jesus who healed people, who fed people, who chased devils out of people, and who drew huge crowds to see him do those things and hear his teaching. This Jesus stands at the beginning of a historical phenomenon which is still happening. Starting with the first generations of his followers after his death—and indeed, during his lifetime itself—other people have carried on the works which Jesus was doing. The outcome of these works has been a new way of being together as human beings. The outcome has been what we term today the church.

How has this happened? How do teachings and feedings and healings and exorcisms lead to a change in the structure of human being itself?

One must first ask, what is human being? Each era and each culture has proposed its own answers, and our twentieth-century Western technological society has developed one of the most interesting. Each man, woman, and child can of course be called a human being; there are billions of us "human beings" (plural) at large upon the earth today. Human being (singular) is what is common to all of us. To be a human being, is to reach out beyond what we can actually reach. We have no ceiling over our human aspirations, but only the arc of the heavens and infinite space. To be human is to know, and to have an open-ended, unsatisfiable desire to know more and more. Human being is not just having, but *being*, this open-ended curiosity to learn. By the same token, to be human is to love, and to have an ever-open, ever growing attraction toward other beings: a drive to embrace them, to nurture them, and to shelter their growth toward perfection and union with our own human being. Human being is not just having, but *being*, this magnetism for other beings.

The philosophical term for the intrinsically infinite reaching of knowledge and love which we not only have but *are*, is transcendence. We experience our transcendence in knowledge and love as an undercurrent within all the particular experiences which we may have in a lifetime. Usually one is not directly conscious of this tacit outward opening of the human spirit, unless one pauses in the midst of activity and thinks about the basic assumptions and capacities that make all of one's particular activities possible.[2]

Some of the most creative work of modern philosophy has been done as an effort to show us how to "catch ourselves in the act," as it were, of transcending.[3] The experience of transcendence is so elusive because it is always hidden within ordinary experiences of playing with children, or mowing the lawn, or reading, or conversing with friends. Analysis which seeks to identify (that is, bring to our notice) the experience of human being's open-endedness, is called phenomenology. One of the tactics which phenomenology uses to throw light upon human transcendence, is to look for experiences where transcendence is thwarted. In other words, transcendence seems easiest to spot when it is not working, that is, when something has gotten in its way.[4]

Instinctively, human beings seem to resist whatever threatens the perceived orderliness of the world. We seem to thirst for meaning even more than for happiness. One can accept a great deal of suffering, if only one can see that it "makes sense" in some way and has a purpose. The chaotic is a threat to mental and physical well-being. We get a kind of negative evidence for the reality of our desire to know and understand, when we notice the vehemence with which the mind resists and attacks something that appears absurd. The mind recoils from the senselessness of violent crime or debilitating illness—just as the body recoils from the pain which these cause and seeks to shield itself from the physical harm they entail. This reflexive recoil from the senseless, this horror of chaos, is an aspect of the fabric of human being itself.

In the same way, human beings resist anything that curtails their freedom. Again, we get vivid testimony to the intrinsic infinity of our outward thrust to love and nurture other beings, whenever that thrust runs into something that wants to prevent it from reaching its target. The human spirit cannot tolerate infringement upon its right to grow, to express itself, and to care for other people and the good things of the earth. There is an irrepressible will to resist whatever diminishes human freedom. That will to resist seems to be part of what we *are* as human beings, not just something which we have or which we learn.

What, then, is human being? Twentieth-century phenomenological philosophy has sketched out an answer in terms of human being's unlimited transcendence in knowledge and love, which comes to light as unconditional resistance to shame and correction.

Although this is a distinctly modern view, it is in accord with the view of the human condition which Christians discern in the Book of Genesis' stories about creation, and in Paul's teaching about the significance of Jesus Christ. The goodness of the things which God made is stressed in the first account of creation, Genesis 1:1–2:4. The second account of the creation, in Genesis 2, stresses the importance of relationships among the first human beings whom God created. This concern with what we today would call human intersubjectivity appears in vv. 18–23:

> The LORD God said: "It is not good for the man to be alone. I will make a partner suitable for him." So out of the ground the LORD God formed every wild animal and every bird of the sky, and brought them to the man to see what he would call them. Whatever the man called each living creature, that would be its name. The man gave names to all the cattle, all the birds of the sky, and all the wild animals. But none of them turned out to be the partner suitable for the man.
>
> So the LORD God put a deep sleep upon the man, and while he was asleep took out one of his ribs and closed up its place with flesh. Then the LORD God built up that rib, taken from the man, into a woman. When God brought her to the man, the man said:
>
> "This one, at last, is bone of my bones
> and flesh of my flesh;
> This one shall be called 'woman,'
> because she was taken out of man."

It has been said that the man is not really human until he meets the woman, because her appearance is the occasion for him to utter the first human lines of dialogue in the scriptures. And those lines are poetry.

Interestingly, Genesis represents the first sin as something that goes

wrong with the human drives for freedom and knowledge, and consequently with human relationship or intersubjectivity. God's command to
the man is recorded in Gen 2:16–17 as:

> "You are free to eat from any tree of the garden except the tree
> of knowledge of good and evil. From that tree you shall not
> eat . . . ."

The woman and the man, of course, decide they will be free to eat of
the tree of knowledge as well, in 3:1–7. After they do so, God calls them
to account, in vv.8–11. The man, who a few verses earlier had been en-
raptured by the sight of the woman, now blames his disobedience on her
and indirectly on God, who had put her beside the man, v.12. The woman,
called to account, blames the serpent, in v.13, and the rest is history.

Paul reads into the Genesis story a foreshadowing of Jesus' own mission. He calls Adam a type or figure of Jesus. In Rom 5:12, 14, Paul says:

> Therefore, just as sin entered the world through one person—
> and through sin, death—and thus death came to all people, in-
> asmuch as all sinned . . . death reigned from Adam to Moses,
> even over those whose sins were unlike the transgression of
> Adam, who is a type of the one who was to come.

Paul goes on to argue, in vv.15–19, that the obedient act of Jesus has
undone the damage which Genesis had depicted as a disordering of the
human drive for knowledge and freedom. As we would put it in phenomenological terms, Jesus sets right the disruption of human intersubjectivity
which stems from a primordial flaw in relationships.

Paul makes further use of the parallel between Jesus and Adam in his
teaching about the resurrection.

> But now Christ has been raised from the dead, the first fruits of
> those who have fallen asleep. For since death came through a
> human being, the resurrection of the dead came also through a
> human being. For just as in Adam all die, so too in Christ will all
> be made alive, but each one in proper order: Christ the first
> fruits; then at his coming, all the ones who belong to Christ.
> (1 Cor 15:20–23)

In other words, our modern experience of human being as an open-
ended turning outward in knowledge and love fits in well with the biblical
theology: God created human beings as good creatures, whose goodness

consisted in the quality of their relationships with each other, with God's other creatures, and with God's own self.

SINFUL MEANING

What went wrong in Paradise is the same thing that continues to go wrong with human being today. Human life in the world is a project of struggling against chaos and the absurdity of death to achieve meaning and order, and at the same time it is a struggle against coercion by physical and social necessities so that one may exercise some degree of freedom. However, because human existence is a being-with-others in the world, our transcendence has to work itself out in relationships between person and person, or person and thing.

Now, theoretically, it *could* have happened that human beings chose to cooperate in their projects of resisting chaos and coercion. But in fact, we *did and do* opt to act out these resistances and to exercise our transcendence at one another's expense.

There is a fundamental flaw in the meanings which we assign to the people with whom we share the world. Remember: a child receives its human being as a gift not just from God, but from its parents as well; this gift consists not just in a physical body, but also in a social identity which is conveyed and maintained through communications. A human being is created, individualized, and personalized by the gift of a name, given many times, in a campaign of address which socializes the child into a member of human communicating society. The name is a symbol around which a person pulls himself or herself together. Just as surely, a human being can be diminished and destroyed through renaming: labeling, racial or sexist stereotyping, ridicule,[5] slander (*diabolon:* hurling across), and other personally diminishing communications to which all who are human are vulnerable. We are creatures of symbol. We are at each other's mercy. And we know it.

Paul and the Christian tradition have a term which aptly describes what we have done with the creative power of symbolic communication: Original Sin. One construes another person not as a neighbor, but as a threat, that is, a possible source of chaos or coercion. Therefore, one launches preemptive strikes designed to diminish the surprise potential of the other and to subdue him or her by physical coercion, manipulation, ridicule, or other tactics. This is called murder: either physical murder, or murder of the spirit. Alternately, one tries to make one's own threatened existence more secure by investing hope and trust in some particular element of the universe, an element that will not really be able to sustain one's being against all threats. This is called idolatry.

Both murder and idolatry are generic terms for human transcendence gone tragically wrong. The flaw goes to the center of human being. It affects human intersubjectivity. There is pathology within the ongoing generation and sustenance of the social structures of our world. We mean each other wrongly. If human being is a being-together in a social world of our own making, and if we cooperatively hold that world in existence by our constant trafficking in meanings, then something is wrong with our meanings. The creative potential of our human ability to affect reality through communications is intact, but perverted. Human transcendence, created good, has gone bad. It is bent out of shape.

REDEMPTIVE MEANING, AND HOW IT SPREADS

As seen by modern phenomenological analysis, this bentness of our human being is *a pathology of meaning.* Its cure will also be a meaning, that is, a communication. Here is where the gospel comes in. For the gospel is a story. Jesus is the Word of God, spoken into the Babel of human meanings gone awry. In simplest terms, the gospel is a message that breaks into the dissonance of competing human transcendences. It brings harmony to the din of human meanings that have been struggling to drown one another out.

The gospel is assurance that there is One beyond the world who cares about the world, and who can sustain the existence of human beings. When this message is effectively proclaimed and received, its meaning liberates people. They no longer need to scramble to guarantee a sphere of operation for their outreaching love and knowledge by adopting an idol for insurance, or by curtailing the outreach of others. The meaning of the gospel addresses "bent" human being and "rebends" it. If the first bending may be called sin, the second is redemption.

Redemption is a healing of meanings. That is to say, it is a substantial modification of the very being of human beings. Our being is a being-together through mutual co-intending of the social world. Without the gospel, that co-intending would be a hopelessly snarled and frustrated competition. The gospel's infusion of meaning allows human beings to intend one another as partners working out their transcendence together.

When the gospel is effective, when it heals and harmonizes human meanings, there are dramatic results of a social nature. For example, the cooperative communitarian social organization of the early Christians in Jerusalem, depicted in the Acts of the Apostles, is a wonder that accompanies the proclamation of the gospel there. The new way of being-to-gether in cooperative human transcendence, made possible by the gospel, is what we call the church. The church is a kind of intersubjectivity: a we-being. To be a member of the church is to participate in the communication of gospel meanings, and in the social consequences of that communication. As we saw in the last chapter, the church is the outcome of the gospel, at the same time that it carries the gospel message, embodies it, and tells it. Church is the name one gives to the social reality that is coming into being where the gospel is healing human meaning.

What I am describing is a symbolic event—which is to say that it is a real event and an event that affects reality radically. Symbol brings persons together in relationship, and it creates the future by transforming the present. Powered by a divine meaning, the gospel transforms human reality through the very processes of human communication.

What processes? Three seem to be at work in our experience as a Christian people. The good news of the gospel seems to be addressing the structures of human meaning in three interrelated ways: by direct proclamation, by prayerful celebration, and by service to human needs.[6]

Jesus' own proclamation of God's Reign also seems to have taken effect in these three modalities of communication. First, Jesus explicitly *taught* the imminence of the Reign of God and its demands. His teaching used concepts from the Hebrew Scripture, elements of his own Jewish-Hellenistic culture, examples from rural and urban life, and insights from his own intimate relationship with the One whom he called Abba, Father. His teaching, as the gospels record it, was insistent and at times confrontational—but never coercive. Above all, Jesus' thoughts and words seem to have been singlemindedly set upon the goodness of a God whose only glory and happiness was to dote upon the men, women and children whom God had created.

Secondly, Jesus *celebrated* his relationship with his Father in prayer and in the liturgical rituals of his people. This relationship, this "Abba experience," was not for Jesus an exclusive possession, but rather a treasure to be shared with all those whom Abba also loved. Jesus, then, also celebrated human friendships. Among the most vivid gospel memories of him are those where he is among the common people: eating with them, conversing with them at length—"pressing flesh," as politicians say. Jesus is a word of God who is broadcast out among the people. He loves to party with all kinds of people; for this, and for their general neglect of fasting and sobriety, he and his followers attract criticism. The memorial which he leaves at the end of his life, to remind his friends of all he said and did and was, is more than bread: the cheer of wine has to be part of it, too.

Thirdly, and perhaps most eloquently, Jesus proclaimed and kicked off God's Reign by *caring* for human needs. He healed the blind and the mute and the lame. They say he fed the people in the desert, like the God of Israel. This service to the material needs of the people also communicated to them the good news that God's salvation was at hand.

In Jesus' ministry, these three ways of expressing and enacting God's Reign were inseparable. Jesus' teaching, his celebration of the relationship of God and people, and his caring service to people's material needs, all supported the same message. The healings would have made little sense without the teaching; the teaching would have been sterile without the joyful personal companionship; and that celebration of friendship, which was so natural for Jesus, would in turn have been hollow and frivolous without the healings and teachings.

To say that the church carries on Jesus' work of proclaiming the gospel, is to say that the church continues to communicate the good news of God's Reign by using precisely the three varieties of effective communication which the Gospels attribute to Jesus. There are *ministries of the word*, which are extensions of Jesus' teaching ministry. These include: evangelization, preaching, religious education or catechesis, Bible study, theology, religious journalism and publishing, and any activity in which Christians reflect upon the gospel message so that they can apply it and communicate it to other people.

There are also *ministries of the sacraments*, which are extensions of Jesus' table fellowship with his friends and his joyful celebration of his relationship to the One who was both his father and theirs. These include: celebration of the Lord's Supper; assisting the community's liturgical celebration as lector, cantor, choir member, musician, minister of the cup, minister of liturgical hospitality, or acolyte; celebration of baptism, marriage, or the other sacraments; carrying the eucharist to the sick; singing the liturgy of the hours; training people for liturgical celebration; composing or designing artistic works to help the community praise God; and every other activity which treasures and recalls the intimacy of Jesus' personal fellowship with his friends and their Father.

Finally, there are *ministries of service*, which are extensions of Jesus' practical care for the physical and psychological difficulties of the people to whom he was communicating God's own care. These include: feeding the hungry; clothing and sheltering those in need; healing the sick; counseling the troubled; burying the dead; all those other traditional Christian charities called "works of mercy"; all efforts to secure the physical, economic, social, and psychological welfare of disadvantaged people; and whatever is done in Jesus' name to relieve the suffering of his sisters and brothers.

To break down the expressive activities into three categories helps to highlight their connection with Jesus' own expressive communication of God's Reign in words and deeds. But the analysis can obscure an extremely important fact: each kind of activity is symbolic of the others. Each is inseparably related to the other two. No one works alone. Jesus' diverse works had one single message: God's Reign is here. The church's diverse works must have the same unity, and they can be effective proclamations only as long as that unity holds.

The gospel is most effectively and faithfully proclaimed, therefore, when there is a healthy balance among the three expressive ministries: word, sacrament, and service. The church's proclamation should be pointing in several directions at once. It should point back in history to Jesus and the great work which God accomplished in him. But ministries of the word—teaching, theology, catechesis—also should be pointing at contemporary church life in order to show to the world what God continues to do through the proclamation of the gospel in its midst. Both the church's life of worship, and its life of service to human need, are properly parts of the message which preachers and teachers reflect upon and talk about.

Similarly, what the church is celebrating in its liturgical life is not only what happened with Jesus twenty centuries ago, but what continues to happen today in the church's life. Liturgical words "refer," so to speak, to the church's presence to contemporary human need, as well as to God's presence in Jesus. Theological reflection helps to clarify what the liturgy celebrates. Catechetical instruction prepares people for the liturgy, and then guides them to assimilate what they have celebrated. Liturgical prayer becomes a source for theological reflection, as well as an impetus for social action.

Finally, Christians' care for the sick and the needy is no shallowly humanistic gesture, but the unavoidable implication of their understanding of the gospel and their participation in the intimacy of Jesus' table fellowship. The word ministries demonstrate their own authenticity when they support ministries of care. The reality of Jesus' continuing "real presence" in the church's liturgical life is underwritten by the church's continuing outreach to the needy. At the same time, ministry to people's material needs constitutes an invitation to them to join in the celebration of Jesus' friendship and to listen to the message proclaimed in Jesus' story.

A LOOK AT CHRISTIAN HISTORY

When these three families of communicative ministries are in touch with one another, the church is healthy. It is our good fortune today that most of us live in churches which enjoy healthy balance and interchange among ministries, churches in which the gospel can therefore be effectively communicated.

But this has not been so in every era of the church's history. It has sometimes happened that one or another kind of ministry wanted to run away with the whole show. Times of struggle or of corruption within the church invariably were times when something was going wrong with the effective symbolic communication of the gospel. This will become apparent in the chapters to follow, as we trace the story of the gospel within human history.

It is beyond the scope of this book—and it may be beyond the abilities of any one author today—to present a comprehensive history of the ministry of the word within the Christian church. Our purpose here is to provide background resources for contemporary women and men who are working in ministries of teaching, religious instruction, catechetical formation, and related areas. Theoretical orientation toward the work of the gospel is certainly a necessary part of the background which such pastoral workers need. These first two chapters have provided a rudimentary theoretical framework to help you understand what you are doing, what you have been called to do, and where it fits into the big picture of the gospel's transformation of the world.

It is also important for you to have a sense of the history of the kind of work which you are called to do, for it is your heritage. One does not understand the gospel, or God's workings with human beings, unless one appreciates the historical dimension of that ongoing symbolic event. This book, then, while not presenting a definitive history of the gospel, does offer a survey to substantiate the theoretical analysis put forward above, and to impart an understanding of the gospel's historicity, including your own place in it.

The following chapters present successive synchronic (or cross-sectional) analyses of the church's communicative process, starting with Jesus' lifetime and then slicing into history at three-century intervals from the first through the nineteenth century. Each chapter describes the general historical situation, then focuses in upon the balance of the three ministries of proclamation and reflection, of liturgical celebration, and of material service—word, celebration, and care, for short. There is a detailed discussion of the personnel, the institutions, the methods, the media, and the contents involved in the teaching activities which were applying the gospel message to the particular needs and circumstances of the era. Each chapter concludes with a summary of the aspects of Christian teaching today which we owe to the particular era under consideration. A concluding chapter looks to the future.

A note of caution is in order before undertaking any investigation into the history of the church. The objective is not to identify some ideal "golden age" which can set the pattern for church practice in our own day. There has never before been a day like ours. The most traditional thing about the Christian churches is their adaptability, their readiness to change to accommodate new needs in new times, while preserving—more or less faithfully, to be sure!—their continuity with the message and work of Jesus Christ. One pleasant surprise, at least, is in store for the reader. The story of the story of the gospel cannot be told without discovering how crucial to its success has been the work of ordinary people, lay folk, who gave their time and talents to its communication.

Notes for Chapter Two

1. Scripture passages have been translated by the author, with the intention of rendering the words of Jesus into contemporary American speech and giving other texts a gender-inclusive sense when that is present in the Greek original. For example, *adelphoi* is the masculine plural term for brothers, although in ancient times it would have been used in situations where a speaker was addressing a mixed audience—situations in which a speaker of American English would have to say "brothers and sisters."

2. For a good, basic discussion of "signals of transcendence," see *A Rumor of Angels: Modern Society and the Rediscovery of the Supernatural,* by Peter L. Berger (Garden City, N.J.: Doubleday & Co., 1969; Anchor Books, 1970), especially chapter 3, "Theological Possibilities: Starting With Man." Berger points to certain "prototypical human gestures" within the human situation—such as hope and the denial of death—which appear to point beyond everyday reality.

3. This is the philosophical project of the great phenomenologist Edmund Husserl, particularly in the *Cartesian Meditations,* translated by Dorion Cairns (The Hague: 1960). An introduction to Husserl's thought may be found in *Husserl: An Analysis of His Phenomenology,* by Paul Ricoeur, translated by Edward G. Ballard and Lester E. Embree (Evanston, Ill.: Northwestern University Press, 1967). Martin Heidegger and Bernard Lonergan, each in his own way, also have pursued the question of human being through the phenomenon of subjectivity as transcendence. For an introduction to Heidegger, see *Martin Heidegger: The Way and the Vision,* by J.L. Mehta (Honolulu: University Press of Hawaii, 1976). Lonergan's own *Method in Theology* (New York: Herder and Herder, 1972 and 1973; Seabury Press, 1979) provides an introduction to the major trends of his thinking, which are set forth in more detail in his *Insight: A*

Study of Human Understanding (London: Longmans, Green & Co., 1958; San Francisco: Harper & Row, 1978). For a short discussion of the ways in which phenomenological analysis of human transcendence has influenced contemporary theology, see the Appendix to Edward Farley's *Ecclesial Man* (Philadelphia: Fortress, 1975), entitled "Phenomenology in Catholic and Protestant Thought," pp. 235–72. Edward Schillebeeckx and Karl Rahner, both of whose theories of symbol we are using in our discussion of the gospel's transformation of human existence, make extensive use of transcendental analysis.

4. I am indebted to Edward Farley for the following analysis of human subjectivity as a twofold refusing of that which inhibits human transcendence. My discussion is essentially a paraphrase of his excellent analysis of human resistance to chaos and coercion. See especially chapter 6 of *Ecclesial Man*, entitled "Ecclesia and Redemptive Existence," pp. 127–49.

5. Farley says on p. 136 of *Ecclesial Man* that ridicule

> . . . is the attempt to violate another's pride or uniqueness-sense by transforming that novel existence into some fixed and at the same time negative category. Ridicule is always both a reduction and a negation. Ridicule . . . attempts to rob the human being of his future-oriented and self-transcending powers by fixing the human being into some undesireable characteristic. . . . Manipulation and ridicule are obviously closely related. It could even be said that ridicule is a form of manipulation.

6. These three ways have been identified by Edward Farley through painstaking analysis of ecclesial existence. Readers who have a taste for phenomenology are encouraged to study his discussion of the process of ecclesial transformation in *Ecclesial Reflection*, (Philadelphia: Fortress Press, 1982), particularly pp. 252–58. The three categories of word, celebration, and care, which will serve in this book to structure our historical survey of the ministry of the word, derive from Farley's analysis. My own view of sacramental or cultic activities, however, is also influenced by the Roman Catholic theological tradition.

Chapter Three

The Teaching of Jesus

Our survey of the gospel's history must begin, of course, with Jesus of Nazareth. It was his proclamation of the Reign of God which began the alteration of human meanings that issued in a new way of being-human-together for us. In this sense, Jesus is founder and foundation of the church.

Our historical information about Jesus, his message, and its reception by the human community comes almost entirely from the books of the New Testament, particularly from the four which we call the Gospels. But those accounts were not meant by their writers to be histories in any modern sense of the word. They do indeed give reliable information about Jesus, but they communicate along with it the significance which that information had for the writers and for the first readers of those ancient books.[1]

One may describe a Gospel as a life and death narrative of Jesus which aims to show his identity and significance for the church. There are four such narratives included in the New Testament, and in each of them *the* gospel itself is already at work. For the gospel is a contagious constructive message—the message which is announcing that God is making a new way of life possible, and which is at the same time bringing that new way of life into reality. In the Gospels, we are seeing both the primitive message of Jesus, and the effect it is having among the first generation of his followers. The gospel which we find in the Gospels, then, is already a gospel at work altering the self-definitions of individuals and communities: a gospel in the act of saving through meaning.

This is strikingly clear when several of the New Testament writers place the announcement of the Reign of God at the very beginning of Jesus' public communication. What he promises comes true while he is saying it. The Gospel of Mark records that:

> . . . Jesus came into Galilee proclaiming the gospel of God and saying, "The time is ripe and the Reign of God is going down now. Repent, and believe in the gospel." (Mk 1:14–15)

41

Luke's Gospel adds more dramatic detail. He locates Jesus' first public teaching event within the Nazareth synagogue, where, in the context
of a liturgical reading and commentary upon the Scripture, Jesus sets out
the program of God's Reign and informs the congregation that this Reign
has indeed begun.

> He came to Nazareth, where he was brought up; and according
> to his custom went into the synagogue on the sabbath day. He
> stood up to read. A scroll of the prophet Isaiah was handed to
> him. He opened the scroll and found the place where it was writ-
> ten:

> "The Spirit of the Lord is upon me,
> because God has anointed me to preach glad tidings to the poor.
> . . . to proclaim release to captives,
> and recovery of sight to the blind,
> to let the oppressed go free,
> and to proclaim a year acceptable to the Lord."

> Rolling up the scroll, he gave it back to the attendant and
> sat down, and all of the eyes in the synagogue were gazing at him.
> He began to say, "Today this scripture came true in your ears."
> (Lk 4:16–21)

The Gospel goes on to show how this prophecy is fulfilled during Jesus' career through his words and deeds. In fact, it is Jesus' teachings, exorcisms, healings, and feedings of the people which spell out the
disconcerting meaning of this shorthand formula, "Reign of God."

It may be that Jesus himself expected the Reign of God to arrive, with
glorious fanfare, during his own lifetime. Certainly Mark's community re-
tains such a memory about Jesus' understanding of God's Reign:

> Jesus said to them: "Amen, I'm telling you, there are some stand-
> ing here who won't taste death until they see that the Reign of
> God has arrived in power." (Mk 9:1)

If Jesus at first expected to accomplish a rather quick and easy opening
of God's Reign, then the mounting difficulties which he encountered in
Galilee and Jerusalem, culminating in his execution, would have come to
him as all the more bitter disappointments. Such an expectation on Jesus'
part would make sense out of the despair expressed in his last words, as
Mark records them:

. . . Jesus cried out with a loud voice, *"Eloi, Eloi, lama sabach-thani?"* which is translated, "My God, My God, why did you let go of me?" (Mk 15:34)

If God had forsaken Jesus, then God had forsaken the one who was supposed to bring God's Reign into the world. This is certainly the most paradoxical aspect of the concept of God's Reign, as the Gospels present it. Nothing about this concept is easy to understand, either for Jesus' first audiences, or for us who ponder it twenty centuries later. Upon this provocative but elusive concept, each generation of Christians have projected their own preconceptions.

However, modern interpreters are better equipped to discover elements of Jesus' own preaching than were their forebears, for several reasons. These include: greater familiarity with the ancient languages of Aramaic and Koine Greek; better understanding of the society and culture of Jesus' time, including its literary expressions; and the interpretive "tool kit" of the historical critical method for analyzing the scriptural texts. For example, it was not until 1774 that anyone took the trouble to arrange the texts of the first three Gospels in parallel columns in order to identify their similarities and differences. Such an arrangement, called a synopsis, is an invaluable aid for figuring out how the Gospels must have been compiled.[2]

Recognizing how prone Christians have been to misunderstand, one must try to reconstruct as exactly as possible Jesus' own understanding of "Reign of God." This is difficult to do. None of the Gospels gives us a definition of God's Reign from Jesus; we have only allusions and similes. To begin with, it is well to note some reasons why such a concept appealed to audiences in Jesus' day and land.[3]

THE SITUATION IN GALILEE AND JERUSALEM, ABOUT 30 C.E.

Before there was a way of being-human-together known as the Christian church, there was a way of being-human-together known as Judaism. Like any social entity, the Jewish people sustained their unity and their national identity through the sharing of meanings. Some of these meanings were national memories. As the books of the Hebrew Scripture reminded them, the Jews had been brought out of Egypt by God, who had thereby made them into a people. They understood one another to be heirs of that great event, heirs of the relationship which God had established between God's self and them at that time. The relationship itself was constructed by another set of meanings, the Law. In the Book of Exodus, the first account of the giving of the Law begins with a self-identification by God:

> I am the LORD, your God, who brought you out of the land of
> Egypt, out of the place of slavery. You shall not have other gods
> besides me. (Ex 20:2–3)

Torah specified how human affairs were to be conducted, and it bore the intentionality of the entire people who through it could understand themselves to be God's people.

Embedded in the meanings of their Law and their history was an understanding of God as someone outside the world who yet cared for the world and who particularly doted upon God's special people. The Law itself was the most intimate expression of God's intention to care for the people. The Jews of Jesus' time thought of the Law not merely as a text contained in scrolls, but as a mysterious entity that was with God even before creation. In the pious sayings of the rabbis, Torah was personified as a kind of companion for God. (This popular belief must have formed part of the background for the Johannine concept of the Logos or Word of God.)[4] Jesus' people imagined or symbolized God as lawgiver, as trailmaster, as mighty guardian, even as husband, of the people. The metaphor of the warrior-king presented itself to the poetic imaginations of Israel's psalmists, and this symbol expressed the Almighty's intention to be personally present and available to God's people. For example, see the "Canticle of Moses" in Exodus 15, where

> The LORD is a warrior, LORD is his name!
> Pharaoh's chariots and army he hurled into the sea (vv.3–4).

Psalm 95 says,

> . . . The LORD is a great God,
> and a great monarch above all gods.
> In God's hand are the depths of the earth.
> The tops of the mountains belong to God as well.

Other psalms, like 93, 97, and 99, begin with the refrain, "The Lord is King." Praise of Yahweh as victorious king seems to have been a popular liturgical theme.

At first, Israel had no king but the Lord. Eventually, the changing political climate brought David to the throne, and necessitated a theological revision of what monarchy was to mean for the people. Experience with the shortcomings of human monarchs, along with experience of their own inability to maintain justice and order in society despite the assistance of the Law, combined to persuade the people that somehow God had not yet quite managed to get a hold of worldly affairs. God was indeed king; nevertheless, the society in which they lived certainly was not the best that the Lord could manage.

The shifting geopolitical situation in the centuries before the birth of Jesus is well known. Jews had repopulated Judea after a generation of exile in Babylon, but they remained subject to the Persian Empire. Alexander the Great swept through the region in the fourth century B.C.E., and his heirs held political control for about 150 years, until Roman power began to grow. Inept administration, along with religious persecution and cultural pressure from Hellenism, led to a Jewish revolt in the mid second century B.C.E., which was successful (unfortunately so, in light of the false and rash hopes it engendered in subsequent generations). There followed about a hundred years of Jewish independence before Palestine fell once again under foreign control and a Roman administration was established.

Jesus' contemporaries, then, shared an interesting complex of meanings centering upon government. Politically, there was among their common national memories a recent experience of independence, and a more distant experience of having been ruled by their own Davidic kings. In light of these memories, the present foreign administration was understood to be anomalous.

Socially, everyday reality for a tax-ridden, exploiting and exploited populace contrasted sharply with the ideal social order projected by the Law and the Prophetic writings. For example, the principle of the jubilee year, as set forth in Leviticus 25, seems never to have been honored. The Law provides that land, in effect, cannot be purchased outright but only leased, because it must revert back every fiftieth year to the original family who owned it. Lev 25:36–37 forbids the taking of interest, for the explicit reason that "I, the LORD, am your God, who brought you out of the land of Egypt to give you the land of Canaan and to be your God" (v.38). But these principles seemed impractical to the modern commercial society in which Jesus lived. Moreover, in Jesus's society Jews themselves were employed in collecting Roman taxes from their own people. (It was from among this particularly despised group of collaborators that Jesus chose some of his followers.) In short, neither the political life nor the everyday social life of the nation was being effectively governed by God.

In light of these interpretations, personal and national longing for an improvement could easily express itself as longing that God, the King of Israel, would summon up the power to rule. In fact, the text of a prayer that was commonly recited in the synagogues in Jesus' day gives us evidence of a popular recognition that God was not yet ruling as successfully as God could rule and ought to rule. The prayer, a Kaddish in Aramaic, expresses a wish that God should establish the Reign of God. The text reads, in part:

> Magnified and sanctified be his great name in the world which he has greated according to his will. May he establish his kingdom in your lifetime and in your days and in the lifetime of all the house of Israel even speedily and at a near time.[5]

"Reign of God," then, was a culturally available cypher for whatever could improve the political, social, or personal situation. In those troubled times, however, "Reign of God" could also be a joke. And a joke it surely was to many who heard a certain intensely serious country dreamer from Nazareth, trying to tell them that the time finally had come when the Lord intended to begin reigning. "Where did this one get all this?" they asked, even in Nazareth itself. "What is the wisdom given him?" (Mk 6:2) In other towns, they were less polite and they asked: "Out of Nazareth can any good thing come?" (Jn 1:46)

For Jesus' contemporaries were not naive. The rolling hills and farmlands of the northern country harbored no center of Jewish learning or power. Greek theaters and schools, perhaps there were. But Jewish learning and power were concentrated in the capital, Jerusalem, in the south. The Temple and the priests were there; and the liturgical sacrifices and prayers that went up to God from Jerusalem were meant to express Israel's deepest understanding of its relationship with its King.

The Temple, with its corps of priests and its liturgy, was the official symbol that pulled together the people of God. Moreover the Law, Israel's other symbol of God's presence and power, had found able interpreters in the Pharisees. These lay leaders believed that the Law, which expressed God's intimate relationship with the people, was meant to be kept by everyone. To help ordinary people to understand and live the Law, the Pharisees undertook to interpret it and define its requirements in terms of the modern situation, in which many Jews had little contact with the Temple aside from paying taxes for its support. This practical concern of the Pharisees served the people well, all in all. And when the Temple was destroyed toward the end of the first century of the common era, only the Pharisaic conception of the Law remained viable. It became the only symbol whose meaning could pull Israel together as a nation as the people dispersed around the globe.

Jesus, however, had a different view of the Law, because he had a more original conception of the relationship which God desired to have with the people. Jesus was in touch with the power of God, which God would unleash through him. The Pharisees were practical men, and reasonable in their attempt to accommodate the traditional meanings of Judaism to the needs of the times. There was nothing practical about Jesus. He came out of the hills of Galilee shouting that God was about to take direct control of things. And he could do more than shout.

GOD'S CARE FOR PEOPLE IN JESUS

Jesus could cast devils out of madmen. Jesus exorcised, healed, and fed people. These deeds in favor of human well-being attracted attention to Jesus message, to be sure. But the point is, these deeds *were the message*. The healings, exorcisms, and feedings were demonstrations of what God's Reign meant. Jesus himself makes the connection explicit in Lk 11:20: "if I'm expelling demons with the finger of God, then the Reign of God has come upon you."

There is a dramatic exorcism story in the fifth chapter of Mark's Gospel. Jesus expels a whole gang of devils from a man whom no one could restrain during the devils' occupation. In a twist that must have seemed humorous to Jewish witnesses and readers, Jesus then allows the devils to take over some two thousand pigs that were feeding on a nearby hillside, and the pigs stampede forthwith to a watery death in the lake below. Pigs were unclean according to the Law, and so good Jews could not have eaten them anyway. Undoubtedly, the livestock were being fattened for sale to non-Jews—perhaps to the Roman occupation forces, who enjoyed pork.

Now, thanks to Jesus, the finger of God has touched the economy of the region. The Reign of God has stirred things up. Who is happy about this development? Presumably the man who got rid of the devils, because he wants to go with Jesus (v.18), and Jesus' other followers. Who is *not* happy that God's Reign has had this strange effect upon human affairs? The devils, and the pig owners! The Reign of God is bad news for devils, who shriek (v.7): "What do you have to do with me, Jesus, Son of the Most High God? I adjure you by God, do not torment me!" The Reign of God is also bad news for pig owners, that is, for those who are making their living through complicity in a situation that is bad for God's people, the Roman occupation. God's power has come meddling in their affairs through Jesus, and the story reports that "they began to beg him to leave their territory" (v.17).

Jesus also acted out God's concern for human happiness when he healed sick people and those with physical and social disabilities. The woman who had hemorrhaged for twelve years is cured of her affliction when she touches Jesus' clothing, according to the stories preserved in each of the synoptic Gospels (Mk 5:25–34; Mt 9:20–22; Lk 8:43–48). Her encounter with Jesus meant something more for her than relief of physical discomfort. She had hesitated to touch Jesus because her disease was a gynecological disorder. Under the Law, a man who touched a menstruating woman became unclean. Most women experienced this regulation as a periodic inconvenience; for this woman, however, the Law functioned to separate her from her husband indefinitely. Some of the experts said that the Law permitted a man to divorce a woman who had an ailment like this one. Jesus' healing has removed a social disability as well as an illness.

Other stories in the Gospels elaborate upon the meaning of encountering God's Reign at work in the healings of Jesus. In the second chapter of Mark, Jesus' reaction to seeing a paralyzed man lowered through the roof is, "Child, your sins are forgiven" (v.5). The proclamation of forgiveness, which is evidence of the Reign of God taking effect, is not welcomed by certain of Jesus' hearers: the scribes, who were learned in the Law. "Why does this one speak that way?" they ask themselves (v.7). "He is blaspheming! Who but God alone can forgive sins?" Who, indeed? Jesus' second word to the crippled man is a command which empowers him to walk and carry his mat so that everyone can see (vv.11–12). Jesus says this healing word "so that you may know that the Son of Man has authority to forgive sins on earth" (v.10). Jesus implies that the power to forgive sins— God's power—and the power to effect a cure by intending it—Jesus' power—are the same.

In the Gospels, then, Jesus' healings and exorcisms dramatize the impact which God's power makes as it breaks out in people's homes and businesses. God's reigning means that the blind see and the lame walk. More than that, however, it means the forgiveness of sins, economic disruption, inversion of social status, and an unsettling reinterpretation of the Law itself. These latter effects of God's coming into power do not lend themselves to demonstration through works of power. These meanings are conveyed through Jesus' prayer, fellowship, and teaching, to which we now turn.

JESUS AND THE CULT: A NEW MEANS OF INTIMACY

The Law and the Temple constituted twin symbols of the presence of God to the people. The Temple was God's dwelling place among the people: it allowed God to be with them. The priesthood was a hereditary office, shared by descendents of the tribe of Levi. The sacrifices which the priests made in the Jerusalem Temple, according to detailed prescriptions expressed within the Law itself, were the people's tangible offering of hospitality to the architect of the universe, their token of recognition of God's dwelling among them. Although the upkeep of the Temple, the purchase of large animals for sacrifice, and the maintenance of the numerous priests constituted a heavy economic burden for a nation that had to pay civil taxes to the forces of occupation in addition to the ten-percent Temple tithe, nevertheless the benefits seemed worth the cost.

The Temple was a grand place of pilgrimage in the capital city, which those who lived elsewhere might visit once a year or once in a lifetime. But the Jewish people had another symbol that, thanks in large part to the Pharisees, brought God's presence home to them in their everyday intimate lives. The Law itself was treasured as an expression of God's relationship with and solicitude toward the people. To keep the commandments, with love and with zeal, was to know that one belonged to God, a God who had given God's self to the people. This was the Covenant, and the good Jew delighted in faithful observance of it. The Pharisees' zeal for the Law was a missionary zeal. They sought to teach and explain the Law so that every Jew, in every town no matter how far from Jerusalem and its Temple, could have the joy of faithful participation in God's greatest gift. For the Law was the expression of God's intention toward the people.

But a learned lawyer's perspective upon life is not necessarily that of a peasant or a shepherd. Jesus criticized the results of the Pharisees' well-intentioned attempt to spell out legal obligations in minute detail. For Jesus, that attempt had had an effect opposite to what was intended. It made the Law a barrier between God and the man in the street or the woman in the home—instead of the window into God's care for human beings that it was meant to be.

Matthew's Gospel records a severe attack by Jesus upon the Pharisees. Although the account surely reflects a situation of heightening tensions between Jews and the Christian sect after Jesus' death, nevertheless it serves to give examples of the kind of minutiae which Jesus found to be oppressive for the common people. "Woe to you, scribes and Pharisees. Hypocrites!" says Jesus in Mt 23:23. "You tithe mint and dill and cummin, and have neglected the heavier things of the law: judgment and mercy and faith." Jesus charges (Mt 23:4) that the people's religious leaders "tie up heavy burdens hard to carry and lay them on other people's shoulders, but they will not lift a finger to move them." In fact, Jesus identifies the Pharisees' interpretation and application of the Law as something that is running counter to God's attempt to rule in power:

> Woe to you, scribes and Pharisees. Hypocrites! You shut down the reign of heaven right in front of people. You don't enter, and the ones who are entering you won't let in. (Mt 23:13)

Jesus puts forth his own interpretations of the Law, and in a number of cases these amount to a program of social reform. Jesus' radical reinterpretation does not overturn the Law as symbol of God's presence to and care for the people. On the contrary, it means to rehabilitate the powerful symbol of the Law so that it functions once again to shape the patterns of human affairs according to God's will for human welfare. At least, that's how Matthew sees things.

Among the stories that come down to us concerning Jesus and the Law, there are echoes of a demand for Covenant justice in the tradition of Israel's prophets. This can easily be seen in the area of what we might term family-relations law. When the Pharisees confront him on the issue of divorce, Jesus makes bold to correct both them and the Mosaic Law itself on the basis of Jesus' own understanding of God's intention. In Mk 10:2–12, we read:

> The Pharisees came up and asked, "Is it lawful for a husband to divorce his wife?" They were testing him. He answered them, "What did Moses command you?" They said, "Moses permitted him to write a certificate of divorce and send her away." But Jesus told them, "It was because of the hardness of your hearts that he wrote you this commandment. But from the beginning of creation, 'God made them male and female. For this reason a person shall leave father and mother, and the two shall become one flesh.' So they are no longer two but one flesh. Therefore let no human being pull apart what God has yoked together."

Again we may ask, who would have been happy to hear this new, stricter interpretation of the Law? Wives, of course—who under some contemporary interpretations of the Mosaic law were at risk of divorce (and the loss of economic and social status) for matters as trivial as bad cooking or the passing of youthful attractiveness. Incidentally, Moses did not permit wives to divorce their husbands.[6]

Jesus seems to have demanded reform in another area of family-relations law, that concerning the obligation to support one's aged parents. There was also an obligation to support the Jerusalem Temple, and the legal experts seem to have subordinated the former duty to the latter in a kind of tax-shelter arrangement. We read in Mk 7:9–14 the following criticism leveled by Jesus:

> Nice going! You set aside God's commandment so you can keep your tradition. For Moses said, "Honor your father and your mother," and "Whoever speaks evil of father or mother shall

die." But you say, "If a person says to father or mother, 'Any support you might have had from me is *korban*' " (meaning, dedicated to God), you permit the person to do nothing more for his or her father or mother. You wipe out the word of God with your tradition which you hand on. And that's not all you do.

Who would have been glad to hear Jesus talk like this? The elderly. Who would *not* have liked Jesus' views on this aspect of the Law? Someone who had been taking advantage of the loophole. Jesus' interpretation would require a person to pay out 10% of income as Temple tax, plus perhaps 20% as parental support: a total of 30%. The Pharisees' interpretation would excuse a person from paying the 20% to parents if that 20% were dedicated to the Temple; the Temple would get twice as much, the person would pocket an extra 10%, but the parents would get nothing. Obviously, the other group whom Jesus' criticism would have displeased would be the Jerusalem Temple personnel, the priests, who were benefitting by the loophole arrangement.[7]

Besides family-relations law, Jesus also takes aim at laws that have to do with the practice of Israel's worship, the cultic laws. These defined who was "clean" enough to join in the official worship of God, and when. We have already seen that Jesus' cure of the woman with the hemorrhage relieved her of the burden of being in constant danger of making her husband, or any other man whom she chanced to touch, ritually unclean or unfit to pray. Jesus does not allow the cure to happen surreptitiously, as the woman wished. Instead, he causes her no little embarrassment by calling attention to what has happened. He permits and endorses the touch that has passed between himself and this "unclean" woman. Christians see this story as Jesus' lifting of the blood taboo which men had connected with menstruation in many religions.[8]

Another kind of taboo or "uncleanness" which Jesus does away with, thus easing the legal burdens upon housewives in particular, is that connected with the selection, preparation, serving, and eating of food. Mark's Gospel not only tells how Jesus did this, but adds an explanation of the customs for an audience which no longer was familiar with them:

> Now when the Pharisees and some scribes who had come from Jerusalem gathered around him, they saw that some of his disciples ate their meals with unclean, that is, unwashed, hands. For the Pharisees, and all Jews, do not eat without carefully washing their hands, observing the tradition of the elders. And when they come from the marketplace they do not eat without purifying themselves. And there are many other things that they

have traditionally observed, the purification of cups and jugs and pots. So the Pharisees and scribes questioned him, "Why do your disciples not follow the tradition of the elders, but eat a meal with unclean hands?" He said to them: "Isaiah prophesied well about you hypocrites, as it is written:

'This people honors me with their lips,
but their heart is far from me;
In vain do they worship me,
teaching as doctrines the precepts of human beings.'

You leave God's commandment but hold on to human tradition." (Mk 7:1–8)

Mark has Jesus give a further explanation later on:

"Don't you get it? Don't you know that everything that goes into a person from outside cannot defile, because it goes into the stomach, not the heart, and passes out into the latrine?" Thus he declared all foods clean. "But what comes out of a person, that is what defiles. From within people, from their hearts, come evil thoughts, fornication, theft, murder, adultery, greed, malice, deceit, licentiousness, envy, blasphemy, arrogance, foolishness. All these evils come from within and they defile." (Mk 7:18–23)

Jesus' understanding of what God wishes in the way of worship from human beings comes into sharpest conflict with that of the legal experts over the details of sabbath observance. The seventh day, on which God rested after the work of creation, according to Genesis 2:2, was supposed to be a day of rest and renewal for all Jews (Ex 20:8–11). Detailed regulations were devised to define and insure what was meant by "rest." For example, food could not be prepared. In order for the women to have a day away from the cooking fires on the sabbath, they had to do double work on the day before, the day of preparation. Despite this, the principle was a sound one, and one around which Jewish family life turned in Jesus' day as it continues to do until the present.

Mark's Gospel records conflict between Jesus and the Pharisees on an occasion when, far from home and previously prepared meals, his hungry followers pick and eat heads of grain as they are passing through a field on the sabbath. Jesus answers the legal criticism with the principle, "The sabbath was made for people, not people for the sabbath" (Mk 2:27).[9] In the next chapter, Jesus is infuriated when the Pharisees watch to see whether he will heal on the sabbath (Mk 3:1–5). Jesus defiantly cures a man with a misshapen hand in front of the legal experts, who then plan to destroy Jesus (v.60) for destroying the sabbath rest. But Jesus actually has honored the sabbath, which is a religious institution meant to honor the completion of God's creative activity in Genesis, because Jesus has completed God's creative work upon the man whom Jesus made whole.

Jesus' radical reinterpretation of the Law serves to rehabilitate this symbol of God's presence among the people. If the symbolic function of the sabbath is to celebrate God's availability and power, then a sabbath which is a day of healing, "works better" than a sabbath which is merely a day of rest from worldly activities. The emphasis is to be placed upon the God who is present through the symbol of the Law, and not upon the material prescriptions of the Law itself. In the same way, Jesus discounts the importance of the material components of Israel's other great symbol of God's presence, the Temple. Mark 13:1–2 presents Jesus' remarks on the occasion when he and his companions, having journeyed to the capital from their homes in rural Galilee, were visiting the impressive Temple compound in Jerusalem.

> As Jesus was going out of the temple, one of his disciples said to him, "Look, teacher, what awesome stones and buildings!" Jesus said to him, "You see these great buildings? There's not going to be one stone left on top of another that won't be thrown down."

The Temple is indeed the effective symbol of God's presence, power, and availability to God's people. But it is by no means indispensable.

Jesus sees beyond the material structures of the Temple and the concrete details of the Law. He gives the impression of having another means of access to the power of God besides these effective symbols. Jesus seems to enjoy a familiarity, an intimacy, with God that is not available to other Jews of his day. He teaches "with authority, not like the scribes" for whom Law and Temple constitute the only availability of God.

Jesus speaks to God with a new degree of intimacy and urgency; moreover, he invites his friends to do likewise. The Gospels say that Jesus often spoke to God in prayer, and they record several instances of what Jesus said to God when he prayed. Jesus' prayers are in one sense typical of those which any devout Jew of his day might offer. For example, the Aramaic Kaddish says:

> Magnified and sanctified be his great name in the world which he has created according to his will.[10]

In Mt 6:9, Jesus tells his friends to pray;

> Hallowed be your name.

The Kaddish continues:

> May he establish his kingdom in your lifetime and in your days and in the lifetime of all the house of Israel even speedily and at a near time.

Jesus' prayer continues (v.10):

> Your kingdom come! Your will be done, on earth as it is in heaven.

The similarities are apparent; but there are important differences as well. First, Jesus' prayer expresses the wish that God's Reign "come"— that is, come immediately, right now. The Kaddish asks that God "establish" God's Reign at some future time, although "speedily and at a near time." Secondly, Jesus' prayer is much simpler and more direct. This is explained in part by the fact that the Kaddish is a formal, official liturgical prayer. Such a prayer would naturally have a more literary structure than a prayer which one composed to teach to Galilean peasants. But more importantly, Jesus' prayer is addressed *to God* and uses the second-person grammatical construction: "your" name, "your" kingdom, "your" will. The more formal synagogue prayer is speaking *about God*, according to its third-person grammatical structure: "his" name, "his" will, "his" kingdom. The "your" of the Kaddish refers not to God but to the human beings gathered to recite the prayer.

Other Jewish prayers, to be sure, often were addressed directly to God and used second-person constructions. Many of the Psalms express intimate, heart-to-heart sentiments. Ps 63, for example, begins:

> O God, you are my God and I seek you;
> My flesh faints for you and my soul thirsts for you
> like the parched earth when there's no water.
> So I have looked toward you in the sanctuary
> to see your power and glory.

This is certainly a prayer which Jesus learned in his youth; it is a prayer which taught Jesus himself how to pray. Yet the intimacy of Jesus' prayer consists in more than its simplicity and its direct, second-person form of address. Jesus calls God "Father"—in his native tongue, "Abba"—which no one else did. "Abba" would translate into American English as "my Dad" or "Daddy."[11] This name for God seems to have been a habitual feature of Jesus' prayer, judging from the frequency with which it appears in the Gospels (e.g., Mk 14:36, Lk 22:42, Mt 26:39, Lk 11:2, Mt 6:9). More importantly for us, Jesus indicates that he is not the only one whose "Abba" God is. The Lord's Prayer is given to the disciples as an instruction in how they themselves are to talk to God (see Mt 6:9 and Lk 11:2). The Christian tradition adopted this custom from Jesus, as is apparent not only in the stories about Jesus recorded in the Gospels, but in other material as well (see Rom 8:15 and Gal 4:6).

Why did Jesus start calling God "Abba"? It is impossible for us, twenty centuries later on the other side of the world, to read Jesus' mind or to psychoanalyze him to uncover the nature of his experience of God. But we can look into his mind and his heart from the outside, that is, through the evidence we have concerning his activities and his message. We can, on this basis, say a few things about what the "Abba experience" must have been like for Jesus.[12] Jesus is someone whose heart is set upon God, whose entire attention, hopes and dreams are completely occupied with God. But the God who so fascinated Jesus is a God whose heart is likewise set upon humankind: upon the happiness, the well-being of the men, women, and children whom God has created. Jesus has, and expresses, an intimate insight into the "will" of God, which is that human beings should be free and happy.

In fact, so intensely certain is Jesus of God's desire for human welfare, that he also experiences an intolerable wrongness when he encounters real human suffering of any sort. But along with this sense that suffering ought not to be, Jesus experiences something else. He finds himself empowered to do something about human suffering on God's behalf. The intimacy of Jesus' relationship with Abba and certitude of Abba's intentions becomes a sharing of Abba's power to heal human hurt. In other words, Jesus' healing power as the agent of the outbreaking of the Reign of God is thus directly connected with his experience of intimacy with his "Abba."

Later generations of Christians would, of course, identify Jesus' unique experience of intimacy with God as Jesus' divinity. Jesus is God and the Son of God, they would say, and "no one knows the Father except the Son" (Mt 11:27). Those early Christian theologians would also identify the force which empowered Jesus to proclaim God's Reign in word and deed—a force arising directly from the intimate relationship between Father and Son—as the third person of the Trinity, God the Holy Spirit. "God anointed Jesus of Nazareth with the holy Spirit and power," they would say. "He went around doing good and healing all who were oppressed by the devil, for God was with him" (Acts 10:38). Moreover, Jesus "received from the Father the promise of the Holy Spirit, and poured it out, as you both see and hear" (Acts 2:33).

The intimacy which Jesus enjoyed with his Father was not something which he could keep to himself. On the contrary, it was meant to be shared and celebrated. Jesus told his followers that God was their Father, too. God's Reign touched their lives when they touched Jesus.

The picture of Jesus which is preserved in the Gospels is that of a man who enjoyed contact with all kinds of people, and particularly with ordinary folk. Mark's Jesus is up to his elbows in people. We see him grasping a hand (1:31 and 9:27), laying his hands on the sick (6:5), jostled by crowds (5:27 and 31), putting his fingers into a deaf man's ears and spitting on his tongue (7:33), laying hands on a blind man and spitting into his eyes (8:23–25), putting his arms around a little child (9: 36), getting perfume poured on his head as he is reclining at the dinner table (14:3). We also see him getting a hug and a kiss from a traitor (14:45), seized by an armed mob (14:46), blindfolded, beaten, roughed up, hit on the head and spit upon (14:65; 15:15 and 19), and nailed to a cross (15:24). Jesus is remembered as having been physically available to people, and vulnerable to them. For the reader, Mark's many mentions of how people have touched Jesus convey an impression of a Jesus whose body is available as an instrument for the arrival of God's Reign. The reader is then prepared for the way in which Jesus speaks of his body at the Last Supper:

> While they were eating, he took bread, said the blessing, broke it, and gave it to them, and said, "Take it; it's my body." Then he took a cup, gave thanks, and gave it to them, and they all drank from it. He told them, "This is my blood of the covenant, which will be poured out for many." (Mk 14:22–24)

Before Jesus, the Temple and the Law had been symbols through which God was present, active, and available to the people. Realistically speaking, these concrete symbols had not been entirely successful in facilitating God's governance of the land and of society. Now God's Reign was taking effect in human lives through the bodily touches of Jesus which healed and fed the people. Jesus' own body, his own personal presence, became the new effective symbol of God's availability to people. This experience of God's availability in Jesus was to become the foundation of the sacramental worship of the Christian church, and particularly of the Christian celebration of the Eucharist.

The custom of celebrating fellowship in the Reign of God with a festive meal seems to have begun well before the last days of Jesus' life. Just as Jesus' teaching and healing activities were directed to all God's people in need, so the table fellowship of Jesus' followers embraced all classes of society. Jesus was noted for seeking out the company of sinful persons and the poor. This scandalized the religious authorities and lay leaders, who expected a religious teacher to be more selective in his associations. Apparently, many were also scandalized by the sheer frivolity of the parties which Jesus used to give. Matthew's Gospel records that Jesus was criticized as "a glutton and a drunkard, a friend of tax collectors and sinners" (Mt 11:19)

After Jesus' death, the early Christian communities would carry on the tradition of meeting for joyful community meals to remember what Jesus had done and to look forward to the day when Jesus would return to "drink again the fruit of the vine" in the Reign of God with them (Mk 14:25). It is not without significance that the Eucharist, the great symbol of God's presence with the people in Jesus and of Jesus' promise to return, is made with two elements. Bread, of course, is a very sensible kind of food that can sustain human life. But wine is hardly a food at all; its only "use" is for gladness. This effective symbol of God's Reign needs both practicality and frivolity. Jesus sets a table where the refreshments are both good for you, and fun.

JESUS' WORDS: THE MESSAGE OF THE REIGN OF GOD

What is it about the Reign of God that makes Jesus and his friends want to celebrate? They are celebrating the kind of God it is who is starting to rule the world. This God cares about the people, and sends Jesus with power to heal, feed, and release the people from evil. This God's heart is set upon human well-being. This God is "Abba" for Jesus and for his friends.

However, this is also a wasteful and foolish God, according to the stories of Jesus. God does not invest wisely in sending good things to human beings. God squanders love and material blessings on those who deserve them least. Jesus' followers are instructed to immitate this prodigal aspect of God's personality. Jesus says in Mt 5:44–45:

> I'm telling you, love your enemies, and pray for those who persecute you, so that you may be children of your heavenly Father, who makes the sun rise on the bad and the good, and causes rain to fall on the just and the unjust.

Luke records a similar instruction:

> . . . love your enemies and do good, and lend expecting nothing
> back; then your reward will be great and you will be children of
> the Most High, for God is kind to the ungrateful and the wicked.
> (Lk 6:35)

Jesus tells Peter he must forgive "seventy-seven times" (Mt 18:22), and
goes on to illustrate with the Parable of the Merciless Official. In this story,
an official who cannot immediately pay off a several-billion-dollar debt to
his king asks for leniency in the form of an extended schedule of payments.
"Have patience with me," he says, "and I will pay back everything" (v. 26).
Instead, the king decides simply to write off the debt and cancel the sched-
uled repayment. The official, however, is not content with this. He calls
in his own investments and demands that a fellow official immediately pay
off a smaller debt. At this point, the debtor proposes the same extended
payment plan which the official himself had proposed to the king. It is rejected again; but instead of forgiving the debt as the king had done for him,
the official has his colleague jailed. When the king hears about this, of
course, he punishes the official. The man's offense is twofold. He has not
shown his colleague the compassion which he experienced from the king.
But more than that, he has rejected the king's generosity. Not wanting to
be written off as a bad debt, he is intent upon showing that he can indeed
repay his huge debt to the king—just as soon as his own investments pay
off.

Jesus' message is that the Reign of God does not run like a ledger
showing profit and loss. If anything, God is a notoriously bad investor. The
Parable of the Prodigal Father (also known as the Prodigal Son, Lk 15:11–
32) makes this point. The younger son has been imprudent and reckless
in frittering away his capital with bad companions, and returns to his home
seeking only to work with the servants. But his father is even more reckless. Having already lost a substantial amount of property through the
son's wastefulness, he goes ahead and spends more on this same son. Having already had his heart broken once, he nevertheless welcomes the son
back with love. In doing so, he even risks alienating the affections of the
older son, the one who has indeed proved to be a good investment in terms
of the property and the love which the father has entrusted to him.

God gives love without our having earned it. God's goodness cannot
be harnessed through the meticulous fulfillment of the Temple sacrifices,
or through faithful observance of the Law. The only thing that accounts for
God's goodness is God's goodness itself. It doesn't seem fair, and it doesn't
make sense, but that's the way it is in the Reign of God.

The unfairness of God is illustrated in a story about labor relations in Mt 20:1–16. An estate owner hires workers for his vineyard at different times of the day, but at day's end each gets the same pay: a full day's wage. The owner has not gotten the maximum return for his money. He has been foolish in squandering extra pay on workers who produced less; and he has done so in such a way that those who worked longest have heard about the inequity and are disgruntled. Again, generosity has no warrant other than itself. This behavior certainly seems reckless by any rational criterion of wise business practices.[13]

Yet Jesus and his followers can and do celebrate the fact that God is going to run the world in this inefficient, unfair manner. The Reign of God is a kind of bad investment; but it is also presented as a challenge: can you be glad that this unwise investor of a God is taking over and reigning? Can you call this old fool of a God your Father? Can you let this God forgive your debts, and can you be as foolish in your relationships with the other citizens of God's Reign? If you can, then you know why Jesus and his friends are laughing, and the secret of God's Reign is yours. John's Gospel makes this theme a part of Jesus' parting words to his friends:

> As the Father loved me, so I also loved you.
> Remain in my love.
> If you keep my commandments, you will remain in my love,
> just as I have kept my Father's commandments
> and remain in his love.
> I have told you these things so that my joy may be in you
> and your joy may be complete.
> This is my commandment:
> love one another as I have loved you. (Jn 15:9–12)

Jesus' joy is the bottom line of the Reign of God. But the joy coexists with a good deal of hardship. The Gospels show God's Reign already breaking out in human reality through the deeds of Jesus; but, paradoxically, they also indicate that one must get to the Reign of God by following Jesus into it. And that is not easy. Mark seeks to show that discipleship entails suffering when he places these words in Jesus' mouth:

> If you wish to come after me you must deny your very self, take up your cross, and follow me. For if you wish to save your life you will lose it, but if you lose your life for my sake and that of the gospel you will save it. What profit is there for you to gain the whole world and forfeit your life? What could you trade for your life? (Mk 8:34–37)[14]

If, indeed, someone wishes to follow after Jesus, the requirements are explicitly presented in the Gospels. Discipleship means an introduction to Jesus through personal encounter; a call to which one immediately responds; a commissioning to tell other people about Jesus; and following Jesus to death.

Personal encounters with Jesus in the Gospels often take the form of healings and exorcisms. Bartimaeus in Mk 10 follows Jesus after having received his sight. Mary Magdalene, Joanna and Susanna accompany Jesus on his preaching tours after they "had been healed of evil spirits and infirmities," according to Lk 8:1–3. For others, personal experience of Jesus takes the form of listening to Jesus and disputing with him. The Samaritan whom Jesus asks for water in Jn 4 begins her relationship with him in this manner.

The personal encounter may lead directly into a call to follow Jesus. Indeed, Mark's account of the sudden call of Simon, Andrew, James, and John combines the initial experience and the summons in one event. Jesus watches the fishermen at work, then tells them, "Come after me" (Mk 1:16–20). They immediately leave their work, without taking time to think. The personal encounter *is* the call. One potential disciple decides not to accept Jesus' invitation when he sees the implications of what he has come to understand about Jesus. His initial encounter takes the form of a discussion:

> As Jesus was setting out on a journey someone ran up, knelt down before him, and asked him, "Good Teacher, what must I do to inherit eternal life?"
>
> Jesus answered, "Why do you call me good? No one is good but God alone. You know the commandments. . . ."
>
> The person replied and said to him, "Teacher, all these I have observed from my youth."
>
> Jesus looked at that person, and loved that person, and said, "There's one thing missing. Go on, sell what you've got and give to the poor, and you'll have a fortune in heaven. Then come and follow me."
>
> But saddened by that word, the person went away grieving, because that person had so many possessions. (Mk 10:17–23)

The story shows that one can have personal experience of Jesus and receive a call to go with him on a journey, yet still decide not to accept the invitation. The journey upon which Jesus was about to set out, in this Markan narrative, was of course the journey to Jerusalem, where he would be executed.

The third aspect of discipleship is that, once one knows Jesus and understands where he is going, one tells others about Jesus and about the encounter which one has had with him. When the Gerasene man in Mk 5 whom Jesus exorcised wanted to go away with him, Jesus

> would not permit him but told him instead, "Go home to your family and report to them what the Lord in pity has done for you." Then he went off and began to proclaim in the Decapolis what Jesus had done for him. . . . (Mk 5:19–20)

The Samaritan at the well is also sent by Jesus to announce good news to her town. John records that she

> . . . left her water jar and went off into the town and said to the people:
> "Come and see a person who told me everything I have done. Could he be the Christ?"
> They went out of the town and came to him. . . . Many Samaritans of that town believed in him because of the word of the woman who testified. (Jn 4:28–30, 39)

Her message is effective, and leads others to have direct experience of Jesus. The townspeople ask Jesus to stay for awhile, and they hear his words at first hand. Then they are able to tell the woman:

> No longer do we believe because of your talking; for we have heard for ourselves, and we know that this is truly the savior of the world. (Jn 4:42)

The fourth requirement of discipleship is that one follow Jesus all the way to death. Few of the disciples whom we encounter in the Gospels meet this criterion. The Eleven who have eaten the Last Supper with Jesus and followed him out to Gethsemani to pray nevertheless desert Jesus and run off when the mob comes to arrest him (Mk 14:50). Ironically, Judas, one of the Twelve, is leading others to follow Jesus, in the sense that they are tracking him down to arrest him. But some of Jesus' women followers do not desert him; these are the disciples who remain with Jesus at his execution. As Jesus dies on the cross,

> There were also women observing from a distance. Among them were Mary Magdalene, Mary the mother of James the younger and Joses, and Salome, who had followed him when he was in

> Galilee and ministered to him. There were also many other
> women who had come up with him to Jerusalem. (Mk 15:40–41)

The profile of the disciple which Mark's Gospel presents is obviously
meant to provide a program for faithful Christian life in an evangelizing
community which is facing the everyday danger of persecution and death.
But the basic pattern of discipleship—experience, share, and follow Jesus
until death—remains the blueprint for all Christian life.

This blueprint is the key to entry into God's Reign. As we have seen,
the meaning of the *call* to discipleship depends upon the kind of God it is
who is reigning, and upon the characteristics of the Reign itself. These
have been specified by Jesus in his gestures of *caring* for people's needs
and *celebrating* both God's recklessly forgiving love of the people and the
people's brotherly and sisterly relationship with one another. In light of
this care and this celebration of intimacy, the call to enter God's Reign
could hardly be anything other than urgent, surprising, even inconven-
ient. Jesus' gospel is more than oral teaching. His message takes effect
through the combined impact of care, celebration, and call.

The first century after Jesus' death saw the growth of the church into
an organization with institutional structures into which caring, celebra-
tional, and teaching functions were departmentalized. In the next chapter
and subsequent ones, we will be able to describe the development of the
ministry of the word in terms of its personnel, institutions, methods, media, and content. However, even within the ministry of Jesus itself there
are foreshadowings of institutionalization, and so this fivefold organizational analysis can be begun now with the earliest stratum of gospel communication.

Personnel: Every disciple is supposed to share the work of telling others about Jesus. However, Jesus also may have experimented with a more
formal arrangement to supplement his own preaching. In all three synoptic Gospels, we find projected into Jesus' career the details of an organization of traveling gospel teachers (Mt 10:1, 9–11, 14; Mk 6:7–13; Lk 9:1–
6). While the story of their commissioning by Jesus may not be historical,
it does reflect the attempts of early followers of Jesus to continue to spread
God's Reign using the same techniques they remembered Jesus himself
using. As the story has it, a group of twelve disciples is called together.
They are given authority to heal and to expel demons, and they are sent
out to preach the Reign of God, to exorcise and to heal. The twelve get
specific instructions. They are to go in pairs, travel without provisions, and
accept home hospitality.

The twelve do as Jesus did. They go through the villages of Galilee,
where they preach the gospel, cast out many demons, treat the sick and

heal them. Afterwards they are said to report back to Jesus, who invites them to "come by yourselves to an out-of-the-way place and rest a little" (Mk 6:31). Luke says that Jesus later appointed seventy-two more preachers, and sent them out with similar instructions. These went "ahead of him in pairs to every town and place he intended to visit" (Lk 10:1). Their message is the same as Jesus' message, and Luke has Jesus assure them that

> Anybody who listens to you is listening to me. Anybody who rejects you is rejecting me. And anybody who rejects me is rejecting the one who sent me. (Lk 10:16)

The twelve and the seventy-two do what Jesus does: they announce God's Reign, they heal, and they rout demons.

Institutions: It would be anachronistic to characterize these two groups as ministers in any institutional sense of the word. There is no positive evidence in the Gospels that the work of Jesus was becoming institutionalized during his lifetime. Indeed, if Jesus himself had expected God's Reign to bring the age to a close in the very near future, he would not have been thinking in terms of establishing ministries at all. Institutionalization of ministry took place in subsequent generations, the very generations in which the Gospel accounts themselves were being written down. The Christian communities whose members composed the Gospels were communities in which a variety of structures of leadership and teaching were emerging. It is not surprising, then, that members of those communities were especially interested in preserving any memories of Jesus that could help to shape the ministerial structures then taking form in their midst.

In this spirit, they recalled what Jesus had had to say about religious institutions of his own day. The Gospels remember Jesus as a great critic of religious institutions. Matthew's community recalls that Jesus told his followers:

> As for you, don't let anybody call you rabbi. You've only got one teacher, and you are all sisters and brothers. Don't call anybody on earth your father; you've only got one Father, the one in heaven. Don't let anybody call you master; you've only got one master, the Christ. The greatest among you must be your servant. (Mt 23:8–12)

Mark, too, portrays Jesus as deliberately provoking conflict between himself and virtually every religious constituency and institution in his society. Jesus disrupts the revenue-producing market within the Temple compound, so that the priests start looking for a way to get rid of him (Mk 11:15–18). He makes fools out of the Pharisees and Herodians when they confront him on the issue of Roman taxation (Mk 12:13–17). Likewise the Sadducees, whom he accuses of failing to understand the Scriptures when they question him about the material details of resurrection (Mk 12:18–27). Likewise the scribes: Jesus delights the crowd at the scribes' expense by catching them in a contradictory teaching (Mk 12:35–37), and then he volunteers a commentary on their demeanor and means of support:

> Watch out for the scribes who like going around in fine clothes, and greetings in the marketplaces, and good seats in synagogues, and the head table at banquets. They eat up the houses of widows while pretending to say long prayers. They're in for a very severe sentence. (Mk 12:38–40)

In Mark's account, Jesus rounds out this attack on religious leaders with a few disparaging words about the Temple itself:

> You see these great buildings? There's not going to be one stone left on top of another that won't be thrown down. (Mk 13:2)

No wonder the religious leadership wanted to destroy this man!

Jesus' vision of the Reign of God takes shape in opposition to the options offered by religious institutions of his day. God's Reign is not authoritarian. It is not elitist: whereas the Pharisaic interpretation of the Law excluded a large fraction of the population from fidelity to the Covenant, Jesus opens God's Reign to everyone. It is not escapist: whereas the Essenes left corrupt society for the desert, where they tried to live the Law perfectly, Jesus proclaims God's Reign as breaking out in the most secular of circumstances. Whether the very phenomenon of institutionalization is something necessary to the effective spread of God's Reign, or something fundamentally at odds with it, remains to be seen. But the memory of Jesus' criticism has made Christian ministers uncomfortable for twenty centuries.

Methods: Confrontation with authority figures seems to have ranked high among the teaching methods employed by Jesus, and certainly it is a striking feature of Mark's portrait of him. Jesus also sought to confront the everyday assumptions and expectations which governed the common people's grasp of their reality. A particularly effective tool for doing this was the parable. Jesus' parables were pointed stories which unsettled the things that people thought they knew about God, their neighbors, and themselves. They pulled the rug out from under the comfortable furniture of the human imagination, and in the ensuing chaos Jesus could clear a space for God's Reign to get a toehold.

One notices in the imagery of Jesus' parables a reflection of the village life of Nazareth when he was growing up: his familiarity with farming, fishing, housework, and commerce. Jesus did not find it necessary to use abstract concepts or rabbinical argumentation to proclaim God's Reign. This message came couched in words accessible to ordinary folks. Moreover, it came with the most concrete of illustrations. Jesus' message is backed up both with deeds of healing, exorcising, and feeding the people, and with an attitude of conviviality and welcoming for all of Abba's offspring.

Media: The voice, hands, and gestures of Jesus are the media which carry his proclamation of the gospel. The only written materials which he uses are texts from the Hebrew Scriptures, which would have been quite familiar both to him and to his audiences. Occasionally we find a Hellenistic proverb attributed to Jesus. Interestingly, several times the Gospels say that Jesus picked up something to use in making a point: a whip in Jn 2:15, to chase livestock out of the Temple compound; a little child in Mk 9:36, to show the kind of person who matters in God's Reign; bread and a cup in Mk 14:23, to express the sharing of life and the shedding of blood which he anticipated as God's Reign would dawn.

Content: The phrase "Reign of God" summarizes the theme of Jesus' preaching. We have noted the resonance of this concept with national memories and expectations of the Jewish people. God's Reign can be thought of as both "coming" and "in your midst." The concept is not only paradoxical, it is susceptible to misinterpretation both in Jesus' own day and in every era since. The memories of Jesus' own teaching, his intimacy with God and other people, and his works of healing, are preserved as a perpetual corrective to every interpretation of this concept, "Reign of God," in ways antithetical to Jesus' own meaning. The haunting paradoxes of the Beatitudes (Mt 5:3–12; Lk 6:20–23) recall to mind the difficulty of forming adequate paraphrases, much less curricula and institutions, for the message of Jesus: happiness is for the poor, the sorrowing, the hungry, the meek, the merciful, and peacemakers.

Notes for Chapter Three

1. In *this* chapter we mean to focus upon what is known, with some degree of historical certitude, about the sayings and doings of Jesus himself during his lifetime. The *next* chapter continues to deal with material found in the gospels, particularly in Matthew and Luke, in order to depict the emergent organization of the first-century church as it proclaims the gos-

pel to an ever-widening audience in the ancient world. For a good intro-
duction to the issues at stake in any attempt to reconstruct the "historical
Jesus" from the Gospel accounts as they have come down to us, see *Jesus
Christ in Matthew, Mark, and Luke*, Proclamation Commentaries, by Jack
Dean Kingsbury (Philadelphia: Fortress Press, 1981). Also helpful is Norman Perrin's *Rediscovering the Teaching of Jesus* (San Francisco: Harper
& Row, 1976). The ground-breaking work upon whose insights many later
scholars have built is Rudolf Bultmann's *The History of the Synoptic Tra-
dition*, translated by John Marsh (San Francisco: Harper & Row, 1963).

2. J.D. Kingsbury, *Jesus Christ in Matthew, Mark, and Luke*, p. 2.
For a modern synopsis, see *Gospel Parallels: A Synopsis of the First Three
Gospels*, edited by Burton H. Throckmorton, Jr. (Nashville: Thomas Nel-
son, 1949, 1979).

3. For a discussion of the Hebrew background of the concept of
God's Reign, see *The Kingdom of God: The Biblical Concept and Its Meaning for the Church*, by John Bright (Nashville: Abingdon, 1953, 1978).
Bright's work begins with the thirteenth century B.C.E., but his treat-
ment of the pre-Davidic period must now be supplemented by Norman
K. Gottwald's *The Tribes of Yahweh: A Sociology of the Religion of Lib-
erated Israel, 1250–1050 B.C.E.* (Maryknoll, New York: Orbis Books,
1979). For a discussion of the geopolitical situation during the four centuries before the birth of Jesus, see parts one and two of Helmut Koester's
History, Culture, and Religion of the Hellenistic Age (Philadelphia: Fortress Press, 1982).

4. Lucas Grollenberg, *Paul* (Philadelphia: Westminster Press, 1978),
pp. 33–4.

5. Norman Perrin offers this translation of a reconstructed text on
p. 57 of *Rediscovering the Teaching of Jesus*.

6. Deuteronomy 24:1 gives the legislation (which is actually in the
form of an introduction to another law, a prohibition against *re*marrying a
woman whom one has divorced if she has subsequently had another husband):

> When a man, after marrying a woman and having relations with
> her, is later displeased with her because he finds in her some-
> thing indecent, and therefore he writes out a certificate of di-
> vorce and hands it to her, thus dismissing her from his
> house. . . .

By Jesus' day, ways were being found to remedy the arbitrariness and
one-sidedness of this law. The Mishnah, a law code published about 200
C.E., and the Talmud, a collection of teachings that coalesced around it,

describe legal procedures to protect the rights of the wife in a variety of circumstances. Marriage and divorce laws are discussed by Judith Hauptman in "Images of Women in the Talmud," pp. 184–212 in *Religion and Sexism: Images of Woman in the Jewish and Christian Traditions*, edited by Rosemary Radford Ruether (New York: Simon and Schuster, 1974).

7. These stories come to us from Mark. Whether they accurately reflect the exact terms of Jesus' own critique is impossible to tell. We may be confident, however, that they still express the gist of Jesus' criticism of the Law. The story about the Temple tax loophole must go back at least to within a generation or two of Jesus, that is, to a time before the Temple was destroyed in 70 C.E.

8. It would seem, however, that not all Christians appreciated the point of this story, judging from sources cited by Clara Maria Henning, "Canon Law and the Battle of the Sexes," in *Religion and Sexism*, pp. 267–91. Henning writes:

> The fear of menstruation is found in discussions of women in general and deaconesses in particular. Thus Dionysius of Alexandria (died c. 264 A.D.) declared that a menstruating woman may not take communion or go to church, and Theodor Balsomon taught that "the uncleanliness of menstruation banished the deaconess from her role before the holy altar." We might further quote Theodores of Canterbury, who declared that "women may not step into a church during the period of their menstruation. Neither lay women nor nuns should attempt this." (p. 273)

Henning regards these restrictions as "a context in which to view a few of the general laws that forbade women all liturgical functions."

9. Here it is not the saying itself, but the radical application of it as a warrant for breaking the sabbath rest, which seems to be original with Jesus. As Rudolf Bultmann points out, on p. 108 of *History of the Synoptic Tradition*, there was a common rabbinic saying to the effect that "the Sabbath is given over to you, not you to the Sabbath."

10. The text is again from Norman Perrin, *Rediscovering the Teaching of Jesus*, p. 57. My discussion of the similarities and differences of the two prayers is based on Perrin's remarks, pp. 57–60.

11. One sometimes finds native speakers of American English in disagreement about whether "Abba" is best translated as "Dad" or as "Daddy." The difference arises because of regional variations in the language which Americans speak. Had Jesus been raised on the West Coast, in the Midwest, or in the Northeastern United States, he would have

called God "Dad." But if Jesus had grown up in the Southeastern part of the country, God would have been "Daddy."

12. I believe that it was Edward Schillebeeckx who coined the useful phrase "Abba experience" to identify the intimacy which Jesus humanly enjoyed with the Father. See Schillebeeckx' insightful discussion on pp. 256–71 of *Jesus: An Experiment in Christology* (New York: Seabury Press, 1979).

13. The unfairness of God, illustrated in this parable, is particularly unsettling when one considers the context in which Matthew has placed it. The lesson follows several verses after Peter has asked the self-interested question that is lurking in the mind of every Christian reader: "Here we have put everything aside to follow you. What can we expect from it?" (19:27)

14. There is perhaps less of Jesus and more of Mark (or Mark's community) in these sayings than meets the eye. They are followed immediately by another saying, which Perrin identifies as an "eschatological judgment pronouncement" that probably originated with a Christian prophet at the eucharistic gathering:

> If anybody is ashamed of me and of my words in this adulterous and sinful generation, that's somebody the Son of Man will be ashamed of when he comes in his Father's glory with the holy angels. (8:38)

See *Rediscovering the Teaching of Jesus*, p. 22. Of course, for the author of Mark's Gospel, the distinction between what Jesus said in person in the time before he died, and what he said through his Spirit and the mouth of a prophet after he rose, would not have been as important as it is to us.

Chapter Four

First Century:
The Apostolic Age

Jesus, who preached the coming of God's Reign, died about the year 30 C.E. without anyone's having noticed a change in the way the world was running. Had God's Reign begun? Had Jesus proved to be a more effective vehicle for God's governance of human affairs than the Temple and the Law? Apparently not.

Temple and Law had endured for centuries as relatively effective means for God to be present, active, and available among the people. But God's availability to the people through Jesus had turned out to be all too fragile and short-lived. Those who had found God present and active in Jesus had also seen Jesus killed. Jesus was gone, and the close encounter with God's Reign was over.

Except that . . . their grief that Jesus was gone turned into certitude that Jesus was *with them again though absent.* Their disappointment was turned inside out. Each experience connected with the fiasco of the crucifixion underwent a radical reversal: those who could not watch one hour with Jesus now were praying unceasingly; those who had denied Jesus now were speaking out about their relationship with him; the men who had run away in all directions now were banding together again; the women who saw Jesus die now were seeing him alive.

The betrayals, desertions, and death were not erased, but conquered. These failures failed to snuff out God's act in Jesus; on the contrary, God's act grasps these ruins of human relationship and raises them into encounters unparalleled since creation. Out of the mud and dust of this human debacle, God raises a new humanity. God begets and births the first of many brothers and sisters.

For this reason, the first generation of Christian preachers can continue to call people to experience God's presence, activity, and availability in Jesus. However, they cannot continue to use Jesus' own preaching formula, "the Reign of God." What has happened no longer fits into that phrase. That phrase had expressed the presence of God in the human presence of Jesus, the availability of God in the human availability of Jesus, the activity of God in the human activities of Jesus. Something new has happened now to Jesus' presence. It is "risen" presence, that is, a presence-in-absence, a presence of the Spirit of Jesus which is directly made possible by the reunion of Jesus with the Father. The "Reign" gets displaced into the future, as the coming event of the reunion of Christ with Christians.

What the Christians preach, then, is the Resurrection of Jesus. They grasp the Resurrection both as a memory of something which God did for Jesus, and as an on-going experience of what God is preparing in the Christian community. If we seek to understand what "Resurrection" meant to the first generation of Christians, we should consider that what the term denotes is a human experience which happens to different people in different ways. Resurrection always means a double inversion of relationships.

For example, Peter's relationship with Jesus before Jesus died must have been one of friendship, of dear companionship. Jesus was to Peter a teacher who opened up hitherto unsuspected possibilities for human being. Peter had great expections of God's Reign, and Peter looked forward to a bright future for himself in the administration of the Reign. These hopes came crashing down when Jesus was arrested. Peter denied that he knew his friend Jesus, and he deserted him (Mk 14:66–72). Jesus died, and that put an end to the possibility of any further relationship. For Peter, who had loved Jesus and lost Jesus, Resurrection was the experience of seeing Jesus alive again and knowing that friendship again was possible (Lk 24:34). The Risen Jesus invites Peter to continue their relationship. The call to follow Jesus is still open, and Peter accepts it. Resurrection for Peter is the renewal of relationship with Jesus.

But how did Jesus himself experience the Resurrection? In one sense, we can't begin to imagine what it means to rise from the dead until it happens to us. Yet it is possible to indicate the same double inversion of relationships in Jesus' experience of the Resurrection as we detected in Peter's. During his career, Jesus enjoyed a close intimacy with the One whom he called "Abba." In moments of prayer, he was absolutely certain of Abba's love and care for him and for all Abba's children. Indeed, this was the heart of the message which Jesus preached. Jesus had relied upon Abba's loving fidelity. When he encountered circumstances of human suffering which called into question Abba's care for people, Jesus found himself empowered to act on Abba's behalf to heal them. Jesus knew himself to be called to be the agent of the coming of the Reign of God, and he obeyed this call. He had every right to expect, then, that God would vindicate him and allow him to lead the people into God's Reign. These expectations were bitterly disappointed when Jesus was tried, condemned, and executed. Jesus' experience of intimacy with Abba turned into an experience of personal abandonment as he died, and the hopes for the Reign of God died with him (Mk 15:34). Resurrection for Jesus, then, is vindication of his trust in God. It is reunion with his Abba and "enthronement at God's right hand" to judge the worldly powers that had put him to death (e.g., Mk 16:19). It is the experience of risen life after death.

For the community of Jesus' followers, Resurrection meant the experience of becoming a church. Before Jesus' death, the bond among Jesus' disciples was a human bond of friendship, of sharing allegiance to the same teacher and a vision of a bright future with him in God's Reign. This friendly bond proved to be weak indeed when the disciples scattered to the four winds as soon as Jesus was arrested. Their "we-being," their intersubjectivity, dissolved. For this community, more properly called now an un-community, the Resurrection was an experience of being gathered back together by the radically new personal presence of Jesus. The Spirit of Jesus reassembled the disciples and added thousands to their number (Acts 2:41). The Spirit became the bond among them. Paradoxically, this Spirit who gathered them and bonded them also scattered them throughout the world. But this sending did not break the bond: it strengthened it.

We have three different names, and three different liturgical feast days, for these three aspects of the Resurrection experience. On Easter we celebrate the experience of seeing Jesus alive and knowing that he still calls us to reconciliation with the Father through relationship with himself. On Ascension, we celebrate Jesus' reunion with the Father. On Pentecost, we celebrate the new presence of Jesus with us through the Spirit who pulls the church together and sends it into the world.

Paul, too, had an experience of the Risen Christ, who identified himself as Jesus—although Paul had never met Jesus before he died. Paul's encounter with the Resurrected One changed him from an energetic persecutor of Christians, into the "Apostle to the Gentiles" and the chief architect of the Christian church (Acts 9:3–7). The oldest parts of the New Testament were written by Paul, and it is in his letters that we find the earliest attestation to the content of the Christian gospel. We may outline Paul's message as follows (based upon 1 Thes 4:14–17; cf. 1 Cor 15):

Christ has died,
God has raised Christ,
Christ is coming back.

And as a corollary:

If you die before Christ comes,
you will rise,
and meet Christ as he returns.
If you do *not* die before Christ comes,
you will be swept up into the clouds,
to meet Christ in the air as he returns.

One notes in Paul that the theme of the Reign of God has been superseded in Christian preaching by the theme of the Resurrection, understood as the Resurrection of Jesus and also the Resurrection of Christians.

The Resurrection is preached as a radically new kind of life. But along with the newness of life in Christ, another note is sounded as well. It is *the same* Jesus who has been raised to this *new life*. It is the same Jesus who had lived and taught and worked among the earliest disciples. Therefore, the Resurrection is a seal of approval on his "old" life as well as the inauguration of a new one for him. Affirming that the Risen One is the same person as Jesus of Nazareth seems to be the intent of the stories of Jesus' post-Resurrection appearances when they stress the material details which allowed his friends to recognize him. Examples are Lk 24:38–42, where Jesus lets his friends handle him and eats a broiled fish before their eyes; and Jn 20:24–28, where Thomas is invited to put his hand into Jesus' side. At the same time, the stories affirm that Jesus is living a new kind of life by depicting his body as able to penetrate into locked rooms (Jn 20:19), dematerialize (Lk 24:31), and levitate (Lk 24:51 and Acts 1:9–11). The two great foundational teachers of the Christian movement, Jesus and Paul, seem to have attempted to deflect curiosity away from a material understanding of resurrection, and focus upon the relational dimension.

In raising Jesus, in making him Christ, God has ratified what Jesus taught about Abba's intentions and has guaranteed that Jesus was right about the outcome of a life given over in obedience to the service of God's Reign. For this reason, the memories of what Jesus had said and done in connection with God's Reign remain important—precious—to the new church as it preaches and teaches the Resurrection.

If the Resurrection is an experience of God's overcoming the heartbreak of broken relationships, that experience is touched off in the ecclesial community as an event of communication. Many who had never known Jesus now come to know the Risen Christ through the Spirit-fired speech of Peter on Pentecost (Acts 2:14–41). But a message is also the detonator for the Resurrection experience of those who had known Jesus very well during his lifetime. The Gospels report that the Easter faith of those women and men has its genesis in a message spoken by (variously) a man, two men, or an angel. In each account, the message has two parts: it first assures them Jesus lives, and it then recalls to them an aspect of their previous relationship with him. In other words, the message recalls them to their trust in Jesus and in Jesus' message itself. Without this message, the material details such as the empty tomb, the stone, and the shrouds, mean nothing. Mark's "young man in a white robe" tells the women who have come to anoint the body of Jesus:

> Don't be shocked. You're looking for Jesus of Nazareth, the crucified. *He has been raised*; he's not here. Look there's the place where they laid him. But go tell his disciples and Peter that he's going ahead of you to Galilee. You'll see him there, *as he told you*. (Mk 16:6–7)

The reader of Mark's Gospel naturally recalls what Jesus said in Mk 14:28, the last time he ate with his friends: ". . . after I've been raised up, I'll go ahead of you to Galilee."

Luke's "two men in dazzling clothes" ask the women:

> Why are you looking for the living one among the dead? He's not here, but *he has been raised. Remember how he spoke to you* while he was still in Galilee, saying that the Son of Man had to be handed over to sinful people and crucified, and on the third day rise. (Lk 24:5–7)

Luke adds the comment, "And they remembered his words" (v.8).

Matthew attributes the same message to an angel, whose "appearance was like lightning" and "clothing was white as snow":

> Don't be afraid. I know that you're looking for Jesus the crucified. He's not here, for *he has been raised just as he said.* Come on, take a look at the place where he lay. Then go quickly and tell his disciples that he has been raised from the dead, and he is going ahead of you into Galilee. You'll see him there. That's it, I've told you. (Mt 28:3, 5–7)

This message is the basis of Resurrection faith. This pronouncement says that Jesus' own message is reliable. The primary datum of the "event" of the Resurrection is not a material, concrete one: not an empty tomb, not thunder or a rolling stone, not heat, light, radiation, or earthquake. It is not even the physical touch of the familiar hands of Jesus, now risen. The material event of Jesus' death proved powerless to touch his relationship with God; and now that that relationship is being reaffirmed, something more than a material event is required. The "event" of the Resurrection is a communication.

Because human being itself is created through communication (as we saw in chapter 2), communication substantially affects subjectivity and intersubjectivity. Communication is ultimately the only thing that can change what I am, who I am, and who we are in our togetherness. The communication that Jesus is risen—the same Jesus who promised that Abba would be faithful—is the communication which inaugurates the church. The church, as a new way of being together, arises out of this gospel.

The gospel changed the world, but it got off to a slow start. In Mark's original account, the first hearers of the message are left "bewildered and trembling," and are too much afraid to say anything to anyone (16:8). In Luke, the women do convey the message to the apostles, "but the story seemed like nonsense and they wouldn't believe them" (24:11). Further experience of Jesus alive within the community was necessary for Resurrection faith.

In this chapter we shall examine the ways in which Jesus' living presence among the Christians enabled them to continue the transformation of human existence which God had set in motion through him. Like Jesus, they too engaged in the interrelated communicative activities of caring, of celebrating intimacy with God and the people, and of teaching. First, however, let us briefly recall the social and political climate of the first century, in which this gospel communication was to take place.

THE SITUATION IN THE MEDITERRANEAN WORLD, 30–120 C.E.

The transforming communication of the gospel began as a renewal movement within the nation of Israel, and then spread throughout the cosmopolitan Hellenistic culture of the Roman Empire. First-century Palestine experienced the tensions of polarization between rural and urban peoples, between priestly families and lay people, between traditionalist and Hellenized Jews, and between the indigenous population and the conquering Romans and their collaborators.[1] While some of these polarities were owing to Palestine's place as a vassal nation of the empire, others are rooted in Israel's own history and geography.

The principal urban center of Palestine was Jerusalem, a city whose economic welfare depended upon its Temple and upon the trade, tourism, and business which the Temple attracted. It was difficult to earn a living in Jerusalem apart from the Temple. The soil was poor, the merchant trade routes bypassed the city, and there was no industry. As a religious center, which was also the seat of the Sanhedrin or religious governing body, Jerusalem was home to a conservatively minded population. The priestly families, the lawyers and teachers, the shopkeepers and hostelers all had a vested interest in the status quo of Jewish religion and Roman government.

By contrast, the population of the countryside was more volatile. They bore the full burden of taxation, whereas Jerusalem enjoyed various religious tax breaks. Absentee landowners profited from the labor of the agricultural workers. Moreover, the remoteness of Roman power bases in the surrounding Hellenistic city-states permitted the expression of nationalistic sentiments among farmers and villagers. At festival times, the influx of these country people into Jerusalem spelled trouble, and the townfolk braced themselves for the inevitable unrest.

The gospel did not begin in Jerusalem, but among the rural population of Galilee. Jesus and his followers traveled about the countryside, visiting villages but avoiding the cities. When at last the Galileans came into the capital, they came up against the Sanhedrin and the Roman authorities, who were prepared to move swiftly and effectively to neutralize them. The methods and the message by which Jesus had galvanized the country people left the inhabitants of Jerusalem unmoved. Eventually the gospel did take root in Jerusalem, but among two marginal groups: farmers and fisherfolk who had emigrated from Galilee, and Hellenized Jews newly arrived from the Diaspora.

Like Pharisaism, Jesus' renewal movement was based among lay people, that is, elsewhere than among members of the hereditary priestly families in and around Jerusalem. Jesus had criticized the Temple, the cultic laws, and many of the customs which these families were interested in defending. Yet the abolition of those things was not part of the program of his first followers. The first Christians in Jerusalem continued to participate, as good lay Jews, in the Temple cult led by the priests, until the destruction of the city in 70 C.E. made that impossible. At that time the Pharisees, who had sought to show that Judaism was more than the Temple cult and should touch the everyday life of every Jew, set about rebuilding Jewish institutions of teaching, worship, and governance. A similar task was facing the Christian church.

Jerusalem, while it lasted, was home to the most conservative of Judaism's people. Within that religious enclave it was possible, in principle, to shun contact with Gentiles, their customs and their culture, and to avoid even those Jews whose occupations, tastes, or lifestyles placed them beyond the pale of cultic purity. The Jewishness of even Jerusalem, however, was insufficient for some, like the Essenes, who isolated themselves in a mountain stronghold where they aspired to keep the Law perfectly. Unlike the Essenes and the conservative factions of the Jerusalem community, many other Jews had adopted Hellenistic culture and customs to a greater or less degree. This was especially true in the Diaspora; and Jews whose homes were spread out across the cities of the Roman Empire regularly traveled to Jerusalem to visit the Temple. Many of these Jews no longer understood Hebrew, which is why the Scripture had been translated into Greek in a document now known as the Septuagint.

If Jews in Hellenistic cities had adopted Greek culture, they had also made their own Jewish heritage available to their Gentile neighbors. It was usual for Jewish communities within the cities of the Empire to sponsor circles of friendly Gentiles who honored and respected Judaism without taking that final step of conversion, circumcision. The existence of the cosmopolitan Jewish Diaspora, with its well-established relationships with sympathetic Gentiles, was a crucial factor in the effective spread of the gospel from Palestine around the Mediterranean basin.

Two other benefits of the Roman Empire were to assist the gospel to travel throughout the known world: Rome's suppression of hostilities and promotion of commerce, and the concomitant high literacy and universal familiarity with a common language, the Koine Greek. These provided optimal conditions for communication among vast numbers of people—the best conditions that the world had yet seen.

The church's first century, then, was a time of translation, of "carrying across": literally, linguistically, and literarily. The gospel was carried physically from town to town and city to city by Christian apostles who claimed experience of the the Risen Lord. They traveled on Roman roads and ships, and when they ranged beyond the regions of Palestine they spoke Greek. The words and stories of Jesus which they repeated had then to be translated from Aramaic, Jesus' mother tongue. References to Jewish customs had to be explained. The oral embodiment of the gospel in the Greek *kerygma* and in communities far removed from Galilee was well under way long before any of the Gospels were written down. Many translations from ear to heart to lifestyle to mouth, then, had to precede the definitive translation of the oral traditions into the written texts which have come down to us.

The first century also was a time of institutionalization. The original followers of Jesus had been wandering charismatics: men and women who left homes, families, and possessions to go with Jesus into the Reign of God. But settled communities of Christians needed resident teachers and caretakers. Gradually the prophets were supplanted by people whom the New Testament calls apostles, bishops, presbyters, and deacons.

This institutionalization was one of several sources of conflict among the early Christian communities who stand behind the writings of the New Testament. Within the communities, there were different patterns of leadership, different social classes, different opinions about the importance of the Jewish heritage, different expectations among urban and rural populations, and eventually differences about doctrinal matters. Finally, from outside the community, there were cultural pressures toward syncretism as well as violent persecutions.

The cultural translation of the gospel message from Galilee to the cities of the empire, the institutional structuring of the church's activities, and the regulation of conflicts within and around the community are known to us from several sources. The most important of these are the New Testament, with its letters and narratives, and contemporary noncanonical letters and summaries of Christian teachings.[2]

These sources afford us a picture of the early churches assembled and animated by the gospel of Jesus Christ. Those churches embodied and precipitated the transformation of human existence through the effective communication of the gospel, and they did so by means of the same three sorts of communicative activities which had characterized the ministry of Jesus: *caring* for the sufferings and material needs of people, *cultic celebration* of the new intimacy with the Father into which humanity now was reconciled, and an evangelizing prophetic *call* which invited growing numbers of people to experience that reconciliation and taught them what it meant.

CARE: THE MATERIAL SUPPORT OF THE CHURCHES

Healing, feeding, and exorcism were activities through which Jesus had proclaimed the Reign of God. Along with his teaching and his prayer, these caring activities effectively set in motion the transformation of human existence which was the church. After Jesus' death, the church experienced Jesus' presence and power as it continued the transformative activities which enacted the gospel.

The Son of the Prodigal Father had been poor in the goods of the world. Sayings and ethical teachings of Jesus which are preserved for us in the Synoptic Gospels depict his career as that of a transient teacher without home, family, or belongings. The rootlessness of Jesus and his followers made a prophetic statement when contrasted with the strong family values promoted by Judaism: the Reign of God was arriving and upsetting the old order of things. Those whom Jesus called to follow him in that wandering life continued after his death to work in the manner in which he had worked, and to teach what he had taught. The wandering Christian prophets remembered a homeless Jesus who had said, "The foxes have holes and the birds of the sky have nests, but the Son of Man has nowhere to rest his head" (Lk 9:58). They are responsible for the preservation within the Christian tradition of teachings such as the following:

> . . . Don't worry about your life and what you're going to eat, or about your body and what you're going to wear. Because life is more than food and the body is more than clothes. What about the ravens: they don't plant or harvest; they don't have any store-houses or barns, yet God feeds them. . . .
>
> As for you, don't go looking for what you are to eat and what you are to drink. Stop worrying. All the nations of the world are after these things, and your Father knows that you need them. . . .
>
> Sell your belongings and give to charity. (Lk 12:22–24, 29–30, 33)

Leaving home to follow Jesus meant leaving family and family obligations as well. Jesus had told his followers:

> If anyone comes to me without hating his father and mother, wife and children, brothers and sisters, and even his own life, then he cannot be my disciple. (Lk 14:26)[3]

Jesus himself seems to have been estranged from his own family. All three of the Synoptic Gospels record that Jesus disowned his mother and brothers in favor of his disciples, his new family (Mt 12:46–50; Mk 3:31–35; Lk 8:19–21). The wandering Christian prophets remembered Jesus as saying:

> Do you think that I came to give peace on the earth? No, I'm telling you, just the opposite. From now on, a household of five will be divided three against two and two against three. It's going to be father against son and son against father, mother against daughter and daughter against mother, mother-in-law against daughter-in-law and daughter-in-law against mother-in-law. (Lk 12:51–53)

Without family, homes, or possessions, then, how did these wander-ing prophets survive? Roaming the countryside as they did, the charis-matic prophets probably found it possible to live off the land. Luke's Gospel mentions that Jesus' disciples picked grain and ate it as they walked along (Lk 6:1). There is evidence that they depended upon bases of support in the villages which they visited.[4] Jesus is said to have received hospitality in several homes in Bethany, for example (Mk 14:3; Lk 10:38; Jn 12:1–2). They also received support from wealthy benefactors, like Mary Magdalene, Joanna, and Susanna (Lk 8:2–3). In the rural regions of Palestine, Jesus' renewal movement would have been comprised of relatively few transient prophets, who lived and spread the radical message of Jesus, along with more numerous settled individuals and households, who sheltered and supported them when they came into town. Indeed, not everyone who encounters Jesus in the Gospel stories is allowed to go traveling with him. In Mk 5:18–19, Jesus tells a man to "go home *to your family* and report to them what the Lord in pity has done for you," although the man is trying to get into the boat and sail away with Jesus.

The sympathetic townfolk did not abandon homes, families, and possessions to follow Jesus; if they had done so, everyone in the Jesus movement would have starved. Instead, as "hearers and keepers of the word of God," they acted as surrogate families supporting the indigent prophets of God's Reign. In view of their care for the homeless preachers, the village-dwellers were assured of their places in the Reign of God by teachings such as that in Mt 25. There, the returning Son of Man judges people according to their generosity:

> . . . The king will say to those on his right: "Come on, you who are blessed by my Father. Inherit the kingdom prepared for you from the foundation of the world. For I was hungry and you fed me, I was thirsty and you gave me drink, I was a stranger and you welcomed me, naked and you gave me some clothes, I was sick and you came to see me, I was in jail and you visited me. . . . Amen, I'm telling you, the things you were doing for one of these least sisters and brothers of mine, you were doing for me." (Mt 25:34–36, 40)

Despite the radical words of Jesus, traditional family structures and household organization had to have remained intact in the Galilean countryside for this kind of teaching to have been supported and preserved. In that stable traditional society, there were customary ways of caring for elderly parents, widowed relatives, the crippled, and the poor. The charismatic prophets had forfeited the security of this system by shirking their responsibilities within it. While they occasionally lightened the social burden by curing someone who was disabled (as we read in Lk 9:1–6, where the Twelve are sent out to preach and to cure but without other provisions), nevertheless it must have been the material needs of the prophets themselves which occasioned the exhortation to generosity. Only later does the radical call to leave everything become domesticated as a spiritual admonition; then, the duty of generosity can be transposed to the poor in general.

As Christianity spread to the cities, prophets continued to rely upon the material support of the communities which they visited. In an urban setting like Jerusalem it was no longer possible to live off the land. Furthermore, because a greater proportion of the city-dwelling Christians were separated from the land and from extended families obligated to care for them in time of need, the urban Christian community had to provide what we today term a "social safety net" for the support of widows, orphans, the poor, and the sick. Matthew's dramatization of the last judgment acquired a broader application, because "the least of Jesus' brothers and sisters" now made up a greater proportion of the urban Christian community. Moreover, in Paul a new profile of the Christian evangelist emerged: one who paid his own way. Paul made his living at the trade of tentmaking, which—unlike fishing and farming, the occupations of Jesus' first followers—was "portable" as he traveled from city to city.[5] This seems occasionally to have engendered the charge that Paul did not act like an apostle because he did not ask the community to feed him, a charge which he answers in 1 Cor 9:1–18 and 2 Cor 11:7–9 and 12:13.

It is Paul who devises the beautiful metaphor of the Body of Christ to speak of the unity between Jesus and the Christian community. Selfish disregard for the material needs of other Christians destroys the Body of Christ, says Paul. It makes the Eucharist impossible, and he reproves the thoughtlessness of the Corinthians in the strongest possible terms:

> When you meet together, then, you're not doing it to eat the Lord's supper, because when you eat, each one goes ahead with her or his own supper, with one going hungry while another is getting drunk. Don't you have homes where you can eat and drink? Or is it that you despise the church of God enough to make those who have nothing feel ashamed? (1 Cor 11:20–22)

Paul was holding Christians in Corinth responsible for the material needs of members of the community. The Corinthian church also had resources to care for the infirm, for Paul lists miracle workers and healers among the community's ministers (1 Cor 12:28–30).

The Acts of the Apostles claims that the members of the Jerusalem church freely gave up their own private property.

All who believed were together and had all things in common; they would sell their property and possessions and distribute them to all according to each one's need. (Acts 2:44–45)

. . . No one claimed that any of one's possessions was one's own, but they had everything in common. With great power the apostles gave their testimony to the resurrection of the Lord Jesus, and great grace was upon them all. There was no needy person among them, for those who owned lands or houses would sell them, bring the proceeds of the sale, and place them at the feet of the apostles, and they were distributed to each according to need. (Acts 4:32, 34–35)

(Acts goes on in 5:1–11 to record the dire consequences of seeking to hold back anything from the apostles.) Apparently, there was even a daily distribution of food (Acts 6:1). The administration of contributed funds and the purchase and distribution of food were the responsibility of those who also preached the gospel. In fact, providing such material assistance itself was a part of gospel transmission. The author of Acts pictures "the Twelve," or Jesus' original followers, delegating this task to assistants or deacons in 6:2–6. However, at least one of those entrusted with the material care of community members, Stephen, continues his work of proclaiming the gospel as a singularly gifted orator and debater, in 6:8–7:53. The story of this soup-line worker ends with martyrdom; he is stoned to death while witnessing to a vision of Jesus standing at God's right hand (Acts 7:54–60).

Acts also records that the proclamation of the gospel was backed up by many works of healing and exorcism. Peter cures a cripple in 3:1–11, and this attracts a crowd and gives Peter the opportunity to preach reconciliation in Jesus. Even Peter's shadow is said to have the power of healing, in 5:12–16. Philip, too, casts out evil spirits and heals crippled people in Samaria (Acts 8:4–8).

In time, the work of healing, like the work of feeding the poor, became organized and institutionalized. The Epistle of James mentions that the healing ministry has been entrusted to the elders or "presbyters":

Is there anybody among you who is sick? Summon the presbyters of the church, and let them pray over you and anoint you with oil in the name of the Lord, and the prayer of faith will save you if you're sick, and the Lord will raise you up. If you have committed any sins, you will be forgiven. Therefore, confess your sins to one another and pray for one another, that you may be healed. (James 5:14–16)

Healing continues to be associated with the gospel of reconciliation as the church carries on the caring work of Jesus.

In connection with the ecclesial activity of care, mention also should be made of the need for judgment in the church. The administration of goods and services within growing communities, and the incorporation of new members from various social strata, inevitably led to conflicts. Jesus himself had declined to act as judge in a property dispute between brothers, according to a story preserved in Luke's Gospel (Lk 12:13–15). But later, Christian communities needed provision for keeping peace among community members, and even for expelling those who would not live by the community's rules. Matthew's gospel accords the necessary authority on the one hand to Peter, one of the Twelve who had traveled with Jesus in Galilee, and on the other hand to the community itself, now settled down with its own resident leaders. In Mt 16, Jesus says to Peter:

> . . . you are Peter, and on this rock I will build my church, and the gates of hell won't stand up to it. I'm going to give you the keys of the reign of heaven. Whatever you tie up on earth is going to stay tied up in heaven; and whatever you untie on earth is going to stay untied in heaven. (Mt 16:18–19)

In Mt 18, the same legal formula of "binding and loosing" is used to set up a procedure for arbitration of disputes within the community:

> If any of your brothers or sisters sin against you, go and tell them their fault just between you and them alone. If they listen to you, you have won over your brother or sister. If they don't listen, take one or two others along with you, so that "every fact may be established on the testimony of two or three witnesses." If they refuse to listen to them, tell the church. If they refuse to listen even to the church, then treat them as you would Gentiles or tax collectors. Amen, I'm telling you, whatever you tie up on earth is going to stay tied up in heaven, and whatever you untie on earth is going to stay untied in heaven. (Mt 18:15–18)

Paul, too, tells the Corinthians not to drag each other into court to settle their disputes, but to find a wise member of the Christian community to arbitrate them. (1 Cor 6:1–9)

By about the turn of the century, Christian churches had codified the rules governing use of the communities' resources. The Didache, an ancient manual of church order dating from about this time, balances the duty of generosity with a warning about its abuse:

Give to everyone who asks you, and ask not back, for the Father wills that God's own blessings we should give to all. Blessed is the one who gives according to the commandment, for that one is guiltless. But woe to the one who receives; for if anyone receives, having need, that one shall be guiltless, but one who has not need shall give account, why he or she received and for what purpose, and coming into distress shall be strictly examined concerning his or her deeds. . . . (1:5)

By this time also, the wandering charismatic prophets had about worn out their welcome in the settled urban churches. While provision is made that prophets and apostles "be received as the Lord" (11:3–4) and given food, nevertheless there are now criteria for the recognition of worthy prophets. They must have a message in accord with what the Didache it self teaches (6:1; 11:1–2), and their behavior must match their teaching. Moreover,

. . . they shall not remain longer than one day; and, if need be, another day also; but if they remain three days they are false prophets. And when apostles depart, let them take nothing except bread enough till they reach their lodging. But if they ask for money, they are false prophets. . . .
And no prophet who orders a table in the spirit eats of it, unless that one is a false prophet. (11:5–6, 9)

The Didache foresees that wandering prophets will wish to settle down in Christian communities. This is permitted if the newcomer has a trade by which to earn a living. If the prophet has no trade, the Didache indicates that he or she should learn a craft so as not to be a "Christ-merchant" (12:3–4).

EMERGENCE OF THE CHRISTIAN SACRAMENTAL CULT

The Christian communities' care for the physical well-being of their members was one of the essential activities through which the gospel took effect and transformed human lives in the first century of the church's existence. Jesus had placed human need above the observance of cultic laws, as we saw in the last chapter when we considered his teachings about the Sabbath, cooking customs, and ritual purity. The Father's care for his children, though communicated through Torah and Temple, could not be bounded by either.

The community of Jesus' followers continued to emphasize care for people as a crucial component of one's relationship with God. Worship and generosity are mentioned in the same breath by the author of the Letter to the Hebrews:

> Let mutual love continue. Do not neglect hospitality. . . . Through Jesus then let us continually offer up to God a sacrifice of praise, that is, the fruit of lips that confess the name of Jesus. Do not neglect to do good and to share what you have, because sacrifices like that please God. (Heb 13:1–2, 15–16)

Matthew's community remembers Jesus' advice that one should postpone sacrifice until one has set right any injustice done to a brother or sister (Mt 5:23–24). For the author of the Letter of James, religion *is* "to care for orphans and widows" (Jm 1:27).

The Jesus movement clearly stood for a relativization of the importance of the rituals of worship. There are no Christian priests in the New Testament. The author of Hebrews views Jesus Christ as the one priest, whose sacrificial death and resurrection has made sacrificial cult unnecessary. Moreover, Jesus' followers continue to participate in Jewish worship services in the Temple and in synagogues for some time after his death.

Yet there are distinctively Christian ritual celebrations among the communities whose stories are told in the New Testament. These celebrations continue Jesus' celebration of God's overwhelming concern for human beings, and they are intrinsically bound up with both the proclamation of the gospel and the community's care for people.

Jesus had celebrated a God who wished for new intimacy with men and women, and who established that astounding intimacy in Jesus. The availability of God in Jesus was quite tangible and concrete—as solid, in fact, as a friend sharing food at the dinner table. Those who responded to God's outreach in Jesus were crushed by the fiasco of Jesus' death; yet these same people experienced the renewal of God's presence, activity, availability, and invitation in a completely unprecedented experience which they called Jesus' Resurrection. Intimate contact between God and human being was reestablished in Jesus, they said. One might pray "in Jesus' name," one might "put on Christ," and one might encounter the Risen Lord in the assembly of the Christian community.

The mystery of the personal presence and power of the Risen Lord became tangible and available for the community by means of symbol, as all personal presence does. Symbol, it will be recalled, is a point in material reality where a person becomes present, active, and available for the sake of relationship with other persons. Jesus was God's symbol; now the Christian assembly becomes symbol for the presence of the Risen Christ. In other words, the Risen Christ imprints the community itself, as well as the individual life stories of Christians, with the pattern of Jesus' own life: the pattern of reconciling intimacy between God and human being.

This reconciliation, constituted by the power of God's desire for human welfare as expressed in Jesus, received ample tangible symbolization in the church's material care for people's needs, as we have seen above. It was also symbolized (that is, made personally effective and real) in the church's preaching of the gospel message, as we shall see below. But both of these symbolizations—the care and the call—generated joy that had to vent itself in celebration. And like Jesus' celebration, this joy was itself fruitful, drawing new friends into the festivity and strengthening old ones. It was in the sacramental celebration of the gospel that Christians became most deeply impressed with their own identity in Christ and fortified for a life of discipleship.

Two rituals in particular stand out in the New Testament descriptions of the affairs of the first Christian communities: Baptism, and the Eucharist. The word "baptism" comes from the Greek word for "dunking,"[6] and "eucharist" means "thanksgiving." Both of these celebrations are to be understood in the context of the proclamation of the gospel. Paul considers the Eucharist an act of Christian prophecy (1 Cor 14:1–25), and he interprets Baptism explicitly as the Christian's first step following Christ through the Paschal Mystery: having died in Baptism, one is sure of rising and meeting Christ at the end of time.

The prophetic dimension of the Eucharist is clearly expressed in Paul's statement: "For as often as you eat this bread and drink the cup, you *are proclaiming* the death of the Lord until he comes" (1 Cor 11:26). Chapter 14 of 1 Cor is concerned with the value of prophecy within the Christian community. In this connection, Paul uses cognates of "eucharist" twice, in verses 16 and 17, to describe what the prophet does in the assembly. (The same word is used by all four accounts of Jesus' institution of the Eucharist: Mk 14:23; Mt 26:27; Lk 22:17,19; and 1 Cor 11:24.) Interestingly, Paul acknowledges that both men and women prophesy in the Corinthian assembly (1 Cor 11:4–5).[7] Two generations later, *eucharistein* is still the job of the prophets, according to the Didache (10:7), even though the Didache prescribes additional prayers of thanksgiving to be offered by the rest of the assembly at the Eucharistic celebration (9:1–4; 10:2–6).[8]

The Eucharist was an evangelizing proclamation for the early church because it began with the table fellowship of Jesus and his followers. Certain meals which they shared were meant as prophetic actions, that is, gestures which demonstrated the meaning and the arrival of God's Reign. There was a custom in Jesus' day for groups of friends to meet regularly for formal dinners at which the Law and the destiny of Israel would be discussed. Ordinarily only observant Jews would be included in the circle.[9] Jesus, however, welcomed tax collectors to his table and held his gatherings in the homes of people outside the Law. Memories of the Last Supper preserved in the Gospels reflect this custom. Moreover, we are told that on the night before he died Jesus instructed his friends to continue to hold such suppers.

The bond of friendship among the followers of Jesus as they had gathered at table was a dimension of the outbreaking Reign of God. Their physical activity of thanking (*eucharistein*) and praising God and eating together with Jesus constituted a symbolization of the personal presence and power of God. Destroyed by Jesus' death, the bond was restored in the mystery which his followers termed Resurrection. They met again for the fellowship meal that had symbolized, enacted, and made real God's intention for human well-being when they had celebrated it with Jesus. But now the meal symbolized Jesus himself as well: the material fact of their gathering and eating provided a locus for the personal presence, availability, and power of the Risen Lord. All that Jesus was, all that he had known and taught of God, all that he had handed over in obedience to the Father as he breathed forth his spirit on the cross, was there for his friends as they did what he had asked them to do: remember him as they made this meal together.

An effective symbol is a body in that it gives the presence and activity of a person a place to be. The bread and wine of the eucharistic meal were the body of the Risen Christ, just as really as the body that had grown up in Nazareth and died on Calvary was Jesus' body. The assembly of the church also was the body of the Risen Christ. To share the eucharistic meal was to be a member of Christ's body, as Paul said.

One became a member of Christ's body by being baptized, which was another ritual celebration of the gospel's taking effect. The Matthean community understood itself to be commissioned by the Risen Lord to "go . . . baptize . . . teach" (Mt 28:18–20). Paul, on the other hand, says that "Christ didn't send me to baptize but to preach the gospel" (1 Cor 1:17). Apparently his coworkers and others followed up upon his preaching by baptizing those whom his message had touched, although Paul admits to having baptized a few members of the Corinthian church (1 Cor 1:14–16).

The Acts of the Apostles dramatizes the effectiveness of Peter's first sermon by giving a body count of the Baptisms which followed:

Those who took in his word were baptized, and about three thousand people joined up that day. (Acts 2:41)

As Acts tells it, great numbers of people who hear the gospel respond by accepting baptism. These include both men and women, Jews and Gentiles; often whole households are mentioned (Acts 8:12; 10:22, 33, 48; 16:15, 33; 18:8). This baptism is "in the name of Jesus Christ" (Acts 2:38) or "in the name of the Father and of the Son and of the Holy Spirit" (Mt 28:19).

Baptism, like the eucharistic meal, was a ritual based upon a custom known in Judaism. John "the Baptist" employed the rite as a sign of repentance and a break with one's former life. The Essenes, too, practiced a ritual of baptism which signified purification from past defilement. In Acts, Christian Baptism continues to connote repentance. Moreover, it symbolizes God's reconciling love and the forgiveness of sins. Peter tells the crowds in Jerusalem,

Repent and be baptized, each one of you, in the name of Jesus Christ for the forgiveness of your sins. (Acts 2:38)

It is Paul who elaborates upon the gospel theme of forgiveness in order to show how Baptism connects the Christian with the Risen Lord. In baptism, one does what Jesus did. One retraces the steps of Christ's Paschal Mystery. The Christian's death *to* sin follows from Jesus' death *for* sin.

How can we who died to sin still live in it? Or is it that you don't know that all of us who were baptized into Christ Jesus were baptized into his death? That means we were buried with him by baptism into death, so that, just as Christ was raised from the dead by the glory of the Father, we too would be able to walk in newness of life. Because if we have become united with him through a death like his, we certainly are going to be united with him in the resurrection. (Rom 6:2–5)

Developing the Pauline tradition, the author of Colossians sets up a parallel between the neophyte's emergence from the water, and Christ's Resurrection. "You were buried with him in baptism, in which you were also raised with him through faith in the power of God, who raised him from the dead" (Col 2:12). Those who followed Jesus into death also are going to follow him into the Resurrection.

Baptism, then, acts out what happened to Jesus. It is more than a personal response to the proclamation of the gospel. Baptism is a dramatization, an effective communication, of the gospel itself.

The terms in which Paul explains the efficacy of Baptism match up with the terms of the ancient *kerygma*, the gospel tradition which Paul himself received and handed on:

> . . . that Christ died for our sins in keeping with the Scriptures; that he was buried; that he was raised on the third day in keeping with the Scriptures; that he appeared to Cephas. . . . (1 Cor 15:3–5)

Paul goes on to assert that Christ is raised as

> . . . the first fruits of those who have fallen asleep. For since death came through a human being, the resurrection of the dead came through a human being too. . . . Everyone will be made alive in Christ. . . . (1 Cor 15:20–22)

The ritual action of Baptism, then, announces that the Christian is dying with Christ, but also that the Resurrection of Christ warrants the Christian's own future resurrection. Both Baptism and the Eucharist are modes of the effective communication of the gospel for the New Testament church.

THE CALL TO ACKNOWLEDGE JESUS AS CHRIST, LORD, AND GOD

The presence of the Risen Christ was of paramount importance in the life of the early church. In the beginning of this chapter, however, we saw that it is impossible to reconstruct the Resurrection of Jesus as a material event. The Gospel accounts give conflicting details about the what, when, who, where, and how in the stories of the empty tomb and the appearances of the Risen Lord.

The "event" of the Resurrection—and one must use the term "event" with caution—was a communication which recalled and confirmed relationship with Jesus of Nazareth. For the first Christians, this event is not historical, because it is not over. As we have seen, this communication kept on happening for them when the gospel was announced and when the symbols of Baptism and Eucharist enfolded them in the dynamic, powerful, personal availability of the Risen Lord. His Resurrection meant his presence-in-absence, the fullness of his Holy Spirit in the church. Moreover, the Resurrection of Jesus meant that each man, woman, and child in the church was irrevocably "in Christ," belonging to Christ's ecclesial body and moving with Christ toward the certitude of her or his own resurrection. What God had done for Jesus was not an event of history for these Christians; it was the presently effective demonstration of what God meant to do for all of them.

The transformation of human existence detonated by the Resurrection spread as a message. We have seen how in the first-century church, the gospel propagated itself in two kinds of messageful activities: caring for human needs, and celebrating the intimacy of Jesus' new life. The third ministry which enabled the gospel to transform human lives was, of course, the ministry of the word. Christians of the first century preached, prophesied, taught, exhorted, debated, testified, catechized, evangelized, corresponded, and, finally, composed the oral traditions of the Jesus movement into written narratives, the Gospels.

The New Testament sources do permit the recovery of some of the concepts, the language, and the understandings which comprised the core of this message, and as might be expected, it is possible to trace lines of evolution over the time span represented in the documents which come down to us. We have seen that Jesus preached the Reign of God but Paul preached the death and Resurrection of Jesus and of Christians. In between these two landmark versions of the gospel, there is at least one other important crystallization: the preaching of the wandering Palestinian charismatic prophets. To them we look for the earliest known articulation of faith in Jesus as Christ and Lord.

Some of these men and women were followers of Jesus during his career; after his death, they carry on the tradition of his preaching. It is they who perpetuate the "sayings of the Lord" which later become one of the sources for the Synoptic Gospels. The prophets speak for the Lord in the Spirit. This is by no means a matter of recalling what Jesus *used to say*. Rather, they announce what Jesus *is saying here and now*. In an oral culture, the impact of this Spirit-filled prophetic testimony must have been enormous. Their preaching evoked the presence of the Risen Lord, experienced as powerfully active in their proclamation. Moreover, the prophets certified their words with deeds of healing and exorcism.[10] At first, it did not occur to anyone to maintain a strict distinction between what Jesus had said before he died, and what he said afterwards through the Christian prophets. (Eventually, however, the writing down of Gospels would allow the "real" Jesus to congeal in the past, so that he and the events of his life would form a historical foundation for the church.)

The Christian prophets said that Jesus had been exalted by God, had been made Christ and Lord, and would shortly return to bring God's judgment to earth. They did not have to preach that Jesus had been crucified and had died. Everyone knew that. They did not have to tell stories about finding an empty tomb, or about seeing Jesus alive and eating fish. Everyone could tell that Jesus was alive and powerfully present in the preaching and healing and exorcisms of the prophets. They did tell people who Jesus was: risen Lord and messiah, exalted to the right hand of God.

By contrast, the *kerygma* which Paul employed was fashioned according to a formula stating that Jesus (1) died, and (2) rose, and (3) was seen by certain trustworthy witnesses. That Hellenistic version was developed to evangelize people who had not heard of Jesus before, and for whom the prophets were no longer able to mount a credible oral proclamation that would evoke Jesus' living presence and power. The reasons for the obsolescence of Christian prophecy are not well understood. It is known that prophets could and did contradict one another, and that there were false prophets who led communities astray. The antidote to this unbridled variation, the written Gospel, which fixed the details of Jesus' message and biography as facts sedimented into the human *past*, seems to have had the inescapable side effect of diminishing the immediacy of Jesus' *living presence* in the communication of the gospel.

Ever since the gospel has been written down into Gospels, Christian ministers of the word have had the task of reconstituting it again as a living word in which the Risen Christ is effectively present. It now remains to determine in detail the *personnel, institutions, methods, media, and content* used in teaching and preaching the gospel in the first century of the church's life. In this investigation, we are not particularly interested in the issues of authority or of leadership. Rather, we want to understand how the Christian communities grew and grew strong through teaching and the other word ministries.

Personnel. Several varieties of ministers of the gospel have already been mentioned in this chapter's discussion of care, celebration, and word in the early church: the wandering Christian prophets, apostles like Paul, presbyters, and deacons. That list lengthens as one examines the New Testament to discover the different names given to those who carry out some aspect of the ministry of the word, as well as what sorts of people are doing that work. Once again, lines of evolution can be discerned over time.

In the Gospels, the generic term for a Christian, literally a follower of Jesus Christ, is "disciple." As we saw in the last chapter, discipleship always entails a personal encounter with Jesus, a call to which one responds, a mission to testify to others about Jesus, and following Jesus to death. Even the concept of discipleship, however, can be seen to undergo development. For Jesus, it meant setting one's heart upon the Reign of God. For the charismatic Palestinian prophets, it meant imitating the teaching and the lifestyle of Jesus. For Mark, it meant risking persecution and death, while refusing to be turned aside by delusions of glory and power. For Matthew's community, it meant understanding, interpreting, and doing the Law of Jesus in conscious opposition to contemporary interpretations of the Mosaic Law. For the author of Luke and Acts, it meant witnessing to the power of the Spirit of Jesus set loose in the world. For the community of the Beloved Disciple, it meant a personal relationship with Jesus that proved itself in love for the other members of the community.

Understandably, different views of the meaning of Christian life led to different roles for those whom the community entrusted with the communication of the gospel message. The Christian prophets at first continued to "work the territory" where Jesus already had announced God's Reign and where support groups of sympathizers already existed in villages and towns. Prophets who ventured into new territory to establish new communities were called "apostles." Jesus himself had sent some of his followers out on their own as apostles, according to a story preserved by Luke. Peter, who had traveled with Jesus as one of the Twelve, is the apostle who evangelizes the city of Jerusalem on Pentecost.

The term "apostle" is one that spans the first three Christian generations. The Twelve, who knew Jesus, were called apostles, but Paul also considers himself an apostle and says that the Jerusalem community concurs. Workers recruited by Paul as helpers and independent evangelists are called apostles, too. While none of the terms which designate ministerial roles in the New Testament has an exact definition, "apostle" seems to denote someone who is sent out and who founds a Christian community. One of the names of recognized apostles that come down to us in the New Testament is that of a woman, Junia (Rom 16:7).[11]

The apostle is the first to announce the gospel to a city. Afterwards, prophets may pass through to visit and guide the new community and to strengthen it by making Eucharist. "Teachers" are also mentioned. Eventually, both teachers and prophets may be resident as well as transient. These roles constitute the only known ministries of the word within many of the early churches, particularly the communities which Paul founded in the Hellenistic cities.

Churches which grew up in proximity to Jewish communities in the cities of Judea, and churches established by the apostles commissioned by those churches, sometimes developed a more formal organizational structure, as will be seen below. One of these was Matthew's community, and the Gospel which it produced gives us fascinating glimpses of a Christian teacher, for surely that is what the author is.

One term in Matthew's Gospel which designates people whom we would call teachers is "scribe," literally one who can read and write. The Jewish scribes were clerks and notaries; some of the more learned were members of the Sanhedrin and served as staff advisers to the leading priests. Most importantly, the scribes read and interpreted the Scriptures and were looked upon as experts in the Law. Therefore, they were respected members of Jewish society.

Matthew portrays Jesus himself as a teacher, but one who is *not* like the scribes (Mt 7:29). Jesus speaks on his own authority, interpreting Scripture without reference to a tradition of teachers. The teaching Jesus in Matthew is comfortable with the scribal technique of citing the Scriptures in his argumentation. On numerous occasions he uses the formula, "Have you not read. . . . " Matthew has the teaching Jesus reaffirm the importance of the Law.

> Amen, I'm telling you, until heaven and earth pass away not an iota, not a dot, will pass from the law, until everything happens. Therefore, whoever breaks one of the least of these commandments and teaches people to do so will be called least in the reign of heaven. But whoever does and teaches these comandments will be called greatest in the reign of heaven. I'm telling you, unless your righteousness is more than the righteousness of the scribes and Pharisees, you're not getting into the reign of heaven. (Mt 5:18–20)

In this context, holiness means scrupulous fidelity to the details of the Law. Matthew even censors the story in which Jesus "declared all foods clean," which comes down to us in Mk 7:1–23. The parallel passage in Matthew's Gospel deletes Mark's statement that Jesus has revoked the food laws (Mt 15:1–20).[12] For Matthew, the ideal Christian scribe knows how to bring forth from the storeroom both the new and the old (Mt 13:52). The Christian teacher shows the continuity between covenants (Mt 26:28), stressing the fulfillment of the Hebrew Scripture in the life, death, and resurrection of Jesus.

Matthew considers teaching so important that he makes the commission to teach one of the elements of Jesus' parting command to the disciples: "go . . . baptize . . . teach" (Mt 28:18–20). Yet, the Gospel cautions Christian scribes against seeking out the social position and the respect that were accorded to scribes in Jewish society:

> . . . Don't let anybody call you rabbi. You've only got one teacher, and you are all sisters and brothers. Don't call anybody on earth your father; you've only got one Father, the one in

heaven. Don't let anybody call you master; you've only got one master, the Christ. The greatest among you must be your servant. (Mt 23:8–11)

These words follow some of the vehement criticism which Matthew's Jesus customarily levels at Jewish scribes. In contrast to Matthew's assessment of what is wrong with the Jewish teachers (those contemporary to Matthew, not to Jesus), Matthew wants the teaching of the Christian scribes to be characterized by humility and by fidelity to the spirit of the Jewish Law as interpreted by the one Christian teacher, Jesus.

The role of the Christian teacher developed in other communities besides Matthew's, of course, but no other has left us such detailed instructions defining the teacher's ministry. In general, as the church spread throughout the Roman Empire the teachers' role probably was fashioned according to the two models available in the culture: rabbinic instruction, and the Hellenistic school of philosophy.

Although Judaism maintained its Temple and the center of its priestly cult in Jerusalem until 70 C.E., there were synagogues in the outlying towns of Judea, in the cities of the Empire, and even in Jerusalem itself. Synagogues were centers of Jewish life, where the Law and the Prophets were read and discussed. The wise man who led this ongoing study, and who instructed the young in Hebrew language and tradition, was the rabbi. (The rabbinate as an ordained ministry, however, was not organized until after the fall of Jerusalem.) Textual study, the custom of gathering for prayerful communal reading of scripture, and homiletic application of sacred texts to the circumstances of everyday life are all aspects of the Jewish teaching tradition which were adopted by the Christian churches.

Learning was held in esteem also among the Greeks to whom the Gospel was carried. In Hellenistic culture, there were formal schools organized at the elementary, secondary, and advanced levels. Philosophical academies attracted students from the privileged classes, and training in the methods of effective communication and argument was deemed the best preparation for entry into almost any business or profession. Inhabitants of the Greek cities could recognize an educated speaker when they heard one, and Christian teachers had to match wits with speakers trained in the traditions of Aristotle, Plato, Zeno, and Diogenes. Paul himself had had a Greek education along with his Pharisaic training "at the feet of Gamaliel" (Acts 22:3).

As Christianity entered Hellenistic culture, it was challenged to communicate the gospel message in philosophical categories (such as body, mind, soul, and matter) that had not been reflected in the teaching of Jesus. Moreover, many among those who accepted the gospel had already been trained in Hellenistic thought and rhetoric. For example, a man with a Greek name, Apollos, is identified in Acts 18:24 as a Jew who is both eloquent (i.e., skilled in Greek rhetoric) and "an authority on the scriptures" (i.e., Jewish learning). Acts 18:25 says that Apollos was catechized— *katēchēmenos*—in the Way of the Lord, and spoke and taught accurately the things concerning Jesus. Apollos is a native of the great academic center, Alexandria, and is found teaching in the synagogue at Ephesus. He receives further explanation about the Way from Priscilla and Aquila, and is able to confute the Jewish scholars in public debates by arguing that the Hebrew scriptures show that Jesus was the messiah (Acts 18:26–28). This teacher's power and rhetorical skills apparently attracted such a following that it created difficulties for Paul in Corinth (1 Cor 1:12). (Are there feelings of inferiority behind Paul's criticism of Greek wisdom in 1 Cor 1:18–25? Paul tells the Corinthians, "When I came to you, brothers and sisters, I did not come with fancy words or wisdom," 1 Cor 2:1.[13])

The teacher's role in the New Testament churches often is hard to distinguish from that of the prophet. We have seen that the first Christian prophets continued the wandering rural lifestyle of Jesus in Palestine. The cultural models upon which their work was based were Jewish prophecy and Cynic philosophy. The Hebrew prophets spoke for Yahweh: "Thus says the Lord!" The great classic prophets were intent on calling Israel back to faithful relationship with God, and to fidelity to covenant justice toward the little people of the land. The prophet's word was God's word, endowed with power to bring about what it declaimed. Bands of wandering prophets also had been known in Israelite tradition. Through these prophets, the Spirit of God had been inexorably active. Moreover, the regions of Samaria and Galilee had for a long time been familiar with the social and ethical teachings of the Cynics, another group whose adherents were homeless wanderers. The Cynic philosophers Oinomaos, Meleager, and Menippus were from the region of Gadara, where Jesus cast out the Latin-speaking demons ("Legion") and allowed them to drown a herd of pigs.[14] These two paranetic traditions—Jewish prophecy and Cynic philosophy—formed the background against which the work of Jesus and his disciples was understood.

But as the church grew and spread through the Empire, the role of the Christian prophet underwent modification just as the teacher's role had done. Peripatetic Cynic philosophers were known not just in Hellenized Palestine but throughout the empire. These philosophers were recognizable by distinctive dress and customs. They espoused a lifestyle free from social conventions, and they freely shared their views in public places. Their message was principally ethical in character, concerned with how one could lead a noble human life in the midst of complex cosmopolitan society. They enjoyed the acceptance of the populace, if not the interest. Paul seems to have been taken for a mediocre example of such a philosopher when he attempted to preach to the people of Athens (Acts 17:16–34). The existence and acceptance of footloose Cynic philosophers among the Hellenized peoples may explain why Greek Christian communities were prepared to welcome their own wandering prophets and to feed them.

What sort of person was called to "discipleship," to lead the Christian life and to serve the community in the role of apostle, prophet, or teacher? The call to accept Christ was universal. Both Jews and Gentiles, slaves and free, men and women, wealthy and workers, were baptized as Christians. To be an apostle, one had to be chosen and sent to witness by the Lord: by Jesus himself, or by the Spirit of Jesus speaking in the community. Experience of the Risen Lord, the ability to speak to crowds and to brave personal danger, an adventurous disposition, and a flair for diplomacy were the preferred qualifications for apostles. (It also helped if one had a business that kept one on the road a lot.) The New Testament names as an apostle at least one woman, Junia (Rom 16:7).

To be a prophet, one had to be filled with the Spirit of Jesus and endowed with the oral skills to make a vividly effective proclamation of the gospel. A flair for drama and for symbolic communication were assets, for the prophets made Eucharist "as much as they wished" (Didache 10:7). Prophets, too, had to be able to endure hardship during their travels and to get along on very little. Women as well as men prophesied in the Pauline churches.

To be a teacher, one had to be thoroughly familiar with the Jewish scriptures, and appreciate their new interpretation in the school of Jesus. Teachers had to understand Jewish history and the place of Jesus within it as the fullfillment of its prophecies. They also had to understand their own times and the complicated world in which they lived, so that they could apply the scriptures and Jesus' teachings to the complex situations which members of their communities had to face. This interpretive and extrapolating work called for patience, ingenuity, and wisdom. If one had Greek rhetorical training, so much the better. Teachers followed up the evangelizing work of apostles by explaining the gospel, helping it to sink in, and preparing Christians to celebrate Baptism and the Eucharist with understanding. The burden of their instruction was moral catechesis, as is evident from the contents of the Didache, "The Teaching of the Twelve Apostles." After the prophets stood up to deliver exciting Spirit-filled "words of the Lord," it would have fallen to teachers to bring the message down to earth, interpret it, correlate it with the received tradition of Jesus' teachings, and apply it to concrete situations. From among the teachers came the impulse finally to set down in writing the stories about Jesus that were in free oral circulation among the communities. It is they who committed the gospel to the Gospels.

Institutions. One of the ironies of Christianity is that a movement founded by such a great critic of religious institutions as Jesus of Nazareth could have developed such complex institutions itself, all the while cherishing the memory of the founder's critique in its scriptural canon. Institutionalization is a natural, sociological process by which complex societies retain their identities over time and insure their own propagation. Where two or three gather, no matter in whose name, for longer than a week, an institution is sure to appear.

We have seen how the ministry of the word was institutionalized within some of the New Testament churches in three roles: apostle, prophet, and teacher. In other churches, particularly those evangelized by apostles from the Christian community established in Jerusalem, another constellation of ministries emerged. This pattern was adapted from the leadership structure of the synagogue, the board of elders or "presbyters." The term elder does not indicate a specific job or function, but responsibility for the welfare of the community in general. Christian presbyters seem to have served on a policy-making council to guide the community. The New Testament does not depict them as successors of the Twelve or as divinely instituted. Nor are they ever mentioned in connection with the Eucharist. Presbyters within the community to which the author of 1 Tim writes, however, are engaged in teaching and are deemed worthy of double honor because of it (1 Tim 5:17). In most churches the board of elders has or is acquiring authority to administer property (e.g., Acts 11:29–30), to dispatch apostles (Acts 15:22–29), and to hear testimony and settle disputes in matters of polity and teaching (e.g., Acts 15; 16:4). Elders in the Johannine community, however, have no authority other than the eloquence of persuasion born out of their personal relationship with the Risen Lord.

In general, then, the work of the elders was to care for the welfare of all facets of the community's life and to oversee its affairs. The term "overseer," *episkopos*, begins to be used as a synonym for elder or presbyter. Our word "bishop" comes from this term, but in the New Testament the terms overseer and elder (bishop and presbyter) are used interchangeably. Interestingly, the New Testament never mentions an *episkopos* in connection with the celebration of the Eucharist, although in the second century the bishop's role would center upon his presidency of the eucharistic assembly.

It is also difficult to determine the precise function of those whom the New Testament calls "deacons." The word is used generically to describe service to the church. As the bishop's assistant, the deacon would rise to prominence in the organizational structure of the second-century church, when for example men and women deacons would assist in the separate baptismal rituals of male and female catechumens. However, it does not seem to have been important to the New Testament writers to define the deacons' exact responsibilities. Phoebe, whom Paul calls his sister in Rom 16:1, is a deacon (*diakonon*).

The presbyteral church structure turned out to be superior, from an administrative point of view, to the relatively unstructured ministry of the word in the Pauline churches. By the end of the first century, boards of elders were being organized in all the Christian churches. An effort was made to validate this innovation in the Pauline churches by anachronistically and pseudonymously attributing its origin to Paul himself. Acts 14:23 claims that Paul and Barnabas appointed elders in the churches of Lystra Iconium, and Antioch. The author of the Letter to Titus has Paul providing for the establishment of presbyteral organization in the church of Crete:

> That's why I left you in Crete, so that you could set right what remains to be done and appoint presbyters in every town on the conditions I gave you: somebody who is blameless, a man of one wife, with believing children who are not open to charges of being licentious or rebellious. Because a bishop as God's steward must be blameless, not a drunkard, not aggressive, not greedy for sordid gain, but hospitable, a lover of goodness, temperate, upright, holy, and self-controlled, holding on to the true message as taught, so that the bishop will be able both to give instruction in sound doctrine and to convince opponents. For there are also many rebels, big talkers and deceivers, especially among the circumcision party. (Tt 1:5–10)

By the turn of the century, the imposition of presbyteral order has not yet been completed. Churches in the Matthean tradition still are guided by teachers who follow Jesus in humility and fidelity to the scriptures, and these churches still look to prophets to preside at their Eucharist. The teachers who authored the Didache quote liberally from the scriptures, especially the Gospel of Matthew, as they transmit the content of their catechesis for the direction of the church's life. They are perhaps the last Christian teachers to have had such influence upon the governance of a church.

These teachers place the authority of their own more ancient ministry behind the institution of presbyteral church order, which apparently has not yet been welcomed in the communities which they are addressing. They advises their readers:

> Elect therefore for yourselves bishops and deacons worthy of the Lord, people who are meek, and not lovers of money, and truthful, and approved; for they too minister to you the ministry of the prophets and teachers. Therefore despise them not, for they are those who are the honored ones among you with the prophets and teachers.

The ministry of the bishops and deacons has to be legitimated, for these communities, by the endorsement of a teacher. It can be so legitimated only insofar as it resembles the ministry of the prophets and teachers, which is already established and revered among these churches (15:1–2).

Methods. The Christian church was born into a culture of orality, and attained its first growth through word of mouth. Today it is difficult for us to set aside the biases of our own literate and post-literate culture in order to understand the dynamics of effective communication in a society without the printed word, let alone telecommunications. The Jesus movement passed through a watershed at the point in its history when the oral gospel was committed to writing, as we shall see below. To grasp the methods of instruction employed by Christian teachers, prophets, and preachers in the first century, one must keep always in mind the extraordinary impact of the spoken word among them. The oral gospel is a living word and its utterance is a "Christ-event."[15]

According to Acts, apostles like Peter preached by addressing large crowds in public places. A work of healing or exorcism may have served to draw the people's attention, after which the story of Jesus' life and death would be told. The apostle would testify that God had raised Jesus and that forgiveness of sins was available through him. Acts insists that this method of open-air preaching was extraordinarily successful, at least in the beginning. At Athens, it yields only a handful of converts for Paul.

The wandering prophets, in the meantime, continued to make contact with the rural communities which had supported Jesus' mission and message. They repeated the stories which Jesus had told, and told stories about Jesus. The prophets kept Jesus' words alive, and the communities perceived that the Risen Lord continued to speak to them through the prophets.

The principal setting in which the prophets spoke the words of the Lord was the liturgical assembly, when the followers of Jesus were gathered in his name to keep the custom of table fellowship which he had taught them. At such meetings, the Hebrew scriptures would also be read and searched for meaning in light of what God had done in Jesus. This practice probably accounts for the embedding of the phrase "according to the scriptures" in the ancient kerygma formula handed on to Paul.

The chief method of instruction for the earliest churches, then, was their participation in liturgical assemblies, in which they heard the words of the Lord from the prophets, read and interpreted the Hebrew scripture, and shared the Eucharistic meal in expectation of the imminent return of Jesus to judge the world. When the practice of liturgical meetings spread to the Hellenistic cities, Christians there added hymns whose poetry explored the meaning of Christ in categories familiar to Greek thought. Examples of these hymns survive in 1 Tm 3:16; Col 1:15–20; Phil 2:6–11; Jn 1:1–5, 10–12, 14, 16. Singing these hymns in the assembly impressed upon the hearts and minds of the people their new identity as members of Christ's body. The theological assimilation of Hellenistic categories to express the Christian message, discernible in Paul's letters and characteristic of the first millennium of Christian thought, undoubtedly gets its start with these hymns.

There was individualized instruction as well. Christian men and women spoke of their faith to others in their workplaces, in the market, and in homes. In Acts we have the story of the evangelization of an Ethiopian traveler by Philip (Acts 8:26–38). Sometimes one had to evangelize individuals without using any words at all. The author of 1 Peter knows that women whose conduct reflects the simple lifestyle of Jesus can win their husbands over to Christ "without a word" (1 Pet 3:1). There are no classrooms for religious education in the New Testament.

Media. The oral gospel was committed to writing during the first century. Some have imagined this event to be a mere verbatim transcription of Jesus' story from memory to paper, or perhaps the compilation of several remembered stories into a unified narrative. Such a conception of the writing of the gospels overlooks the intrinsic interaction between medium and message. The prophetic oral delivery of the words of a living Jesus brought about what it signified. The spoken "words of the Lord" functioned as effective symbols; that is, they provided a material sensible event in which Jesus personally became present, available, and active. There was confirming evidence in the healings and exorcisms which the prophets and apostles performed in Jesus' name.

Yet there seems to have been disconfirming evidence as well. Jesus did not come back soon, as his followers were expecting. His friends grew old, got sick, and died. There was trouble with the Jewish authorities, and then with the Romans. Moreover, there were quarrels within the community. It even happened that prophets spoke in contradiction to one another. Jesus' powerful presence in the Spirit in the prophetic word did not seem to be enough to get the community through. Or so it must have seemed to the second and third generations of Christians—particularly those charged with helping community members absorb and integrate the gospel message in relation to the events of their daily lives: the teachers.

Besides having Jesus present, the community also needed him to be absent.[16] His life and death had to be consigned to the past if the church was to have a future. The community needed him as an "other advocate" with the Father, distinguishable from the "other advocate" who was the Holy Spirit and who remained present with them as their helper in their own time. The power of the Holy Spirit had to be unleashed by the definitive separation of Jesus and by his symbolic relocation in the past, in the future, and at God's right hand—in other words, elsewhere than in the volatile words of the prophets. Jesus had to go away.

> Simon Peter said to him, "Lord, where are you going?"
> Jesus answered,
> "Where I'm going, you can't follow me now,
> but you are going to follow later. . . .
> I will ask the Father and he'll give you
> another Advocate to be with you forever. . . .
> I won't leave you orphans; I'll come to you. . . .
> And now I've told you this before it happens,
> so that when it does happen you may believe.
> *I will no longer talk much with you.* . . .
> When the Advocate I'm sending from the Father gets here
> —the Spirit of truth that procedes from the Father—
> this Advocate is going to testify to me. . . .
> But to tell you the truth,
> it's better for you if I go away.
> *Because if I don't go,*
> *the Advocate won't come to you.*
> But if I go, I'll send you the Advocate."
> (Jn 13:36; 14:16, 18, 29–30; 15:26; 16:7)

With the writing of the Gospels, the facticity of Jesus' death finally begins to sink into Christian consciousness. The events of his life and death are recorded with pen and ink as events of the past. The Resurrection, too, can for the first time be understood as a historical event, for the written narrative situates it in time. That is the function of narrative: to map out the time and space of reality.

Teachers trying to make sense of the conflicting testimony of the prophets and of the troubles the community encountered despite Jesus'

Resurrection must have perceived the need for a standardization of the gospel, a concrete criterion against which individual prophets and evangelists might be judged. This standard Gospel would also have to explain why Christians should encounter suffering. Perhaps the first attempt in the direction of standardization and authority was to identify the oral lineage of teachers: their "apostolic" pedigree. Unlike the prophets, whose license to speak was the compulsion of experiencing the Risen Lord, teachers were teachers precisely because someone had taught them. One can still discern a distinctive Matthean school, for example, in comparison with that of the Beloved Disciple. The time came when teachers took it upon themselves to set down their own "official" story of what Jesus had said and done. In that first Gospel, the Risen Lord does not speak at all (for, as scholars agree, Mark's original literary composition concludes with verse 16.8).

The text then had to be put into circulation, that is, certified for use within Christian catechesis. There, it is not the Risen Lord but the teacher who speaks. Once the Gospel of Mark has been written and accepted, Jesus cannot say anything else through the prophets. The fluidity of the oral tradition congeals. That took a while, to be sure; for other Gospel writers from other traditions would in the next generation congeal Jesus' words into slightly different shapes.

By the end of the first century, prophecy is dying out. Teaching relies now upon written sources. The church has written narratives about Jesus which are read aloud in the liturgical assembly. The prophets are coming in from the cold and settling down in the communities. Something has been lost.

But something has been gained as well. With Jesus' life, death, and Resurrection consigned to the facticity of the Christian past, and with his glorious return and the resurrection of Christians projected out into the future, a dynamic tension has been set up in time. This development coincides with the fading of the Christian hope that the Parousia soon would arrive. Jesus' presence-in-absence through the other helper, the Spirit, propels the community forward in time toward its certain fate: away from Jesus, but toward the King of Glory. We see here that the mystery of what God does in Jesus can now take effect symbolically according to what we have described as the second level of symbolic function. Beyond presence, symbol is empowerment through the persuasive projection of an ideal vision of future relationship upon the present in such a way that the dissonance between vision and reality pushes the present into alignment with the ideal future. What makes this possible is a fixed, written text in the hands of a Christian teacher. There must be distance between vision and reality for the one to affect the other.

Where prophetic utterances had evoked the simple presence of Jesus, now that "Jesus is history" in a text, the ministry of the word involves a more complex process. Teachers and evangelists at the end of the first century face the new task of making the written word a living word. They have to bring the stories of Jesus to life, but in three dimensions: as a definite message delivered by someone in the past, as interpretive tools for issues that arise in everyday living, and as a guarantee for the future of the individual and of the entire cosmos.[17]

Oral communication remains important. It is the medium of the liturgy, and it is the principal medium of instruction. The letters of Paul and of other apostles occupy a place midway between the oral delivery of the kerygma and the written text of a Gospel. The epistles are indeed written transcriptions of oral instructions. That is the way letters were written in the ancient world. Paul likely would have dictated what he wanted to say to a scribe. Naturally, the letters lack the smooth narrative structure of a Gospel, and are composed instead of short and relatively independent discourses and arguments about a number of topics. Yet as texts, the epistles too congeal and cement the kerygma, and its interpretation, into a certain solid facticity which later teachers and preachers will cite as authoritative. (Not so authoritative, however, that they refrained from editing them and interpolating post-Pauline passages!) This sedimentation incorporates other earlier speech forms: fossilized hymns, proverbs, slogans, liturgical formulae, midrash, and secular rhetorical flourishes.

The Gospels, too, bear traces of earlier fragments of the preaching of apostles and prophets. Sayings of Jesus that had floated along in the oral tradition, adhering to any number of different contexts according to the exigencies of particular preaching situations, now have become anchored into historical settings. Miracle stories, moral exhortations, traditions about the crucifixion, appearance stories, infancy stories, and so forth, have been sculpted by the Gospel writer to fit the narrative which situates Jesus in the Christian past and future.

Content. Much has already been said about the content of the catechesis which nourished the growth of the church in the first century. In general, that teaching sought to interpret the present life circumstances of each Christian man and woman so as to disclose a dynamic connection between him or her and what God did and would do in Jesus. Paul's insistence that Christians who died with Christ in Baptism must necessarily rise with him upon his return is an excellent example. Moral instruction formed a large part of first-century catechesis, as one can see both in the references which Paul's letters make to his own teaching, and in the Didache. Instruction also treated the events of the life of Christ, seen now as historic, and the expectation of Christ's return, symmetrically placed at the end of time.

But the greatest doctrinal achievement of the first century was the clear articulation of belief in the divinity of Jesus Christ. This belief would receive dogmatic definition in the fifth century at Chalcedon in the affirmation that Jesus is truly God and truly human. That definition is based upon evidence of what was believed and taught in the first-century church—evidence found in the New Testament itself.

The early Palestinian Jesus movement and the apostolic church in Jerusalem proclaimed that God had exalted Jesus who had been crucified, but these adamantly monotheistic Jewish Christians have left us no clear indication that they identified Jesus as divine. If Jesus was "Son of God" for them, that appellation connotes that he was God's special chosen messenger. Moreover, it seems that they understood the bestowal of the status of son upon Jesus to have taken place at some point in his life (i.e., after his conception). Typical of this understanding is the story of Jesus' baptism in Mark's Gospel:

> . . . Jesus came from Nazareth in Galilee and was baptized in the Jordan by John. As soon as he came up out of the water he saw the sky being ripped open and the Spirit, like a dove, descending on him. And there was a voice out of the sky: "You are my dear son. I am so glad about you!" (Mk 1:9–11)

In this story Jesus' sonship is announced, and presumably conferred, at the beginning of his career. He is presented as a man who has been singled out by God for a mission. Accounts of early apostolic sermons recorded in the book of Acts convey a similar interpretation of the relationship between Jesus and God. Peter is said to have addressed the Jews gathered in Jerusalem in the following words:

> Jesus the Nazarene was a man commended to you by God with mighty works, wonders, and signs, which God did through him in your midst, as you yourselves know. This man, given up by the set plan and foreknowledge of God, you killed, using lawless people to crucify him. But God raised him up, releasing him from the pangs of death, because it was impossible for him to be held by it. . . . Therefore let all the house of Israel know for certain that *God has made him both Lord and Christ, this Jesus whom you crucified.* (Acts 2:22–24, 36)

Peter conveys the same message to Gentiles in Acts 10:36–43, that God has selected Jesus for special work and has raised him up. A similar theme also is attributed to Paul, who is said to identify Jesus' reception of sonship as the Resurrection:

> We are preaching the good news to you that what God promised our ancestors God has brought to fulfillment for us, their children, by raising up Jesus, as it is written in the second psalm, *"You are my son; today I have begotten you."* (Acts 13:32–33)

In these passages, Resurrection is understood as the vindication and exaltation of Jesus, who had been executed as a criminal. God's identification with Jesus is a judgment affirming Jesus' life and teachings, so it is necessarily subsequent to them. In other, later passages of the New Testament, however, the identification of God and Jesus is pushed back in time to the beginning of Jesus' life, and indeed to before the beginning of time. Luke's Gospel has Jesus' mother Mary conceive him "by the power of the Most High" so that "the child to be born will be called holy, the Son of God" (Lk 1:35). John's Gospel places the identification between Jesus and God still earlier:[18]

> In the beginning was the word,
> and the Word was with God,
> and the Word was God.
> This one was in the beginning with God.
> All things came to be through this one,
> and without this one nothing came to be. (Jn 1:1–3)

This Word or *logos*, who exists before anything else, is God's Son and is missioned to the world, the Gospel says:

> Because God loved the world so much that God gave God's only Son, so that everyone who believes in him would not perish but have eternal life. For God did not send God's Son into the world to condemn the world, but so that the world would be saved through him. (Jn 3:16–17)

In this Johannine christology, the Son of God is at last identified as God.

The first century church, then, is in possession of a teaching that Jesus is the Christ, God's chosen one; Jesus is the exalted Lord, the one whom God has vindicated and raised up despite his death; and Jesus is God's Son, the enfleshment of divinity which existed before the world itself. The relationship between Jesus and God is not a closed system, but a relationship into which Christians enter "in Jesus' name." They do so through these teachings, and also through the sacramental celebrations of Baptism and Eucharist and through caring for the material needs of Jesus' least sisters and brothers. This relationship is the foundation of the reconciliation which was offered in Jesus, and it is the ground for the Christian hope in resurrection for those who are reconciled in Jesus.

LEGACY OF THE FIRST-CENTURY CHURCH

- Gospels
- many sayings of the Risen Lord
- access to Resurrection experience through stories
- a historical time-line for the church
- the doctrine of the divinity of Jesus
- leadership organization: presbyters, bishops, and deacons
- a network of urban churches
- a trans-national outlook on God's intent for human beings
- cultural and linguistic translations of Jesus' message
- the metaphor "Body of Christ" for the church
- profiles of discipleship
- profiles of Christian teaching
- critiques of abuses of authority by teachers
- a distinctive Christian hermeneutic of the Jewish scriptures
- a distinctive ecclesial identity in contrast with Judaism and Hellenism

Notes for Chapter Four

1. For background in these and other aspects of first-century Palestine, see: Gerd Theissen, *Sociology of Early Palestinian Christianity*, translated by John Bowden (Philadelphia: Fortress, 1978), and *The Social Setting of Pauline Christianity*, edited, translated, and introduced by John H. Schultz (Philadelphia: Fortress Press, 1982); Werner H. Kelber, *The Oral and the Written Gospel* (Philadelphia: Fortress Press, 1983); Helmut Koester, *History and Literature of Early Christianity* (Philadelphia: Fortress, 1982); Ronald F. Hock, *The Social Context of Paul's Ministry* (Philadelphia: Fortress Press, 1980); John Knox, "The Ministry in the Primitive Church," pp. 1–26 in *The Ministry in Historical Perspectives*, edited by H. Richard Niebuhr and Daniel D. Williams (New York: Harper & Row,

1956; San Francisco, 1983); and Nathan Mitchell, *Mission and Ministry*, (Wilmington: Michael Glazier, 1982).

2. Among non-canonical sources, the most important is the Didache, or *The Teaching of the Twelve Apostles*. In this chapter I will be using, and sometimes updating, the translation published by Philip Schaff (New York: Funk & Wagnalls, 1889), third edition, which presents the Greek text and the translation side by side. Important information about the early church also is found in letters written just after the turn of the second century; for example, those of Ignatius of Antioch and Clement of Rome.

3. Conspicuously omitted by this saying (or, perhaps more accurately, by its editor), is mention of women's leaving husbands to follow Jesus. However, there is evidence that they did so in Lk 8:2–3.

4. This is the thesis of Gerd Theissen. See his arguments on pp. 17–23 of *Sociology*. He states on pp. 22–3:

> Our investigation of the local communities has shown that they are to be understood exclusively in terms of their complementary relationship to the wandering charismatics. The radical attitude of the wandering charismatics was possible only on the basis of the material support offered to them by the local communities. . . . In turn, the local communities could allow themselves to compromise with the world about them because the wandering charismatics maintained such a clear distinction. The two social forms of the Jesus movement were both associated and distinguished by a gradated pattern of norms.

5. Theissen points out on pp. 37–8 of *The Social Setting* that:

> It is immediately evident that fishermen and farmers turned itinerant preachers had to give up their work if they were to missionize in rural environs. They could not pack up and carry along their fields and lakes as one might one's tools. Peter the fisherman is forced by necessity to accept the "privilege of support"; Paul the craftsman can afford to renounce it.

For a fascinating study that takes seriously the fact that Paul worked long and hard at a trade which defined his place in society, see R.F. Hock, *The Social Context of Paul's Ministry*. Aside from the parallels to Greek philosophical *thought* which may be found in Paul's writings, Hock points out that in working as an artisan, Paul is following the *practice* of some Greek philosophers.

6. But Thomas A. Marsh makes a distinction between two Greek

cognate verbs, *baptein*, "to dip in," and *baptizein*, "to immerse." He notes that it is the latter form, used by Jewish translators in connection with ritual baths, which is reserved to describe Christian rituals of baptizing. See his discussion on pp. 28–9 of *Gift of Community* (Wilmington: Michael Glazier, 1984).

7. Yet 1 Cor 14:34 seeks to muzzle the prophecy of women! Either the irascible Paul is here caught in an inconsistency (vis-à-vis 1 Cor 11:4–5), or 1 Cor 14:33–6 is a post-Pauline interpolation, or the passage is indeed Pauline but cannot be applied to unmarried women prophets. Elisabeth Schüssler Fiorenza argues for the third option; see *In Memory of Her* (New York: Crossroad, 1984), pp. 227–33, and note 81 on p. 240.

8. Bernard Cooke argues for the prophetic character of the early eucharistic celebration in *Ministry to Word and Sacraments* (Philadelphia: Fortress, 1977), pp. 529–30, where he states that.

> . . . the eucharistic breaking of bread is essentially an act of evangelic proclamation. It is a "proclaiming of the death of the Lord until he come" (1 Cor 11:26). . . . (T)he action of eucharistic blessing is one of recognizing the saving act of God, of proclaiming his great deeds as these find culmination in Christ's death and resurrection, of expressing the conversion and dedication of life that are appropriate response to the gospel.

9. Gregory Dix's clasic study *The Shape of the Liturgy* (London: A & C Black, 1945; New York: Seabury, 1982), presents evidence linking the Christian Eucharist with the formal supper of a *chaburah* rather than the yearly Passover supper. According to Dix, a *chaburah* was an informal society of friends "banded together for purposes of special devotion and charity, existing within the ordinary Jewish congregations. . . ." Because the strictly observed customs are familiar to scholars through rabbinic sources, Dix is able to reconstruct a plausible account of Jesus's instructions, gestures, and intentions on the last occasion when he shared this meal with his friends, and to comment upon how these things must have been received among the first few generations of his followers. See pp. 50–70. Joachim Jeremias, however, holds that the Eucharist is indeed based upon the rituals of the Passover celebration, as the Synoptic Gospels say. See *The Eucharistic Words of Jesus*, translated by Norman Perrin (Philadelphia: Fortress Press, 1966), especially pp. 26–62.

10. The function of miracles to certify the words of prophetic preaching is reflected in "the longer ending" of Mark's Gospel, especially Mk 16:15–20.

11. The notation on this verse in the revised edition of the New American Bible reads:

> The name Junia is a woman's name. One ancient Greek manuscript and a number of ancient versions read the name "Julia." Most editors have interpreted it as a man's name, Junias.

See the Revised Standard Version for such a mistranslation. See also Elisabeth Schüssler Fiorenza's discussion, *In Memory of Her*, p. 47, and note 13, p. 65.

12. Observance of Jewish dietary laws is still recommended in the Matthean churches after the turn of the century, if Schaff's interpretation of the Didache is correct. In 4:2 the Christian is advised:

> If you are able to bear the whole yoke of the Lord, you will be perfect; but if you are not able, do what you can.

13. Paul himself was "a learned man," as Geraldine Hodgson points out in *Primitive Christian Education* (Edinburgh: T. and T. Clark, 1906), p. 22. Hodgson identifies in Paul's writings, or in speech attributed to him, three citations from classic Greek authors: Aratus in Acts 17:28, Menander in 1 Cor 15:33, and Epimenides in Tit 1:12; see pp. 22–3.

14. See Donald R. Dudley, *A History of Cynicism* (Chicago: Ares, 1937, 1980).

15. So says Kelber in *The Oral and the Written Gospel*, p. 101.

16. This paradox is disclosed to present-day scholars like Werner Kelber who analyze the symbolic efficacy of the gospel. It was not apparent to first-century prophets, although some teachers evidently recognized the need for an authoritative text condensing the Jesus traditions into the facticity of something past and settled. I interpret passages of the Johannine Last Discourse as poetic expressions of the intuition that the voice of the Risen Christ speaking through the prophets would cease, but that this departure of Jesus would intensify, not extinguish, the activity of the Spirit.

17. One can at this point begin to speak of the Christian foundational documents as mythic, in the sense that they serve to explain and legitimate the existence of the church while interpreting human being in relation to it. The phenomenology of myth has generated an extensive body of literature. For a basic introduction to the concept of myth, see John Dominic Crossan, *The Dark Interval* (Niles, Ill.: Argus Communications, 1975).

18. The proper way to translate the first verse of John's Gospel is a matter of contention among scholars. Raymond E. Brown mentions some

of the objections to the formula "the Word was God"; see Brown's commentary on *The Gospel According to John,* The Anchor Bible (Garden City, New York: Doubleday & Company, 1966). However, Brown himself opts (on pp. 3 and 5) in favor of the formula as reflecting

> the Johannine affirmative answer to the charge made against Jesus in the Gospel that he was wrongly making himself God (10:33; 5:18). Nevertheless, we should recognize that between the Prologue's "the Word was God" and the later church's confession that Jesus Christ was "true God of true God" (Nicea), there was marked development in terms of philosophical thought and a different problematic.

Chapter Five

Fourth Century:
The Eclipse of Antiquity

The gospel of reconciliation announced by Jesus in the Palestinian countryside had made its way into major cities of the Roman Empire during the first century of the common era. We have seen that the gospel took effect then and there in the transformation of human lives through the church-building activities of caring for people's needs, celebrating the intimacy of God and humankind in Jesus, and communicating the invitation to all to share a new way of living.

Having examined how the gospel got started with Jesus and with the first few generations of his followers, our historical survey continues now with another glimpse of the church, somewhat later in time. The fourth century was in many ways a watershed in the story of the gospel. Governmental sanctions against Christians were lifted in the year 313. The church grew in numbers and influence, in an era when the Roman Empire itself was beginning to show signs of strain and decay. Doctrinally and liturgically, this period represents a classical age for Christianity. The early church's theological interpretation of Christian revelation culminated in the trinitarian definition of 325 at Nicea and the christological definition of 451 at Chalcedon. The church's experience of its own being and mission achieved vividly effective sacramental expression in ritual celebrations of initiation and reconciliation: Baptism, with its Catechumenate, and canonical Penance.

From our twentieth-century vantage point, we can see that these crystallizations of the gospel are owing both to the heritage of Jesus, and to the interplay of historical and cultural factors in the fourth century. Christians of that era did not conduct ecclesial affairs in exactly the same way as their ancestors of the first century. The church "changed" because it continued adapting its activities to the needs of the times just as the first Christian generations had done. Nevertheless, Christians of the fourth century were quite concerned to insure that their gospeling activities, particularly their teaching, retained its apostolic authenticity.

110

Practices which authentically and effectively expressed Jesus' offer of reconciliation for people of the fourth century—such as public penance, the catechumenate, or the female deaconate—cannot be expected automatically to work as well in any other era. The historian who wishes to understand them is careful not to wrench them out of the culture in which they made sense. Doctrinal definitions, too, must be understood in their own time and place, with particular attention to the language in which they are framed. The catholicity or universality of the Christian faith consists not in transcending culture, but in its ability to penetrate and transform any culture.

In the last chapter we saw that first-century Christians had affirmed the belief that Jesus is God. The early Christian imagination tended to associate the divinity of Jesus with his Resurrection, for which the Gospel texts had provided a historical location" in time. Christians of the first century stood with the Beloved Disciple at the empty tomb of Jesus and there confessed their faith in Jesus as Christ, Lord, and God. During the ensuing centuries, the focus of reflection upon the divinity of Jesus seems to have moved backward in time: from tomb to womb, as it were. Already in John's Gospel, Jesus had been identified with the pre-existent Word of God through whom everything else had been made. To the "incarnation" of this Word in human flesh was assigned a place in history: the moment of Jesus' conception. Like the Resurrection, the Incarnation too came to be regarded a historical event. Like the Resurrection, which was "about" each Christian's fate as well as that of Jesus, the Incarnation too was "about" the humanity of each woman, man, and child as well as that of Jesus. Humanity, *our* humanity, had been taken up into divinity in Christ "when" the Word became human.

Reflection upon the nature of human being itself had long been a concern of the Hellenistic philosophers. As people with philosophical training accepted the gospel's invitation, they brought into Christianity both their philosophical questions and their tools of inquiry. In the second century, the great African academic center of Alexandria already had a theological school headed by Pantaenus, a baptized Stoic philosopher. He was succeeded by Clement, a man learned in Greek philosophy and literature, and by Origen, also famous for his erudition. None of these philosophers was ordained while at Alexandria. In the early third century under Origen, the school at Alexandria had two divisions: one for basic catechesis, and another for advanced studies in exegesis and theology. Origen taught in the advanced division, whose curriculum included preparatory work in liberal arts and philosophy as well as religious studies.[1]

The advanced division was closed down when Origen lost his job about the year 230 after a quarrel with the bishop. Origen's teaching career continued succcessfully for another two decades in Caesarea in Palestine, however, before he was martyred. By the fourth century, the experiment of the Christian academy was over. Christians received instruction in their faith only through preaching, especially preaching addressed to the cate- chumens. Theological training for clerics could be obtained privately through association with the bishop or older clerics.

The distinction between clergy and the rest of the baptized had emerged only at the end of the third century, after ministry became a full- time job first for the bishop and then for the presbyters. Whereas "bishop" and "presbyter" were terms used interchangeably in many New Testa- ment texts, the early second century saw the development of the mono- episcopate, that is, the organization of each church with a single bishop having responsibility for all its church affairs. The role of the bishop grad- ually grew more important. In general, presbyters assisted the bishop in his cultic and teaching duties, and deacons and widows assisted him with community relations including administration of the church's goods for the welfare of the poor. However deacons also took a distinctive part in the eucharistic celebration and in the baptismal ritual, where both women and men deacons were needed. The earliest extant reference to a Christian cleric as a "priest" appears in a document dating from about the year 190.

Teaching was still recognized as a separate ministry in Rome at the beginning of the second century. Thereafter, the functions of teaching and prophecy, which had been such distinctive marks of the New Testament church, gradually were absorbed into the bishop's role. As the churches grow, the third-century bishop shoulders responsibility for all of the gos- peling activities characteristic of ecclesial transformation. He is the shep- herd and care-taker of the community. He administers property used for relief of poor Christians, especially those who have suffered persecution. He guards the community's integrity, wielding authority to admit people to Christ's body and to exclude anyone who does not follow the Christian way. He supervises the catechumenate and appoints those who provide catechesial instruction. He presides at liturgical celebrations: the Eucha- rist, Initiation, Penance, and Ordination. He is beloved and revered as the head and exemplar of the community. Moreover, the Roman imperial bu- reaucracy recognizes him as the individual through whom official business may be conducted with the community.

At the same time that this profile of the bishop is taking shape, a cer- tain stratified organization also is emerging in the Christian community itself. When the church assembles for worship, only those who have been baptized are admitted to the eucharistic celebration. The catechumens, who are preparing for Baptism through the instruction and other practices of the catechumenate, depart from the assembly after the prayers, read-

ings, and preaching known as the Liturgy of the Word (or Mass of the Catechumens). They are recognized as a separate order, the order of
catechumens, in contrast to the order of the faithful. By the same token,
Christians seeking readmission to the church after apostasy or some other
grave sin also must undertake works of penance like the catechumens, and
like the catechumens they are excluded from the Eucharist. They make
up an order of penitents. A Christian's degree of participation in the assembly depends upon the order to which he or she belongs—penitents,
catechumens, or the faithful. It is not long before Christians begin to regard those who preside at the liturgical assembly as a fourth order, the
clergy.

While the persecutions persist, however, this stratification is to some
extent upset by martyrdom. A martyr is a "witness," one who declares that
Jesus is Lord in front of the civil authorities. A Christian who survives such
an experience returns to the community with a unique status. Such a "confessor" needs no ordination to preside at the eucharistic celebration. Confessors who have spoken for Christ "in chains" can speak for him to
reconcile sinners to the church. The phenomenon of martyrdom, then,
tends to level the status of the different orders in the church up to the
fourth century.[2] When the Roman state officially recognizes the church's
right to exist in 313, the leveling influence of martyrdom no longer ame-
liorates the stratification of the Body of Christ.

As we turn now to an examination of the ecclesial activities of care,
liturgical celebration, and teaching in the fourth-century church, we find
that the historical documents which make up the bulk of our source material are more numerous and better understood than the ones preserved
from the first century. A variety of genres are represented among the ancient texts which have come down to us. There are catecheses, or instructions written to be spoken as sermons to those preparing for Baptism; there
are also numerous theological essays and dialogues which follow conventions of argumentation established by Hellenistic rhetoric. Historical com-
pilations and liturgical instructions come down to us. Church councils have
left records of their decrees, and pilgrims have left accounts of the customs
they observed in the churches which offered them hospitality during their
travels. Private correspondence among Christian leaders also has been
preserved—all thanks to the patient recopying of manuscripts by anonymous Christian men and women in later centuries. Besides texts, there is
physical evidence dating from the fourth century itself in the form of inscriptions on monuments, tombs, and public buildings. Even the architectural design of early church structures tells something of what went on
inside them. Alongside all of these documents, inscriptions, and designs,
there also exist corresponding pagan sources which help us to understand

the distinctiveness of the Christian forms within their contemporary culture. From about the turn of the fifth century comes the earliest extant
account of church life seen through the eyes of a woman: Egeria's chronicle
of her pilgrimage to Jerusalem.

THE SITUATION IN THE ROMAN EMPIRE IN THE FOURTH CENTURY

The enforced peace which the Roman imperial administration had
brought to the Mediterranean world facilitated trade and communication
among many nations, and thereby provided an almost ideal medium for
the spread of the gospel message and way of life during the first few centuries of the common era. Periodic government persecutions of Christians
gave way in 313 with the Edict of Toleration of the first Christian emperor,
Constantine, who moved the imperial capital east to Byzantium, his Nova
Roma, renamed Constantinople. The empire embraced a hundred nations, but along its 10,000-mile frontier many others waited for a chance
to seize for themselves something of the prosperity and civilization enjoyed within the Roman sphere. Though they were called Barbarians, Germanic peoples had been trading with the Romans for centuries and had
filled the ranks of the Roman legions in the West. Pressured by the bel-
ligerence of tribes from the distant Mongolian plains and by the growth of
their own populations, these European peoples had begun crossing into
imperial territory either peacefully or by conquest.
     Some of the peoples entering the Christianized empire had them-
selves already been baptized, although by adherents of a variety of Christianity called Arianism. The Goths received Arian Christianity from
Bishop Ulfilas in the fourth century. It was in response to the teaching of
Arius that the Council of Nicea in 325 had defined that the Son of God is
"of one substance" with God. But many in the church still agreed with
Arius' understanding of the nature of Jesus Christ: that he was more than
a man but less than God. The controversy was bitter and long-lasting, and
it entangled relationships between the church and the empire. Constantine himself was baptized on his deathbed in 337 by an Arian bishop.
     Germanic, Persian, and African peoples menaced Roman order from
outside the empire; but within imperial society, erosion of another sort
was at work. The empire maintained itself by its armies and its bureau-
cratic administration, and these in turn were maintained by heavy taxation. In both the military and the government, corruption and inefficiency
fed off one another and produced general disillusionment with traditional
social values and virtues which the best Greek philosophy had nurtured

and prized. The Hellenistic culture gradually was losing its ability to inculcate civic virtues in the young.

Philosophy was deteriorating; which is to say that the educational system, as agent of the socialization of the middle and upper classes, produced fewer and fewer of the sort of citizens who could find personal meaning through participation in the civic, economic, or military life of the empire. Higher education was becoming preoccupied with form at the expense of substance. Schoolboys were taught to compose technically correct stylized speeches about persons or occasions out of the past; the validation of this rhetoric in present experience was never considered. The masses of the people, even those who had received this hollow education in logic and literature, were receptive to the exotic cosmologies offered by mystery religions and by gnosticism, among other systems of ideas imported from the Eastern reaches of the Empire and beyond. These promised an interior, personal, mystical achievement of meaning to many who were disillusioned with the traditional public civic virtues. The appeal of Christianity itself can be understood within this context.

Yet in the fourth century, philosophical education had not yet completely lost its power and attraction. Julian, a nephew of Constantine who would succeed him as emperor, and who was unfavorably impressed by the violent dissension among the Christians at his uncle's court, turned to the traditional Hellenistic philosophical heritage. He found it possible to obtain an excellent liberal education in the academic centers of Athens and Nicomedia. As a young man, Julian had secretly been initiated into a mystery cult, but he continued to participate publicly in Christian worship for political reasons. Unusually abstemious in his personal habits, the Emperor Julian earned the respect of his people and his troops. He also earned the title "Apostate" from the Christians when he sought to restore the old Roman civic values by restoring the cult and the real estate of the pagan religions throughout the empire.

During his brief reign, Julian issued a regulation concerning school teachers that had the effect of excluding Christians from that vocation. It is significant because of the light it throws on fourth-century imperial educational practice. From elementary training, to the grammatical school, to higher training in rhetoric, instruction invariably focused upon classical Greek and Roman literature, for which the legends of gods and goddesses provided the themes. One learned to write by copying their names; one learned public speaking by composing orations on their behalf. It is clear that teachers and students alike regarded the divinities as literary, not religious, figures. In no way was this public education understood to be *religious* education. Certainly the Christians could not have so understood it, for they never hesitated to send their children to public schools. Moreover, there were Christians serving as teachers in the public schools, although not everyone in the church approved of that.[3] Julian decreed that it was immoral for anyone who did not believe in the gods, to give instruction in classic literature which mentioned the gods.

This short-lived restriction spurred some Christians to attempt "literary" paraphrases of the New Testament books and start Christian grammar schools which would base their instructions upon those compositions instead of the classic authors. This brief experiment was the exception that underlined the rule: it was the universal custom for Christians in the empire to be educated alongside pagan citizens. Neither Christian elementary schools nor theological academies existed again until monastic and cathedral schools developed—several centuries later in another culture altogether.

Yet the church of the fourth century did not lack well-educated and articulate teachers: its bishops, its preachers, and its catechists. Their erudition was a hybrid born of the gospel and of Hellenistic philosophy and rhetoric, and bred in controversial engagement with issues long under discussion in the Hellenistic academies. In the catechumenate, the church had an effective institution for socializing and educating new Christians. Throughout the era of the Roman persecutions, the church had developed a remarkably cohesive social structure. Its close-knit community life, always attractive to people beset by the anomie of the deteriorating Hellenistic culture, became with the lifting of persecution a magnet for growing numbers of women and men in the cities and then in the countryside. By the fourth century, Christians occupied positions of power in government and in the military as well as in the academy. The Emperor Constantine's conversion was as much the result as the cause of this fact.

The legalization and imperial establishment of Christianity, its subsequent growth, and its ongoing dialogue with Hellenistic thought all made their impact upon the ecclesial activities of care, cult, and gospel call in the fourth century.

CARE: ADMINISTRATION OF RELIEF SERVICES FOR A GROWING COMMUNITY

By the time the Empire legalized the church in 313, all ministry had become the responsibility of the bishop. He was chief care-giver, liturgical celebrant, and teacher of the faithful; although to be sure, these responsibilities were delegated to many other men and women under the bishop's direction.

With imperial recognition came new civil status for the bishop. His judgments in disputed cases now carried the force of civil law. In the mind of the people, the bishop's role acquired aspects of the role of the civil governor. For several centuries, the trend in civic life had been to lessen citizens' responsibility for and involvement in their own government, so that the emperor had become a dictator ruling through appointed representatives. Constantine went so far as to provide a daily loaf of bread and free entertainment to the lowest-class inhabitants of Constantinople, although they were denied the vote.

An interesting and somewhat parallel development was taking place in the church. In the first century, Paul had envisioned the Christian community as Christ's Body. Each member was a distinctive part of the body with a distinctive task to accomplish. Each part needed the others. Gradually, however, another metaphor supplanted Paul's image of mutually interdependent ministries. People began to regard Christ's Body as an entity apart from themselves, one meant to shepherd and rule them. A new metaphor, "mother church," seemed to project an active parental ministry caring for passive, helpless, childlike people. This ministry was personified in the figure of the bishop, who was expected to be shepherd, magistrate, and mother all in one.[4]

Such a job description made sense in the culture of the fourth century, owing in part to its similarity with the role of the ideal Byzantine emperor. Indeed, in that culture the images of parental church and parental bishop did facilitate the continuance of aspects of ministry of Jesus, particularly his care for the well-being of the sons and daughters whom Abba loved.

The imperial dole took the edge off the hunger of the poorest Christians, but there was still great need for assistance to the destitute and the homeless. While persecutions had lasted, many Christian families lost their breadwinners to martyrdom; many others had their homes and possessions confiscated. The material support of such victims of imperial sanctions was the responsibility of the Christian community as a whole. When property was donated for the upkeep of these and other widows and orphans, it was the bishop who administered the property. This arrangement continued even after the end of the persecutions, when Constantine ordered that confiscated property be returned to the churches. The need of poor Christians alone justified the church's acquisition and administration of material goods.[5]

Seeing to the upkeep, use, and distribution of church property occupied a sizeable portion of the bishop's attention. He was assisted in this work by male and female deacons and by widows—although the latter group undoubtedly included recipients as well as distributors of the charitable assistance.

Under the bishop's leadership, the Christian community established hospitals, shelters, orphanages, and homes for wayward youth in response to social and material needs. Martin of Tours, who introduced the monastic way of life into Gaul in the late fourth century, continued his own established practice of providing for the needy after he was chosen bishop by acclamation of the people. Hospitality for travelers was a distinctive Christian ministry. This custom stretched back in time to the Galilean townspeople who had welcomed the wandering Jesus and his followers. On a sight-seeing pilgrimage through the Holy Land about the year 400, Egeria wrote:

> On Saturday evening we proceeded onto the mountain, and, arriving at some monastic cells, we were received very hospitably by the monks dwelling there, and they offered us every courtesy. Since there is a church there with a priest, we stopped there for the night. Early on Sunday morning, accompanied by that priest and the monks who lived there, we began climbing the mountains one by one. . . . [6]

Throughout a trip of several years' duration, Egeria seems to have been able to rely on hospitality from Christian communities at every stopover. She relates that they supplied her party with provisions and customarily gave her gifts. First in the East, and after the fourth century in the West as well, monasteries became centers of charitable works for the welfare of the poor and travelers.

The ministry of healing, too, survives in the church of the fourth century. This work resists institutionalization, for Christian healing is wrought by ascetics by virtue of their unusual personal sanctity. Wherever bishops are known as healers, their power is attributed to their saintliness rather than their office. Healings also are reported at the tombs of martyrs. However, the church supports hospitals, and the first asylum for lepers is established by Basil, the bishop of Caesarea. In the sacramental anointing of the sick, presbyters use oil blessed by the bishop as a kind of medicine. Though the bishop may not personally visit the sick person, his healing touch is brought in the form of the ointment through which he has sent his health-giving blessing.

THE CLASSIC AGE OF CHRISTIAN CULTIC CELEBRATION

The anointing of the sick, which could be understood both as a liturgical ritual and as a gesture of physical care for a human being in need, illustrates the close connection between varieties of ecclesial activity which in essence are effective symbolizations of the gospel. Here it is impossible to draw a line between *cult* and *care*.

Nor can one draw a line between *cult* and *catechesis* in the third- and fourth-century practice of Christian Initiation. Entry into the Christian community entailed a period of moral instruction, followed by the rituals of Baptism, Chrismation, and Eucharist, followed by a period of "mystagogical" instruction explaining the significance of the rituals.[7] After Initiation, the principal means of continuing instruction for the faithful was the bishop's sermon, and it was embedded in the weekly celebration of the Eucharist.

By the fourth century, Christian Initiation rituals had grown rather elaborate, even sensuous, and their power for effective communication can hardly be doubted. The men, women, and children who assembled on the day before Easter to be baptized had already prepared for the experience by several years of instruction, and several weeks of intense moral catechesis, prayer, and fasting. Their stomachs were empty as they prayed with the bishop and listened to scripture readings all night long. The bishop exorcised them, and in the middle of the night he blessed the icy cold running water in which they would be immersed. The men and the women separated and undressed completely, taking off even their jewelry and unpinning their hair. The bishop blessed two jars of oil: the oil of exorcism and the oil of thanksgiving. The first would be used as a kind of soap, and the second as a perfume.[8]

Each candidate for baptism was lathered with the exorcising oil, then went down into the water with a deacon. A presbyter standing by the water took hold of him or her, and three times asked the candidate to affirm belief: in God the Father, in God's Son, and in the Holy Spirit. After each affirming answer, the candidate's head was pushed under the water. Since the time of Paul, this ritual had signified that the Christian died with Christ.

The newly baptized Christians emerged from the cold water, dried off, and put on new white clothing. Then they rejoined one another and the rest of the Christian assembly, who had gathered to celebrate the Eucharist with them. First, however, the neophytes were rubbed with the fragrant oil of thanksgiving. The bishop laid his hand on each one and prayed aloud that he or she would receive the Holy Spirit. Then the bishop kissed each new member of the church. After more prayers, the newly baptized and chrismated Christians exchanged the kiss of peace with the whole community. Then, for the first time, they celebrated the Eucharist together.

The new Christians would have been told very little about the rituals of Initiation and Eucharist before they participated in them. Therefore the bishop's sermons at Easter, during Easter week, and for the Sundays until Pentecost were devoted to explaining the meaning and significance of these rites. The whole community received a "refresher course" each year as the mystagogical sermons and the experiences of their newly baptized brothers and sisters reminded them of their own conversion and reception into the church.

During the centuries when Christians were persecuted and their meetings had to be kept secret, this kind of Christian Initiation promoted internal cohesion in the community and strong "horizontal" bonding among the Christians. But the situation began to change after Christianity became legal in 313 and then became the official imperial religion in 380. The increase in sheer numbers of candidates applying for Baptism, the expansion of the church, and its spread from the cities to the countryside all tended to decrease the personal intimacy of the Initiation ritual. The community grew too large to assemble in one place to welcome new members at the Easter Vigil, and the bishop could not stand over five or ten baptismal tanks at once. So candidates were baptized without the bishop in outlying communities; later, he would travel around to anoint by hand those who already had been partially initiated through the immersion ritual.

Within several generations, the majority of the population in the urban centers of the empire had been baptized. Now the typical candidate for baptism was a child of Christian parents. The ritual steps of initiation still were performed in sequence, but with greatly diminished significance. An infant was carried through exorcisms, anointings, washings, and a little taste of the Eucharist, with godparents vouching for her or his (future) faith.

For such a child, becoming a Christian was virtually an accident of birth, not a decision to join a select, cohesive, and persecuted community. By the fifth century, nevertheless, infant baptism was becoming the custom, for a variety of reasons. Augustine had used the already established practice of infant baptism in constructing his theology of original sin. His teaching in turn provided a rationale for baptizing infants: one must "remove" this sin, lest they die in it and be excluded from Christ forever. The infant mortality rate was high. Moreover, infanticide and abortion were culturally accepted means for limiting family size. As the population within the empire shrank (and the surrounding barbarian population swelled), a policy of infant baptism encouraged parents to regard even the youngest life as one that should be joined to the Body of Christ.[9] If "christening" babies ensured that more of them survived, the empire would have more citizens to resist the influx of barbarians.

Paradoxically, some Christian parents who chose not to baptize their infants saw their sons and daughters postpone Baptism for many years. Some pagan converts, too, entered the catechumenate but delayed Baptism until death was near. For these people, the attraction of Christian community life was not strong enough to override the fear of failing to live up to its moral standards. Once Christianity had become legal and commonplace, it was perceived as a personal burden rather than a daring adventure undertaken in the supportive company of heroic martyrs. The community, for its part, had not yet devised a realistic procedure for rehabilitating Christians who though baptized continued to fall into sin, as we shall see below. In the meantime, many deemed it prudent not to test the efficacy of Baptism until the existential likelihood of major sinfulness lay behind them. Less sincere were those who accepted Baptism lightly for the sake of the social and political advantages that came to be associated with it by the end of the fourth century.

The practice of Christian Initiation imparted stratification to the Christian community, separating its members into two classes: catechumens, and the faithful. It also imparted order to the calendar. The season of Lent, when the fasts, prayers, and instructions of the catechumenate intensified in preparation for Initiation at the Easter Vigil, came to be observed by the whole community in solidarity with the *competentes* (or *photizomenoi*) who had submitted their names for Baptism. The rest of the liturgical year arranged itself around the central event of Initiation, but many of the popular feast days seem to have been adapted from pre-existing pagan celebrations held about the same time.

The pagan understanding that a religious celebration should include a sacrifice was one of the factors that led third- and fourth-century Christians to regard the Eucharist as a sacrifice and the bishop as a priest. To be sure, the Letter to the Hebrews hundreds of years earlier already had associated Christ and his achievement with the Jewish priests and the Temple sacrifices. It had done so, however, in order to declare that sacrifices henceforth would be unnecessary. Therefore the Eucharist was explained as *the same* sacrifice that Jesus had offered: his own body and blood made present again, not a new sacrifice. The priesthood of the bishop, then, consisted in a personal identification with Christ during the offering of Christ's sacrifice.

As the churches grew too large to assemble in one place, bishops delegated presbyters to preside at eucharistic celebrations in outlying areas, so that presbyters too became priests. (Deacons, however, who stood in for the bishops in practically every other task except presiding at the Eucharist, never came to be considered priests.[10]) For the first time in the fourth century, the legalized and growing church was able to erect special structures to house the liturgical assembly. For the first time, the bishop wore special clothing as a badge of his office when he presided over the assembly's eucharistic celebration.

The liturgy itself became more elaborate in this era. The civil authorities had declared Sunday a day of rest, so slaves did not have to rush off to work. There was time for longer prayers and more expressive rituals. A variety of ritual styles developed in the different patriarchal sees: Jerusalem, Constantinople, Antioch, and Alexandria in the East, and Rome in the West. The cities of Gaul developed their own distinctive style, too. As the prayers grew more ornate, it became necessary to write them down so that the words and actions might be properly executed.

In the fourth century, the liturgy is becoming something that must be done *for*, rather than by, the people. The man who stands in Christ's place to offer his body and blood to the Father must himself receive a liturgical validation to do so. There is evidence of a ritual of "ordination" practiced among Christians in New Testament times, although it seems not to have been the only basis for one's ability to lead the community's Eucharist. (Prophets and, later, confessors made Eucharist without having been ritually ordained for it.) However, when Christians of the fourth century chose their bishop-priests by acclamation, other bishops laid hands upon them to empower them for this ministry. The bishop in turn called out other men to assist him as presbyters.

The suddenness with which this vocation could overtake a man is illustrated by the experience of Ambrose, a level-headed young provincial governor in fourth-century Italy. Performing his civil duties one day in 374, he intervened to prevent a riot when the partisans of two rival contenders for an episcopal see had met to select a bishop. Ambrose ably defused the situation, which so impressed the mob that both sides shouted his name for bishop. At the time he had not yet even been baptized, but that was taken care of and within a week he had been ordained deacon, presbyter, and bishop.

Bishops ordained the presbyters and the deacons whom they had called to assist them in the work of teaching, liturgical celebration, and caring for the well-being of the community. In fourth-century Antioch and Constantinople, women are regularly ordained to the diaconate. The Council of Chalcedon in the mid-fifth century legislates that women must be at least 40 years old before ordination. Other legislation from the fourth century suggests that women served as presbyters, too, until that time.[11]

Ordination, Eucharist, and Initiation were three of the public liturgical celebrations in which the church cultically proclaimed and experienced the transforming power of Jesus' message. The gospel of reconciliation also gave rise to a fourth public cultic event, known as canonical Penance.

Forgiveness of sins was the heart of Jesus' announcement of the out-breaking of God's Reign. Baptism signified the reconciliation of the men and women who accepted Christ, and Eucharist their ongoing union with him and one another. These effective symbolizations were meant to begin and sustain the transformation of human lives which Jesus had set in motion. In fact, they did not always "work." What should not have happened, *did* happen: Christians failed to live up to the new life that had been given to them. In the face of persecution, some renounced their Baptism and left the Christian community. Besides the scandal of apostasy, there were other sins among Christians, including murder and adultery, for which the bishop would formally exclude someone from the company of the baptized.

Being shut out of the cohesive, supportive Christian fellowship must have been a powerful and painful sanction. We know that many lapsed Christians sought to re-enter the church during times when the persecutions eased up. The second and third centuries saw lively controversy over whether, how, and on what terms, a Christian who had publicly broken his or her baptismal commitment might be readmitted into Christ's Body. Some saw in the New Testament an indication that there were sins that could never be forgiven (Mt 12:32; 1 Jn 5:16; Heb 6:6). Others said that Christian sinners could be forgiven again after Baptism, but only once (or, once during life and once again on their deathbeds). Consensus emerged that readmission to the church should be made possible, but not easy.

By the fourth century, a re-entry procedure had developed that combined the three kinds of ecclesial symbolizations—word, ritual, and alms—in effecting a sinner's reconciliation. The procedure resembled Christian Initiation in that it lasted for a period of months or years, provided the encouragement and assistance of many members of the community, and entailed a person's entry into a separate "order" of Christians, the Order of Penitents.

Lapsed Christians who wished to rejoin the church would approach the bishop, admit their sins, and accept his decision whether it was necessary to undergo the public discipline of canonical Penance. (For lesser sins and for people of lesser social standing, forgiveness was possible through private repentance, works of charity, and participation in the Eucharist and community life.)

Someone whose sin had occasioned scandal and public harm to the church would be enrolled in the Order of Penitents with a brief liturgical ceremony not unlike the rite of admission to the catechumenate. Rules for penitents differed from place to place. In general, penitents were set apart from the community, excluded from the eucharistic celebration, and submitted to exorcisms. They might stand on the steps of the church edifice to ask for the prayers of community members going in for the Eucharist. They might have to wear special clothing, and they were certainly under close scrutiny by other Christians. They had to fast, give alms, and perform works of charity if they could. In some places the discipline for Penitents was extremely severe. They could not hold public office, go to the circus or the theater, engage in marital relations, or enter the clerical state. Sometimes these restrictions lasted for years, or for life—even after the sinner had been formally reconciled to the church. It was no wonder that many people, especially those who hoped for careers in public life, would postpone Baptism rather than risk incurring such socially debilitating penalties.

When the assigned period of penitence was completed, there was a public liturgical ceremony of readmittance to the church. The bishop imposed hands upon the chastened sinners or anointed them with oil, and pronounced the forgiveness of sins and reconciliation. The entire ritual process of canonical Penance, involving words and deeds and extending over a significant part of one's lifetime, was particularly effective in the church of the martyrs.[12] Thanks to the cohesive horizontal bonding of the community, exclusion was painful and one took to heart the prayers and admonitions of Christians from whom one had been estranged. Comparatively few sinners (and virtually no clergy) ever went through canonical Penance, but everyone in the congregation shared in the experience of this ritual process because of its public character. However, it began to lose its effectiveness when the persecutions ceased and the bonding of the Christian community weakened. Regulations for penitents grew stricter, but bishops grew more reluctant to submit people to them, and fewer Christian sinners came forward to seek so rigorous a reconciliation to a less and less select community. By the sixth century, canonical Penance was hardly ever observed; while in Ireland, a new form of ritual celebration of reconciliation began to take shape.

Third- and fourth-century regulations for canonical Penance make a connection for the first time between sex and the Christian cult. Those who have been ritually enrolled in the Order of Penitents must abstain from marital relations with their spouses. This seems to have been understood as a kind of fasting from something the sinner found pleasant, without regard for the effect upon the spouse or upon the stability of the marriage itself. Neoplatonic philosophy, with its distrust of physical things, had begun to influence Christian attitudes about the resurrection and the worth of the human body. At the same time, Ordination was seen in parallel with Baptism and Penance, both of which signaled the forgiveness of sin and admitted one to a new order within the church. Presbyters and bishops, now viewed as "priests," were encouraged to fast and do penance before leading the celebration of the Eucharist. The Hebrew Scriptures had imposed a ritual taboo against sexual intercourse by requiring Jewish priests to abstain from this "unclean" activity before taking their turn in performing the sacrificial rites of the Temple. Now that there was a Christian sacrifice and Christian priests, it seemed fitting to apply the ritual taboo to the Christian cult. Regulations began to appear that demanded sexual continence of Christian priests before they celebrated the Eucharist. The more frequent the celebrations, the greater the continence demanded, until it seemed opportune to forbid clergy to marry at all. Legislation restricting clerical marriage began to appear in the fourth century, but it was never to become entirely effective.

Of the seven rituals that would be recognized as "sacraments" a thousand years later, the fourth-century church knows public, elaborate, episcopal celebrations of five. Ordination, Eucharist, Penance, Baptism, and Confirmation, with the last two undergoing a gradual separation from their original unity in the rite of Initiation. The sick are anointed in appropriately private, informal rituals, which nevertheless involve the "long-distance delivery" of the bishop's blessing via the healing oil which he has liturgically consecrated. Marriage, although recognized as the normal mode of Christian life, is not yet regularly celebrated in the Christian cult. Nor do married people constitute a separate order; they are simply the rank and file of people in the Body of Christ.

CATECHESIS, THEOLOGY, AND DOGMA

The teaching of God's word took many forms in the fourth century: catechetical instruction to prepare new Christians for Baptism; mystagogical reflection upon the mysteries celebrated in the cult; parental sharing of scriptural stories with children in the home; homiletic exhortation to upright living; philosophical exploration of age-old questions about human nature in light of the Christian good news; apologetic arguments addressed to proponents of pagan systems of thought; doctrinal controversy among learned lay Christians and clergy; dogmatic definitions of the truths of faith by bishops gathered in councils. The rich liturgical life of the community nourished this teaching, while the church's concrete outreach to the poor backed up the words with substantive evidence of their truth.

Rustic catechumens and philosophers alike wanted answers to the same questions. What is a human being? What is the value of this life which we live? Who am I, and what should I do with the years allotted to me to become a fully human man or woman? The church answered in terms of the being of God's own self, and of God's Son, Jesus Christ.

Christians affirmed, with the author of John's Gospel, that God had become a human being, Jesus Christ, who remained at the same time fully God. Nevertheless, many Christians found the views of Arius convincing. He taught that Christ was surely like God, but not the same as God. But consensus was established at the Council of Nicea that Arius's understanding was incorrect, heretical. The Nicene Creed called Christ

> the only Son of God,
> eternally begotten of the Father,
> God from God, Light from Light,
> true God from true God,
> begotten, not made,
> one in being (*homoousion*) with the Father.
> Through him all things were made.
> For us human beings (*anthrōpous*) and for our salvation
> he came down from heaven. . . .
> and became human (*enanthrōpēsanta*).[13]

The definition was made in the Greek language, and it employed a Greek philosophical concept: substance, *ousios*, that which underlies an entity and accounts for its independent being. The creed was stating that Jesus and God were the same stuff: Jesus had the right stuff. Some harbored misgivings about attributing stuff to God at all—especially those Eastern Christians for whom Greek was mother tongue as well as philosophical jargon. Yet the Nicene formula of consubstantiality served to consolidate the Christians' certitude that Jesus indeed had what it took to be able to do what they claimed he had done: reconcile the world with the Father.

Christological controversies continued, however, with energy and interest such as it is difficult for us to imagine today. A second milestone in the dogmatic articulation of the Christian faith was passed at the Council of Chalcedon in the middle of the fifth century. Defining in Greek again, the Council said that Christ is both God and a human being. His stuff is the same as God's, but it is also the same as our stuff. Christ is *homoousion* with the Father in his divinity, but *homoousion* with men and women in his humanity. He has, therefore, two natures (*physesin*) but one person (*prosōpon*) and one subsistence (*hypostasin*).[14]

The meaning of this definition has been mooted ever since. Our words "nature," "person," and "subsistence" are not really English words at all, but anglicized versions of the fifth-century Latin terms used to translate the conciliar definition in the West. Each of these terms has taken on connotations foreign to the Chalcedonian intention in the course of the subsequent development of modern languages, including the English which we speak. In contemporary American English, "nature" connotes the great outdoors; "person" connotes the psychological structures described by Freud, Piaget, and others; and "subsistence" connotes the minimum income necessary to stay alive. However, it is probably not too far from the original meaning to say that the conciliar definition affirms that Jesus Christ is the personal union of divinity and humanity. The mystery of his being eludes exact definition, now as then.

Defining it was difficult, yet the *reality* of the reconciliation wrought in Christ was vividly present to the Christian community. They experienced their own unification in the celebration of the Eucharist, while in Baptism and Penance they witnessed the joining, or the rejoining, of sinful men and women to Christ's Body. In the face of this experience, and of its undeniable power to transform human living, they were baffled at the continuing power of sin which seemed to exert a counterforce against the efficacy of Christian worship, teaching, and good works.

About the turn of the century, one of the greatest of all Christian teachers took up this problem. Augustine reasoned that the disobedience of Adam and Eve made every human being guilty at birth (although Jesus and Mary were exempt). Expanding on the Greek idea that the human soul like the body is inherited from the father through his semen, Augustine suggested that the original sin also passed onto each human soul through the act of intercourse in which the person was conceived. The ancient philosophers were ignorant of the mother's genetic contribution, and thought of her merely as a fertile matrix in which the semen could grow. Jesus would have escaped Original Sin because there was no human semen involved in his conception, while Mary was exempted because the human body and soul of Jesus needed a "clean" medium in which to grow. Incidentally, this notion confirmed Augustine in his neoplatonic belief that the more physical something is, the less perfect it can be; and something as physical and irrationally spontaneous as the human orgasm must always be sinful, even within Christian sacramental marriage.

The human rational soul, created in God's image (Gen 1:27), was severely damaged by the effects of Original Sin, Augustine reasoned, and this explained why it was so difficult to live a virtuous life, even with the help of Christian community life and the church's prayers. Greek thinkers, too, had been preoccupied with the difficulty of charting a virtuous life in a decadent world. Christian moral teaching adopted many of the values, maxims, and examples that were current in contemporary pagan literature. The Jewish Scriptures were another source of moral instruction.

Conversion of life and training in common human virtues like honesty, marital fidelity, and industry seem to have constituted the greater part of the task of the catechumenate. Christian life was a matter of *praxis*, not *gnosis* (that is, doing, not knowing). Secular and sacred erudition took a decidedly second place to the ability to lead a life worthy of one who was born again in Christ.

To "teach" a Christian, then, was no simple matter. We may distinguish here several senses of the term "teaching." By the second century, the term could connote apostolic authority. In this sense, the teaching of the church consists in its reliable transmission of the message of Jesus. Both the Christian Scriptures, and the bishop, had authority to teach what Jesus meant.[15] But that authority may be distinguished from the *skill* or the art of effective teaching. Bishops have the authority to teach authoritatively; that is precisely why it is they who appoint teachers who have the knack for making the message of Jesus come alive and address the catechumens in terms of immediate relevance to their own lives. The church of the fourth century is concerned about the quality of its teaching, in both senses. Conciliar definitions safeguard the integrity, the apostolicity, of Christian teaching; but at the same time, master teachers like Augustine and John Chrysostom give instructions about how one may effectively catechize.

Theology, as a ministry of the word, is a teaching activity that falls somewhere in between these two senses of teaching. It has neither apostolic authority, nor direct efficacy in the lives of the Christian faithful. Yet it serves both kinds of teaching, because it nourishes the understanding of the teachers themselves, bishops and working catechists alike. We may conclude our investigation of the fourth century with a brief survey of the personnel, institutions, methods, media, and content used in its Christian teaching.

Personnel. Teaching, like all ministry in the fourth-century church, is the responsibility of the bishop. He oversees the catechumenate and the progress of the catechumens in the Christian life. The bishop himself may deliver the concluding instructions as the catechumenate reaches its climax in Lent. He appoints and supervises catechists, virtually all of whom by this time are clergy: deacons or presbyters. Because the catechumen must learn a way of life as well as doctrine, the instruction of the catechist is supplemented by the example, advice, and companionship of a sponsor. This godmother or godfather eventually will accompany the catechumen to the baptismal font and assist in the rite of Initiation along with the deacon and the presbyter. In the case of young people born into Christian homes, the parents are the principal catechists and sponsors in the faith. Documents preserved from the fourth and early fifth centuries give us a glimpse of how bishops guided parents in providing religious instruction for children, as we shall see below. Bishops also provided leadership for the formal instruction of the catechumenate and set the standard both for teaching and for theological reflection.

But who taught the bishops? There were no seminaries, and independent theological faculties were a thing of the past (and the future) after Origen. It is evident from their writings that bishops like John Chrysostom and Augustine received the best classical education that the pagan world could offer. Bishops came from the privileged, educated class of imperial society. Hellenistic philosophical studies formed their intellects. Equipped with this secular training, they were able to interpret the gospel message to people of their time and culture. Some bishops came to reject the value of their Greek philosophical and rhetorical formation; but they could not theologize without it.[16] And when, in later centuries, this classic education broke down, Christian theology itself virtually ceased.

Classic education was geared above all to produce effective speakers. Chrysostom means "gold mouth." Education in the rhetorical school gave one the skill to compose convincing arguments both in speech and in writing, and Jerome insists that rhetorical skill is essential for a Christian teacher. Augustine regrets that some preachers and teachers are lacking in speaking skills; educated converts must be warned not to laugh at them.[17]

Institutions. The catechumenate, the first institution for Christian religious education, is well established in the church of the fourth century, although it will not outlive the fifth. The institutional structure of the catechumenate seems to have influenced the contours of two other church institutions: the process of canonical Penance, and the clergy. Penitents are treated like catechumens: recognized as a separate order, excluded from the Eucharist, prayed over, and exorcised. Clergy, too, form a separate order, and many of their functions correlate with the needs of the catechumens: ritual initiation, moral instruction, and mystagogy. When authority is "institutionalized" in the church, it is placed in the hands of the bishop—largely so that he might ensure the integrity of Christian teaching.

Uniquely characteristic of the catechumenate is the provision of training which includes the elements of the Christian message and the scriptures, as well as the discipline of the Christian way of life. Catechumens do not hear much about the Christian cult, however, for the liturgical symbols are explained in full only after Initiation. More than a learning process, the catechumenate is a process of decision. The candidate makes a choice to enter, and the community decides to accept him or her. After several months or years of training, the catechumen must decide whether to submit his or her name for Baptism, and community members must certify whether the candidate has demonstrated conversion of life.

Egeria reports that candidates for Baptism are assembled on the first day of Lent before the bishop and the priests.

> One by one the candidates are led forward. . . . Then the bishop questions individually the neighbors of the one who has come up, inquiring: "Does he lead a good life? Does he obey his parents? Is he a drunkard or a liar?" And he seeks out in the man other vices which are more serious. If the person proves to be guiltless in all these matters concerning which the bishop has questioned the witnesses who are present, he notes down the man's name with his own hand. If, however, he is accused of anything, the bishop orders him to go out and says: "Let him amend his life, and when he has done so, let him then approach the baptismal font." He makes the same inquiry of both men and women. If, however, someone is a stranger, he cannot easily receive Baptism, unless he has witnesses who know him.[18]

As the gateway into the Christian community, the catechumenate institutionalized the selectivity of Christianity. Secrecy and safeguards against enemy infiltration surely were necessary during the persecutions, and Christianity was not the only religion to have institutionalized such practices. The Greek and oriental mystery religions also kept their rituals secret before initiation.

Comparison of the early catechumenate with Greek and Jewish cultural parallels gives us some indication of what Christians may have borrowed from them. Christian initiation resembled the mystery cults not only in the secrecy of its rites, but in the vividly sensuous nature of its initiation, which was calculated to produce unforgettable experiences for the neophytes.[19] The notion of mutual choice by community and catechumen is reminiscent of the Jewish concept of election, particularly among groups like the Essenes and the Pharisees. This exclusivity among the Christians was perhaps made necessary by the persecutions; it is strikingly opposed to Jesus' policy of extending forgiveness before conversion was demonstrated. The first-century Essenes in particular asked new members to undergo a probationary period of testing and aescetic practices, although the theology of election itself is characteristic of the Jewish scriptural heritage as a whole.

From both their common Jewish heritage and contemporary Jewish educational practice, Christians were familiar with the rabbinic teaching tradition. Jewish learning above all cherished the Scriptures by continuously meditating on them, memorizing them, and interpreting them for new situations. The rabbis also emphasized the duty of parents to provide for religious formation at home. In both synagogue and Jewish home, the Law was to be not only studied but also done. Likewise, the catechumenate stressed both intellectual and moral formation in a program of instruction that relied heavily upon the Scriptures.

Perhaps more significant than the catechumenate's borrowings from its cultural milieu is the Christians' rejection of certain other elements. Unlike the Jews, Christians at this period did not found elementary schools to teach their children to read—undoubtedly because the Christian scripture was written in Greek, which everyone still understood.[20] Unlike the Essenes of old, the fourth-century Christians did not flee from the world in order to give or to receive religious instruction. The catechumenate existed in the midst of everyday life. And unlike the mystery cults, Christianity was not hampered by the lack of intellectual formation.[21] On the contrary, the Christians' participation in secular schools, their immersion in cultural, political, economic, and intellectual life, and their ongoing dialogue with the major Hellenistic philosophical movements shaped not only the Christian theory and practice of teaching, but the socio-religious movement that was Christianity itself.

Methods. Though they did not found schools, fourth-century Christians have left us records of their great concern to ensure that the gospel was taught effectively. There are several full-scale works that deal with educational methodology, and the works of many other authors devote some attention to the process of and preparation for teaching.

John Chrysostom's *On Vainglory and the Right Way for Parents to Bring Up Their Children*[22] discloses his views on instructional techniques, and more importantly shows that the bishop of Constantinople expects the primary religious education of children to take place in the home. He recommends that parents tell Old Testament stories to small children to displace the tales of Greek heroes in their imaginations, to illustrate moral behavior, and to prepare the girls and boys to hear them read in the liturgical assembly. New Testament stories should not be told until adolescence. Both mothers and fathers are to share in the storytelling.

The bishop is sensitive to the communicative power of such seemingly innocuous things as observing quaint pagan customs, or giving a Christian child a pagan name. He also recommends that common virtues like patience and self-reliance be instilled in young Christians. So concerned is Chrysostom to keep Christian sons from adopting the lax sexual mores of the Hellenistic culture, that he tells parents not to allow boys even to see any young women servants. (Readers of Chrysostom's instructions immediately note that they are meant for the wealthy class of Christians. Some of the bishop's advice pertains more to gentlemanliness and ladylikeness than to Christianity itself.)

Chrysostom seems almost modern in his appreciation of the effectiveness of behavior-modification techniques. Besides suggesting that the fear of hell be used to restrain youthful passions, he urges parents to point out the good example of the boy's peers who model proper behavior. The bishop advises parents to arrange their son's marriage and introduce his future bride to him before he begins his professional training. This gives them more leverage in forming his character:

> If you sing the maiden's praise for her beauty and her comeliness and all the rest, adding that "she will not endure to be your mate if she learns that you are slothful," he will reflect deeply, seeing that his ultimate happiness is imperiled. . . .
>
> Say to him: "All who know your bride—her father and mother, her servants and neighbors and friends—are deeply concerned for you and your way of life, and will report to her." Bind him then with this fetter, the fetter that makes virtue secure.[23]

The young person should often receive praise from the bishop and should be given to understand that this makes the parents proud. Since Christian youths must not attend the theater, with its ribald and suggestive entertainments, parents should devise wholesome amusements for them and give them gifts. Young people should receive an explanation why they are forbidden to go to the theater:

> And let the father take the boy in the evening when the theater is ended and point to the spectators coming out and make fun of the older men because they have less sense than the young and the young men because they are inflamed with desire. And let him ask the boy: "What have all these people gained? Nothing but shame, reproach, and damnation. . . .
>
> "My child, spectacles such as those, the sight of naked women uttering shameful words, are for slaves. Promise me not to listen to or speak any unseemly word and go your way. There it is impossible not to hear what is base; what goes on is unworthy of your eyes." As we speak to him, let us kiss him and put our arms around him, and press him to show our affection. By all these means let us mold him.[24]

Chrysostom understood well the needs and emotions of young people, and the power of parents to form them in habits compatible with the gospel.

Even in the informal catechesis of the home, the telling of Bible stories formed an important component. For catechists and preachers, facility in biblical exegesis was considered an indispensable tool. Jerome, who insisted that the Christian teacher have an ample secular education, is adamant about careful study and knowledge of scripture as well.

However, the exegesis of scripture was practiced in the fourth-century church according to rules of interpretation quite different from those familiar to us. We have transcripts of a series of catechesial lectures delivered in Jerusalem during Lent and Eastertide of the year 348 by a presbyter named Cyril, who soon would become bishop of that church.[25] Cyril makes extensive use of scriptural citations; at times, they comprise more than half his text. He takes it for granted that the Old Testament pertains to the life and death of Jesus, in minute detail. Cyril's exegesis often finds Christ speaking in the Hebrew Scripture; otherwise, he assumes that the text must be speaking about Christ. This catechist is convinced that the whole Bible is one single unified story of the salvation in Christ, and therefore he easily ignores even the grossest considerations of genre and historical context.

The modern reader is amused to find Cyril regaling the catechumens with lines from the Song of Solomon. He assures these new Christians that Christ will say to them:

> "Behond, thou art fair, my love; behold thou art fair. Thy teeth are like flocks of sheep new shorn"—because of the confession of a good conscience; and further—"which have all of them twins"—because of the twofold grace, I mean that which is perfected of water and of the Spirit, or that which is announced by the Old and by the New Testament.[26]

If it seems that Cyril has drafted this Hebrew poetry into the service of doctrinal battles to which it conscientiously objects, nevertheless there is a sound principle underlying Cyril's effort to employ the scriptures in his catechesis. He intends to teach "to the best of my power with the proof from the Scriptures." As he tells his hearers,

> concerning the divine and holy mysteries of the Faith, not even a casual statement must be delivered without the Holy Scriptures; nor must we be drawn aside by mere plausibility and artifices of speech. Even to me, who tell you these things, give not absolute credence, unless you receive the proof of the things which I announce from the Divine Scriptures. For this salvation

which we believe depends not on ingenious reasoning, but on demonstration of the Holy Scriptures.[27]

Cyril urges the new Christians to read the canonical books of the Bible, and suggests that the list of their names be memorized as he recites and comments upon it.

The fourteenth lecture's discussion of the Resurrection ransacks the Old Testament for even the faintest allusions to words that appear in the Gospels. Using the Greek Septuagint translation, Cyril purports to show the catechumens that the season, the time, the place, and many other details had been foretold by the Prophets and the Writings. Where would Jesus be buried? The Song of Songs says, "I went down into the garden of nuts" (Song 6:2). From where would he arise? "(I)n a cave of the rock, close to the outer wall" (Song 2:14). At what season would Jesus rise? "The winter is past, the rain is past and gone" (Song 2:2). At what time of day? "Prepare thyself, be rising at the dawn; all their gleaning is destroyed" (Zeph 3:7).

In spite of his expressed preference for Scriptural catechesis, Cyril does not hesitate to employ philosophical categories in his teaching. In a lecture meant as a summary of the others, one simple enough "for children," Cyril says:

> . . . learn what you yourself are: that as man you are of a two-fold nature, consisting of soul and body. . . . Know also that you have a soul self-governed, the noblest work of God, made after the image of its Creator: immortal because of God who gives it immortality; a living being, rational, imperishable, because of Him who bestowed these gifts: having free power to do what it wills.[28]

A keen awareness of the niceties of contemporary theological disputes about the being of Jesus Christ underlies Cyril's teaching elsewhere in the same "simple" lecture:

> Believe also in the Son of God, One and Only, our Lord Jesus Christ, who was begotten God of God, begotten Life of Life, begotten Light of Light, who is in all things like to him who begat, who received not his being in time, but was before all ages eternally and incomprehensively begotten of the Father: the wisdom and the power of God and his righteousness personally subsisting. . . .

(R)eigning together with the Father, and creating all things for the Father, yet lacking nothing in the dignity of Godhead. . . .[29]

Cyril also differentiates the orthodox Christian doctrine of God from dualistic heresies and from a variety of idolatries, all of which probably were familiar to many of his hearers.[30] Cyril's own editorial comment upon this heady material—"I know, however, that I am talking much, and that the time is already long"[31]—is followed by another seventeen paragraphs before the catechumens are dismissed!

Cyril had a unique opportunity to enliven his catechesis by referring to the physical proximity of the sites of the crucifixion and the Resurrection. His mystagogical lectures were delivered in the church built over the place of Jesus' tomb, which Cyril in his own youth had seen and could describe. For the catechesial lectures, the people gathered in the basilica next to the hill of Golgotha, which had been paved and was an open courtyard. Apparently the group went outdoors into the courtyard itself when Cyril wanted to impress upon their memories the reality of what had happened to Jesus.[32]

About fifty years after Cyril gave the lectures whose transcripts have come down to us, Egeria went on pilgrimage to the same Jerusalem community and described the customary Lenten catechesis there. According to her, there is instruction for three hours each morning for seven weeks. After services, the candidates for Baptism are exorcised and

> . . . a throne is placed for the bishop in the major church, the Martyrium. All those who are to be baptized, both men and women, sit closely around the bishop, while the godmothers and godfathers stand there; and indeed all of the people who wish to listen may enter and sit down, provided they are of the faithful.[33]

Egeria reports that the bishop teaches in Greek, but that a priest simultaneously translates his words into Syriac for the catechumens who do not understand Greek. Liturgical readings from the Greek scriptures also are translated. For visitors like Egeria who understand neither Greek nor Syriac, "there are other brothers and sisters who are bilingual in Greek and Latin and who explain everything to them in Latin."[34]

About the turn of the fifth century, a deacon and catechist in the North African city of Carthage asked the bishop of a nearby town to give him some guidelines for teaching catechumens. In response, Augustine of Hippo wrote a treatise of catechesial content and method entitled *De Catechizandis Rudibus*, "on catechizing the uninformed ones," that is, those approaching the catechumenate for the first time. This remarkable manual sets forth well-reasoned principles of teaching method, and reflects the practical insights of a seasoned teacher. Augustine, who was a bishop and a great writer of philosophical theology, also spent time instructing ordinary men and women.

He cautions the catechist to take up one theme at a time and to relate everything to the love of God. The message should be adapted to the capacities and interests of the learner, and the learner should be seated and made comfortable, especially if he or she begins to yawn. A little levity now and then is good for the inquirer, and the catechist should be cheerful and joyful.

Augustine deals with the catechist's own discouragement, or "burn-out," as we might say.

> I would not have you be disturbed because you have often seemed to yourself to be delivering a worthless and wearisome discourse. For it may very well be that it was not so regarded by the one whom you were endeavoring to instruct, but because you were earnestly desiring to have something better for your hearers, on this account what you were saying did not seem worthy of others' ears. For my part, I am nearly always dissatisfied with my discourse.[35]

Augustine knows that catechists can lose their enthusiasm for a number of reasons: because they would rather be doing something else, because they are sick and tired of saying the same simple things over and over again, because of stress and overwork, or because the catechumens fail to give any sign of having listened or understood. For fifteen centuries, Christian teachers have taken heart upon reading that the greatest theologian of the ancient world shared experiences like these.

Augustine's manual gives evidence that Christianity was attracting converts from all segments of society and with a variety of intellectual backgrounds. Special strategies are suggested for businesspeople and for those who already have received secular higher education. Augustine suggests that a candidate who is engaged in the commerce of Carthage should receive instruction that focuses on the instability of worldly riches. If the candidate is familiar with philosophy and "well versed in liberal studies," the catechist should quickly cover points of doctrine which may already be familiar through private reading and pause only on those upon which the candidate asks for further explanation, "assuming on our part only so much of the magisterial tone . . . as the person's humility, which has brought him or her to us, is now seen to permit of."[36] The cultured candidate needs guidance in choosing among the works of pagan authors those which are compatible with the Christian message.

Candidates trained not in philosophy but in the rhetors' schools require a different instructional strategy. Augustine feels that they need lessons in humility, and especially must "learn not to despise those whom they know as shunning more carefully faults of character than faults of diction."[37] Since rhetorical training in that era emphasized style at the expense of substance, candidates with such training might look down upon the inelegant expression of some Christian preachers and of the Koine Scriptural texts themselves. Therefore,

> . . . they should be taught to listen to the divine scriptures, so that solid diction may not seem mean to them merely because it is not pretentious, and that they may not imagine that the words and deeds of men, of which we read in those books rolled up and concealed in fleshly coverings, are not to be unfolded and revealed so as to convey a meaning, but are to be taken literally. And as regards the actual value of a hidden meaning . . . and the power of these concealed oracles to sharpen the desire for truth and to shake off the torpor induced by surfeit, such persons must have this shown them by actual experience, wherein something which failed to stir them when set plainly before them is brought to light by the unraveling of some allegory.[38]

For the Latin-speaking Augustine as for the Greek Cyril, use of the Scriptures is an indispensable component of catechesial method. In Augustine's view, the catechumen must learn not just what the scripture says, but how to listen to it.

Media. Yet by the fourth century, the plain style of the Scriptures clearly is a source of embarrassment to cultured Christians like Augustine. When Julian the Apostate forbid instructors who believed in Christ to teach the works of pagan literature, two Christian professors undertook to translate the Septuagint and the New Testament *into Greek*—a Greek, that is, "literary" enough to be used in schools. They rewrote the Pentateuch as they imagined Homer would have done it, turned the historical books into Greek dramas, and recast the teachings of Jesus as Platonic dialogues. Fortunately, Julian's early death soon brought this experiment to a close.

Yet in the West, by the end of the fourth century very few people understood Greek at all, although it remained the language of the liturgy in Rome. Latin translations of the Gospels were circulating by the middle of the second century. Most of the Bible was translated into Gothic in the fourth century,[39] a task for which a Gothic alphabet had to be invented. Latin was the native tongue of Jerome, who learned Greek and Hebrew so that he could translate the scriptures for Latin-speaking Christians. Literacy also was decreasing in the fourth century. An early monastic rule from that period anticipates that Christians entering the monastery might need to be taught how to read the Scriptures.

But the chief medium of Christian instruction was word of mouth. Cyril and Augustine both *spoke* to catechumens, though Augustine envisions a supplementary program of directed reading for the best educated among them. When Scripture was used in catechesis, preaching, or worship, it was read aloud. Private study was the prerogative of very few; and those few most likely read aloud even to themselves. In fact, the creed itself was not even supposed to be written down. This custom undoubtedly reflects the necessity of secrecy in the early church; but even Cyril, who uses the articles of the creed as the very outline of his lecture course, nowhere writes them down in collected form.

Orality was the characteristic mode of communication of the culture as a whole. The function of literacy, while it lasted, was to facilitate training in the intricacies and flourishes of stylized rhetoric: fancy speaking. Fewer and fewer scholars read for the sake of learning, or chose writing as the medium in which they would pass their wisdom on to later generations. Christians learned to read so that they could read the scriptures aloud to other Christians. Yet even this diminished sort of literacy became scarce after the fourth century.

Content. We have seen that the books of the Old and New Testaments provided most of the material used in fourth-century catechesis. Without modern historical understanding or literary criticism, however, Christian scholars developed ways of interpreting the scriptures that seem strange to us today. Although at times, fourth-century catechesis seems to distort biblical material beyond any semblance to the texts' own intentions, nevertheless the "proof-texting" is not completely arbitrary. The texts are used to demonstrate and underscore the gospel message that God has become human so that human beings can be reconciled with God.

This message receives formulaic expression in the abbreviated statements of the Creed. Catechumens commit the creed to memory along with the words of the Lord's Prayer. Both of these provide the outline of the "curriculum" of instruction in the catechumenate. The great theological controversies and doctrinal definitions of the fourth century are kept separate from the simple, solid instruction intended to sustain the faith of Christians.

Catechesis stresses moral instruction, for conversion of life is the expected response to the gospel and is therefore the goal of the catechumenate. Moral catechesis is supported not only with Scripture texts, but also—if the catechist has sufficient education to know them—with judicious use of pagan authors and philosophical or rhetorical methods of argumentation. The example, the advice, and the admonishment of all Christians, but particularly parents and those appointed as sponsors for catechumens, give substance to this moral instruction.

The content of fourth-century catechesis, then, comes out of the three ecclesial activities of care, celebration, and proclamation. Its moral exhortation inculcates a lifestyle of concern for the material well-being of others. For youth, this focuses on sexual morality because the well-being of women and children depends on inheritance through legitimacy of birth. The good works of Christians and especially of their leaders also contribute to the formation of new church members. Catechesis is geared closely to liturgical celebration in that the catechumenate prepares for Initiation, mystagogy explains the rites, and liturgical preaching takes place in the midst of the assembly gathered for worship. The call of the gospel is heard through the scriptures which catechumens learn to interpret and revere, if not to read.

LEGACY OF THE FOURTH-CENTURY CHURCH

- Bible translation in a Germanic language
- Nicene Creed
- vestments
- edifices built specifically as "churches"
- Sunday a day of rest in civil law
- all-male presbyterate
- the Trinity as a dogmatic definition
- Original Sin as a theological theory
- treatises on educational methods and theory
- clergy as a special class of Christians

Notes for Chapter Five

1. For a discussion of the Alexandrian theological faculty, see William Barclay, *Train Up a Child: Educational Ideals in the Ancient World* (Philadelphia: Westminster Press, 1959), pp. 214–19. See also H.I. Marrou, *A History of Education in Antiquity*, translated by George Lamb (New York: The New American Library, Mentor Books, 1956), pp. 434–38; and M.L.W. Laistner, *Christianity and Pagan Culture in the Later*

Roman Empire (Ithaca, N.Y.: Cornell University Press, 1951, 1967), pp. 56–63. The historical reconstructions in this chapter are based on those works and on the following: Bernard Cooke, *Ministry to Word and Sacraments* (Philadelphia: Fortress, 1977); Nathan Mitchell, *Mission and Ministry* (Wilmington: Michael Glazier, 1982); George H. Williams, "The Ministry of the Ante-Nicene Church (c. 125–325)," pp. 27–59 in *The Ministry in Historical Perspectives*, edited by H. Richard Niebuhr and Daniel D. Williams (New York: Harper & Row, 1956; San Francisco: 1983); Joseph Martos, *Doors to the Sacred* (Garden City: Doubleday, 1981); Pierre Riché, *Education and Culture in the Barbarian West*, translated by John J. Contreni (Columbia: University of South Carolina Press, 1976); and E. H. Gifford's "Introduction" to *The Catechetical Lectures of S. Cyril, Archbishop of Jerusalem*, volume 7 of A Select Library of Nicene and Post-Nicene Fathers of the Christian Church (Grand Rapids: Wm. B. Eerdmans, 1955). For an insightful discussion of the social and cultural history of the third and fourth centuries, see Will Durant, *The Age of Faith*, volume 4 of The Story of Civilization (New York: Simon and Schuster, 1950).

2. Bernard Cooke points out that many of the martyrs had previously occupied no position of importance within the community, and that "the position of martyrdom as the ultimate expression of Christian life made for a radical egalitarianism in early Christianity." See *Ministry*, p. 60. Williams says that a confessor who physically suffered in witnessing to the faith "is ranked as a presbyter or deacon by a kind of ordination in blood and in the Spirit without the laying on of hands." See "The Ministry of the Ante-Nicene Church," pp. 39–40.

3. Tertullian said that Christians were forbidden to be schoolmasters or professors of literature, but permitted Christian students to attend the secular schools. See Barclay, *Train Up a Child*, pp. 239–41.

4. This insight is Bernard Cooke's; see pp. 66–7 of *Ministry*.

5. One way in which the church acquired real estate and other wealth was through the bequests of prosperous Christians. Durant remarks that "property was being left in rising amounts to individual churches." Steps had to be taken to insure that the bequest became the church's property and not that of the clergy; otherwise when the clerics died they would in turn bequeath it to their own children. See *Age of Faith*, p. 45. Durant says (p. 50) that Pope Damasus was reported to be "an *auriscalpius matronarum*, a scratcher of ladies' ears—i.e., an expert in wheedling gifts for the church from the rich matrons of Rome." On the other hand, the story is told that Cyril of Jerusalem pawned his church's property for the poor during a famine. Apparently a theater patron later spotted an actress costumed in a gold-embroidered cape that had been

given by Constantine to one of Cyril's predecessors as bishop of Jerusalem. She had bought it from a merchant who bought it from Cyril. The story was told to the Emperor Constantius by Cyril's opponents in an effort to discredit him. See Gifford's "Introduction" to Cyril's *Catechetical Lectures*, pp. v–vii.

6. *Egeria: Diary of a Pilgrimage*, translated and annotated by George E. Gingras (New York: Newman Press, 1970), p. 51. The ebullient Egeria often persuaded her hosts to accompany her on treks over rough terrain to out-of-the-way spots. The translator supplies the word "courtesy" for *humanitatem*, and remarks:

> Egeria uses *humane* and *humanitas* to render the notion of hospitality. The terms had become specialized among Christians to describe those acts of charity relating to the reception of pilgrims. . . . Egeria was lodged in a *xenodochium*, a hospice maintained by bishops, laymen, and especially monks for the reception of pilgrims, the poor, and the sick. The full ritual of hospitality consisted of the sending of a delegation to meet the pilgrim, an examination of his credentials . . . the kiss of peace, the washing and anointing of feet, the offer of refreshments, especially fruit, the provision for material needs, and an invitation to participate in the prayers and liturgy of the community.

See pp. 167–68.

7. For background and interpretation of the development of the catechumenate, see *A History of the Catechumenate* by Michel Dujarier, translated by Edward J. Haasl (New York: Sadlier, 1979).

8. This detail of ancient grooming customs is given by Thomas A. Marsh in *Gift of Community* (Wilmington: Michael Glazier, 1984), p. 122.

9. See Durant, *Age of Faith*, pp. 76–7, who writes:

> [T]he church blessed abundant motherhood, and sternly forbade abortion or infanticide; perhaps it was to discourage these practices that her theologians damned to a limbo of eternal darkness any child that died without Baptism. It was through the influence of the church that Valentinian I, in 374, made infanticide a capital crime.

10. Williams's essay "The Ministry of the Ante-Nicene Church" details the development of the roles of bishop, presbyter, and deacon in relation to one another. Williams, however, finds evidence in fourth-century

conciliar legislation that in some localities deacons did offer the Eucharist up until that time; see pp. 57–8.

11. See the evidence presented by George E. Williams on pp. 64–5 of "The Ministry in the Later Patristic Period," in *The Ministry in Historical Perspectives.*

12. This sociological analysis of canonical Penance is owing to that presented by Martos on pp. 326–28 of *Doors to the Sacred.*

13. The text of the creed that is used for worship by Roman Catholic communities in the English-speaking world fails to express the inclusiveness of the Greek terms *anthrōpous* (human beings, not just "men") and *enanthrōpēsanta* (was made human, not "man"). Greek had another term for the human male: *anēr.* For the Greek text of the Nicene Creed, see H. Denzinger and A. Schönmetzer, editors, *Enchiridion Symbolorum: Definitionum et Declarationum de Rebus Fidei et Morum* (Barcinone: Herder, 1963), p. 52, no. 125.

14. Greek text and Latin translation appear in Denzinger-Schönmetzer, *Enchiridion,* p. 108, nos. 301 and 302.

15. For analysis of the development of the notion of authoritative church teaching, together with illustrations from ancient texts, see Robert S. Eno, *Teaching Authority in the Early Church* (Wilmington: Michael Glazier, 1984). Also insightful is Cooke's discussion in *Ministry,* pp. 235–73 and 420–22.

16. Rejection of secular learning was not so common in the fourth century as it would later become. Augustine valued philosophical training, though he looked askance at the outcome of rhetorical and sophistic education. In the mid-fifth century, clerics began to regard the renunciation of classical literature as part of their renunciation of all worldly matters. Pierre Riché reflects on these developments in *Education and Culture,* pp. 98–9. In the sixth century pope Gregory the Great, Riché sees a man who anathematized the culture of antiquity yet was unable to exorcise its traces from his own writings; see pp. 145–57 of *Education and Culture.* See also Durant's appreciation of Gregory in *Age of Faith,* pp. 519–24.

17. *De Catechizandis Rudibus,* translated and introduced by Joseph Patrick Christopher (Washington: The Catholic University of America, 1926), p. 45.

18. See Egeria's *Diary,* pp. 122–23.

19. For an account of the initiation ritual in the cult of Isis, see Harold R. Willoughby, *Pagan Regeneration: A Study of Mystery Initiations in the Greco-Roman World* (Chicago: University of Chicago Press, 1929), pp. 184–92. Willoughby stresses that such vivid rituals made the cults attractive to many people.

20. Barclay notes that the Mishnah and the Talmud frown upon the

study of Greek by Jews; see *Train Up a Child*, pp. 38–9. Nevertheless many Jews were well versed in Hellenistic culture, and many knew their scriptures only in Greek translation. Exceptions to the general rule that Christians did not found religious elementary schools occur in Syria and in the remote territory of Antinoe. See Marrou, *History of Education*, pp. 432, 434, 438; and n. 8 on p. 573.

21. S. Angus quotes Aristotle's (fourth century B.C.E.) criticism of the cults: "It is not necessary that the initiates learn anything but that they should receive impressions and be brought to a suitable frame of mind." The mystery religions seem never to have developed a theology, and this vagueness made them unattractive to most educated people. See *The Mystery Religions and Christianity: A Study in the Religious Background of Early Christianity* (London: John Murray, 1925), pp. 262–70. Conversely, Angus remarks on p. 267 that "Christianity, by construing under the forms of reason what had been first vouchsafed to faith, stood the test of criticism which so often resulted in the evaporation of the vague ideas of ancient Mysteriology." Many scholars attribute the cults' inability to survive through periods of persecution to the lack of any sustained intellectual and moral formation—such as developed in the catechumenate.

22. Translated by M.L.W. Laistner as an appendix to *Christianity and Pagan Culture.*

23. *On Vainglory*, paragraph 81.

24. *On Vainglory*, paragraphs 79, 78.

25. There is uncertainty about the date, and therefore about whether Cyril had yet become bishop when he delivered these lectures. See Gifford's "Introduction," pp. xliii–xliv and iii–iv.

26. Lecture III:16.

27. Lecture IV:17.

28. Lecture IV:18.

29. Lecture IV:7. As native speaker of Greek, Cyril avoids the term *ousia*, "substance," which recently had been canonized by the Council of Nicea. Gifford discusses this choice of terms on pp. xlvi–liii of his "Introduction," and remarks on p. lii:

> The confusion arising from the uncertainty in the use of these words had been the cause of strife throughout the Christian Church for more than twenty years before the date of Cyril's lectures; and though it was declared at the Council of Alexandria (362) to be but a controversy about words, it had long been and afterwards continued to be a fruitful cause of dissension between men who, when forced to explain their meaning, were found to be in substantive agreement.

That Cyril abstained from introducing into his elementary teaching terms so provocative of dangerous controversy, is a reason for commendation, not for censure.

30. Lecture IV:4–6.
31. Lecture IV:20.
32. See Cyril's references to the geography, e.g., Lectures IV:10, X:19, XIII:23.
33. Egeria, *Diary*, p. 123.
34. Egeria, *Diary*, p. 126.
35. *De Catechizandis*, p. 17.
36. *De Catechizandis*, pp. 39–43.
37. *De Catechizandis*, p. 43.
38. *De Catechizandis*, pp. 43–5.
39. According to Durant, *Age of Faith*, pp. 46–7, Bishop Ulfilas decided not to translate the Books of Kings because he thought it would be dangerous to place such militaristic texts in the hands of the Goths.

Chapter Six

Seventh Century: Feudal Bondings

We have seen how effective a story the gospel was in the fourth century. Ecclesial activities and institutions like the catechumenate, the episcopate, canonical Penance, parental instruction, and hospitality were functioning as means to transform human existence by establishing within everyday life the personal presence of the God who was Abba to Jesus. The message that this God willed the well-being of the people, and had sent Christ to reconcile them, was indeed being celebrated, taught, and enacted within every stratum of the civilized societies of the Roman Empire.

Christ's presence to fourth century society often evidenced itself in Christians' criticism of secular institutions: the immorality of the theaters and baths, the conspicuous consumption of the wealthy, or, for a time at least, the brutality of military life. More often, however, elements of secular society became the building blocks for the church's own activities. This was strikingly illustrated in Christian teaching itself, which employed techniques of communication already well developed in the secular educational system. As in earlier centuries, the gospel was taking flesh within human society as a distinctive modification of the common meanings which constituted that society. If, as we have seen, the church is not *a being* but *a way of being human*, then in the fourth century the church was *a way of being Roman*.

Being Roman was a vastly different experience in the seventh century than it had been in the fourth. The migrating Germanic and Slavic peoples who had breached the frontier of the old empire were energetically warring among themselves. The emperor in Constantinople no longer could project power westward to control or to defend the Italian Peninsula, Gaul, and Africa. To the east, the Persian Empire threatened the Byzantine, and the armies of Islam had begun their advance around the Mediterranean.

For the common people in the lands where the church had been es-

145

tablished, these political disruptions meant poverty, famine, and damage to family life. Sons were conscripted for military service, daughters were raped by passing armies, property was pillaged or taxed away, and croplands were trampled or left unplanted. Not every year was a year of war in every place; but the centuries of unrest took their toll. The population of the old empire declined in numbers and in standard of living. For the common people, it became increasingly difficult just to stay alive. All one's wits, energy, and imagination had to be focused upon the material necessities of making a living.

Classical culture deteriorated. Literacy waned, and the symbolic competence of the people also regressed. Few enjoyed the social and civic experiences that had provided the context in which conventional concepts like Paul's first-century "Body of Christ," or Augustine's fourth-century "City of God," could make sense. Increasing numbers of Christians came from peoples who had never developed a complex culture like the Hellenistic culture of the Roman Empire. The symbols of the gospel message now meant something quite concrete and material, if they meant anything at all.

Nevertheless, the gospel continued to transform human life. The symbols which effected this transformation, allowing God to be personally present among the people of these so-called dark ages, reflected the changed mentality and material conditions that characterized human existence in that era. At the Christian grass roots, so to speak, new forms emerged which spoke to the material needs and concrete imaginations of the people. From these symbols, a new and classically Christian culture eventually would flower.

A great variety of symbolically effective ecclesial activities and institutions embodied the gospel in the early medieval period, about the sixth through the eighth centuries. In Ireland, a new custom of celebrating reconciliation made use of the tribal customs of the people to build up a new quality of Christian existence among them. In Italy, bishops administered vast landholdings after the secular organization of the economy broke down. In Constantinople, religious artworks called icons were cherished as the books of the illiterate. On the European continent and in the British Isles, monasteries gave material organization to human time, labor, and, eventually, learning, and thereby served as centers for evangelizing rural districts. The seeds of a new Christian educational system can be discerned not only in the monasteries, but in parish and cathedral schools organized at this period.

Interestingly, the one sort of symbolization of the gospel that is missing from the early medieval picture is theology. There was no doctrinal development comparable to that represented in the dogmatic definitions of Nicea and Chalcedon. No learned treatises of any significance survive from this era.[1] In fact, the term "theology" itself had yet to acquire its modern sense of systematic study and analysis of the truths of faith. Among the writers of the ancient Greek-speaking church, the term "theology" had been used in reference only to doctrine about the trinity and unity of God. The ancient Greek Christian writers seem to have had no specific technical word to denote the kind of discourse in which they engaged. It is only from the vantage point of modern times that scholars refer to that discourse as "patristic theology"—a term which obscures the fact that women engaged in this discourse along with "the fathers." Nor did the monks and nuns writing before the thirteenth century use the term "monastic theology" to describe their work, which inherited the spirit and intentionality of earlier Greek and Latin Christian writers. In early medieval times, the term "theology" denoted instead an experiential knowledge of God given by the Holy Spirit in prayer, a knowledge that was integrated with the manual labor and communal life characteristic of the monastic ideal. "Theology" was a way of life, not a specialized academic enterprise as it was to become in the high middle ages and remains for us today.

THE SITUATION IN THE SIXTH, SEVENTH, AND EIGHTH CENTURIES

The change from classical to medieval culture was a gradual one. It took centuries for the Byzantine imperial administration to grind to a halt, and the feudal system did not evolve to displace it over night. Political and cultural transitions came more rapidly in some places and some periods than in others, and these changes were all but invisible to the people who were living through them.[2]

The barbarians who moved into imperial territory respected the Roman way of doing things. In the cities of Western Europe and North Africa, the buildings still stood, the aqueducts still worked, Roman roads and ports still funneled commerce into the old marketplaces, Roman law still was honored, and the people spoke and read Latin. Yet by the mid sixth century, Germanic immigrants had set up their own administration in the midst of the old imperial superstructure: Vandals in Northern Africa, Suevi and Visigoths on the Iberian Peninsula, Franks and Burgundians in Gaul, and Ostrogoths in Northern Italy—where in Ravenna the Byzantine Emperor also still maintained an administrative outpost. Within Gaul, Roman customs, culture, and literacy proved more tenacious in the south than farther north.

As a general rule, the cities of the barbarian kingdoms preserved

the Roman way of doing things longer than the rural areas did. Characteristic of the Roman way were the Latin language, literacy, and an
urban church pastored by a bishop and his presbyters. In the sixth-century countryside, however, one heard a more rustic and barbaric form
of Latin among the common people, if not on the estates of the old
wealthy families. The people on the land intermarried with the im-
migrating Germanic and Slavic peoples, and the barbaric tongues began
to fuse with Latin to create gradually the modern European languages.
Evidence of the illiteracy of Europeans in the seventh century comes
not only from the scarcity of books composed at that time, but from
deeds and other documents which bear identifying marks rather than
signatures. The leaders of the first Gothic and Vandal peoples to penetrate imperial territories seem to have adopted Roman civilization and
allowed their children to learn to read; but the rank and file of the people
were forbidden to do so. Physical education and military training were
deemed more important for barbarian sons.

Apart from the estates of the gentry, some of which still preserved
libraries and instructed their sons in the classics, the ability to write and
to read became a rare and specialized skill. Before making contact with the
Roman Empire, some of the Germanic peoples already had religious leaders who possessed the ability to write their own language in Runic char-
acters. But they regarded writing as an almost magical skill, and letters as
signs that evoked the protection of invisible powers. This attitude toward
the written word persisted in the generations who settled within the territories of the old empire, and it was carried over to the Latin writing that
was used for contracts, deeds, wills, and tomb inscriptions—not to mention the Christian liturgical books.

In an otherwise illiterate society, notaries drew up and interpreted
such civil documents. If there was in a rural area a Christian priest who
could read and write, he would be called upon for "clerical" duties that
included the writing of documents as well as the celebration of the liturgy.
Not every district had a priest, however. Christianity had spread primarily
to *the cities* of the Roman Empire. Outside the cities, Germanic and Slavic
tribal religions, folk customs reflecting the old Roman and Greek cults,
and a variety of superstitious practices relating to the life-sustaining tasks
of agriculture and hunting, characterized the religiosity of the country people. These persisted for centuries alongside and within Christianity after
missionaries had brought the gospel to rural Europe, and they live today
in all forms of Western Christianity.

Roman civilization had been urban, but the Christianized cities
grew unsafe as their concentrated wealth attracted first the Germanic
raiders and later the Saracen, Magyar, and Norse invaders of the eighth

through tenth centuries. Wealthy citizens moved with their retainers to their country villas. These could more easily be defended, and could become economically self-sufficient by producing all of the goods needed for everyday life. So began the feudal system, a pattern of decentralized economic, social, and military organization.[3] In return for protection and management by a local strongman, the people on the land gave him money, produce, and service, becoming "serfs." A wealthy household might also have "slaves," people captured from among the Slavs (as yet unchristianized), the Saracens, or other infidels, who were owned outright. A priest living in the countryside, though considered a freeman rather than a serf or slave, still would be expected to provide whatever civil service the local lord might require. Monasteries established in rural areas also became owners and administrators of the surrounding lands with their serfs.

In times of war either between Christian kingdoms or against infidel invaders, the local lord gathered men from among his serfs and rallied to fight for his own lord, the king. In practice, between the king and the serfs there often were several layers of lords owing fealty "upwards" and protection "downwards."[4] The human qualities which made such a society viable included military, agricultural, and domestic skills, loyalty, fidelity, and good hard work. People participated in their society with shovels and shuttles, not with oratory or literature. The human intelligence and ingenuity that built feudal Europe must not be underestimated; nevertheless, it was a quite concrete intelligence. The ability to read was superfluous for kings and local lords, serfs and slaves alike. Laws were encoded in oral traditions. One could always hire a cleric or scribe to write out a legal document on rare occasions when such a thing was needed. To the practical people of early medieval times, the oral tradition must have appeared a sturdier repository of law than the written word. Documents are fragile; the written word is vulnerable to fire, flood, theft, forgery, tampering, mold, insects, and rodents.

The Latin legacy, then, was becoming unavailable to most people in the West. The living languages which they spoke were diverging in pronunciation and in vocabulary from the classical speech of the Roman empire-builders. The skills of reading and writing were becoming not only rare, but magical. No longer the ordinary means of communication, the written word became for the people a kind of mystical power given to a few but irrelevant for the everyday life of most men and women.

Moreover, the Greek legacy was lost in the West to all but a handful of scholars during these dark ages. Geographically and politically separated from the Greek-speaking world and the emperor in Constantinople, even men who were regarded as great teachers could not understand the

language in which the Gospels had been written. Only in port cities did
Greek survive into the sixth century, thanks to the maritime trade with
the Eastern Empire. While the Greek philosophical and literary heritage
was preserved in Constantinople and later would be reimported to Europe, it ceased to be a resource for European cultural life after the fifth
century. So thoroughly had Christian scholars forgotten about Greek philosophy, that they thought the term "philosophy" itself meant physics,
medicine, or the occult.

Even while Roman schools persisted in the cities ruled by the Barbarian kings, the instruction available in them had lost its invigorating contact with human experience. Rhetorical education long had emphasized
literary forms at the expense of substance. Now, much scholarly activity
consisted in summarizing and excerpting works from the past. Just as the
straitened circumstances of the times had made common people preoccupied with the material level of existence, so it seemed that scholars too
were less interested in theoretical or analytical thought than in compiling
collections of miraculous occurrences, unusual exploits, strange beasts, fa-
bles, beliefs, and all manner of curiosities.[5] Such was the character of their
own literary output; such was what they understood the Scriptures themselves to be; hence, the predominance of allegorical interpretations of the
scriptural stories. On the European continent, this limited and impoverished literary activity was carried out in a language that was no longer spoken by the common people, and perhaps not even by the scholars
themselves except on formal occasions. A somewhat different situation
prevailed in Ireland and Britain, as will be seen below.

As political turmoil deprived a dozen European generations of the leisure and the civic experience to carry on the classical cultural traditions,
so several generations of social reorganization under the Merovingian
kings set the stage for the cultural revival of Pepin and Charlemagne
toward the end of the eighth century. The Holy Roman Emperor, before
being crowned in 800, had brought to his court the British scholar Alcuin
who fostered the establishment of cathedral and cloister schools throughout the Frankish lands, primarily for the education of clerics as imperial
administrators.

By the time of Charlemagne's reign, the northern advance of Islamic
armies and culture into Europe already had been turned back at Tours in
732, exactly one hundred years after the death of the Prophet Mohammed.
But the Muslims were more successful in Northern Africa and in Spain,
which they entered in 711 and where their administration lasted into the
thirteenth century. From the eighth century onwards, then, Islam became
both a military and a cultural influence upon the lives of Christians in the

Mediterranean world. In the twelfth and thirteenth centuries, Arabic translations would allow Christian scholars to reacquaint themselves with much of their own classic cultural heritage.[6]

In the eighth century, then, the gospel was at work upon a planet culturally more pluralistic than ever before. The gospel had first been heard among Jews, whose ancient culture was integrated into the world-wide Hellenism established by the Roman Empire. Even in the fourth century, the Greek language and the waning Hellenistic culture still were providing for Christian teachers, writers, and preachers a common frame of reference for communication of the gospel. But by the close of the eighth century the situation was quite different, and one may count several distinct human worlds coexisting in the eastern hemisphere. The Byzantine Empire still sustained a Greek Christianity preserving many of the customs familiar in earlier times, but it was under military, cultural, and political pressure from the Arabs to the East. Moreover, this culturally rich Greek Christianity was out of touch with Latin Christianity to the West. There, elements of a decrepit Roman civilization were combining with the folk customs, laws, tastes, and traditions of the Germanic and Slavic peoples to shape a new Christian culture in Europe. Islam challenged the gospel both in the East and in the West. Judaism survived as a minority culture within each of these worlds: in Islamic lands, in the Byzantine Empire, and among the Germanic, Slavic, and Latin peoples who were merging to form Europe. As merchants, traders, and scholars, the Jews facilitated communication among these diverse human cultures to an extent far out of proportion to their numbers.

By the eighth century, all of the major cultural forces which would shape the modern world were in place, save one: the imperialistic thirst of Europe's swelling population for the wealth of the Far East—as yet "undiscovered"—which would draw new empire-builders to the Americas and to sub-Saharan Africa. The events of the ensuing centuries cannot be understood without considering the part the gospel played in them. Already in the early medieval period, the picture is becoming quite complex. In this book, however, it is necessary to set some limits to our investigation. Because this book is meant for Christians who received their faith through peoples who were living in Eastern and Western Europe in medieval times, our survey of the gospel's story focuses on cultural and political developments in those parts of the world. We turn now to an investigation of the ways in which the gospel's message took effect through activities of care-giving, cultic celebration, and teaching in Europe of the sixth through the eighth centuries.

PROPERTY AND POLITICAL POWER FOR THE CHURCH

Jesus' own announcement and enactment of God's Reign consisted in activities which we have called care-giving, as well as in his teaching and his celebration of reconciliation between Abba and Abba's children. Jesus' care-giving activities included the dramatic healings and exorcisms which he performed in God's Spirit and his miraculous feats of feeding people in the desert as God had done before. We have seen that the first- and fourth-century churches continued to care for people's material needs, in the tradition of Jesus' own ministry. Understandably, the interpersonal caring of Jesus became complex and institutionalized in subsequent generations, as Christians following his example tried to care for greater and greater numbers of people.

By the seventh century, the church's care-giving function has become complicated indeed. In many places, the church acquired immense political power and greater wealth than that of the king. For us looking back, and surely for the people of those days, it is and was difficult to see the theological connection between these developments, and the gospel preached by the poor and apolitical Jesus of Nazareth. We may maintain that the needs of the poor were the only justification for the church to acquire property and power in the first place. This statement becomes not merely an explanation, but a criterion for criticism as well, as we seek to grasp and evaluate how the early medieval church carried out its caring ministry. In fact, the temporal power of the church sometimes helped, and sometimes hindered, the transformation of human life which is the outcome of the gospel effectively administered.

After the church was legalized in the fourth century, it began to play an increasing role in civil government. By the pontificate of Gregory I, at the turn of the seventh century, the pope ran Rome and administered revenues from surrounding territories for the emperor, who lived in Constantinople. He was "the emperor's banker and paymaster."[7] This situation came about partly by default, as the civil authorities crumbled in the face of the barbarian influx; partly by gradual accrual of wealth to the papacy through generations of bequests of property from well-to-do Christians; and partly because the old first families of Rome whose sons traditionally had entered imperial service now were bringing their considerable political acumen into the ranks of the clergy. Not only did the pope feed the impoverished citizens of Rome when the emperor's representative proved unable to do so; he also raised an army to defend the city against the Lombards.

In other cities, the situation was similar. It has been estimated that by 700 the church owned one quarter of the farmland of Europe. Bishops had the responsibility of managing this property and the serfs who worked the land. As administrators of the urban churches, the bishops also distributed the produce of the farms. In the countryside, the abbess' or abbot's job included the management and defense of the surrounding lands and the people on them.

The three activities of business, government, and militancy, then, which Christians of an earlier age had deemed improper for bishops, were by the seventh century added to their job descriptions.[8] For Rome, Pepin made this de facto political arrangement official in the middle of the eighth century by turning over to the pope Italian territories which the pontiff would govern as a secular head of state.

Ironically, the ecclesiastical power of the popes in this era was not so great. While the bishops of Italy, Africa, and sometimes Spain and Southern Gaul, looked to the pope for supervision, the churches beyond the Alps were administered by regional metropolitans. These northern churches consecrated their own bishops and held their own synods, calling on the pope for mediation when they could not settle disputes among themselves. But Augustine of Canterbury, whom Pope Gregory I sent as a missionary to England at the close of the sixth century, organized there a church that thought of itself as Roman. So did the churches organized in eighth-century Germany by Boniface, also a missionary bishop who had been consecrated in Rome. Their monasteries, owing allegiance to Rome, counterbalanced the autonomy of the Frankish clergy and contributed to the eventual consolidation of authority by the papacy.

The ecclesiastical organization of the European churches in this era was a patchwork of contrasting patterns. As we have seen, Christianity first spread to the cities of the Roman Empire, and it survived there—more or less intact, depending upon the local conditions of the barbarian political reorganization. But the countryside had not been thoroughly evangelized before the Germanic and Slavic immigrations began. In some places, wealthy Christians had founded private chapels on their country estates, but these remained isolated from the life of the city churches and from the bishops. In the sixth century, then, much of rural northern and eastern Europe that technically fell within the see of a metropolitan bishop was in reality pagan territory. Some of these lands had never heard the gospel, while in others, the political upheavals and heathen immigrations had drowned it. Both Rome and Constantinople sent missionaries to those areas, sometimes to the consternation of their nearby but unevangelically minded bishops.

For example, Christianity had been established in the imperial province of Britain in the second century. However, when in 597 Augustine came from Rome to Kent, in the southeast of England, he found himself among heathen Germanic tribespeople, although there was still a British Christian church on the other side of the island, in Wales. It is likely that the early British Christians originally had evangelized in Ireland, for there were a few Christians there when Patrick arrived in the middle of the fifth century. The Irish church in turn sent missionaries back to evangelize Northern England in the early seventh century; about the same time Irish missionaries also spread out across Gaul and into northern Italy.

Those Irish missionaries founded monasteries abroad like the ones they had at home. There had been no cities or towns in Ireland when Patrick evangelized there. Society was made up of clans, and the church that grew in Irish society was organized by monasteries rather than by episcopal sees. The clan elected the abbot and provided for the upkeep of the monastery and its monks. In turn, the monastery became the clan's religious and educational center, a social and spiritual focal point for this tight-knit social group. A bishop who was not also an abbot had no administrative power, and might carry out his ceremonial liturgical duties under the supervision of an abbess or abbot. This model of administration translated well to rural regions on the continent wherever the social organization of the resettled Germanic people happened to resemble that of Irish tribal society. Needless to say, there was conflict when the Irish missionary monks, working with their accustomed autonomy, came within the orbit of an urban bishop. Within a generation or two, the Irish monastic rule was supplanted by that of Benedict.

About a century later, in 719, the English nobleman and Benedictine monk Boniface was sent from Rome to evangelize in Germany. He, too, established monasteries as an effective means of symbolizing the gospel among rural, agricultural and forest-dwelling peoples. Boniface understood the concrete mentality of these people quite well. He is said to have impressed them by chopping down a sacred oak tree without being killed by its evicted god. But Boniface's mission was to the city churches as well. Himself a bishop but without a see, Boniface tightened up church discipline and established better communications between local bishops and Rome.

In Central Europe, a few Irish and Frankish missionaries had sought to establish a Latin Christianity in the late eighth and early ninth centuries. However, the Slavs appealed to Constantinople for missionaries who could preach and celebrate the liturgy in their own language. They were sent the brothers Methodius and Constantine (later called Cyril), who had been born in the bilingual city of Thessalonika where both Greek and a Slav dialect were spoken. Though Methodius was a monk and Cyril became one, they enfleshed the gospel not in a monastic foundation but in a linguistic one. The western monasteries were civilizing the people by caring for the land; now Cyril and Methodius would cultivate the distinctive national identity of the Slavs itself. What today we might call "indigenization" was in its time a powerful gesture of caring for the cultural integrity of a people. Inventing an alphabet, Cyril translated the scriptures and the liturgy, and in so doing invented a new literary language, Old Church Slavonic. Methodius, who several times visited Rome and was there made an archbishop, worked to ensure good relations between the Slav churches and the pope, who approved their vernacular liturgy. After Methodius and Cyril died, however, the Frankish clergy succeeded in having the Slavonic liturgy suppressed.

For the most part, the seventh century church took seriously its duty to care for the material needs of the people. By modern standards, this duty was carried out in ways that compromised the independence of secular and religious affairs, and moreover affronted the human dignity of serfs and especially of slaves. The success of this church's efforts may be seen in the facts that the population of Europe gradually rose, the economy reorganized itself in the growth of the feudal system to which the church was a partner, and Christianity gradually displaced the Germanic folk religions by proving its God more powerful than their pantheon in warmaking, agriculture, and social organization. However, the church failed to express the gospel as care-giving toward the Jews. The Christian symbolization of the gospel for the Jews was the pogrom, the very antithesis of care for their human needs.

DIVINE-HUMAN INTIMACY IN CONCRETE TERMS

Jesus had celebrated his intimacy with Abba and with Abba's children in his prayers and in his customary friendly companionship with the disciples, particularly at table. From this dimension of Jesus' gospel, the church's sacramental liturgy had emerged. The church of the seventh century continued to express the gospel in its liturgy and in paraliturgical practices of popular piety.

Understandably, the social and economic conditions that were shaping the lives of the people also shaped their celebrations. In particular, the scaling down of the symbolic imagination to the concrete level had a distinct effect upon the liturgical expression and actualization of faith. The material elements of ritual and art became issues in themselves. Grace and salvation were thought of as if they were concrete things handed over by God's man, the priest, whenever the proper concrete conditions were fulfilled.

The kinship bonds of the Germanic tribes also figured into sacramental practice. Unlike the secular city-state or the church of antiquity, to which one belonged by virtue of a personal choice, the barbarian clan was held together by the concrete bond of blood. The church capitalized on this familial bond in cases of mass conversion, and baptized whole tribes at once. Later, when the baptized people still clung to rituals that had been part of tribal life, another sacrament — "confession"—was used to root out these heathen practices and so to weaken the tribal bonding.

In the ancient church, sacramentality had meant that one related to God horizontally, through a cohesive community of converted Christians. In early medieval times, however, the only horizontal social bonds left intact were the pagan bonds to one's clan and its gods; therefore, sacramentality meant that one must learn to relate to God vertically, that is, apart from the social ties to one's own people. The church's devaluation of the family, its promotion of clerical celibacy, and the elevation of the ranks of the clergy "above" the common people all were due in part to this shift in God's perceived location.

Such a reorientation could not have been accomplished through the catechumenate, an institution whose effectiveness was owing to its ability to mediate faith horizontally. But the catechumenate was no longer available; it had faded away after infant baptism became common in the fifth century. The simplified ritual process for initiating infants was the only baptismal rite available for admitting barbarians en masse to the church. The period of instruction required before baptism had been drastically reduced, or waived altogether. To the concrete early medieval mind, the physical pouring of the water seemed sufficient to accomplish the personal change which earlier Christians had thought required years of instruction, prayer, fasting, almsgiving, and community support. This change now was understood concretely rather than conventionally: as washing away a stain, rather than joining a new community.

First in Ireland, then on the continent, the European church devised another ritual celebration to perfect the sociological conversion from paganism left incomplete by instant baptism: confession. An outgrowth of the monastic practice of fraternal correction, confession eventually supplanted canonical penance as the church's liturgical way of celebrating reconciliation.[9] Canonical penance had become ineffective when the church ceased to be a select, voluntary community of would-be martyrs. Unlike canonical penance, confession was private, personal, repeatable, applicable to the "little" sins of everyday life, and available to every Christian. In keeping with the concrete mentality of the times, it submitted the penitent to physical punishments such as fasting, whipping, and surrender of property.

We know something of what was dealt with in confession, because we have Penitentials, or handbooks matching sins and penalties, that were compiled for the use of monks who heard confessions in those days. The Penitentials make fascinating reading as mirrors of everyday medieval life.[10] Following folk custom and Irish tribal law, a penalty could be commuted by the payment of a fine in lieu of physical punishment. The lists of the sins common among Celtic and Germanic peoples included the use of an amazing variety of spells, potions, charms, and tricks by which they expected to do good or ill to others or themselves. To be sure, the common people of earlier Hellenistic times had had a repertoire of folk practices no less extensive, if we can judge from the detail in which they were condemned by Christian preachers like Cyril of Jerusalem and Theodore of Mopsuestia, who admonished catechumens:

> Service of Satan is clearly that a person should follow astrology and with the positions and motions of the sun, the moon, and the stars for the purpose of traveling, going forth, or undertaking a given work . . . (These are) service of Satan: the purifications, the washings, the knots, the hanging of yeast, the observances of the body, the fluttering or the voice of birds and any similar thing.[11]

The medieval Penitentials include a great number of similar superstitious practices in their lists of sins, and assign severe penances for them. At times, the harshness of the penance seems due to the fact that the magic has successfully brought about the injury or death of another person; in other words, the Penitentials take the efficacy of the practices for granted! Many of the Penitentials that come down to us are collections that may have originated in Ireland but were edited on the Continent in the ninth or tenth century or later, by people who no longer understood their allusions to magical rites. This is evident in the way the sins are grouped. For example, a section headed "Gluttony" might include penalties for consuming human or animal urine or feces in the same list as drunkenness and overeating. One wonders what the tenth-century editor thought of the appetites of his or her forebears.

The Penitentials also document the fact that the monk-confessors sought to suppress other folk customs which undoubtedly strengthened clan bonds but have no link to superstition that is apparent to us; for example, keening for the dead. As with all other offenses, sins of superstition carried greater penalties for clerics than layfolk, for men than for women. Similarly, penalties were greater for sins that injured clergy than for those that injured layfolk.

By getting the people to admit that they still practiced elements of their former folk religion, and by concretely punishing them for it, the monks eventually purged most of the paganism from the Irish and the Germans. The people's loyalty to the old customs and to the clan gradually was transferred to the church, particularly as concretely embodied in the monastery, and to the pious practices, feasts, fasts, and rituals which punctuated time in the Christian calendar.

As missionary monks spread Christianity in rural areas where no bishop was close by, there was a further development in the ritual process of Christian initiation. Adults and infants were baptized by a local presbyter, often regardless of the time of the liturgical year. Later, they received a sealing or confirmation of their baptism from the bishop himself, either by traveling to his city or by waiting for him to visit them. In this way, Confirmation came to be recognized as a separate sacramental ritual: a physical contact between the bishop and each Christian symbolizing the unity of the church even among Christians who lived far away from one another and shared no common blood.

The changing social and geographical situation of the church in the seventh century also contributed to the eventual sacramentalization of marriage after the eleventh century, when a liturgical wedding ritual did emerge. But at the time when missionary activities were bringing Germanic and Romanized peoples into contact in the seventh and eighth centuries, a difference in marriage laws between these two cultural groups made it necessary for the church to intervene to set policy for judging the validity of marriages and the procedures for divorce.

The demographic changes taking place in Europe around the seventh century enriched the church with greater ethnic diversity, which naturally altered and enriched Christian sacramental celebration. But can the shift in the average Christian's symbolic competence from the conventional to the concrete level also be regarded as a circumstance that enriched Christian sacramentality? In the seventh century, many church leaders thought not. Interestingly, those who complained that the people's religion was superstitous or idolatrous invariably belonged to the upper classes, that is, they did not have to make their bread with their own hands.

The iconoclast controversy in the Eastern church illustrates this well. While Byzantine Christians had forgotten Latin, they retained the mystical incarnational insights of early Greek writers and the diversity of oriental liturgical rituals. In the seventh century these factors were coming together in the formation of the Byzantine liturgy. Devotion to the Mother of God, *Theotokos*, expressed itself both in that liturgy and in popular practices. The people also revered their saints, particularly those who had been generous to the poor and the oppressed. Ordinary Christians found meaning and guidance for their own lives in the stories of the Gospels and the lives of the saints. To make those stories tangible, artists created special holy images of Jesus, Mary, the apostles, and other saints, and the people cherished them. These icons were venerated in churches and in Christian homes.

An implicit theology lay beneath the creation and veneration of icons. It held that God, ineffable and untouchable and sublime spirit, nevertheless took flesh in Jesus and became involved in earthy existence. God's will to be present, active, and available for human beings generously expressed itself in God's identification with material, secular reality—an identification which in some way deified the everyday without making divinity common. (Those would not be sentiments that an ordinary person could have put into words; nevertheless, the veneration of the icon said as much.)

Literate Christians, however, suspected that few of the common people really knew the difference between God and a picture of God. Indeed, it seemed that icons and relics were sometimes regarded as magic tokens possessing an occult influence that could stave off misfortune. Moreover, the neighboring Muslims permitted no representative art at all, and their ideas were becoming a cultural influence in learned circles. The upper classes recognized that it was in their interest to obliterate those concrete signs that the sacred penetrates the secular world. In 726 the emperor Leo III decreed the removal of all icons from churches. He was supported by the higher clergy and the military, but when his soldiers implemented the order the people rioted. Although the arguments of the iconoclasts stressed the transcendent and immaterial nature of religion, in practice they sought to destroy not only the arguments and the images of their opponents but their concrete bodies as well. This physical persecution did little to convince the people of the superior efficacy of words over physical things. More than one hundred years of controversy and violence ensued, but the working people of Constantinople, the monks, and the lower clergy continued to venerate their icons.

The iconoclast movement failed. Icons and other forms of religious art continue to be an important means by which Christians celebrate God's involvement in the world. Throughout the centuries, there has always been the danger that people could mistake the icon, the statue, the relic for the provident care of the loving God which it was meant to represent. Indeed, even the material species of the eucharist would sometimes be idolized from afar rather than consumed in recognition of Christ's body. Yet the presence of these material elements both in the church's sacramental rites and in its paraliturgical popular cults insures that the church cannot forget the immanence of God in this world, a world which, though material, is very good and a fit place for people to experience God's parental care. Moreover, it insures that people can have access to this divine immanence and care even if they are unable to articulate or comprehend

the theory of it. The material elements of the Christian cult teach the un-
learned, and at the same time they keep the learned in touch with the fact
that the mystery of God's intimacy with us ultimately is unspeakable. They
prevent the powerful from isolating the realm of religion from the realm
of everyday socioeconomic concerns, and they assure the weak of God's
involvement in their own toil.

To conclude our examination of the seventh century's celebration of
God's intimacy with human being in Jesus, we must mention developments in the role of those whose job it was to lead the cult: the priests, the
bishops, and those vowed to follow a rule of life which included ritual celebrations of the word. The medieval stratification of society into kings,
lords, and vassals led people to visualize the church also as a stratified society with the pope "on top," layers of clergy, layers of monks and nuns,
with the common lay people on the bottom. The term "hierarchy" in
Greek had connoted a revelation of God in the midst of human society—
a hierophany. Hierarchy now came to mean the stratified pyramidal structure of the church, or more exactly, the clergy who occupied the top of the
pyramid. This conception made very good sense in medieval society.

If the lord was the king's man, and the serf was the lord's man, then
the priest was God's man and had the duty of administering God's property. He had the keys to the gate of heaven and served as a mediator or
steward distributing God's stuff to the people. To be sure, the concretizing
tendency evident in this conception was balanced by the church's insistence that the priest's ritual actions worked because they represented the
actions of Christ, not because of his own personal worth.

It has been estimated that one man in 25 was a cleric in early medieval
times. Although monasticism had begun as a lay movement, by the seventh century more monks were seeking to be ordained either because of
the liturgical needs of the people whom they were serving as missionaries,
or because of the perceived superiority of the ordained state over the lay.
Among women, the monastic life remained a lay way of life, but it continued to be perceived as superior to married life and was increasingly circumscribed by ecclesiastical legislation.

As we have seen, the political and demographic developments of early
medieval times modified the bishop's role. As the rural population increased, it was no longer feasible to have the bishop preside at a common
Eucharist for the entire church, or indeed even at a common initiation ritual. Bishops of northern European churches lost some of their administrative autonomy to Rome, but they did establish their jurisdiction over
abbots, abbesses, and monasteries, even those originally founded by independent Irish monks and nuns. Oftentimes bishops came from among
the monks, patterned their households after the monastery, and related to

the town clergy (called canons) who lived with them as an abbot directing a monastic community. The country clergy, by contrast, did not adopt the monastic life, but instead lived much like the common people. Like the serfs, they often worked for the lord of the manor and may have felt a stronger allegiance to him than to the far-off bishop. The rule of celibacy, already observed by town clerics or canons who led a common life in the cathedral house, was imposed on rural clergy as well, largely to emphasize their difference from the serfs among whom they lived and to promote their independence from the local feudal strongman upon whose bounty a family's livelihood would depend.

Because their liturgical tasks required that they be able to read, the town and country clergy and the monks and nuns remained literate, although to different degrees. After the imperial educational system disappeared, few members of medieval society besides the clergy and the cloistered were able to read. The church's leaders—bishops, abbots, and abbesses—had to provide the means of perpetuating literacy skills among men and women who served the church. Therefore those whose ministry had been celebration now took on ministries of teaching as well.

A MESSAGE FOR THE MASSES

When Jesus announced and inaugurated God's Reign, his teaching spelled out the meaning of his good works and his celebration of intimacy between God and human being. The churches of the first and fourth century continued to enact the gospel through ministries of the word. Drawing upon the rich intellectual resources of their cultures, these churches produced first the Christian Scriptures and then many brilliant theological discussions of them and of Christian existence itself.

The early medieval church, however, produced nothing remotely comparable to the foundational literary documents left by earlier generations of Christians. The intellectual climate of the seventh century was impoverished. People lacked several of the preconditions for theology: peace, leisure, literacy, a secure livelihood, access to the thought of past and contemporary theorists of being and existence (i.e., philosophy), and the motivating opportunity to argue with proponents of varying points of view. Conditions of life in the Western church had reduced the symbolic imaginations of most people to their lowest common denominator: concrete and literal meanings.

On the other hand, this church evangelized where the intellectual fourth-century Christians had never gone, especially in rural territories and among barbarian peoples. The message delivered there was simplified, concrete, and eventually quite effective. As we have seen, ecclesial activities of care and cult were important to this evangelizing effort. Along with these activities went moral instruction, preaching, teaching, and other ministries of the word. The organization of work, prayer, and study in medieval monastic life exemplifies the evangelizing interplay of care, cult, and call during this era.

It would be unwise to make sweeping generalizations about the kind of secular and religious education available in the sixth through eighth centuries in Europe and northern Africa. A person who had the means, the leisure, and the motivation still could arrange for private instruction in pagan classic literature. The secular schools had closed at the end of the fifth century in southern Gaul and Lombard Italy, but wealthy families still maintained tutors.

Yet a degeneration of learning had been in progress for several centuries even while the imperial schools had lasted. Prose was clogged with decorative phrases and devoid of inspiration. A "wilful archaism"[12] became fashionable in writing and in instruction. At this cultural low point, common pedagogic practice abandoned classic authors in favor of compiling school texts for grammatical instruction that were based on the lifeless literature then in vogue. Ironically, these textbooks became the common means of transmitting Latin letters for many generations. Also popular were historical and scientific summaries that gave "just the facts," dispensing with foundational argument, but pleasing a decadent literary taste by including accounts of marvels and monsters, usually unsubstantiated.

Latin prose and poetry had little appeal for the barbarian warlords. But the immigrant peoples were quite interested in any learning that might be of practical use to them: medicine, law, and applied sciences such as architecture and surveying. The attitude of church leaders toward classical learning was equally pragmatic. They recognized a need for basic literacy and good speaking skills among those who would instruct the Christian people. Some few, like Cassiodorus, wanted considerably more. He planned a full-scale Christian university for Rome at the end of the sixth century, where he hoped the scriptures could be interpreted with all the cleverness and insight that had characterized pagan literary studies in an earlier day. Despite political upheavals, he did succeed in establishing a monastic center of learning in southern Italy that lasted for a generation.[13]

Most church leaders regarded the flowery rhetorical techniques of late Latin culture as a hindrance rather than a help in communicating the gospel to the common people. Curiously, the classical learning which had so well fitted bishops to be theologians up through the fourth century was counted as a liability for them in the sixth. Not a few of those called to the episcopal state from among the aristocracy found it difficult to put aside the habits of thought and expression learned from rhetors and from classic texts.[14] The European church ultimately placed its priority upon addressing simple solid preaching to the masses of newly converted barbarians, rather than upon developing a literarily sophisticated theology for the edification of a privileged few. This option for the "low road" in the ministry of the word seems to have been a wise one, although in consequence the historian finds a meager literary output from the sixth through eighth century.

Exceptions to the "low road" option in religious education are found in the British Isles and in Constantinople, which did not experience such severe demographic upheavals as those on the western European continent. The Eastern capital maintained a Christian university from the fourth through the fifteenth century. The scholars assisted Cyril in translating the Gospels into Slavonic. Ireland fostered a brand of monasticism that prized both secular and theological learning form the sixth century onwards. Irish monks and nuns wrote both in Latin and in their vernacular, and they concerned themselves with biblical exegesis in the seventh and eighth centuries. After the Greek monk Theodore became Archbishop of Canterbury in the late seventh century, the English too developed centers of theological learning.

The Irish and British educational legacy was taken to the Continent by the missionary monks who founded monasteries there. Boniface, the eighth-century "apostle of Germany," was a Saxon monk who had taught at English monasteries for the first half of his career. His contemporary Bede composed the scholarly *Ecclesiastical History;* but all of Bede's other works are didactic treatises written for his pupils. At the end of the eighth century, it was the English monk Alcuin who headed up the educational and ecclesiastical reforms of Charlemagne. Teachers like Boniface, Bede, and Alcuin represent the cream of the theological talent in their day. Their considerable scholarly skills, however, were devoted to providing basic religious education for the common people.

To conclude our discussion of the ministry of the word in the sixth through eighth centuries, it remains now to examine in more detail the personnel, institutions, methods, media, and content employed in that ministry.

Personnel. Bishops continue to bear the responsibility for ensuring that the gospel is preached and taught in an effective and authentic manner, but their task is a difficult one. The growth of the European population contributed to the bishop's increasing isolation from the people, especially from those living in rural areas. Liturgically, the bishop no longer initiated each Christian or presided at a Eucharist around which his whole church assembled. Catechetically, the bishop no longer instructed candidates for Baptism or preached the mystagogical sermons of Eastertide to the whole community. The bishop's role became privatized: he was father and teacher primarily of the group of town clergy, the cathedral canons, who lived the common life under his direction. He taught them; it was they who preached to and instructed the people of the town.[15]

In the countryside the rural clergy also preached and taught, but their resources for these tasks were more meager than those of the clergy who lived with the bishop. The country clergy were woefully underprepared for their work, even by contemporary standards. They saw the bishop only on his rare visits outside the town, and in Gaul perhaps also at yearly synods, although the latter were dying out by the mid eighth century. Unlike the town priests, these clerics were from society's lower classes and had learned their letters in childhood from other rural clerics. Many country priests could not read well enough to decipher the Vulgate, and so had to base their preaching upon the creed and legends of the saints.

If in the fourth century a bishop could count upon Christian parents to impart moral catechesis and a basic understanding of salvation history to their children, that was no longer the case in the seventh century. The newly baptized but not-quite-converted barbarian people passed on to their boys and girls a mixture of folk lore, Christian legend, and superstition. Although godparents were obliged to teach the creed and the Lord's Prayer to those whom they had sponsored as infants at Baptism, the faith which people received through the natural processes of socialization was something in between orthodoxy and paganism.[16]

This cycle of ignorance and syncretism might have repeated itself indefinitely, had not a new kind of evangelist appeared on the scene: the monastic missionary. Independently of the resident bishops and their clergy, but usually with the backing of Rome, the monks and nuns moved through Europe: southward from England and Ireland, and northward from Rome. These missionaries evangelized in places where the people already were nominally Christian. The houses which they established became centers of Christian life, from which ordained monks instructed and preached to the rural populace. At first there was conflict between monastery and bishop; in later generations, the best bishops were men who had been educated in the monasteries. Women joined their missionary brothers in the evangelizing work of founding and administering monasteries. Boniface's colleagues included several women; the names of Lioba, Chunihilt, Berthgyth, and Tecla come down to us.[17] The instruction which women received there was identical to that available to men. In seventh-century England, the abbess Hilda founded and administered a double monastery for women and men, where she taught and also directed the program of studies.

Institutions. The monastery was Europe's most effective institution of evangelization and catechesis. Its roots were in the tradition of the ascetic Christian anchorites of the Mideastern deserts, but European monasticism developed its own distinctive way of embodying the gospel. Whereas the desert fathers had lived alone, in Europe the winter was cold, the nights were long, and the ascetics found it more practical to live, work, and pray together. The desert fathers had shunned human society altogether, but Europe's monasteries became a gospel presence in the territories of the old empire and beyond. Individual men and women "left the world" to enter the monastery; but, paradoxically, this meant that the monastery could be a collective evangelizing presence, dwelling with the people in whose neighborhood it was established. Several scholars have observed that monasteries well nigh absorbed all ecclesial ministry.

Early medieval monasteries were organized according to a variety of codes; for example, the Columban rule for the Irish and the Benedictine rule, which eventually supplanted the others. Benedict had in the sixth century set up a schedule for the monastic day which specified times when one would work at some physical task, pray, and read. That meant that the monks and nuns, like the clergy, needed literacy skills; and the monks and nuns were in a better position than the clergy to provide these for themselves, as we shall see. Originally most monks and nuns were lay people, but the needs of the countryside for sacramental ministers led the monks to seek ordination.

Monasteries were schools of asceticism and Christian life before they became schools transmitting sacred and profane learning.[18] The monastic vision of Christian life included the practice of reading (or hearing) and reflecting upon the scriptures and pious writings, as well as vocal prayers from the psalter and liturgical books. Monks and nuns learned to write so that they could reproduce books; few other people were doing so. In the seventh century, with widespread poverty and exploitation of children especially in the cities, many boys and girls fled or were given to monasteries, where at least the necessities of life were provided. The children of the wealthy also might be dedicated to monastic life by pious parents. These child nuns and monks had to be taught to read and write Latin and to pronounce or chant it correctly. The better students would also learn the meanings of the words. An oblate was theoretically free to choose to leave the monastery when he or she grew up, and monastery alumni accounted for a good portion of the few literate lay men and women in early medieval times. Providing formal education for lay people had not originally been among the purposes of the monastery; but eventually, custom permitted the education of externs alongside future monks and nuns.

So began the monastic schools. However, the evangelizing work of the monasteries was much broader than the formal religious instruction given in their schools. Monks preached at the celebration of the Eucharist at the monastery and in chapels in the surrounding neighborhood. The quality of this preaching usually was superior to that of the country clergy. Bishops, recognizing this, began to seek monastic training for their own clerics. The influence of monastic training upon clerical education persists to this day in many Roman Catholic diocesan seminaries.

Another sort of school developed out of the makeshift process in which young men were prepared for clerical tasks in the cities and towns. The older priests taught boys to read so that they could serve as liturgical lectors. Cathedral schools were established in the cities, and parish schools in the countryside.[19] The quality of instruction varied widely, according to the abilities of the pastor or canon in charge. These schools remained under the control of the bishop, but many bishops had the good sense to borrow ideas, techniques, manuscripts, and even instructors from the monasteries. Therefore the monastic philosophy of education, which situated learning within a larger program of manual labor and spiritual development, fertilized the episcopal schools almost from their beginnings. These schools were the direct antecedents of the medieval universities.

Methods. Preaching and intentional instruction were the two formal methods by which the gospel message was expressed to the people of the early medieval era. These methods were employed in different settings, but have several characteristics in common.

Preaching was of course addressed to the community at large during the Sunday liturgical assembly. The quality of the preaching depended upon the talents and preparation of the preacher, and as we have seen, could be quite poor in rural areas. Clerics were encouraged to speak simply and in the vernacular. A missionary monk who did not know the local dialect would use an interpreter, who might be a ransomed slave—heathen peoples being fair game for slave traders. The monasteries produced bilingual preachers by taking in local boys to be raised and educated alongside young monks from the founders' homeland; the natives and the immigrants learned one another's languages.

Because preaching was the only means of religious formation and evangelization for the majority of the people, church leaders attempted to help clerics improve their pulpit performance. Preaching manuals appeared, and homilaries were compiled to make a selection of classic sermons available to priests who could not compose their own.[20] Although scripture had been a favorite focus of preaching up to the sixth century, most seventh-century preachers were too unfamiliar with the Bible to find in it subject matter for their sermons. Instead, the typical sermon consisted of moral exhortation, illustrated by tales of the exploits of the saints. This approach fostered credulity, not faith, as preachers sought to manipulate people into proper behavior by overwhelming them with the wonders and horrors of the supernatural. The legends of the Christian saints appealed to the popular imagination because they were similar to the legends of heroes and gods that had been a part of traditional tribal culture.

The intentional instruction given in the monastic and ecclesiastical schools also favored the concrete over the abstract. In the monasteries, young monks were divided into groups of ten and assigned to an older monk. In parishes and in cathedral centers, the number of children gathered around a cleric for instruction also would have been small. Primary education consisted in learning first the alphabet and the sounds of the letters, then the technique of reading and pronouncing a text correctly. Counting and basic computational skills also were taught to children. The first, often the only, text which the child learned to read was the Latin psalter. Monks and nuns had to know the psalms in order to fulfill their liturgical duties, but the psalter was the basic text for secular children as well.

Primary education was considered complete when the young person could recite all 150 psalms from memory. This accomplishment might take as long as three years, because the children did not understand what they were memorizing. They were taught correct pronunciation and inflection of the Latin words without learning their meaning. Only a few went on for further studies, and countless monks and nuns must have spent their lives "saying prayers," singing the Latin office, and copying manuscripts without understanding their meaning.

The study of Latin began the second phase of education for a few of the young people. Knowing this language would give them access to the thought of earlier Christian generations and of selected pagan classical authors, as represented in whatever manuscripts the monastery or cathedral happened to possess. (Practically no one knew Greek, although the iconoclast persecutions in Constantinople did bring some Greek monks, with manuscripts, to exile in and around Rome in the eighth century. Only Europe's Jews knew Hebrew, but Christians did not consult them for help in understanding their scriptures.) Instruction seems to have taken the form of a conversation or dialogue, but disputation and controversy were avoided. The students liked riddles, and they liked to look through the Bible for stories of nature miracles: Jonah, the crossing of the Red Sea, the miraculous draught of fishes. Exegesis was not taught to students; only in his or her further independent studies would a scholar delve into that esoteric field. Knowledge of scripture seems to have been equated with the ability to recite passages from it.

Unlettered Christians were expected to have memorized at least the Apostles' Creed and the Lord's Prayer in the vernacular, and their godparents were responsible for teaching it to them.

The instructional techniques of the seventh-century church were fitted to the concrete imagination of a people who lived close to the earth and worked hard to earn their living in a precarious political and economic situation. (They even thought of writing as plowing parchment or, more aptly, plowing the wax tablet upon which lessons and first drafts were inscribed.) Abstract thought eluded them; and given the choice between a picture and a thousand words, they chose the picture. Western Christians sided with the iconodules in Constantinople, for their own churches were decorated with wall paintings and statues. The vivid word-pictures of contemporary hagiography and of scriptural miracle stories provided the images which housed their religious meanings, and homilists catered to this taste. Faith meant adhering to the material details of the gospel story of Jesus, as listed in the creed. Morality meant outward confirmity with laws; motivation was not considered. Even church leaders saw no difference between coercion through fear, and persuading people to do the right thing for the right reason.

Learning was a tour de force of memorization without understanding. Praying was saying the words correctly and singing them beautifully. Knowing the scriptures was reciting the list of Jesus' ancestors from one of the Gospels. Searching the scriptures was forecasting the future by random citation of texts. Christian life was being in the right place at the right time according to the daily monastic schedule or the yearly liturgical calendar, whose feasts and fasts had displaced the pagan cycle of holidays. This concrete mentality, so characteristic of the early middle ages, is less a stage in the historical development of the Christian religion, than a stage in the cognitive development of a new Christian people. Centuries earlier, in the Hellenistic world, other Christian people already had received and expressed their faith in far more sophisticated, abstract terms. The scriptures which those earlier Christians produced do abound in abstract conventional and critical thought. It is interesting that a less sophisticated people, when confronting these alien documents, seek out their allegorical and moral sense. The concrete mindset of the early medieval scholars led them to interpret the Bible allegorically, just as the conventional mindset of nineteenth- and twentieth-century theologians would lead them to interpret it along dogmatic lines.

Ironically, it was the early fifth century bishop Augustine of Hippo, himself possessed of a mind almost modern in its familiarity with the subjective structures of existence, whose writings showed the medievals how to undertake the allegorical interpretation of scripture. Augustine thought of the scriptures as having something for everybody, from the *rudes*, to the alumni of the rhetors' schools, to the philosophically astute. The appeal of the Bible's stories to the medievals proved Augustine's point.

Media. We have already mentioned most of the media through which the gospel was addressed to the seventh-century church. Word of mouth remained the most important one, used in preaching and for dialogical instruction in the schools. This was done in the local dialect of the people, although Latin was necessary for advanced studies, for communicating with Christians outside one's own region, and for understanding the liturgy. The monastic rule prescribed that nuns and monks spend time each day reading, which often meant that they read aloud to one another. The barbarians were peoples who loved to sing and dance, but their traditional ballads preserved pagan beliefs and their dances affronted the missionary monks' ideas of morality. To displace the pagan songs, Christians composed vernacular hymns and popular ballads with acceptable themes. It has been suggested that liturgical dance also was a part of early medieval life.[21] The Christian calendar reinterpreted the seasons of the pagan year.

Seventh-century Christian scholars wrote books specifically for the purpose of facilitating instruction, and usually these were in Latin. However, the Irish monks composed works both in Latin and in their native tongue; and in Eastern Europe a new written language, Slavonic, was devised to translate the scriptures and the liturgy so that people could understand them. The techniques of mass printing were as yet unknown in the western world. Books were copied by hand, and they circulated slowly. The sight of a finely lettered and decorated manuscript apparently impressed even people who could not read it. It is thought that the miniature pictorial "illuminations" decorating the pages served as an instructional aid when a literate Christian read to an illiterate one. The barbarians liked pictures, and the walls of churches were decorated with them. In the East, icons expressed an incarnational theology that the people held very dear.

Content. What were the specific claims of the gospel which transformed the early medieval Europeans slowly into Christians? These people had gotten where they were by conquest, and they were still trying to conquer the forests of Europe to carve out farmlands. The Christ preached to them was one who had conquered through violence—the violence of his own death—and whose blood had won for his people a better life in the world to come. Christ the hero, head of the Christian people, attracted the men and women of a society which was led by warlords. As the lords themselves accepted Christ's lordship, the people too transferred their allegiance to him. Eventually it would become impossible to make war in Europe except in the name of Christ.

The gospel which the medieval Europeans received made behavioral demands upon them as well. For a start, they must give up their pagan folk rituals and blood feuds. The barbarians' marriage customs already were more chaste than those of Roman society; but the new Christians must learn to abstain from marital relations on Sundays and during Lent. As the generations passed, there were added the refinements which eventually shaped feudal society as a web of justice among unequals, and which modeled the monk and nun as the ideal Christians stewarding a graced created world.

The rewards for conformity were no less awesome than the punishments for transgression. Materialists though they were, the medieval Europeans had imaginations concrete enough to make heaven and hell more real than the produce of their fields or the charms of their spouses. These imaginations responded to a gospel that came to barbarian ears in vivid stories of Jesus, the apostles, Mary, and the saints.[22] They took many things literally, and they tended to personify good and evil. They felt strongly and acted upon their feelings. Tragically, when they heard a gospel story that Jews had killed Jesus, they felt honor-bound to get even. They did so in the only way available to the concrete imagination.

LEGACY OF THE SEVENTH-CENTURY CHURCH

- Romanization of the Western church
- hell, imagined as a place of vividly concrete torments
- monasteries in Northern Europe, founded by the Irish
- private celebration of Penance ("confession")
- copying of manuscripts by monks and nuns
- standardization of the liturgy, featuring "Gregorian chant"
- large-scale adaptation of the gospel for non-literate people

Notes for Chapter Six

1. See M.L.W. Laistner, *Thought and Letters in Western Europe A.D. 500 to 900*, revised edition (Ithaca, N.Y.: Cornell Univ. Press, 1957), pp. 169, 176; and David Knowles and Dimitri Obolensky, *The Middle Ages*, vol. 2 of The Christian Centuries (New York: McGraw-Hill Book Company, 1968), p. 57. Those references concern the situation in Italy

and in Gaul, but as we shall see the literary hiatus extended throughout Christendom. The most significant religious work written in the seventh century was the Koran.

2. For general background on the early medieval period, the following texts are particularly helpful: Laistner, *Thought and Letters;* Knowles and Obolensky, *Middle Ages;* Pierre Riché, *Education and Culture in the Barbarian West From the Sixth Through the Eighth Century*, translated by John J. Contreni (Columbia: Univ. of South Carolina Press, 1976); and Will Durant, *The Age of Faith*, vol. 4 of The Story of Civilization (New York: Simon and Schuster, 1950).

3. Durant describes feudalism as: "the economic subjection and military allegiance of a man [i.e., a family] to a superior in return for economic organization and military protection." See *Age of Faith*, pp. 552–79 for a discussion of the feudal system.

4. Segments of European peoples remained "unfeudalized." Durant says that feudalism:

> never matured in northern Italy or Christian Spain, and in the Eastern Empire the great landowners never developed military or judicial independence, nor that hierarchy of fealties which seemed in the West essential to feudalism. Large sectors of Europe's peasantry remained unfeudalized: the shepherds and ranchers of the Balkans, eastern Italy, Spain; the vine growers of western Germany and southern France; the sturdy farmers of Sweden and Norway; the Teutonic pioneers beyond the Elbe; the mountaineers of the Carpathians, the Alps, the Apennines, and the Pyrenees.

See *Age of Faith*, p. 553.

5. See the analysis of the themes of sixth-century writing offered by Riché, *Education and Culture*, pp. 40–3. See also Knowles's discussion of "Christian Culture in the West," pp. 155–62 of *Middle Ages*. But in sixth-century Italy, several scholars including Boethius and Pope Gregory I made more substantive contributions; see Laistner, *Thought and Letters*, pp. 85–113.

6. For a wealth of historical and cultural information about early Islamic civilization, see Durant, *Age of Faith*, pp. 153–307.

7. So says Knowles, *Middle Ages*, pp. 58–9. Durant says of Gregory I:

> To every poor family in Rome he distributed monthly a portion of corn, wine, cheese, vegetables, oil, fish, meat, clothing and

money, and every day his agents brought cooked provisions to
the sick or infirm.

See *Age of Faith*, p. 521.

8. The irony of this situation is brought out by Roland H. Bainton in
"The Ministry in the Middle Ages," in *The Ministry in Historical Per-
spective*, edited by H. Richard Neibuhr and Daniel D. Williams (San
Francisco: Harper & Row, 1956, 1983), pp. 82–109, especially pp. 82–7.

9. For discussions of the development of confession or private penance, see: Bernhard Poschmann, *Penance and the Anointing of the Sick*,
translated and revised by Francis Courtney, S.J. (New York: Herder and
Herder, 1964), pp. 81–138; and Paul F. Palmer, S.J., editor and com-
mentator, *Sacraments and Forgiveness: History and Doctrinal Development of Penance, Extreme Unction, and Indulgences*, vol. 2 of Sources of
Christian Theology (Westminster, Md.: Newman Press, 1959), pp. 139–
52.

10. Translated excerpts of several penitentials may be found in John
T. McNeill and Helena M. Gamer, *Medieval Handbooks of Penance: A
Translation of the Principal Libri Poenitentiales and Selections From Re-
lated Documents* (New York: Columbia Univ. Press, 1938).

11. Quoted in M.L.W. Laistner, *Christianity and Pagan Culture in
the Later Roman Empire* (Ithaca, N.Y.: Cornell Univ. Press, 1951), pp. 6–
7.

12. The phrase is Laistner's; see *Thought and Letters*, p. 36.

13. For contrasting accounts of this experiment, see Riché, *Education
and Culture*, pp. 129–35; and Laistner, *Thought and Letters*, pp. 95–
103. Durant credits Cassiodorus with initiating the monastic practice of
copying manuscripts, to which the world owes the preservation of the writings of antiquity; see *Age of Faith*, p. 99.

14. Riché discusses the conversion of Pope Gregory I away from his
classical education, which nevertheless left its imprint on his writings; see
Education and Culture, pp. 145–52. Riché attributes the desire for simplicity in expression to the fact that "the church was turning wholeheart-
edly to the urban and rural masses," p. 93; see also the discussion on
pp. 91–9.

15. As Cooke says, "the bishop is becoming, in actual practice, more
the 'father of the clergy' than the 'father of the community' "; see *Ministry*,
pp. 85, 256, 259.

16. This is not to say that preachers did not exhort parents to give
children Christian instruction; see Riché, *Education and Culture*,
pp. 448–49 for examples. The point is that the parents did not understand
the Christian tradition well enough to teach it effectively.

17. Riché, *Education and Culture*, pp. 433–36.

18. This is Riché's thesis; see *Education and Culture*, pp. 100, 109.

19. Local church councils were making regulations for both episcopal and parish schools in the sixth century; see Jean Danielou and Henri Marrou, *The First Six Hundred Years*, vol. 1 of The Christian Centuries, translated by Vincent Cronin (New York: McGraw-Hill Book Company, 1964), p. 442. The Carolingian reforms at the turn of the ninth century sought to establish these schools throughout western Europe. For further background on these institutions, see: Cooke, *Ministry*, pp. 260, 363; Knowles, *Middle Ages*, pp. 159–160; and Riché, *Education and Culture*, pp. 124–29.

20. See Riché, *Education and Culture*, pp. 489, 93–4. However, Bainton suggests that if people recognized that there was poor preaching and took steps to improve it, this can only have been because there was also effective preaching to be heard and the difference was noticeable; see "The Ministry in the Middle Ages," p. 100.

21. By Riché, *Education and Culture*, pp. 492–93. See also Marilyn Daniels, *The Dance in Christianity*, (N.Y.: Paulist Press, 1981), pp. 22–33.

22. Durant's characterization of the themes of Pope Gregory I's writings conveys the texture of the early medieval Christian message:

> His *Dialogues* were loved by the people because they offered as history some of the most amazing tales of the visions, prophecies, and miracles of Italy's holy men. Here the reader learned of massive boulders moved by prayer, of a saint who could make himself invisible, or poisons rendered harmless by the sign of the cross, or provisions miraculously supplied and increased, of the sick made whole and the dead restored to life. . . .

> Hell is no mere phrase; it is a dark and bottomless subterranean abyss created from the beginning of the world; it is an inextinguishable fire, corporeal and yet able to sear the soul as well as flesh; it is eternal, and yet it never destroys the damned, or lessens their sensitivity to pain.

Age of Faith, pp. 522–23.

Chapter Seven

Tenth Century:
Thine Is the Kingdom and the Power

As the first millennium of the gospel's work was drawing to a close, there was cause for pessimism about its success. Jesus' vision of the Reign of a loving Abba seemed far from realization; indeed, in many ways it was so distorted as to be effectively forgotten. The quality of human life was deteriorating in the Western world, despite the nominally Christian character of the civilization being forged there. Within the church, some aspects of the caring and the cultic ministries had developed into grotesquely distorted caricatures of the work of Jesus. From outside the church, nonchristian invaders gave Europe no peace, disrupting whatever economic and political reorganization Europe's kings and queens might attempt. These societal disruptions ensured that several promising cultural revivals begun in the ninth and tenth centuries would be short lived.

European Christians felt surrounded and beset by strangers. Along Europe's southern coast, there were Saracen pirates in the Mediterranean who laughed at the gospel. Around the Baltic and North Sea and in large areas of east central Europe, there were fiercely pagan Norse and Slavs. Europe's Christians experienced frustration in their economic and political affairs, and estrangement in their relations with militant foreign powers. These experiences are reflected in the doctrinal discussions of the ninth, tenth, and eleventh centuries. For example, the controversial issue of predestination called into question the power of human action to affect the ultimate conditions of existence. Utter pessimism about the material world led the Bogomil sect to deny the incarnation, while other christological controversies, over the *"filioque"* and adoptionism, expressed the suspicion that God's Son was in some way a stranger within the Trinity.

Christians of the tenth century vested all their hope in the belief that God's identification with Jesus—whether it be by adoption or by generation and co-spiration of the Holy Spirit—had enabled Jesus to accomplish for humankind what people felt powerless to do for themselves: the establishment of a realm of peace, order, and justice. For them, however, this

174

realm existed nowhere on earth; it lay in the future, in heaven. Earth came to be regarded as a place of exile where strangers held the power and Christians were strangers. (Later, people in the eleventh century would give these considerations an ironic new twist, deducing from them a mandate to use military force to end the exile by routing the strangers from Palestine.)

The tenth century, then, is a transitional period in the history of the gospel, although of course the people who lived in that time could not have perceived it as such. It is for today's historian to identify the conditions which prepared the way for significant developments in later centuries.

For example, the feudal system was working in spite of frequent Norse and Saracen raids and occasional famines and plagues. The population of Europe was growing gradually. Monasteries were thriving, and in fact were becoming so economically successful in western Europe that many would stand in need of reform in the next century. The monasteries continued to evangelize by instructing their inmates and the neighboring populations in the Christian faith. In addition, the western monasteries were developing all the prerequisites for the appearance of a more sophisticated systematic theology in the eleventh and twelfth centuries: libraries, literacy, the custom of reading and thinking about scriptural and other texts, an economic organization that freed up some leisure hours for the pursuit of higher studies, and the manpower and womanpower to engage in cultural pursuits such as writing and teaching. Besides the monastic schools and the cathedral schools, the tenth century also saw the organization of centers for the study of canon and civil law, which would contribute to the development of systematic theology in later centuries.

The tenth century is transitional not only for the social and cultural reorganization of Europe, but also for the church's perception of its place vis-à-vis society and culture. Already well established was the experience of stratification in feudal society, mirrored in the stratification of clerical and lay classes within a hierarchical church. But thanks to the circulation in the West of certain neoplatonic concepts in a manuscript newly translated by an Irish scholar, in the tenth century some men and women began to see *metaphysical* as well as social significance in the church's hierarchical organization. In other words, God was "above" the people *in being* as well as in social space. This conceptuality allowed a new sort of justification for the church's pyramidal hierarchy. Pope, bishops, priests, nuns, and monks all stood between the people and God not only because they stood a few rungs up on a social ladder, but moreover because they participated to a grander degree in the very being of God.

This metaphysical hierarchy of being made sense on its own terms to a handful of scholars of the tenth and eleventh centuries. For them, it functioned as a plausible theory explaining the secular powerlessness, estrangement, and sense of religious exile that many of their contemporaries experienced. In this context, the power of the clergy was enormous. People powerless to improve the conditions of their earthly exile sought to prepare a more comfortable place for themselves in that other, more real place, the world to come. With the help of the clergy, activities "here" could bring benefits "there"; and the practice of earning indulgences began to take shape. The clergy, however, by virtue of their ontological superiority, could also bring the reality of "there" into the here and now. A new understanding of the Eucharist was emerging: this new theory emphasized the power to "change" bread and wine into the body and blood of Jesus; that is, to displace a lesser reality with a greater one. On the other hand, a cultic event such as the Baptism of a prince could have quite tangible effects upon the secular political realities of Europe.

We do not find any text of the tenth century giving coherent expression to these ways of experiencing divine power. Nevertheless, in the popular religious imagination, they prepare a foundation for both the theology and the military adventurism of the eleventh century. Then, the popes would call for a holy war to accomplish what secular forces had been unable to do: displace the Muslim occupants of Jerusalem with Christian ones; and Anselm would pen the classic christological treatise *Cur Deus Homo* to explain the incarnation as an event of the penetration of lesser being by greater.

THE SITUATION IN TENTH-CENTURY EUROPE

If Christian Europe found the tenth century a dark age of pessimism about a human existence that was experienced as an impotent exile, the situation was completely different in the contemporary Islamic world. Muslim civilization had synthesized the learning of the ancient Greeks, the wisdom of India, and the poetry indigenous to Arab peoples. The scope of Arabic learning in that era is impressive even by modern standards.[1] The scholar al-Biruni, born late in the tenth century, has been called the Leonardo of Islam, so all-embracing was his learning. Islamic scholarship extended well beyond the Middle East, for there were intellectual centers in Sicily, Spain, and Egypt. Mathematical, medical, and philosophical treatises written or translated by Muslim scholars later would transmit to Christian Europe the learning that would stimulate Aquinas and spark the Renaissance.

The Muslim administration in Palestine was generally tolerant of Christians, both those who resided there and those who came on pilgrimage. In the ninth century there were 11,000 churches in countries administered by Muslims. Hundreds of Christians worked in the Muslim civil service, and the Muslims kept peace between rival Christian sects. There were public celebrations of religious festivals by Christians and others.[2] Jews likewise prospered under Muslim rule, and they conducted trade both with the Muslim powers who controlled the Mediterranean and with Christian communities in Europe. But traders whose ships plied the Mediterranean had more to fear from Muslim pirates than from civil authorities. Saracen piracy, compounded by the raids of the Vikings on coastal cities, virtually closed the ports of Europe in the ninth and tenth centuries. The impossibility of trade hindered the economic recovery which Charlemagne desired. The people fearfully regarded the seas as a source of marauding strangers, rather than a highway bringing friendly trade and prosperity.

However, by the end of the tenth century the Norse leaders were accepting Baptism. History records that Christianity was imposed on Denmark in 974, and on Norway in 995, although these attempts did not immediately achieve the complete conversion of the people. Northern invaders who had settled on the coast of France and along the Seine quickly assimilated the Christian way of life, and the first Norman monastery was founded about 940. In this era, too, northern Slavic peoples who had settled into an agricultural way of life finally began to accept Christianity. The leader of the Poles was won to Christianity by his Bohemian wife and was baptized in 966.

As early as 867, Byzantine missionaries had been evangelizing the Russians in an effort to reduce the political threat to the empire posed by those people. The existence of a stable Christian community in Kiev can be documented from the early years of the tenth century onwards, but the conversion of the people followed the Baptism of Grand Duke Vladimir about 989. In view of the political advantages it secured for both sides, his conversion has been termed "an act both of faith and of statesmanship."[3] But other Slavic peoples who had settled along the Baltic coast retained their traditional religious practices until the twelfth and thirteenth centuries, when the gospel reached them through monastic and military evangelization campaigns.

In southeastern Europe, between the Adriatic and the Black Sea, the Bulgars, Serbs, and Croats had begun to accept Christianity in the ninth century, although they vacillated in acknowledging the authority of Byzantium or of Rome, according to prevailing political pressures. Greek Christianity appealed to the Balkan Slavic peoples, because the Slavonic liturgy and literature which it offered them were more congenial to their own culture than were the Latin rites of Rome. The Bulgarian church en-

joyed a period of lively literary production during the tenth century, which
in turn fostered the spread of Christianity and the foundation of numerous
monasteries. Bulgarian Christians shared their Slavonic translations and
original works with Christians in Russia, where these works would become
the seeds for a flowering of Russian Christian literature in the next century. Serbia, however, was until the twelfth century allied like Poland with
the Roman church. Between the northern and the southern Slavs, in the
region that would become Hungary, there settled a non-Slavic immigrant
people, the Magyars. After several generations spent terrorizing Italy and
Germany, in the late tenth century the Magyars too accepted Christianity—the Roman version, again for political considerations.

In contrast to Muslim scholarship and the literary creativity of the
newly converted Slavic peoples of eastern Europe, the cultural life of western Europe was in eclipse. The northern sea raiders had overrun Ireland
and ransacked monasteries, putting an end to Irish learning for a time.[4] In
the late eighth and ninth centuries, Charlemagne had labored to unify the
West, through programs such as reform of the law, standardization of the
liturgy, and establishment of schools. This Carolingian cultural revival
lasted only about a century.[5] John Scotus Erigena, whose translation of a
neoplatonic philosophical work was to become so influential, was working
toward the end of this period, but he found no peer or student with whom
to share and sharpen his ideas.[6] Otto in Germany and Alfred in England
also attempted political unification and cultural renewal which earned for
both the epithet "great" but which nevertheless did not survive the tenth
century. These brief revivals of learning by the Irish monks and nuns,
Charlemagne, Otto, and Alfred all foundered because the political and economic order upon which they depended could not be maintained. The
Carolingian age, however, did last long enough to pass on to us a legacy
of recopied manuscripts of ancient classical works.

Yet the modest achievements of Western monastic and cathedral
schools continued throughout the tenth century and beyond. The monasteries of Fulda, Corbie, Reichenau, St. Gall, and many others had re-
nowned libraries and harbored scholars. Schools were established in Paris,
Auxerre, Corbie, Reims, Liege, and Chartres. In many western European
localities, vernacular literature had its beginnings in this era, as the songs
and legends of traveling storytellers began to be written down. Among the
well to do, interestingly enough, girls were more likely to learn to read
than boys were. It was the young ladies who had the leisure to listen to
ballads, or read them to each other, as they worked in the home at textile
arts, while their brothers were away learning the practical skills of knight-
hood. Hroswitha, like numerous other high-born women in tenth-century
Germany, received a kind of higher education after entering a monastery.

She was a gifted poet and playwright who wrote fluent Latin. She was familiar with a number of pagan classics, and used their forms as models for
her own work, which sought to communicate edifying Christian themes.

Books, copied and bound by hand, continued to be rare and expensive. Only those manuscripts deemed to be particularly edifying, suitable
for instruction, or interesting by virtue of the wonders they recounted,
were likely to be widely copied. Such works became in turn the more influential ones in the formation of the rising generations. Works attributed
to famous authors, like Augustine or Bede, were especially esteemed. For
example, a ninth-century Byzantine emperor sent to his French counterpart as a gift the Greek manuscript of several neoplatonic treatises which
had erroneously been attributed to the Dionysius who was the only male
convert the Apostle Paul made in Athens (Acts 17:34).[7] It was the author's
supposed identity, more than the merit of his ideas, that made them so
appealing. At the emperor's request, Erigena translated this book into
Latin, making it available to later generations of Christian theologians. The
Irish scholar himself borrowed the metaphysical ideas of this "pseudo-
Dionysius" when working out his own theology.

Erigena's *De divisione naturae* interprets all of reality in relationship
with God, as part of a cosmic flowing out and flowing back to God. Many
of his positions are uncanny foreshadows of twentieth-century process theology. Erigena enumerates four kinds of being: uncreated creating being
(i.e., God, conceived as source of everything); uncreated noncreating
being (i.e., also God, conceived as the end to which all things return and
rest); created creating being; and created noncreating being. God stands
at the beginning and at the end of everything else as the source of its being.
There are presages of twentieth-century existentialist philosophy in Erigena's thought as well, for he says that heaven, hell, and the Garden of
Eden are not places but conditions of the soul.

But Erigena is a writer of the ninth century, not the twentieth. To us,
a "created creating being" would be none other than a human being. To
Erigena, the category included "prime causes, principles, prototypes, Platonic Ideas, Logos, by whose operation the world of particular things is
made."[8] While this pre-modern thinker did indeed discern a non-divine
agency at work in the world, nevertheless he was not yet ready to recognize that it belonged to human being, the "subject of history" so called by
our contemporaries. Instead, Erigena postulated another layer of reality,
elsewhere than here, as the realm where immaterial patterns and prototypes somehow mediated being between God and the lowly world of created uncreating things here below. Not until the political upheavals of the
eighteenth century would men and women begin to realize that power lay
not in their stars but in themselves.

For other thinkers of the middle ages, however, the philosophy of Pseudo-Dionysius and of Erigena would reinforce the popular impression that the material world was moved by powers beyond the control of humankind—though of course people suspected that they could influence the powers a little bit, by means of the Christian cult.

In the tenth century monasteries as yet possessed relatively few books; however, they had come to own a great many other things. Some parishes and cathedrals, too, held extensive properties. Ironically, perhaps, the wealth which these properties generated did not go to the monks, nuns, or parish people. In early feudal society, many monasteries and parishes in turn were owned by wealthy lay people or by absentee clerics, and the distribution of their revenues was little governed by gospel considerations. The tenth century saw the beginnings of a monastic reform movement that was to flower in the eleventh and twelfth.

Increasing political difficulties, doctrinal differences, and incongruences of clerical style had separated Eastern from Western Christians for several centuries. The mid eleventh century would bring the definitive break between the two segments of Christianity, which after excommunicating one another would be known as Catholicism and Orthodoxy. Among the complaints which Greek Christians made against the Latin church were that Roman clerics added the word *"filioque"* to the Nicene Creed, demanded clerical celibacy contrary to the example of the apostles, used unleavened bread for the Eucharist, and shaved their beards. Shortly after the Great Schism of 1054, the leader of the Western church preached a military incursion into territories where Eastern Christians lived. The Crusaders enlisted in this holy war in order to take the Holy Land away from its Muslim inhabitants and give it to Christians. However, they seem to have killed Christians and Muslims in roughly equal numbers, since all dark-skinned peoples looked alike to the fair Crusaders. About the year 1000 another fair adventurer, the Viking Leif Ericson, led an expeditionary force westward to an attractive place which he called Vinland, where there were other dark-skinned people. Several Norse expeditions to the North American continent are recorded in sagas which Christopher Columbus studied while preparing for his own voyage of discovery.

It seems clear that cult overshadowed both care and call in the tenth century. The church construed the intimacy of the divine-human relationship in terms of a divine superpower whose sacramental penetration of human reality diverted the church's attention and resources away from caring for people's physical well-being. These are still "dark ages" for theoretical understanding and teaching of the gospel message. Coercion is preferred to persuasion; and what little intellectual activity there is is preoccupied with the superreality of the divine realm to the neglect of the human. Yet it is still possible to trace out the gospel's transformation of human existence during this century in terms of care, celebration, and word, although many of our findings will be of gospel efficacy gone awry.

USES AND ABUSES OF PROPERTY AND POWER

We have used the term "care" to identify those ecclesial activities which serve the physical needs of human beings, in fidelity to Jesus' own work of healing and feeding the people. Such activities normally require the use and administration of material goods, and therefore they can be subverted by human greed. The redirection of the church's material resources away from the poor and into the coffers of the rich had become a serious impediment to the gospel's work in the tenth century.

Besides greed, there were more subtle ideological factors underlying the abuses of church wealth and power in this era. *In theory*, religious leaders discounted the value of the physical world and pointed to the greater reality of the world of the spirit. *In practice*, that very theory served to legitimate the control of material resources by those who could claim a kind of control over spiritual resources through the cult. For instance, a cleric who performed a spiritual service would expect material payment for it.

The term "care" itself changed in meaning. Souls rather than bodies became the principal object of the church's care—a distinction foreign to the mind of Jesus. The *cura animarum* was the clergy's job, to be carried out in a sacramental praxis preoccupied with the invisible world and all but blind to the needs of the present one. Priestly power, in the eyes of the people, consisted principally in "changing" bread and wine at the Eucharist, and "loosing" the bonds of sin in confession. These cultic activities no doubt made their minds easier during a human existence which they perceived as a temporary exile; but they did not comfort their bodies.

In fairness to the ecclesiastical leaders of the tenth century, we must recall that contemporary experiences of political impotence and recurrent foreign invasion had built up the impression that their world was not their real home. The "most real" needs of the people were perceived to be spiritual ones, and church leaders gave priority to addressing those. In addition, the collapse of the old Roman imperial administration centuries before had thrust upon pope and bishops extensive secular responsibilities which in more settled times they might never have sought for themselves. By the tenth century, it had long been accepted practice that church leaders must wheel and deal in politics, in real estate, and even in military matters.

At the level of the local Christian community in the rural parish, historians assume (in the absence of detailed records) that church funds were duly allocated for the care of the indigent and the socially displaced.[9] Certainly the monasteries would have continued their work of providing for the needy and managing the agricultural tasks of their serfs so that there was food enough for all (although by this time few monks did the manual labor themselves). In the cities, bishops and other wealthy Christians no doubt gave alms to the poor, challenged perhaps by the example of their Muslim and Jewish business associates. But interestingly, the fact that so little information about tenth-century Christian charitable practices has come down to us indicates that people of that era considered these activities relatively unimportant.

We get indirect evidence of the common people's perception of the church's administration of its property in the Bogomil movement, which began among tenth-century Bulgarian peasants and influenced the Balkan peoples for several centuries. The members of this sect adopted certain Near Eastern dualistic views, and they condemned the material world as the creation of the devil. They experienced everything material as evil; for them, no element of the physical world could possibly be a sign communicating the parental love of God. Interestingly, their assessment of contemporary ecclesiastical charity did nothing to dissuade them from this view. On the contrary, it led them to place the church, its sacraments, clergy, and institutions on the side of the devil and matter, condemning all alike. That the Bogomil views, though pronounced heretical, were persuasive enough to last five centuries is a telling indictment of the church itself. A heresy denying the goodness of the material world and the sacraments would seem to be an impossibility in a church whose care and whose sacramental life effectively communicated God's love to the people.

In feudal Europe, wealth came out of the earth in the form of agricultural products, livestock and wild game, fibers, fuel, building materials, precious metals and stones. Land was owned by those powerful enough to defend it and to manage it properly so that both landlords and serfs got the food, clothing, and shelter which they needed to survive. From an economic point of view, there was no difference between the ways in which church properties and other properties produced wealth. A parish church received its revenue from the produce of whatever fields and forests belonged to it, just as a monastery did, and just as a country estate did. Any of these wealth-producing units could be owned by a lay person, who would take for himself or herself a part of the revenue of the parish, monastery, or estate. From an ecclesiastical point of view, there were two disadvantages to this arrangement. First, the church's material resources were going into the pockets of wealthy lords and ladies. And secondly, these proprietors had control over appointment of the pastors, abbots, and abbesses who would manage their properties. The latter was called lay investiture, and could lead to a conflict of interest for clerics who owed their positions to secular governors.

If in peacetime the Christian gentry did what they could to get their hands on lucrative church real estate, in times of invasion the heathen raiders, too, were attracted to the monasteries and churches. Both kinds of assault weakened church life and obscured the original purpose for which the church held property: the material relief of the poor. In the tenth century, western monasticism was at a low ebb but reform was on the horizon. At Cluny in Burgundy, Abbot Odo tightened up the observance of the monastic vows and restored order and discipline in his congregation. The "Cluniac" method of organizing monastic life spread from there across much of western Europe during the next two centuries. Cluny had been placed directly under the authority of the pope, and it demanded that its daughter houses give their allegiance to the abbot of Cluny. In this way, it managed to escape interference from local bishops and lords alike. The Cluniac monasteries in turn helped to strengthen the central papal power in Europe.

The gradual strengthening of the authority and prestige of the papacy during the later middle ages would have astonished any citizen of tenth-century Rome. Powerful Roman families of that era kept the city's civil and ecclesiastical government tied up in knots with endless intrigues and corruption, leading to a quite rapid turnover of popes: there were twenty-five between 900 and 1003.[10] For an age whose theology discounted the reality of the material world, the tenth century produced ecclesiastics who seemed inordinately interested in claiming their share of its goods. They bought and sold bishoprics, and on occasion the papacy itself. This practice was condemned as simony (payment for spiritual power, Acts 8: 18–20), but the real object of the sale was of course the revenue and the political power that went with church office. The corrupt ecclesiastical leaders of this era also treated women as commodities which they could use without providing for them the social and economic protections of Christian marriage. Later reformers would seek to impose celibacy upon clerics to curb this sexual abuse, but also to prevent the sons of clerics from inheriting the considerable church property which their fathers might have amassed.

The avarice which spoiled the church's caring ministry in the tenth century is all the more pathetic when we consider that Christians of that era denied the real value of the very things that they were so eager to possess and consume. Their ideology displaced God's reign to a far-away heaven, but they sought to manipulate heavenly affairs with the same scheming tactics they employed in earthly politics. This manipulative stance toward spiritual matters expressed itself in their cultic practice, as we shall presently see.

We have little indication, in the evidence that comes down to us, that tenth-century Christians saw the world around them as the place where a loving God was providing freely and generously for their human welfare. Yet this vision, which was the vision of Jesus, cannot have been entirely lost among the Christian people. This vision of Abba's largesse must have been transmitted somehow—perhaps through the poor, for it reenters the gospel's story two centuries later when Francis falls in love with Poverty.

DOLING OUT WHAT CHRIST HAD EARNED

The church's administration of its property no longer spoke to the people of God's parental care for their physical needs. Therefore, its cultic ministry also lost its focus of celebrating the intimacy of the divine-human relationship. Instead of distributing bread to the poor and then enjoying with them the free and unlimited gift of relationship with the Father through Jesus, it seemed that many clerics got things exactly backwards. They enjoyed the bread of the poor and then "distributed" to them small measured parcels of grace.

Impoverished in so many ways, the church of the tenth century found it difficult to imagine the infinite generosity of God. Christians looked to the socio-economic organization of their world for a kind of model for understanding the divine-human "economy." The *cura animarum*, or care of souls, was managed by methods not unlike those employed in the management of large agricultural estates. The church's spiritual wealth was thought to consist in the "merits" which Jesus had accrued through obedience during his life and death. This capital, though it was limitless, was to be spent judiciously in return for the proper performance of certain tasks. Clerics earned quantities of it by carrying out the eucharistic ritual, and could apply what they earned where they wished; for example, to cancel out the eschatological punishment which some sinner was facing. Even lay people could earn shares of the merits of Christ by saying words and doing deeds to which ecclesiastical authorities had attached "indulgences."

How had it happened that Christians came to construe their relationship with God as a kind of invisible ledger sheet? This image was no doubt fostered by pastoral practices that grew up around confession, that is, the Celtic method of celebrating reconciliation imported to the European continent by the Irish missionary monks. As we saw in the last chapter, confession was designed to mold the behavior of new Christians in rural tribal societies. Confessors consulted standardized lists of sins and the penances associated with each of them. Typical penances consisted of fasts that lasted for a specified number of days, weeks, or years.

Only after the penance had been completed would the confessor pray for God's forgiveness for the sinner. This custom was different from that observed in later centuries and in our own day. Up to the ninth century, the ritual of reconciliation went as follows: confession of sins, assignment of penance, completion of penance, prayer for God's forgiveness, and readmission to the Eucharist. In the tenth century, the order was changed to the one familiar to us today: confession of sins, assignment of penance, absolution from sins, readmission to the Eucharist, completion of penance when and if possible. The confessor's prayer for God's forgiveness for the penitent developed first into a pronouncement that the penitent was absolved *from the duty of completing the remaining penance* in case of approaching death, and then into a pronouncement of the absolution *of sin itself.*

But in the ninth century, when the prayer for forgiveness was supposed to follow the penitential practice, an obvious pastoral difficulty arose: what if the penitent died before completing the penance? This was taken care of in two ways. An infirm penitent could have his or her penance commuted to the saying of specified prayers; this gave rise to the idea that prayers or good works were in some way interchangeable with corporal punishment and could be used to remit it. But the penitent who died still "owing" some punishment was thought to get the chance to work off the debt after death, in "purgatory." It was a short step from there to the idea that the prayers of a living person could lessen the time a dead one had to suffer.

It must be remembered that people in this era doubted the value of human decision; they doubted that human efforts ever could amount to anything in this, our place of temporary exile. Everything in their social and political experience told them otherwise. Our modern ideas about personal initiative, decision, and commitment could never have entered their minds. So perceiving themselves as the bumbling inhabitants of an unimportant second-rate material world, they turned to those whom they perceived as having one foot in the more real, more intensely existing realm of spiritual things. They turned to priests, who shared in the ontological intensity of God's own being, and who therefore had special powers. Priests could bring divinity into the common matter of bread and wine, and moreover they could fix up the eternal harm that invariably seemed to result from the exercise of human freedom in the material world.

To be sure, the priest's power was understood to come from Jesus and to be given for the sake of all God's people. The very fact that their gloomy world could be brightened by the incursion of divinity into it in the Eucharist, and by the expectation of a better life hereafter, expressed for Christians of the tenth century God's intention to accompany them in their exile and lead them home. The dimension of celebration may be hidden behind the ledger sheets of tenth-century cult, but it is not entirely lacking.

Yet if we are to understand the ecclesial experience of those people, and indeed of the generations who followed them, we must not overlook the economic side of their cultic practice. If by saying mass a priest "earned" and "dispensed" parcels of Jesus' merit, people would offer him money to get him to say as many masses as possible. Monasticism had begun as a lay movement, but the prospect of spiritual and monetary gain influenced abbots to have their monks ordained, and eventually some monks said masses all day long. Similarly, monastic prayers and penances were viewed as meritorious. Wealthy people endowed houses of religious men or women in order to receive the benefits of their continuous prayers, especially after death.

Both monastic life and the life of the ecclesial community "in the world" followed the cycle of the liturgical year, with its traditional feasts and seasons. By the tenth century, some 25,000 saints had been recognized in various locations across Christendom. It is to the popular cult of the saints that one must look for evidence of real exuberance in the tenth century's "celebration" of the intimacy between God and humankind. Saints were those who had made it through the earthly exile and found their way home to God. The people regarded the saints as their earthly guides and their friends and advocates in the heavenly kingdom. Many of these holy men and women were officially recognized by having their feasts commemorated in the liturgical calendar. In addition, the people treasured relics of the saints, especially their bodies or parts of their bodies. It seemed advantageous to seek the help of a saint in the presence of his or her relics. The concrete imaginations of simple people attributed spiritual power to the relics themselves; possession of a scrap of cloth or bone seemed to them to entail possession of some influence over the saint.

The times were perilous, and people felt that they needed all the help they could get. There was a brisk market for relics, just as there was for masses. The phenomenon was by no means limited to the simple people; for the same abbots who had all their monks ordained to say thousands of masses also enriched their monasteries by collecting the remains of saints and saints' possessions.

Another sort of popular celebration of human intimacy with God was the pilgrimage. People traveled to the site where a saint had lived or the saint's relics were preserved. The most awesome pilgrimage to be undertaken was the trip to Palestine, where Jesus himself had lived. If the tenth century experienced the world as a place of exile from God, the pilgrimage represented the trip home from exile. The way was dangerous and difficult, but the observance of cultic customs, fasting, and begging seemed to provide some protection and to guarantee a safe arrival at the journey's end. Christians who went on pilgrimage were symbolizing their trust that there was indeed a way back to God, one marked out by Christ, the church, and the saints who had preceded them. Christians who received pilgrims passing through their neighborhood saw the journey of these strangers as a dramatization of the possibility of following Christ back to God. Evangelistic considerations aside, the pilgrimage afforded high adventure to many women and men whose lives were otherwise circumscribed by the boundaries of their own village or farm. (Unfortunately, the metaphor of holy journey was extended from the pilgrimage to the crusade or religious military expedition.)

The people's sense that life was an exile in a world opaque to the grace of God led them to prize those special instances where the realm of the spirit seemed to touch down into their mundane experience: relics, holy places like monasteries, holy people like priests, and above all the sacrament of the altar. They treasured the eucharistic presence of Jesus. Their imaginations took comfort in the utter reality of this real presence, which was their assurance that God had not left them alone in their exile. Small wonder that one could not see or taste Jesus in the eucharistic elements: sight and taste belonged to the material world, and the level of being of these senses was not up to that required to apprehend the superreality of Jesus' miraculous presence in the sacrament. The tenth century doubted its eyes rather than its Lord.

Interestingly, the tenth century represents a hush in the theological discussion of the nature and possibility of Jesus' eucharistic real presence. In the previous century, Erigena had ventured to explain that presence in terms of symbol, and the monks Radbert and Ratramnus had launched a vigorous philosophical debate. In the following century, Berengarius would reopen the discussion. But it is as if the tenth century regarded eucharistic presence as so vital and yet so fragile a miracle that it must not be probed too far. We may suggest that this mystery of God's *cultic* presence was overloaded, so to speak, by the failure of the church to present God to the people through *care*. The cult, particularly the eucharistic cult, became a precious slender thread linking heaven with earth while the cable of care unraveled.

MAKING CONNECTIONS BETWEEN THIS WORLD AND THE NEXT

The ministry of the word is the ecclesial enterprise of interpreting the received message of the gospel so that it can be retold to, and understood by, each succeeding generation of human beings. In our own day the reinterpretation has had to be rapid in order to keep pace with the development of social and scientific thought. The methods, media, and message of evangelization have changed more in the last three decades than they did in the three centuries between the years 700 and 1000.

In general we may say that the concrete announcement of salvation through Jesus Christ, which had been devised for the first generations of barbarians, continued to be the mainstay of teaching and preaching for their descendants and for the other nations who subsequently joined the church. To this general statement, however, three qualifications must be added.

First, as we have seen, by the tenth century the cultic dimension of the church's life was being made to carry almost the entire weight of the Christian people's experience of God's presence, activity, and availability in their midst. This upset the balance of the three ecclesial activities of care, celebration, and word. Ideally, Christian teaching should be able to draw equally upon each of these activities as sources. What the gospel message is "about" is a new way of living as exemplified in people's care for one another, in their celebration of new intimacy among themselves and God, and in the call they hear and transmit from their biblical tradition.

But for tenth-century teachers, it became nearly impossible to synthesize these three sources. There was more scandal than edification to be gleaned from considering the church's use of its property. There was reluctance to probe the mystery of God's presence in the cult. Sacramentality had been drained out of the ordinary and concentrated in a few special persons, acts, and elements which served to link earth's exiles with their heavenly home. Therefore, teachers and preachers alike concentrated their effort upon instilling a reverent, almost magical awe of cultic persons and things. Like their predecessors, they favored themes of moral exhortation and the lives of the saints.

Second, cultic activities were becoming so important to the tenth-century church that it was easy to lose sight of the equal importance of the ministry of the word (and, indeed, of caring ministries too). People equated salvation with gaining access to a share of the "merits" of Jesus. Such access was to be had through the Eucharist, through confession, through other rites, prayers, pilgrimages and the veneration of relics.

These liturgical and paraliturgical actions "worked" (that is, awarded merit to the doer) as long as the proper actions and words were completed with the right intentions. This satisfied the concrete imagination of the age. Whether one also *understood* what one was correctly doing seemed inconsequential. Therefore, involving the faithful in religious instruction got lower priority than involving them in religious ritual. To be sure, Charlemagne had legislated that the minimum religious knowledge expected of all the baptized was the ability to recite the Creed and the Lord's Prayer in the vernacular. Conscientious pastors would try to ensure that the people understood the basic meaning and implications of the words which they recited. Yet perhaps not by coincidence, this was also the era when the Romance languages had diverged so far from Latin that uneducated people could no longer understand the words of the western liturgies. No one thought that odd except the eastern Christians who still prayed in languages intelligible to themselves.

Third, it seems curious that the tenth century was theologically silent concerning soteriology (i.e., theory of the conditions and means of salvation), while the eleventh century would resume the discussion of soteriological issues laid open in the ninth, as we shall see.[11] Yet there is a latent but compelling soteriological interest at work in the manuscripts which tenth-century authors did produce. Their pious and partisan biographies and historical chronicles seek in a concrete way to sort out the relationship between human deeds and human destiny. Therefore these writers embroider their narratives of factual events with miraculous interventions by heaven into the affairs of earth. Even Hroswitha, the most gifted writer of this period and a woman familiar with some of the works of classical antiquity, chose the forms of epic poetry and drama as the vehicles of her reflection on the relationship between nature and grace.

Aside from these stories, which were soteriologies in their own way, the tenth century added little that was new to the personnel, institutions, methods, media, and content employed in the ministry of the word.

Personnel. Responsibility for addressing the gospel to the church remained with the bishop. Priests instructed the people from the pulpit, and parents instructed children in the home. Monks and nuns catechized and otherwise educated many who were fortunate enough to come under the influence of the monasteries. As missionaries, the monks and nuns continued to go out among pagan peoples and invite them to accept the gospel. Often they did this under the direct sponsorship either of the pope or of the emperor and the patriarch of Byzantium.

Like feudal society, the church had many classes: ordinary people, monks, nuns, several degrees of lower clerics, several degrees of bishops, with the pope on top. The cult being the most signficant means of access to the things of God in the tenth century, these classes were differentiated according to the degree of participation in the liturgy that was permitted to each of them. Interestingly, those least active in cultic activities often were most active in caring.

But if we take into account the many contexts in which the ministry of the word had to take place, this interpretive ministry seems to have been distributed among all the classes of the tenth-century church, lay as well as clerical. In fact, if it is true that the most effective evangelization one receives is that given in childhood, then the ministry of the word was distrubuted in *inverse* proportion to the ministry of cultic celebration, but in *direct* proportion to caring ministry, in the classes of the tenth-century church.

This broad distribution of the ministry of the word was obscured when preaching came to be restricted to those authorized for cultic ministry. In early medieval times, the missionaries who evangelized the immigrant pagan tribes in Europe had preached vigorously among them. Most of those missionary monks and nuns were not ordained. Their commission to preach the gospel came from their own Baptism. As we have seen, conflicts arose between the early missionary monasteries and the bishops of neighboring towns. These conflicts were resolved in part through legislation that limited the pastoral activities of monasteries, at least in areas of Europe that had been Christian for several generations. Such legislation was intended to protect and promote the pastoral initiatives of local bishops, by forbidding any but diocesan clergy to preach. Therefore, in western Europe the monasteries of the tenth and eleventh centuries abandoned the pastoral care of the people who lived nearby. Apparently the parish priests were unable to satisfy the hunger of the people for the gospel, for the eleventh century was to see a resurgence of unauthorized lay preaching, much of it judged by bishops to be heretical.

Institutions. The Christian family continued to transmit knowledge of Christ and Christian living to the rising generations of the tenth century.[12] The other traditional agencies of teaching then built upon the foundation received in the home: parish and monastic schools, and liturgical preaching.

While monasteries were becoming less active in the evangelization and catechesis of ordinary Christians, their schools continued to develop for the educated few a "monastic theology" which was a holistic method of study, prayer, and work. In these schools were trained the monks and nuns who passed on Christian learning, along with the texts embodying the Christian message, to the subsequent generations who would organize Europe's first universities in the twelfth century.

The medieval university had two other "ancestors" that were active in the tenth century: parish or cathedral schools, and law schools. The traditional cathedral school continued to educate future clerics and other young people in both secular and sacred sciences.[13] A century earlier, Charlemagne had envisioned universal free education, and in some places his dream had begun to take shape during his lifetime. Carolingian legislation promoted the establishment of both monastic and cathedral schools in France and western Germany. The momentum of this educational revival was slowed, but not entirely lost, in subsequent generations. German schools seem to have thrived during the tenth century thanks to the prosperity achieved under Otto the Great.

In addition, about the end of the tenth century law schools were organized in several metropolitan centers, especially in Italy. Here, lay persons taught along with clerics—unlike the monastery schools, where only monks and nuns taught, and the cathedral schools, presided over by canons. It was an age when civil and ecclesiastical affairs were intertwined and increasingly complex, so that the new legal scholarship branched out into consideration of the nature and relative authority of church and state. Some of the law schools were predecessors of universities; moreover, the body of legal theory which they compiled would contribute directly to the organization of theology itself as an academic discipline within the university. In comparison with the monastic theology, which was to be another important source of high medieval academic theology, this legal theory was thoroughly secular. Where the monastic theology was a way of life involving prayer and work in a context of Christian community, legal thought arose from an entirely different praxis: trade, war, statecraft, and government, in all of which the church was quite active.

In forbidding lay people to preach, the tenth century took a decisive step in the institutionalization of the ministry of the word. Since preaching always had been the most public and visible of the word ministries, clerics now came to be perceived as *the* official and public ecclesial ministers of the word. Thus the institution of the priesthood came to embody the ministry of the word along with the ministry of the sacraments. Priesthood *was* ministry. Ministry now meant public celebration of the cult and public preaching. As these public activities gradually gave to the term "ministry" its modern narrow definition, the more private sorts of word ministry— and virtually all of the caring ministries—seemed to fall between the cracks. Institutions which grew up to support them no longer would be perceived as ministerial.

Ironically, although the tenth-century church entrusted greater responsibility for transmitting the gospel call to the cleric, it is difficult to identify in that era any contribution to the ministry of the word made by the clerical institution par excellence, the papacy. After the tenth century, to be sure, the popes gradually would consolidate the power and prestige of their office, making of it the greatest pulpit in the world. But during the tenth century, the papacy was such a contradiction to the gospel that one is thankful the popes had then no interest in teaching.

Methods. This transitional century saw no innovation in teaching or preaching methods; however, traditional practices were gradually developing toward the emergence of the stylized academic *disputatio* of the high middle ages.

Relying on the supreme efficacy of the cult, tenth-century evangelists were happy first to baptize monarchs—indeed, whole peoples—and later to instruct them. The leaders of the Slavs perceived Christianity as a means to political salvation in *this* world; therefore, they shrewdly chose affiliation with either Roman or Byzantine Christianity, according to the political advantages to be gained. Those who catechized these peoples subsequently enlarged upon their desire for this-worldly advantages in order to present Christianity as a means of securing for themselves and their people a place in the world to come as well. As the Germanic tribes had done before, whole Slavic nations followed their kings and queens to the baptismal font or river. These converted masses received religious instruction later, principally through preaching at the liturgy and through the example of missionaries.

Monasteries, though weakened by the political and economic setbacks of the ninth and tenth centuries, continued to develop the integrated way of life that came to be known as monastic theology. The Rule was imparted to young nuns and monks by example and by oral instruction. Although ritual practices were taking up an ever greater portion of the monastic day, the Rule specified that time was to be set aside for reading and for study. Therefore, the tradition of memorizing and commenting upon scripture continued.

Both monastic and cathedral schools offered formal instruction in matters of Christian faith. A master would open the pages of the Bible and work through a text, commenting and making references to the interpretations offered by earlier authorities. The "class notes" which the master used in this activity were the marginal comments, or glosses, laboriously written along the edges of the page next to the scriptural text. A Bible could become quite heavily glossated with a lifetime of notes. By the eleventh century, masters were copying the glosses over onto separate sheets. Collections of these comments were rearranged according to topic, and a new genre of theological work was created: the book of *Sentences.*[14]

The systematic arrangement and encyclopedic intent of these collections would set them apart from the varieties of religious literature used in the tenth century: topical treatises, lives of the saints, and scriptural commentaries. Yet those traditional genres also were rooted in the teaching situation. One motive for committing one's instruction to writing seems to have been that the students did not retain it when it was given orally. It is interesting that among the Gospels, that of Matthew received almost exclusive attention during this period, for the First Gospel is the one whose perspective is most distinctively that of an ecclesial teacher.

Media. The tenth century received the gospel in both the spoken and the written word, as well as in many other media. The word was the vernacular. With scores of dialects in use across Europe, preachers and teachers labored to interpret the Christian message in speech which the common people could understand. The missionary impulse was a major force behind the development of European tongues into written, literary languages. When Christian leaders were in turn recruited from among newly Christianized nations, they had to learn something of a church language. In the West, this would be Latin; in Eastern Europe, Slavonic. The Germans and Norse had a harder time of it than the Slavs. But for everyone, the difference between the language of proclamation and the language of celebration tended to widen the gulf perceived between the efficacy of the cult and the efficacy of understanding. The former was shrouded with mystification, while the latter was demoted to a kind of extra frill inappropriate for lay people.

Yet there was an element of celebration even in the written word, for the tradition of manuscript illumination continued. The ninth-century Irish Book of Kells was so beautifully decorated that it was called a work of angels pretending to be human. Pictorial representations of gospel themes remained an important medium of communication, because the number of people who could both read and understand written languages remained small. The walls of church buildings were painted or frescoed with biblical scenes, a practice which Charlemagne had promoted to assist in the religious education of the illiterate.[15] The northern peoples built wooden churches in their forests and carved figures of the saints out of trees which formerly had housed their gods. In Italy, Romanesque church structures displayed frescoes or mosaics depicting the spiritual world within, and a plain, solid brick exterior to the outside world.

The theological silence of the tenth century was in some sense filled by the music of the liturgy. A great portion of the monastic day was given over to the mass and to the liturgy of the hours. The monks and nuns were not content to "say" these prayers; they sang them. The traditional liturgical chants which we call Gregorian after their great promoter originated well before this period, but the ninth and tenth centuries were an era of great creativity among monastic composers. It became possible to add to the repertoire of traditional chants because a system of naming the notes, and eventually of writing down a melody on a musical staff, was being developed in the tenth and eleventh centuries. These innovations enabled people to record and remember new chants. Both men and women sang the liturgical chants, but not together.[16] As the pictures on church walls communicated Bible stories to people who could not read them in books, so the melodies of the plainchant communicated a feeling of transcendence and divine presence to people who could not understand the words.

Content. The gospel message as conveyed to the peoples of the tenth century was both concrete and adapted to use categories which their social and political experiences had prepared them to understand. As the cult assumed central importance in the church's life, the people were instructed in proper cultic observances: how and how often to confess sins, how to complete penances, when to receive the Eucharist, when to present infants for Baptism, and so forth. Redemption was presented in story form. All Christians were supposed to be able to repeat the Apostles' Creed, with its narrative account of Jesus' life. The stories of the saints' exploits provided illustrations of the Christian virtues.

On the other hand, several of the most significant concepts at work in the tenth-century gospel were never stated as propositions at all, although they formed the background of the stories. We have already referred to these several times: the interpretation of the world as a place of exile; pessimism about the possibility that human beings might achieve anything good by their own initiative in this exile; devaluation of the worth, and even the reality, of the material world; anxiety about the threat of powerful strangers invading one's home; and the promotion of the "other" world of heaven to the status of a world more real and more valuable than this one and the true home of the Christian.

These were less doctrines than attitudes, and they underlay not only the stories of popular catechesis but the theological controversies as well. The ninth-century christological disputes had reflected a certain anxiety about the status of God's Son within the Trinity, which had implications for the status of humanity itself. In Charlemagne's time, anathemas had flown between Rome and Spain in a dispute over whether the formula "adopted Son of God" was adequate to describe Jesus' relationship with the Father.[17] Spain also seems to have been the source of a liturgical innovation that would spread throughout the Western church and contribute to its schism from the East: the addition of the phrase *Filioque*—"and from the Son"—to the Nicene Creed. At issue was the technical definition of the relationship of the Holy Spirit to the other trinitarian persons, that is, whether the Spirit proceeds from the Father (alone), or from the Father and from the Son. Anathemas flew between Rome and Byzantium on this issue in the late ninth century and again in the eleventh. It is ironic Christians should become estranged from one another over the nature of trinitarian intimacy.

The ninth-century controversy about predestination also contributed to the atmosphere in which the gospel was communicated in this era. A monk named Gottschalk had offered a new presentation of the theories of Augustine, to the effect that God had already set each human person on the path either to eternal life or to death, and individuals were powerless to do good works. The best scholars of the day, including Erigena, produced treatises defending either Gottschalk's position or the opposite view, which had not been doubted between Augustine's time and their own: that since the Creator wills all to be saved, the means to salvation are provided. For the first time since the end of Antiquity, however, it was now possible to imagine that that was not so. Gottschalk grasped the possibility and went insane.

In the wake of the unsettling ninth-century theological disputes, the tenth century preserved its sense of equilibrium by turning its attention to the reassuring experience of intimacy with God in the Christian sacraments and other cultic practices. Both of these things—the ninth-century controversies, and the tenth-century experience of the cult—formed the background for the theological breakthrough of the eleventh century.

Then, theology would receive its academic name and identity, and the work of systematization would begin in earnest with the books of *sententiae*. Anselm would give to the church a definitive statement of soteriology in his work *Cur Deus Homo*,[18] which still influences the Christian imagination in our own time. Anselm reasoned that Adam and Eve had put all human beings into a situation from which it was impossible for us to extricate ourselves. Drawing on his own social experience of feudal class stratification as well as his ecclesial experience of "paying off" the punishment for sin through penitential practice, Anselm proposed that God had become a human being in order to pay off an infinite debt. Adam and Eve had committed an infinite offense, and incurred infinite punishment, simply because they had sinned against someone who was infinitely "above" them by any scale, social or ontological. It had to be a human being who made satisfaction for this offense, yet no mere human being had the status required to do so adequately. Until . . . God became a human being.

As God, Jesus was able to make infinite satisfaction; as man, Jesus was able to do so on behalf of all women and men. Because Jesus' sufferings made an infinite satisfaction for our sins, he restored the right order to the universe. Anselm's theory put medieval minds to rest concerning the place of human beings in the universe. His "satisfaction theory" of soteriology gave a solid foundation to the people's understanding of the cult as a means of "dispensing" the merits of Jesus among Christians. It made very good sense in its own time.

Anselm was one of several eleventh-century teachers to use a dialectical method in developing his theology. Berengar of Tours was another, and he sought to use dialectic to clarify the reality of the presence of Jesus in the Eucharist, upon which so much of contemporary piety depended. Berengar said that any "change" which occurred in the bread and wine was a spiritual one, for the elements could not both *be* and *not be* bread and wine at the same time. He was roundly refuted by Lanfranc and others, who while less metaphysically astute in their thought than Berengar, more faithfully expressed the experience of the people. Berengar's opponents and church authority agreed: the substance of the bread and wine indeed was "changed" at mass. In 1215 the Fourth Lateran Council would define this event as "transubstantiation."[19] Perhaps no better formula could be found to safeguard the reality of the real presence, availability, and activity of Christ in the Eucharist for people of that era, whose religious imaginations were quite concrete and whose experience of ecclesial transformation was almost exclusively cultic. The critical understanding of symbolic function, and the broader experience of ecclesia, which together would permit a more adequate appropriation of eucharistic reality, lay far in the church's future.

LEGACY OF THE TENTH-CENTURY CHURCH

- absolution after confession but before doing penance
- musical notation
- outlook upon the earth as alien and alienating: a place of exile
- preaching by clergy only
- the trickle-down theory of reality: popular Platonism
- word and care subordinate to the sacramental system
- Poland, Russia, Hungary, Denmark, Norway as Christian nations
- Cluniac reorganization for monasteries

Notes for Chapter Seven

1. Will Durant remarked in 1950:

What we know of Moslem thought in those centuries is a fragment of what survives, what survives is a fragment of what was

produced. . . . When scholarship has surveyed more thoroughly
this half-forgotten legacy, we shall probably rank the tenth century in Eastern Islam as one of the golden ages in the history of
the mind.

See p. 257 of *The Age of Faith*, volume 2 of The Story of Civilization (New
York: Simon & Schuster, 1950).

2. Durant lists the sorts of evidence that lead the historian to this
conclusion, on pp. 218–19 of *Age of Faith*.

3. By Dimitri Obolensky, on p. 314 of *The Middle Ages*, volume 2
of The Christian Centuries, by David Knowles and Dimitri Obolensky
(New York: McGraw-Hill Book Co., 1968). The historical picture offered
in this chapter is built from data presented by that work and by: Durant,
Age of Faith, M.L.W. Laistner, *Thought and Letters in Western Europe
A.D. 500 to 900* (Ithaca, N.Y.: Cornell University Press, 1931, 1957); Bernard Cooke, *Ministry to Word and Sacraments* (Philadelphia: Fortress
Press, 1977); D.M. Hope, "The Medieval Western Rites," in *The Study
of Liturgy*, edited by Cheslyn Jones, Geoffrey Wainwright, and Edward
Yarnold, S.J. (New York: Oxford University Press, 1978), pp. 220–40; Joseph McSorley, *An Outline History of the Church by Centuries*, ninth edition (St. Louis: B. Herder Book Company, 1954).

4. Durant, *Age of Faith*, pp. 499–500. Durant also looks at things
from the Vikings' point of view in a colorful discussion on pp. 502–10.

5. Laistner devotes the third and largest part of *Thought and Letters*
to the accomplishments of the Carolingian Age in education, theology, literature, and philosophy. He remarks (on pp. 321–22) that

> The age of Pippin had come upon the Western world like a
> spring, to be succeeded by the long and radiant summer of Char-
> elmagne's reign. Then the autumnal decline which set in soon
> after his death was for a space arrested by a short but brilliant
> Indian summer under Charles the Bald. The civilizing agent on
> which these princes relied—and there could have been no
> other—was the church.

Durant discusses the educational projects of Charlemagne on pp. 465–66
of *Age of Faith*, and concludes on pp. 471–72 that the Carolingian renaissance

> might have ended the darkness three centuries before Abelard
> had it not been for the quarrels and incompetence of Charle-
> magne's successors, the feudal anarchy of the barons, the dis-

ruptive struggle between church and state, and the Norman, Magyar, and Saracen invasions invited by these ineptitudes.

6. Erigena and his ideas are discussed by Laistner (who notes that Erigena was a layman) on pp. 323–29 of *Thought and Letters*. Knowles remarks that Erigena's work,

> with all its technical, linguistic and perhaps also dogmatic infel-
> icities was the only attempt between Augustine and Nicholas of
> Cusa [d. 1464] to use a philosophical system, or rather a scheme
> of things, derived principally from Plotinus, to express the whole
> of Christian theology.

See *Middle Ages*, p. 137. Durant's sketch of Erigena portrays his wit as well as his intellect, on pp. 477–79 of *Age of Faith*. Legend has it that Erigena was stabbed to death by the pens of his students, which is literarily if not literally true. Laistner remarks that

> it would not be easy to find another thinker of equal intellectual
> stature whose contribution to human thought aroused so few
> echoes either amongst his contemporaries or with posterity.

7. Besides Dionysius, "a woman named Damaris and a few others" also joined Paul and believed when the gospel was preached in Athens, the seat of ancient philosophy. It is thought that Pseudo-Dionysius was a fifth-century author of Syrian extraction who was responding to critics of Christianity by proposing a system of Christian mysticism built out of cur-rent neoplatonic concepts. See Laistner, *Thought and Letters*, pp. 245–46.

8. See Durant, *Age of Faith*, p. 478. For discussions of Erigena's positions, see pp. 477–78 in *Age of Faith*; and Laistner, *Thought and Let-ters*, pp. 324–28.

9. See, for example, Cooke, *Ministry*, pp. 368–69.

10. Or twenty-three, plus two anti-popes.

11. Rome was too busy with political intrigues to produce teachings on these soteriological issues. The catalogue of official church teachings edited by H. Denzinger and A. Schönmetzer, the *Enchiridion Sym-bolorum* (Barcinone: Herder, 1963) lists only one pronouncement for the entire tenth century: the decree canonizing St. Ulrich (no. 675).

12. Or so one must assume, given that Christianity itself continued to

exist. It is interesting, however, that contemporary records or descriptions of this are hard to come by.

13. Cooke points out that because the teachers in these schools were canons, there continued to be "a sizable group of ordained presbyters devoted basically to educational work." See *Ministry*, pp. 260–61; see also p. 367.

14. Knowles explains that *sententia* originally meant "selection" but came to mean "opinion" or "pronouncement" as the collections became more selective. Attempts to harmonize the sentences were made, the *summae sententiarum*. In the mid twelfth century, Peter Lombard wrote his *Four Books of the Sentences*. His contemporary Abelard named an academic discipline with his book *Theologia*. See Knowles, *Middle Ages*, pp. 206–07, see also Durant, *Age of Faith*, p. 941.

15. Durant says that some of the frescoes which Charlemagne had painted on his palace walls at Aachen could still be seen there until 1944, when they were destroyed. See *Age of Faith*, p. 479.

16. With the development of polyphony in later centuries, the absence of women's voices at worship was particularly noticed. To make up for the lack of higher voices, boys were taught to sing the soprano parts. These boys were castrated to keep their voices high, rather than admit women to liturgical choirs. Yet, in some localities at least, men and women must have continued to sing the divine office together up until the twelfth century, when conciliar legislation was enacted against it.

17. There seemed to be a scriptural precedent for this formula, in Acts 2:36, 10:38, and 13:33. For background on "adoptionism," see Knowles, *Middle Ages*, pp. 49–51.

18. The title *Cur Deus Homo* has been translated "Why Did God Become Man," although of course the Latin noun "*homo*" means "human being." The work takes the form of a dialogue between Anselm and a pupil, Boso. It is translated by S.N. Deane in *Saint Anselm: Basic Writings* (La Salle, Ill.: Open Court, 1962, 1974), pp. 171–288.

19. As Knowles points out, Berengar's difficulties "were in essence grammatical rather than theological"; see *Middle Ages*, p. 238, and the discussion of the issues on pp. 237–38. Richard P. McBrien's analysis of Berengar's position also is helpful. McBrien recalls that in subsequent centuries, sacramental theology would identify three components of the symbolic efficacy of the sacrament: the *sacramentum tantum*, including the bread, wine, words, and actions of the eucharistic ritual; the *res tantum*, or union of the church with Christ; and the *res et sacramentum*, the body and blood of Christ. The *res et sacramentum* is symbolically effected by

the ritual, and in turn it symbolically effects the union. This "middle step," however, was not apparent to Berengar, who was seeking to make sense out of the connection between the ritual elements and their ultimate salvific effect. See *Catholicism* (Minneapolis, Minn.: Winston Press, 1981), p. 739.

Chapter Eight

Thirteenth Century:
Reintegrations

The thirteenth century is at once the bright summit of the middle ages, and a turning point for the gospel's story. This age gave the Christian church a theological synthesis of faith that has been second in importance only to that bequeathed us by the generation of catechists who wrote the books of the New Testament. It is a golden age of Christian teaching, because it is an age concerned with restoring the primitive proportionality of sacramental celebration, care for human need, and reflection on the gospel in the life of the church.

In contrast with the tenth century, the thirteenth shows the evidence of gradually progressing transformations in human social consciousness. The Crusades have opened up trade with the East; and trade has brought new goods to improve the material wellbeing of the people, as well as new ideas to challenge their thinking. Increasingly, the conditions are there— social, economic, intellectual, political—to enable people to move beyond the concrete level of understanding. They become conscious of the complex interrelationships in their world. As we have seen, theologians from the eleventh century onward began to be concerned with synthesizing the diverse truths expressed in earlier Christian writings, arranging them in books of "Sentences" to bring out their innate connectedness, developing a theology that can be called systematic. They did the mental work of distilling, refining, abstracting propositions (or dogmas) out of scriptural texts, where these truths had been embedded in narrative, poetry, admonition, or other rather concrete literary forms.

Concrete understanding, as was discussed in chapter one, is that which is available to the mind which can reason about absent things through mental handing of the concepts which stand for them. In our own culture, children aged 7 to 12 typically reason concretely with religious symbols, as do some adults. *Conventional* understanding is that available to the mind which reasons not only by relating concepts to one another, but also by relating relationships (of concepts) to one another. In our culture, this facility appears in adolescence. Certain conditions must be present in the environment for the individual to develop conventional understanding; among them would be the challenge of complex events which cannot be adequately understood or dealt with in concrete terms, and the unfolding of personal relationships beyond the family.

While it is certain that some people reasoned at the conventional, and even the critical, level during the early middle ages, the thirteenth century brought such widespread challenges to human social and intellectual understanding that many more people were enabled to reason about their world in ways which we may term conventional.[1]

Something analogous developed in the economic sphere. The twelfth century saw a great growth in population and in prosperity. There were enough peasants now so that some could leave the land, go to the towns, learn trades, and produce a kind of wealth that was no longer directly agricultural. With the growth of towns and the increase of tradespersons, the barter system had to give way to a *money* system.[2] Money is a token which, by convention or common agreement, stands for the real value that inheres in something else. A dollar bill is equivalent to a loaf of bread, except that it is easier to handle but harder to eat.

Money was a truly ingenious invention, and also a mixed blessing. The history of money is exceedingly complex. Coins were in use, of course, since ancient times, even in farming societies; but money became more important the more complex a civilization became. The value of bread is its ability to nourish; but the value of gold is whatever people agree that it will have. Their agreement may take the form of agreeing to want it intensely enough to labor for it. As the nineteenth century would recognize, money made it possible to separate or "alienate" those who did the value-producing work from the value that they produced. (This insight of Karl Marx's is at the foundation of his economic theories. Communism is in principle a plan for reuniting workers with the value they produce.) On the positive side, however, the switch to a money economy signals that development from concrete to conventional understanding which supports complex urban civilization. Agreement about the value and use of currency is one of the conventions which binds people together into post-agrarian societies.

Dogma is to faith as money is to economic life: an abstract symbolization of real value into a form that can be more easily handled and transmitted. The use of money permitted more complex and exact economic relationships within high medieval society, and the use of dogmatic statements similarly permitted clarification of thought and teaching in the life of faith. For example, the dogma of the Trinity encapsulates the teachings of the entire New Testament about the relationship between Jesus and the

Father. To say that one believes in, or to baptize someone in, "the name of the Father and of the Son and of the Holy Spirit" is to use a few words to express assent to and participation in the many New Testament stories, invitations, admonitions, and so forth.[3] Abstract theological formulae are easier to reason with than are the biblical stories and poetry from which they are derived. Yet the disputations of the medieval "schoolmen," as the great thirteenth-century theologians were called, could seem as dry as a dollar bill to those seeking spiritual nourishment. Simultaneously with the development of systematic theology, there emerged among the Christian people a movement prizing devotion over disputation, a spirituality tempering the ministry of the word in this golden century. It was the creative tension between precision of mind and devotion of heart which found voice in the new expressions of faith of the thirteenth century.[4]

Besides the emergence of the money economy and systematic theology, a third development helped to move many people's imaginations from the concrete to the conventional level. The growth of towns and trades meant that serfs were leaving the land and finding new identities as townspeople. They broke the concrete ties that had held them to the soil where they were born, worked, and died. They affiliated themselves with a city and with a guild, both of which existed as human conventions; or, they traveled as traders. The experience of mobility and freedom did not touch everyone, and of those it touched, not everyone transcended the concrete level of understanding. But for a growing number of women and men, these experiences expanded the symbolic imagination so that they could appreciate abstract thought in religious as well as economic and political matters.

This phenomenon of new patterns of affiliation transformed the church's structures as well, and several new forms of religious life emerged, including that of the traveling mendicant friars. In the tenth century, as the serf had identified with the land, so the monk or nun had identified with the monastery. Now, however, several orders of religious men appeared which had neither the physical stability of monastic life nor its steady means of producing life's necessities from the soil. Their coherence was couched in terms of a papal mandate rather than concrete ties to a single locality. The influence of the papacy grew, for people were prepared now to understand the possibility, indeed (and for the first time) the necessity, of a superterritorial authority transcending that of local bishops and priests. Scholars, too, drew together at Europe's new universities. Increasingly, people could see "the big picture" in which the parts of the church were related to the whole. Both dogma and the traveling friars became a kind of currency whose circulation helped to bind the church together under the headship of Rome.

These orders of men generated "second orders" for women, but the women did not travel or beg. They stayed within monastic houses, and their life resembled that which was traditional for nuns. However, there would indeed be a manifestation of new patterns of affiliation and economic organization among religious women: the Beguine movement. The Beguines stepped outside the boundaries of home and family life to establish Christian sisterhoods which were self-supporting and engaged in charitable works. Their innovative character is comparable to that of the friars, to whom history was kinder.

The growing prosperity of the eleventh and twelfth centuries enabled people to see their earthly environment in a more positive light: the "exile" seemed not quite so desolate as it had in earlier straitened times. People rediscovered God's immanence, availability, activity, address within creatures. Paradoxically, in circumstances of plenty it became possible to embrace *poverty* as a deliberate choice, in imitation of Jesus's own attitude toward the things of the world.[5] The tenth century's ontological devaluation of this world had gone hand in hand with perverse avarice on the part of many who grabbed up whatever they could of the world's supposedly worthless things. The thirteenth century's new vision of God's availability in creation raised the level of the perceived ontological worth of the world, restoring the sacramentality of ordinary things. But this vision set hearts free from greed. The poet Francis of Assisi wrote:

> All praise be yours, my Lord, through all that you have made,
> And first my lord Brother Sun,
> Who brings the day; and light you give to us through him.
> How beautiful is he, how radiant in all his splendour!
> Of you, Most High, he bears the likeness. . . .
> All praise be yours, my Lord, through Sister Earth, our mother,
> Who feeds us in her sovereignty and produces
> Various fruits with coloured flowers and herbs. . . . [6]

Francis loved the world for the same reason Jesus did: it embodied Abba's care for men and women. This poem celebrates the experience of Abba's care through material things. Francis saw that any attempt to *possess* these things would spoil the experience of receiving them as a free gift, spoil the celebration. Poverty, on the other hand, was what made the world transparent.

Francis established a way of life designed to enable men and women to celebrate the free gifts of God. The Franciscan ideal called for poverty, itinerant preaching, and manual labor. When the labor did not bring in sufficient sustenance, the friars might beg. In effect, the poor man of Assisi radically reordered the caring and celebrating dimensions of ecclesial existence. This new alignment of celebration with poverty (rather than with possessions) *was* the message that the Franciscans preached. The impulse to teach, which was to become quite strong in the Franciscan movement within a generation of the founder's death, thus originates in the praxis of an ecclesial way of life that can celebrate intimacy with God through material things which one declines to possess or control.

For the thirteenth century's other great order of teachers, the Dominicans, the need to study, to reflect, and to teach arose directly from the mission for which they were founded: preaching to the faithful to protect them from heresy. If we may say that the sons and daughters of Francis started with celebration of God's care and found that it impelled them to call others to share their new vision of the gospel, then we may also say that the sons and daughters of Dominic traversed the same territory but in the opposite direction. The Dominicans started with zeal for presenting the gospel's call, and as they strove first to understand that call and then to preach it to the people, they found themselves impelled to a lifestyle of poverty that gave new meaning to the sacramental celebrations, particularly that of reconciliation, to which they called the people.

Both of these orders, and others, were working out a new integration of the three dimensions of ecclesial activity: care for physical needs, celebration of intimacy with God in Jesus, and words calling to conversion of life. Moreover, various groups of lay people, from the villages to the universities and palaces, also were rediscovering the centrality of care to the gospel. Not just the three ecclesial activities, but their interdependent efficacy, was recognized. This recognition spelled the beginning of the end of the early-medieval idea that the cult all by itself (i.e., baptism, reconciliation, or the mass) could bring the gospel to fruition.

By this time, however, much more was at stake than ideas. Vast material wealth and political power had been built, and continued to depend, upon the early-medieval soteriological monopoly of the sacraments. The idea that Jesus had been poor was dangerous to these interests, and so it was declared to be heretical. Moreover, the majority of the common people still persisted in the concrete religiosity of their forebears. Their hearts were touched when their neighbors shared goods with them in Jesus's name; but their minds clung to a quasi-magical sacramentalism as the only way home from earthly exile.

Yet a great revival of the ministry of the word, and particularly all kinds of teaching, accompanied the reintegration of care, celebration, and word in some quarters of the thirteenth-century church. Friars, other clerics, and lay men and women[7] were attracted to Europe's universities, where theology reached the heights of systematization in the medieval *summae.* Among the Franciscans, Bonaventure, and among the Dominicans, Thomas Aquinas were stellar teachers at the University of Paris. They and other "schoolmen" organized everything that was known about God, Christ, and Christian living into powerfully logical books of theology. For source material, these men drew upon the work of past writers, both Christians and non-Christian philosophers, and also upon their own experience—which included of course their everyday life in the church of the thirteenth century. The *summae* therefore reflect the laws, the liturgical practices, the social customs, even the medical and botanical lore, of that era.

Despite the richness of their sources and the power of their intellects, the schoolmen nevertheless lacked one ingredient in their theology which every literate person in our own day takes for granted: they lacked sensitivity to historical change. In other words, they assumed that the church as they found it was identical with that of the New Testament in all details. As the first systematic theologians since antiquity, they built a sturdy structure to accommodate all aspects of faith and practice in the church which they knew; but as medievals, they left no room for growth.

The systematizations of theology and of canon law in the thirteenth century represent an achievement analogous to an individual's growth from concrete to conventional understanding. Experience working *within* the new mode of thinking must precede the move *beyond* it to critical understanding—and the perception that reality is subject to historical change is the foundation of the critically understanding mind. After the triumph of conventional understanding in the thirteenth-century *summae*, subsequent centuries would begin to examine their unchallenged assumptions, root metaphors, contradictions of fact, methodologies, and so forth.[8] That was the beginning of the modern mind, and the task continues into our own day.

Interestingly, the transition from concrete to conventional religious imagination showed different results in women than in men. The new men's religious communities, the friars, created the summaries of systematic theology as triumphs of abstracting thought. The new women's religious communities, the beguinages, created new organizations for providing social services, as we shall presently see.[9]

THE SITUATION IN THIRTEENTH-CENTURY EUROPE

Medieval Europe was on the move. The old ties to the land, the local lord, the monastery, the diocese, were weakening. New ties were being forged: to the city, the guild, the non-stationary religious community, the international church headquartered in Rome. Economically, the transition from local-agricultural work to industrial-commercial exchange was underway. Religiously, preachers took to the road to take the gospel among the faithful. Militarily, knights "took the cross" and went on expedition to reclaim the Holy Land. Everywhere, strategies were shifting from defensive to offensive as new weapon systems evolved in business, theology, and war.

Several military campaigns were undertaken between 1095 and 1291 to liberate Palestine from its Muslim administration. These "crusades" were regarded as holy wars, and the spoils sought by Christian soldiers were spiritual as well as material. One crusade even moved against French people belonging to the sect called Albigenses.

In Eastern Europe, non-Christian nations were still making incursions into Christianized territories. The Mongols invaded Hungary and Poland, the Tatars occupied Russia. Meanwhile, the work of converting the Slavic peoples continued. The evangelical thrust of the new mendicant communities extended to the establishment of missions in Persia, India, and China.

The Roman church of the thirteenth century sought to consolidate its political power and its ecclesiastical organization. The Fourth Lateran Council enacted some seventy canons on church discipline. Popes used the cultic weapons of interdict and excommunication to manipulate the civil authorities, who had a sturdy arsenal of their own with which to lean upon the papacy when political considerations warranted. In 1302, the papal bull *Unam Sanctam* expressed the theory behind the relationship between church and state from the papal point of view, in the "doctrine of the two swords":

> . . . Christ has established two swords or powers in the church
> —the one temporal, the other spiritual. The latter he has com-
> mitted to the priesthood, the former to the kings; and both being
> in the church, have the same end. . . . Should the temporal
> power turn aside from its prescribed course, it becomes the duty
> of the spiritual power to recall it to its true duty. It is of faith that
> all men, even kings, are subject to the pope. . . . [10]

In the tug of war with secular powers, the papacy concerned itself not only with the stakes but with the very rules of the game. For example, Pope Innocent III sought to invalidate the Magna Charta, in which English barons had achieved limitations on the absolute power of their king.[11]

More significant than the power struggles between ecclesiastical and secular monarchs in the twelfth and thirteenth centuries were two new phenomena expressive of the gospel's continuing transformation of human existence: the universities, and the Beguines. Lay men and friars played an important role in the evolution of the former, while lay women predominated in the latter.

The medieval universities had their antecedents in the cathedral schools, and they grew into independent entities as the towns grew into cities. Institutionally, they first were organized when students formed themselves into guilds with power to guarantee the quality of the instruction which they would receive from their teachers. As the cities attracted the new wealth pouring into Europe from revitalized international trade, so the universities attracted the ancient learning that was trickling back into Europe from the Islamic world, where the Greek classics had been preserved. Thirteenth-century scholars not only imported ideas but coordinated what had already been available to them, and ancient texts also emerged from backwater monastic libraries within Europe, where they had long lain unnoticed. The classic authors, particularly Aristotle, along with their Islamic commentators, brought new information to the universities in the fields of philosophy, science, mathematics, law, and medicine. Moreover, they brought a novel approach to knowledge itself, one that was experimental rather than allegorical and authoritative. This approach was welcome in the universities, but not at the older monastic schools. The application of new methods of investigation and analysis to traditional texts and practices resulted in the systematic theology which was the crowning achievement of the thirteenth century's ministry of the word.

The universities bore some institutional relationship to the ecclesiastical hierarchy, but the Beguines were completely a grass-roots movement. In various cities, first in the Netherlands and then in Germany and Italy, pious matrons and spinsters[12] came together to perform works of charity and to support one another in Christian sisterhood. The occasional university faculty and the occasional beguinage were suspect of heresy throughout the thirteenth and fourteenth centuries. While the universities nevertheless managed to continue their corporate existence, the beguinages were either disbanded or absorbed into the traditional orders of nuns.

The heresies of the twelfth and thirteenth centuries also bear witness to the urgency of the church's need to maintain a healthy evangelical balance among its constitutive activities.[13] For some, the rediscovery of the material world's sacramentality did not happen in time. The world-deprecating views of the Bogomils came into France with the international trade and were taken up by those called Catharists or Albigenses, who proposed a powerful critique of the church's wealth and its cult. Their own teachings are known to us only second-hand, through the records of those who destroyed them. But thousands of people found those teachings so true to the gospel that they died rather than abandon them. In the face of massive military suppression,[14] their ideas went underground, to emerge in the Reformation of the sixteenth century.

REDISCOVERING THE POOR CHRIST

The comparative prosperity of the twelfth and thirteenth centuries rehabilitated the material world as God's "symbol," the place of human encounter with God. Francis of Assisi became poor so that he could more easily appreciate the richness of creation — that is, the generosity of the Father of Jesus. Devout Christians who shared a vision like that of Francis sought to aid people in distress so that they, too, would once again be able to feel God's parental care in the goodness of their own material existence. There was a flowering of works of charity, and of new religious associations to promote them.

This new materialism had an ugly side as well. Some ecclesiastics regarded this world as the place for punishment of sin and the arena for a downright physical confrontation with the evil of heresy. When persuasion and argumentation failed, they vanquished errant ideas by disposing of those who entertained them. Torture, execution, and anti-population warfare were deemed to be legitimate weapons in the struggle for orthodoxy; for the most part, they were wielded by the secular arm and blessed by the sacred.[15] The tactics of Inquisition and Crusade seem hardly to belong to the same church which produced saints who kissed the decaying flesh of lepers and sold themselves into slavery to ransom captives. Yet it was so. If Francis could see God immanent in Brother Sun, and Thomas could discern Aristotelian forms immanent in matter, then by a pernicious corollary the Inquisitors could sniff out[16] evil thoughts immanent in people— and then snuff out thinker along with thought.

When the pope called on Christian nobles to mount a holy war against Albigensian populations in southern France, it was the prospect of acquiring heretics' property that motivated many to take up arms against their neighbors. One of the worst "heresies," at least from the official ecclesiastical perspective, was the Albigensian criticism of the church's property and the way it was managed.

This criticism seems to us to be a symptom of the imbalance between caring and cultic ministry, an imbalance which in places had become quite scandalous. Indeed, reforms were attempted by the church hierarchy itself, particularly through the Fourth Lateran Council. Canons 16 and 17 called for a simple lifestyle for clerics. Canon 29 forbade clerics to hold more than one benefice. Canon 31 forbade the sons of priests to be appointed to their fathers' parishes. Canon 32 forbade bishops to siphon off the income of parishes for themselves. Other canons sought to eliminate various forms of simony.[17]

Moreover, the Albigensian ideas were a symptom of the changing macroeconomic situation in Europe. The traditional means of support for the clergy had been agricultural: the tithes of produce from parish and monastery lands. But the value of these was declining against the new varieties of wealth being produced and enjoyed in the cities: artifacts of the crafts men and women, fine goods brought by traders, and capital gains through investment. The increasingly centralized administrations of church and state drained away the deflated resources of pastors and bishops. It is therefore understandable that the initiative in providing for the material needs of the common people passed away from the monasteries and the parish clergy, and was taken over by new caregivers like the Beguines and the Hospitalers, and by the civil authorities.

With monasteries and cathedrals in somewhat straitened circumstances, it is remarkable that many of the monks, nuns, and bishops managed somehow to continue their traditional works of charity. These included providing hospitality for travelers and taking care of the sick. Church law required parishes to fund relief for the poor. But as the population grew and became more urbanized and mobile, it became more common for a hospice or hospital to be founded by a wealthy lay person and administered by an association of lay men or women. Sometimes the association or confraternity would develop into a religious order. There were thousands of hospitals for lepers, and they are credited with the gradual eradication of the disease in Europe. Other specialized charitable foundations included those which cared for foundlings, and those which maintained bridges and roads.

In eleventh-century Palestine, the Muslim administration had permitted the establishment of a hospital in Jerusalem for Christian pilgrims. Its staff was reorganized in the twelfth century into a religious order, the Knights of the Hospital of Saint John, or Hospitalers. Their vows included the military protection of Christians, and they were active in the battles of the Crusades. The Hospitalers and two similar orders, the Knights Templars and the Teutonic Order of Knights, were famous throughout Christendom for their charity and their success in battles against the Saracens. Returning home, they were given vast properties in Europe. The Templars consolidated their holdings in France. Their wealth and power were so great by the early fourteenth century that the king regarded them as dangerous rivals and cruelly suppressed them. The Teutonic Order put down a pagan revolt in Prussia, and it subdued and ruled the Baltic lands between Poland and Russia in the thirteenth and fourteenth centuries. That the ruthless massacre of (even pagan) civilians and the tender care of the sick poor could be undertaken by one and the same religious community shocks our sensibilities, but it did not seem incongruent to many during the late middle ages.

Besides the lay associations and the medico-military knights, there were lay "third orders" connected with several of the new communities of friars, as well as independent groups of Beguines. The Franciscans, Praemonstratensians, Dominicans, and others evolved third orders when married and single lay men and women sought to affiliate with these orders so as to share their vision, spirit, and rule of life. With the support which this solidarity afforded them, the lay people were encouraged to engage in caring activities such as visiting the sick and relief of the poor. The lay sisters and brothers provided much-needed services to displaced and disadvantaged persons in an urbanizing society. Moreover, their contact with the clerical and cloistered[18] members of their communities helped to carry the concerns of the real world back to those individuals and keep them in touch with the grass-roots church.

In contrast to the third orders, the Beguines had no special guiding vision other than the gospel, and no sponsoring clerical community. First as individuals, and later in groups or beguinages, certain Christian lay women became distinguished within their towns and cities for their good works and pious lives. They came primarily from the new bourgeoisie or from the nobility, and they worked to provide health care, communal child care, clothing, and shelter to the needy of the cities. The new prosperity of the age had made it possible for some women to remain unmarried, while as yet society provided few options to employ women's energy outside the home or cloister. The Beguines pioneered in organizing the talents of women to respond to the needs of a changing society. The gospel itself was the impulse behind their efforts, for sharing prayer and Christian sisterhood was a key component of the Beguines' way of life. Wealthy women sponsored the participation of poor country women in the beguinages. The movement also included some men, known as Beghards.

The Beguines were more concerned with sisterhood and service than with orthodoxy, and some beguinages shared the heterodox beliefs that were common in their neighborhoods. This was one factor in their eventual suppression. But the threat which some ecclesiastics perceived in the Beguines was more economic than doctrinal in character. Their way of life, in which their goods and energies were devoted to the service of human needs, posed a powerful critique of the contemporary administrative practices of clerical authorities. Like the mendicant friars, the Beguines were demonstrating the feasibility of a "low-overhead" style of caring for people's material welfare. But unlike any other phenomenon in the church up until then, they were an idea conceived and executed entirely by women. It was not an idea whose time had come.

DEVOTIONS AND DEFINITIONS

The recovery of vision which enabled Christians of the twelfth and thirteenth centuries once again to experience the world as God's symbol also gave them a taste and a talent for religious celebration. God became for them a *presence* more than a future, and heaven seemed quite close to earth. A new age of intimacy had superseded the sense of estrangement and exile which had clouded earlier centuries. The profusion of liturgical and paraliturgical celebrations gave voice to this experience and also nourished it. Moreover, the schoolmen's reflections upon their church's liturgical life issued in a sophisticated sacramental theology.

Popular customs like the pilgrimage and the veneration of relics continued, but the piety of the high middle ages took a decidedly personal turn. People doted on Jesus and his mother, Mary, and were particularly fascinated by the human relationship between them. It is said that Francis of Assisi built the first Christmas creche, to represent the touching symbol of God's approach to human beings reaching out in the form of a helpless homeless baby. Jesus the child, Jesus the crucified, Jesus the "bread of angels," even Jesus the "mother," captivated the imagination of the people of the thirteenth century. Jesus as the one who stays with us and nourishes us became the focus of an intense devotion to the Eucharist. Corpus Christi was celebrated as an important feast day, and Thomas Aquinas composed the liturgical prayers for it including the hymn "Pange Lingua."

> Sing, O tongue, the mystery of the body glorious,
> and of blood beyond all price, which, in ransom of the world,
> fruit of womb most bountiful, all the peoples' King poured forth.
>
> Given to us and born for us from an untouched maid,
> and, so sojourning on the planet, spreading seed of Word made
>   flesh,
> as a dweller with us lowly, wondrously he closed his stay.
>
> In the night of the Last Supper, with apostles while reclining,
> all the ancient law observing in the food by law prescribed,
> food he gives to twelve assembled, gives himself with his own
>   hands.

Word made flesh converts true bread with a word into his flesh;
wine becomes the blood of Christ, and if sense should fail to see,
let the pure in heart be strengthened by an act of faith alone.

Therefore such great sacrament venerate we on our knees;
let the ancient liturgy yield its place to this new rite;
let our faith redeem the failure of our darkened sense.

To Begetter and Begotten praise and joyful song,
salutation, honor, power, blessings manifold;
and to him from both proceeding let our equal praise be told.[19]

The monks and nuns intoned the tight Latin of these verses with the restrained emotion of the plainchant; but the Latinless people also celebrated Corpus Christi out of doors with festival, pageantry, and a jubilant procession through the town. Devotion to Jesus in the Eucharist led to the custom of elevating the consecrated bread for adoration at mass from the twelfth century onwards; and in the fourteenth century to the custom of placing the host in a transparent monstrance upon the altar for the people's contemplation. This preference for a visual experience of the blessed sacrament unfortunately meant that people did not consume the sacred species as often as they had in earlier times.

In celebrating the humanity of Jesus and his nearness to themselves, the people of the middle ages naturally were attracted to the one to whom Jesus owed his humanity, his mother. Christians of the Eastern churches always had cherished *Theotokos*, God's mother, and their devotion to her was profusely expressed in their icons, church edifices, liturgy, and religious thought. These deeply impressed the crusaders and pilgrims who went to the holy land, and the marian cult traveled back to western Europe with them. Scripture says little about Mary, but Luke's story of the moment of the annunciation—the moment when the word became flesh thanks to a girl's assent—captivated the hearts of medieval Christians. They loved to repeat the angel's words to the maid of Nazareth: "Hail, full of grace! The Lord is with you" (Lk 1:28). The monks and nuns had 150 psalms and numerous other prayers to recite in their "divine office"; but the people had their own vernacular office of 150 "Hail Marys," puncuating every decade with the Lord's Prayer. This was the rosary.[20]

Medieval women and men loved Jesus as a member of a human family, although his real father was God. Perhaps this helped them to recognize that marriage is a sacrament. An official ritual for celebrating marriage emerged in the eleventh century,[21] and when theologians of the twelfth century first came up with the list of seven sacraments, matrimony was

one of them. Nevertheless, the thirteenth century inherited enough of the
old pessimism about the goodness of things material to persist in the belief
that sexual intercourse always was at least a little bit sinful. For people of
that age, "sinless mother" would be a contradiction in terms—even more
of a contradiction than "virgin mother." Faith preferred the lesser contradiction, and interpreted the term *parthenos* in Lk 1:27 gynecologically.
The virginity of Mary was celebrated as the miraculous means of God's
saving penetration into human history.[22] This view reinforced the practice
of requiring celibacy of those who presided at Eucharist. The two moments of Christ's enfleshment were aligned: as the word had become flesh
in the womb of one who was virgin, so he should become enfleshed eu-
charistically in the hands of one who was virgin—or at least unmarried.

Increasingly, grace was imagined to come through the hands of the
clergy alone, owing to a liturgical development. In the thirteenth century,
the Sacramentary, that is, the Mass book containing the "priest's part" of
the liturgy, was replaced by the complete missal, containing all the "parts"
of the choir, the congregation, and the priest. The presider was then required to say everything himself, duplicating what the people and the
choir said. Gradually it was forgotten that the liturgy is the service of the
whole church.

Yet, the cultic dimension of Christian life remained so vivid and important to the people of the high middle ages that it gave a certain tactical
advantage to bishops and popes in their disputes with civil authorities. A
pope who excommunicated a king, that is, excluded him from participation
in sacramental celebrations, thoroughly discredited him in the eyes of his
subjects and compromised his power to rule. If excommunication did not
bring a monarch around to the pope's way of thinking, interdict surely
would. By interdict, a pope or bishop forbade the celebration of the liturgy
either within a specified territory, or in proximity to a specified person.
That meant that the Eucharist, Baptism, and sacramental Reconciliation
would be unavailable to the people until the interdict was lifted. Popes
also felt themselves empowered to release subjects from their oaths of allegiance to civil leaders, and to dissolve contracts and deeds of ownership.
Though inconceivable in our day, these cultic weapons were extremely
effective in a society in which the sacramental cult was of paramount importance.

The twelfth- and thirteenth-century Christians, for whom sacramental celebration was such a significant component of Christian life, took time
to reflect upon their cultic experiences and produced an impressive body
of theory about them. They refined the definition of a sacrament so as to
distinguish the central liturgical rites from customs of secondary importance. Peter Lombard recalled that Augustine had held that a sacrament

is a sign of a sacred thing, and Berengar held that a sacrament is the visible form of an invisible grace. On this basis, Lombard counted seven sacraments.[23] But later theologians wanted more precision. They proposed that a sacrament is an efficacious sign of grace. For example, Thomas asserted that a sacrament is a sign and a sacrament gives grace; but as a medieval thinker he was unable to show how it could happen that a sign *as sign* produced grace.[24]

These scholastic ruminations about the nature and number of sacraments hardly touched the exuberance with which the common people celebrated the activity of God incarnate in their world and in their sacraments. Paradoxically, however, these theological formulations did find their way into textbooks which later centuries unwisely used to introduce very young Christians to their sacramental heritage. It became clear that, while the people's sacramental life is a rich source for academic theology, the latter can squelch the former.

Popular devotion to the Eucharist, and the fruits of academic reflection, came together in the Fourth Lateran Council's canonization of the technical term "transubstantiation" to affirm the reality of Christ's presence in the Eucharist.

> . . . There is one universal church of the faithful, outside of which there is absolutely no salvation. In which there is the same priest and sacrifice, Jesus Christ, whose body and blood are truly contained in the sacrament of the altar under the forms of bread and wine; the bread being changed (*transsubstantiatis*) by divine power into the body, and the wine into the blood, so that to realize the mystery of unity we may receive of him what he has received of us. And this sacrament no one can effect except the priest who has been duly ordained in accordance with the keys of the church. . . . [25]

This definition culminated a centuries-long discussion of the way in which Christ might be present in the eucharistic bread and wine.

THE REBIRTH OF THEOLOGY

The ministry of the word embraces the proclamatory activities which invite people to hear and accept the gospel, along with the reflective activities which help the gospel's messengers themselves to understand it and express it in ways meaningful to the people to whom they are sent. Theology is a reflective refining of the gospel.

In the universities of the thirteenth century, the academic enterprise of theology went forward with great energy. The medieval *summae* are the most famous legacy left to us by the Christians of that time; but they were not the principal link through which faith was being transmitted. As we have seen, the gospel was at work in activities of care and celebration. Moreover, the gospel call reached the common people in the traditional activities of preaching and catechesis, addressed to them by men and women many of whom had never been to university. Few of the thirteenth century's Christians had any idea about the theological discussions going on in the academic centers of their cities, although the fruits of those discussions would wield tremendous influence over the ministry of the word in subsequent centuries.

The universities were part of a culture rich in contrasts. The same church which cared tenderly for orphans and lepers also waged war against the populations of Palestine and southern France. Francis of Assisi contemplated the wounds of Jesus with such compassion that corresponding marks appeared on his own body; while the inquisitors stigmatized suspected heretics with tortures more imaginative than mere crucifixion. There were social contrasts between the way of life in the countryside, and the new urban civilization taking shape in the growing towns. New religious associations were forming and taking over some of the functions formerly done by the old. New manuscripts of very old works were being studied, and they showed the medieval scholars that the ancients had found it possible to grasp the one in the many—to arrange all human knowledge in a unified whole. The desire to unify knowledge and society was the impulse behind the systematizing efforts of both the theologians and the canon lawyers. It is characteristic of the conventionally understanding mind.

Nevertheless, the understanding of the majority of the people remained quite concrete. The subtle weapon of logical disputation which Dominic used against heretics was available only to a few. Moveover, strategies of evangelization still were circumscribed by an earlier age's exclusive reliance upon the cult. Since the proper performance of ritual had been deemed sufficient for salvation even when the people lacked understanding, the *teaching* of the faith had for centuries received low priority. Therefore, the champions of orthodoxy in the twelfth and thirteenth centuries found scant foundation to build on in the Christian people's understanding. Their religiosity had been allowed to remain at the level of the magical, the credulous, the mythic. They had different myths, but the same level of understanding, as their pagan ancestors of six centuries before.

Two sorts of leaven held promise for raising the mass of the people's religion: disputation, and devotion. For someone like the twelfth-century monk Bernard of Clairvaux, the two seemed mutually exclusive. He looked askance at Abelard's project of reasoning about faith, and he upbraided those who pursued learning for its own sake. Bernard was an eloquent preacher who had the gift of infecting both rich and poor with his own faith that God was intimately present in Jesus Christ and in the beauties of creation. Yet the thirteenth century did find a way to accommodate this vision within the enterprise of theology itself. Indeed, the creative tension between love and logic, devotion and dispute, the concrete and the abstract, seems in retrospect to be the defining characteristic of the medieval ministry of the word. It vibrates throughout the personnel, institutions, methods, media, and content involved in the thirteenth century's ministry of the word.

Personnel. As we have seen, the care-giving role of bishops and priests, monks and nuns was diminishing because of economic and demographic factors at work in the high middle ages. Monasteries had been canonically excluded from proclamatory ministry as well, with the result that diocesan clergy increasingly came to look upon preaching as their own proper work. However, preaching was still understood to be secondary to the sacraments in importance, and one of the principal objectives of clerical preaching was to lead people to sacramental celebration, particularly Penance. The responsibility of bishops to provide teaching for their people was underscored by the Fourth Lateran Council's censure of those who failed to do so.

In the mendicant friar, medieval Europe had a new kind of priest. Unlike the diocesan clergy, friars traveled from place to place to preach. They were usually more educated and had better developed communication skills than the parish priests. Their mission or mandate to teach came not from a local bishop but from the central authority in Rome, as part of an effort to reform and revitalize the religious instruction available to the people. Nevertheless, after the friars moved on, diocesan clergy had the task of sustaining whatever conversion and Christian renewal their preaching had inspired.

The friars were attracted to the universities to get the education they needed for effective preaching. Some also remained at the universities as members of the theology faculties. The Dominicans organized themselves so that every young friar had an opportunity to pursue higher studies, to the extent of his ability. Franciscans and Augustinians, too, were among the thirteenth century's leading scholars. Because these teachers had confreres who were walking the dusty roads and talking with ordinary men and women, they were able to keep in contact with the living faith of the Christian people. This fact is as significant as the rediscovery of Aristotle in explaining how the thirteenth century's masterworks of theological synthesis emerged.

Not all the teachers were friars, and not all the friars were teachers. While some friars battled grassroots heresy by instructing the people in orthodoxy, others sought to further the proclamation of Christian truth through the inquisition. The Beguines were among many who suffered for the gospel at their hands.

Institutions. In several dioceses in the twelfth century, heresy was perceived to be so threatening that bishops set up an "inquisition" in each parish: a panel of a priest and two lay people to find out who might be entertaining and teaching notions contrary to the Christian faith. In the thirteenth century, the inquisition was centralized and placed in the charge of the Dominicans and Franciscans.

By all accounts, heterodox teaching had become such a hindrance to the gospel that drastic measures were needed. One historian asserts that "the towns in western Europe were honeycombed with heretical sects."[26] Having gone without adequate cognitive formation in faith for many centuries, the people were susceptible particularly to the dualistic ideas they encountered when they left the land and moved to the cities. The inquisition was, so to speak, a ton of cure administered when it was already too late for an ounce of prevention.

The Catharist or Albigensian position generally denied the goodness of the material world and regarded it as the creation of the devil. From this idea it followed that the church's sacramental rituals, along with sexual intercourse and the possession of material goods, became suspect. The creation-denying tenor of these views made it more difficult for church leaders to hear the Catharists' valid criticisms of ecclesiastical abuses connected with the liturgy, celibacy, and property. Many shades of understanding, conviction, and good will were present on both sides of the battle lines. Heresy was a phenomenon much feared by the ordinary people themselves, and mob violence was perhaps a greater threat to one who professed novel opinions than was civil or ecclesiastical persecution. The inquisitors would imprison and interrogate suspected heretics, and those who were found guilty would be handed over to civil authorities for (further) punishment. The ecclesiastical inquisition may be interpreted as an effort to introduce some semblance of due process into a situation on the verge of dissolving into civil disorder or occasionally even mass hysteria.

However, the process of interrogation had none of the safeguards for human rights which we associate with the notion of due process. When the inquisition moved into a town, a general invitation was issued to all heretics to come forward and confess their errors. Then people were encouraged to denounce any of their neighbors, or their civil or religious leaders, whom they thought to be heretics. The accusers remained anonymous, and the accused were taken into custody. By law, torture was permitted only once during their interrogation, but this seems to have been interpreted to mean once during each session of interrogation. The accused had no lawyer.

An institution far more conducive to the propogation of the gospel was the medieval university. The growth of the prosperous cities, peaceful relations among the nations of Europe, and the rediscovery of ancient learning were among the factors that made it possible for scholars to collaborate at these international centers in the pursuit of greater understanding both of the gospel and various fields of human science and letters. The University of Paris was a kind of guild of teachers. It grew out of the church schools of the city, particularly the cathedral school, and in the thirteenth century its institutional unity consisted in the fact that all its teachers were licensed by the chancellor of the Cathedral of Notre Dame. Scholars of many nations could converse with one another in the universal language of the learned, Latin. The universities spawned the first real theologians since antiquity; but unlike the Christian scholars of antiquity the medieval scholastics were not bishops. In other words, the administrative work of the chancery and the deliberative work of theological science now were distinct.

A relatively small portion of the Christian population attended universities, but elementary schooling was widely available. The fourth Lateran Council legislated that every cathedral must hire a teacher of grammar (i.e., basic literacy skills), while archepiscopal sees must also have teachers of philosophy and canon law. Canon 11 of the Fourth Lateran Council required:

> . . . that not only in every cathedral church but also in other churches where means are sufficient, a competent master be appointed by the prelate with his chapter, or elected by the greater and more discerning part of the chapter, who shall instruct *gratis* and to the best of his ability the clerics of those and other churches in the art of grammar and in other branches of knowledge. In addition to a master, let the metropolitan church have also a theologian, who shall instruct the priests and others in the sacred scriptures and in those things especially that pertain to the *cura animarum*. To each master let there be assigned by the chapter the revenue of one benefice, and to the theologian let as much be given by the metropolitan. . . . [27]

By the middle of the thirteenth century every parish was required to have a school, although it is difficult to discover the extent to which this directive was obeyed. In addition to these church-sponsored schools, which were conducted by clerics, the prosperous cities also supported secular schools to provide specialized training for business and industry, and lay people taught in those. Young people of the urban working classes received their vocational training through the apprenticeship system, under guild sponsorship. The medieval guilds were imbued with a religious atmosphere—as was almost everything in that era—and so the craftsperson's socialization into a trade association strengthened his or her affiliation with the church and its practices.

The pontificate of Innocent III (1198–1216), and the Fourth Lateran Council which he convened, represent high points of efficient, effective temporal administration of the church in Europe. The institutions of papacy and ecumenical council provided a centralized authority which promoted the ministry of the word. We have already mentioned two other medieval institutions which first were made possible by the existence of this central authority, and then in their turn helped to strengthen it: the new communities of mendicant friars, and the crusades. On the other hand, institutions which did not tend to enhance the trend toward centralization of authority, such as the beguinages and the local lay associations of charity, gradually were absorbed into other institutions or disappeared altogether.

Methods. Though universities and schools signal the rising prosperity and concomitant literacy of the high middle ages, preaching remained the principal vehicle of the religious formation of the people. Sermons provided more than edification; they must have had some entertainment value as well, for the people heard them not only at liturgical services but on market days, at festivals, at political gatherings, and on street corners. Popular sermons were punctuated with tales of wonders and miracles, and their main theme was moral exortation. People felt free to talk back to the outdoor preacher.

Contemporary legislation shows how important the church considered preaching to be. The Fourth Lateran Council in 1215 decreed:

> Among the things that pertain to the salvation of the people of God, the food of the word of God is above all necessary. . . . It often happens that bishops, on acount of their manifold duties or bodily infirmities, or because of hostile invasions or other reasons, to say nothing of the lack of learning, which must be absolutely condemned in them and is not to be tolerated in the future, are themselves unable to minister the word of God to the people, especially in large and widespread dioceses. Wherefore we decree that bishops provide suitable men, powerful in work

and word, to exercise with fruitful result the office of preaching; who in place of the bishops, since these cannot do it, diligently visiting the people committed to them, may instruct them by word and example.[28]

The Dominicans, who called themselves the Order of Preachers, offered their services to bishops as a band of evangelists who were made to order for this task.

In the parish churches, the Dominicans told stories and exhorted the people to live uprightly. In the universities, however, they and the other friars practiced a much more sophisticated method in their ministry of the word. These scholastics brought human reason into conversation with the traditions of Christian faith. The sources of their teaching were several: the scriptures, ancient Christian writings, contemporary ecclesial experiences and customs, and texts containing the wisdom of Jewish, Islamic, and Hellenistic thinkers. In their teaching, they set up the faith as a compendium of true propositions, with the necessary logical corollaries; and they proceeded to examine these one by one. To present a point of doctrine, a teacher would state the issue, introduce arguments against the orthodox position, then refute them and present arguments in favor of it—drawing from all of the available sources.

This method seemed blasphemous to many in the thirteenth century, even within the universities. For one thing, it quoted pagan authorities like Aristotle, along with Jews and Muslims, in the same breath with the Christian scriptures. Secondly, it subjected scriptural assertions and church doctrines to a systematic examination which, at least rhetorically, set forth grounds on which they might be disproven. Here human reason seemed to be in full partnership with faith in grasping the reality of the divine-human relationship.

At various times, the teachings of Aristotle and of Thomas Aquinas were banned at Paris. Thomas' adaptation of Greek philosophy often has been compared with the adaptation of Marxist philosophy by contemporary liberation theologians, which has lately come under ecclesiastical scrutiny. Yet the schoolmen were careful to distinguish between the matters which could be known through the power of the human intellect, and matters which could be known only through divine revelation. In fact, this distinction was a theme of much of their reflection. The nature of revelation itself seems not to have attracted their critical interest. Interpretation of scripture continued the traditional method of seeking out the allegorical and spiritual meaning of texts. One historian remarks, "Spiritual interpretation also served to keep many brilliant and curious clerical minds from the brink of boredom and possible heresy."[29]

The dialectical method would have yielded the curriculum of a course of lectures, or the format of a formal discussion. The method is also reflected in the structure of Thomas' *Summa theologica*. That work presents 631 questions, with ten thousand pros and cons. It is an organizational marvel.[30]

While alien thought was being welcomed into the Christian universities, Christian missionaries and soldiers were going abroad into alien lands. The crusades ultimately failed in their purpose of gaining political control over Palestine for Europe, but they did stimulate European interest in foreign peoples even beyond the Middle East. Violence proved to be a poor method for evangelizing either heathens or heretics, though the medievals earnestly tried to make it work and the Teutonic Knights did have some success with it among the Slavs. The more benign tactics tried by mission-minded medievals included persuasive argumentation, and studying the language and culture of the non-Christian peoples. Thomas Aquinas sought to present the elements of the gospel message to learned non-Christians in his *Summa contra Gentiles*. The Franciscan tertiary Raymond Lull founded a school for missionaries on the island of Majorca, where they could study Arabic and Chaldean in order to prepare to refute the teachings of Islamic philosophers. Against Islam, these methods had little success. But in the Far East, missionaries were able to establish Christian communities in the thirteenth and fourteenth centuries. There were 30,000 Christians and a cathedral in Beijing in 1328.[31]

Media. Those great literary achievements, the theological *summae*, were media for examination of the faith by a comparative few in their own day, and they transmitted the medieval synthesis to subsequent generations of scholars. Besides those literary masterpieces, thirteenth century Christians also produced architectural masterpieces to express their faith: the gothic cathedrals. Unlike the *summae*, these spoke to the common people and the scholars alike. The cathedral stood in the center of the city, organizing the urban environment around itself. Generations of craftspeople labored to build it and beautify it with designs expressing their belief in the immanence of divine care in human events and in common things.

Within the cathedral, biblical poetry was sung in plainchant. One also heard new liturgical compositions in polyphony. New liturgical sequences and hymns were composed and set to music. The liturgy of the word was embellished and presented in dramatic form, so that eventually the "mystery plays" had to be moved out of doors. These dramas became part of the yearly cycle of festivals which marked out time for the Christian people.

The written word was not yet a common medium of gospel communication. More people were learning to read, but books were still quite expensive. The cost of producing a whole Bible made private ownership almost impossible. It took a year to copy the Bible, and a year's income for a parish priest to buy a copy. Several hundred lambs or sheep had to be killed so that their skins could be made into pages for the book. The hand-lettered tome, when finally complete, would be too massive to carry around anyway. Nevertheless, some people did own copies of the Gospels or the New Testament, in Latin. In the late twelfth century a merchant named Peter Waldo paid some scholars to translate the Bible into the dialect spoken in his southern French town. When he read it, he came to the conclusion that Christians should be poor like Jesus. Waldo embraced evangelical poverty and attracted a following; but his disciples developed a critique of priestly authority that caused Rome to number the Waldensians among heretics running amok in France. Local councils in France then restricted lay ownership of the scriptures.

Content. The gospel had come a long way from the hillsides of Galilee to the lecture halls of Paris. But despite the complexification of the scholastic theological method, the thirteenth century did recapture that ecstatic joyful celebration of intimacy between the Father and Jesus which the first apostles had recounted. The gospel was expressed and heard as a call to unity.

At the interpersonal level, and for the common people, the thirteenth century's gospel was told in stories of the intimate love of the virgin mother for her son, of the savior who died for his brothers and sisters, of the saintly individuals who had walked in their footsteps. People were encouraged to see that in their own everyday world, those footsteps were still there for the following. Daily life and neighborhood were made a part of the big picture of God's plan.

At the institutional level, for religious leaders, the gospel was a call to another kind of intimate unity: the charity of an organization well administered and responsive to the changing needs of a growing and maturing world. The challenge of widespread heterodoxy called forth the institutional responses of conciliar legislation, reform of church teaching and practice, new religious orders following new rules of life, and, tragically, the inquisition. Each of these sought to facilitate the unification of the Christian people.

At the intellectual level, for the scholars, the gospel's call to intimacy was experienced as an impulse to coordinate the diverse activities of reasoning and believing, and to pull together the welter of Christian beliefs into a systematic unified whole. Scholars discerned in Jesus' message a guarantee that truth is one, and their massive works synthesizing secular and sacred knowledge still bear witness to the depth of their trust in that ideal.

As we have seen, the essential unity and interdependence of ecclesial caring, celebrating, and teaching reasserted itself in the thirteenth century. Each of these three activities received an infusion of new life through reintegration with the others. The subsequent course of events would show, however, that this reintegration was too little and too late. Centuries of neglect of the Christian education of the masses meant that the flowers of scholastic theology bloomed beyond the reach of most Christians. Centuries of abuse of church property meant that vested interests were now too strong for the reforming councils and popes to overcome. Therefore, from our vantage point we can see that the thirteenth century's recovery of the integrity of the gospel was only partial. Neither the brand of "heretic," nor the repressive measures of dealing with heresies so branded, helped the church to hear the elements of the gospel that were finding a voice outside official church channels of communication. "Heretics" would continue to address forgotten elements of the gospel to the church.

LEGACY OF THE THIRTEENTH-CENTURY CHURCH

- systematic theology as an academic discipline
- many gothic cathedrals
- friars
- third orders: lay (especially female) affiliates of the friars
- several universities
- the rosary
- the missal
- some Christmas customs
- festival of Corpus Christi
- apostolic communities of women
- "transubstantiation" used to define Eucharist
- the Inquisition
- *summae:* textbooks of systematic theology
- ecclesiastical mandate for parish schools
- enculturation of the gospel in the Far East
- many liturgical compositions: text and plainchant or polyphony

Notes for Chapter Eight

1. Although the hypothesis of a stage change in the modal level of human consciousness cannot be proved, and although it may lead to a de-

ceptively oversimple view of history, nevertheless the hypothesis does bring to light a certain congruence in many of the diverse events and teachings of the thirteenth century to be presented in this chapter. Conventional analysis and synthesis also had been done in antiquity, and may be discerned in the doctrinal disputes leading up to the definitions of the councils of Nicea and Chalcedon. See, for example, Bernard Lonergan's conclusions in *The Way to Nicea: The Dialectical Development of Trinitarian Theology*, translated from the first part of his *De Deo Trino* by Conn O'Donovan (Philadelphia: The Westminster Press, 1976), and especially his remarks on pp. 136–37. Lonergan asserts that the Nicene dogma marks "the transition from the prophetic oracle of Yahweh, the gospel as announced in Galilee, the apostolic preaching and the simple tradition of the church, from all of these to Catholic dogma."

2. For background, see Will Durant's discussions of "The Progress of Industry" and "Money" on pp. 621–30 of *The Age of Faith*, vol. 4 of The Story of Civilization (New York: Simon and Schuster, 1950). This work and the following ones support aspects of the account of the church in the high middle ages to be presented in this chapter: Steven Ozment, *The Age of Reform 1250–1550: An Intellectual and Religious History of Late Medieval and Reformation Europe* (New Haven: Yale University Press, 1980); Joseph McSorley, *An Outline History of the Church by Centuries*, ninth edition (St. Louis: B. Herder Book Company, 1954); David Knowles with Dmitri Obolensky, *The Middle Ages*, vol. 2 of The Christian Centuries (New York: McGraw-Hill Book Co., 1968); Charles Poulet, *A History of the Catholic Church*, translated and adapted by Sidney A. Raemers (St. Louis: B. Herder Book Company, 1946); Bernard Cooke, *Ministry to Word and Sacraments: History and Theology* (Philadelphia: Fortress Press, 1977); Joseph Martos, *Doors to the Sacred* (Garden City, N.Y.: Doubleday and Company, 1981).

3. Steven Ozment suggests that the theologians who used new dialectical method

> may be compared with the new class of money-rich merchants who emerged at this time and also upset tradition because as men of wealth who did not own land, they did not fit into the accustomed social divisions of clergy, nobility, and peasantry. Scholastics equipped with dialectic were to the intellectual history of the Middle Ages what merchants equipped with new business methods were to its social and political history—a seemingly alien body, intruders within traditional medieval society, who both fascinated their conservative critics and challenged previous perceptions and ways of doing things.

See p. 6 of *Age of Reform.*

4. See Ozment's discussion of "The Spiritual Traditions" on pp. 73–134 of *Age of Reform.* For several centuries, the harmonization of devotion and reason often was more an ideal than an actuality. Ozment says on p. 78 that Jean Gerson, who was chancellor of the University of Paris at the turn of the fifteenth century

> once pointed out that just as honey required a honeycomb, devotion needed to be structured by an erudite and orthodox mind. Conversely, the honeycomb needed to be filled: the ideas of the mind must also warm the heart and lead to activity in the world.

5. Yet in the early fourteenth century the Inquisition would brand as heresy the proposition that Jesus and the apostles had no possessions; see Joseph McSorley, *An Outline History,* p. 460.

6. Translation from *Christianity Through the Thirteenth Century,* edited by Marshall W. Baldwin (New York: Walker and Company, 1970), pp. 356–57.

7. Durant, for one, says that women studied at the University of Bologna in the thirteenth century and taught there in the fourteenth. See *Age of Faith,* p. 917.

8. Some historians therefore suggest that the fourteenth century, not the thirteenth, was "the most intellectually fertile period of the Middle Ages and . . . became such because of the difficulties created by the great system builders of the thirteenth century"; see Ozment, *Age of Reform,* pp. 17–9.

9. This branching in cognitive development—with men going toward more complex systems of *theory* and women going toward more complex systems of *care*—corroborates empirical findings recently reported by Carol Gilligan, a developmental psychologist. Gilligan criticizes the developmental schemes of Jean Piaget and Lawrence Kohlberg as reflecting exclusively male experimental populations, so that by their scales most women appear to be "arrested" at a concrete stage. Gilligan finds that women develop maturity in moral reasoning in terms of care rather than principled judgment. See Carol Gilligan, *In a Different Voice: Psychological Theory and Women's Development* (Cambridge, Mass.: Harvard University Press, 1982); and John Michael Murphy and Carol Gilligan, "Moral Development in Late Adolescence and Adulthood: A Critique and Reconstruction of Kohlberg's Theory," *Human Development* 23 (1980), pp. 77–104.

10. Cited on p. 535 of Poulet, *History of the Catholic Church.*

11. McSorley, *Outline History,* p. 379.

12. "Spinster" is a term for a new phenomenon in an industrializing economy: a woman who earned her own living in industry (e.g., by spinning) rather than by marrying and keeping house for a man whose wages would support himself and her. A matron is a married woman. The origin of the name "Beguine" is disputed. Men who followed the way of life developed by the Beguines were called Beghards. A community of Beguines is called a beguinage.

13. Durant remarks, "The wealth of the church, however proportionate to the extent of its functions, was the chief source of heresy in this age." See p. 767 of *Age of Faith*, and the discussion of "The Finances of the Church," pp. 765–68.

14. Pope Innocent III called for a military crusade against the nobles of Southern France, and offered as incentives both plenary indulgences and title to the lands to be conquered. The northern French nobility who answered the pope's call overran the south, and at Beziers they massacred 20,000 men, women, and children. See Durant, *Age of Faith*, pp. 774–75.

15. For an account of the tactics of the Inquisition, see Durant, *Age of Faith*, pp. 780–83. He concludes that "the number of those sentenced to death by the official Inquisition was smaller than historians once believed," and gives representative statistics. For example, "in seventeen years as an inquisitor Bernard Gui condemned 930 heretics, forty-five of them to death." It is not known what percentage of convicted heretics lived out their days imprisoned in solitary confinement. See also McSorley, *Outline History*, pp. 411–14, who asserts that while Pope Innocent IV "insisted that civil leaders must at once enforce the law requiring the death penalty" and authorized the use of torture, nevertheless the popes "were unquestionably active in opposing the general tendency to judge hastily and to punish cruelly." These contrasting statements appear two pages apart in the *ninth revised edition* of McSorley's work, which bears a 1942 imprimatur and was used as a textbook in Catholic colleges in the 1940's and 1950's. It is likely that these mutually contradictory affirmations are evidence of the fact that it remained extremely difficult for the church to tell, teach, and hear the truth about this painful era of the gospel's history.

16. The Dominican friars who worked in the Inquisition were called *domini canes*, Latin for "Lord's dogs."

17. See the translations on pp. 307–13 of Baldwin, *Christianity*.

18. The friars, even the Franciscan friars who had begun as a lay movement, quickly became clericalized. The "second orders," for religious women, were cloistered. See Eleanor Commo McLaughlin, "Equality of Souls, Inequality of Sexes: Woman in Medieval Theology," pp. 213–

66 in *Religion and Sexism: Images of Women in the Jewish and Christian Traditions*, edited by Rosemary Radford Ruether (New York: Simon and Schuster, 1974), especially pp. 241–43.

19. Translation from Durant, *Age of Faith*, p. 965, where the Latin verses also appear.

20. The practice of meditating on fifteen different events in the life of Jesus and Mary while saying the Hail Marys developed later. The use of a form of the Hail Mary as a prayer dates from the twelfth century; but the phrase "pray for us now and at the hour of our death" may have been added during the fourteenth century, when plagues were sweeping across Europe. The prayer received the final form in which it is recited today in the sixteenth century.

21. See Martos' discussion, "From Secular to Ecclesiastical Marriage," on pp. 419–35 of *Doors to the Sacred*.

22. Preoccupation with the gynecological aspect of the doctrine of Mary's virginity detracts attention from an important idea conveyed in the Lukan text. Luke has the angel say, in answer to Mary's question, that God affects human affairs *not* by penetration or intrusion, but rather by a gentle "overshadowing." The Lukan text suggests a shift in metaphors away from a masculine model of divine agency.

23. See Martos, *Doors*, pp. 65–74; and Baldwin, *Christianity*, pp. 207, 209. The medieval theologians could quote Christian writers of antiquity without having a sense that the church of antiquity had sacramental celebrations that were different from their own. For example, Peter Lombard writing on Penance quotes Jerome's dictum that Penance is "the second plank after shipwreck," Baptism being the first. But Lombard misses the central point of Jerome's metaphor: there is not likely to be a *third* plank, and one is very fortunate to have found even a second! In Jerome's church, an individual could be admitted to canonical Penance once or at most twice, but Lombard did not know that. Lombard assumed that the medieval practice of relatively frequent confession was also the way of the ancient church, and he writes that one "is allowed to do penance often, but not to be baptized often." See the text on pp. 209–10 of Baldwin, *Christianity*.

24. This is the thesis of Karl Rahner in "Introductory Observations on Thomas Aquinas' Theology of the Sacraments in General," *Theological Investigations* vol. 14 (New York: Seabury Press, 1976), pp. 149–60. "The relationship between the 'sign' function and the instrumental causality of the sacraments as Thomas presents them," Rahner says on p. 151, "is not fully thought out in its ultimate significance." This problem remained within sacramental theology until our own day.

25. Translation given by Baldwin, *Christianity*, p. 300.

26. Durant says this on p. 770 of *Age of Faith*. See also Knowles's discussion of heresies on pp. 365–75 of *Middle Ages*.

27. Translation given by Baldwin in *Christianity*, p. 305. See also Durant, *Age of Faith*, p. 914, who asserts that parochial schools became common throughout Christendom.

28. Translation given in Baldwin, *Christianity*, pp. 304–05.

29. See Ozment, *Age of Reform*, pp. 66–7.

30. On the method and organization of Thomas' *Summa Theologica*, see Durant, *Age of Faith*, pp. 966–67. Concerning the interminable objections and refutations, Durant comments:

> The method occasionally wastes time by putting up a straw man to beat down; but in many cases the debate is vital and real. It is a mark of Thomas that he states the case against his own view with startling candor and force. . . .

31. See McSorley, *Outline History*, pp. 466–67.

Chapter Nine

Sixteenth Century: Reformations

If the thirteenth century was a flower blooming, the sixteenth was a seed pod cracking open. Cross-pollination of experiences in intellectual, economic, political, and religious life brought vigorous human growth and an exponential increase in knowledge. Consequently, the historical era of the Protestant and Catholic reformations requires of us who seek to understand it greater effort, insight, and compassion than any previous period. In that tortured century, Christianity became self-conscious and self-critical about its transmission of the gospel to an unprecedented degree. To examine it is to examine developments which continue to provide the agenda for the religious reflections of thoughtful women and men in the late twentieth century.

It is correct to speak of *two* concurrent reformations in the sixteenth century, although the emergence of Protestant Christianity customarily is termed "the Reformation" and the Catholic reform movement is called "the Counter-Reformation."[1] The centralized Roman ecclesiastical authority had permitted situations which spurred some churches in Western Europe to separate themselves from it; but it also mounted its own sweeping reforms that eventually eliminated many of the abuses that had sparked the original controversies. Catholic renewal manifested itself in great mystics, missionaries, and educators; in the religions communities which they founded; and in the legislation of the Council of Trent, implemented by a series of reforming popes. Protestant renewal manifested itself in visionaries and the changed lifestyles and patterns of worship which they inspired, as well as in the establishment of new ecclesial societies. Factions on both sides were seeking to safeguard the integrity of the gospel while insuring that institutional structures would remain—or, become—effective means for communicating the message of God's parental care to even God's simplest people.

The reformation era brought home to sincere Christians a sobering, and characteristically modern, realization. The great enemy to be faced in communicating the gospel in Europe henceforth would be neither hostile governments nor invading heathens nor illiteracy nor poor roads nor folk customs, as in earlier times—but other sincere Christians. While the new medium of the printing press brought vastly expanded capacity for teaching, a great portion of its output pitted Christian ideas against other Christian ideas.

Much ink, and much blood, were spilled in the struggles to sort out the divine from the human. In medieval times, it was that very interpenetration of divine and human which had inspired scholars to praise the mysterious wisdom of God while marveling at the tidy hierarchy of beings within which each creature found its place. Now, however, the place of human being itself within that order became problematic. Divine ordinances were progressively unmasked as human institutions. Means were sought to purge these accretions in hopes of restoring the essential, divine structures of the church. Conventional customs and procedures were criticized.

It is the special talent of the critical mind to notice that human subjectivity plays a creative role in building the very systems through which reality engages it. As we have seen in the last two chapters, from the concrete religious understanding of the early middle ages developed conventional ways of thought which were manifested in the systematic theology of the universities and in the organization of new religious orders. Now, in the sixteenth century, conventional thought was in turn giving way to critical, which typically calls into question the systems and organizations achieved by conventional thought. Also characteristic of critical religious understanding is concern over the subjective state of one's own being. Individual conscience assumes new importance over against conventional mores and the morality of the group. Faith is construed as a personal relationship rather than as unquestioned membership in a corporate entity like the church.

New insights like these are unsettling when they first occur in any human life. In the life of the church, they occasioned severe turmoil but led eventually to ways of thinking and teaching that were more adequate to the modern world. This chapter can offer only the briefest summary of some of the developments leading to and coming from the Protestant and Catholic reformations, but this will allow us to carry the thread of the gospel's story through into our own times.

THE SITUATION IN SIXTEENTH-CENTURY EUROPE

The peasants, townsfolk, nobility, nuns, monks, and clergy of Europe were relatively well-off in the year 1500, if one compares conditions at that time with those in the previous two centuries. There had been several generations of steady prosperity, and a consequent increase in numbers and longevity of the population. Nine people out of ten still lived in rural areas, but the towns had begun to grow again. In the fourteenth century, weakened by severe famine, people living in high-density housing such as cities and monasteries had been ravaged by several waves of bubonic plague, spread by flea-bearing rats along the trade routes from the East. For monasteries and universities, the famine and plague years meant disruption of scholarly work. Those institutions ceased to nurture scholars of the caliber of Thomas and Bonaventure to carry on the work of those great medieval teachers. The Hundred Years War between England and France, 1337–1453, disrupted families and sapped resources for five generations. But ecological and social conditions were right for a renewal of prosperity in the sixteenth century.

However, the scars of the plague, famine, and war years were not easily healed. Among the most debilitating was the church's lack of forward-looking clerical leadership to guide its adaptation to a world whose horizons were expanding. Today we use the term "spirituality" to denote a style of life and prayer that orients all one's temporal concerns toward the service of the ultimate value, God. The middle ages had evolved varieties of clerical spiritualities, ranging from that of the settled monasteries to that of the wandering friars. There were also lay spiritualities which proved most viable when coordinated with clerical leadership, as in the "third orders." Other varieties of lay spirituality, as we have seen, became or were adjudged to be heterodox and eventually were suppressed as heresies.

But in the difficult days of the fourteenth and fifteenth centuries the healthy development of lay spirituality was thwarted just at the time when the need of the people for religious consolation was greatest. Clerical advice for lay people who wished to live a perfect life typically urged them to imitate the monks and nuns in their prayer, self-examination, and worldly affairs.[2] The "Devotio Moderna" movement, begun in the mid fourteenth century by a lay man, modeled itself after monastic piety. No vision emerged to show how the everyday life of married women and men might mirror God's love and care for them. In effect, the church neglected the emotional needs of the increasing numbers of people caught up in the complexities of urban commercial affairs. Unconventional manifestations of spirituality, and in particular the writings of mystics, came under a cloud of official suspicion. In the centuries before the Protestant Reformation, there is a continuous record of emergent lay spiritualities which are either suppressed or absorbed into clerical movements.[3]

The late fifteenth century also saw the beginning of the age of world exploration and conquest by European nations. Portugal, Spain, France, England, the Netherlands, and other countries sent merchant ships around Africa and across the Atlantic in quest of a good trade route to the wealth of the East. Christopher Columbus' accidental discovery of a "New World" in 1492 signaled the beginning of the race for European settlement of the two American continents. Other traders would establish European outposts, then colonies, in Africa. As in the years after the barbarian invasions, Christians would encounter peoples of different cultures to whom they must address the gospel.

The new vistas in trade and exploration were complemented by new vistas in understanding of what it means to be a human being. The recovery of classical letters, law, and medicine within medieval universities had made available a world view divergent from the traditional Christian hierarchy of being: a humanistic view in which humanity, not divinity, was the center and criterion of reality. This view proved attractive to men and women engaged in worldly affairs, for whom the church had devised no viable spirituality. It also appealed to monarchs who found themselves enmeshed in power struggles with ecclesiastical officials. Its most vivid manifestation appeared in the fine arts, as a celebration of the perfection of the form of the human body. In artworks, as often in law and philosophy, this humanistic view though deriving from pagan classics could be harmonized with religious sensibility, resulting in a fine emphasis upon the humanity of Jesus as disclosive of the divinity within him. The rationale of this Renaissance, or rebirth of the classical hellenistic veneration of humanity's perfection, is expressed by one scholar as follows:

> Every department of life should be subject to the rational control
> of man; the stress was laid in art on perspective, in statecraft on
> diplomacy, in business on bookkeeping, and in war on strategy.
> . . . Among the areas to be explored were alike the new worlds
> beyond the seas and the learning of classical antiquity.[4]

For the humanist, religion becomes but one of several components of the harmoniously organized personality.

Although religion was expected to fit harmoniously into the humanist personality, it no longer functioned to unify people politically. In the sixteenth century, religious differences became instead both symptom and cause of political division and violence. Over several centuries, the nation states of Europe had been consolidating their power through alliances, wars, and strategic marriages. Despite the centralization of its own power, the papacy had not been able to keep pace with them. With nationalistic sentiment on the rise, changing economic conditions caused the papacy to rely increasingly on cash revenues from the countries of Europe, while monarchs for their part sought to find ways to control the flow of currency out of their jurisdictions. In France the king forbade the export of money to the Vatican, so the papacy relocated for the greater part of the fourteenth century to Avignon, within France, in order to have access to funding. Finance continued to be a great problem for church administration even after the papacy was restored to Rome, and criticism of financial practices provided the proximate cause for Martin Luther's dispute with ecclesiastical authorities which set the Protestant Reformation in motion.

Without the media revolution started by the printing press, however, Luther's protest might have had no more effect than those of scores of idealistic men and women before him who had challenged ecclesiastical abuses. The press, with moveable type, together with the availability of paper in quantity, made it possible to produce books and pamphlets cheaply, quickly, and abundantly as never before. For centuries, professors of theology had been holding their spirited disputations. However, they had been heard only by as many people as could fill a lecture hall, and they had affected only that smaller number who had the skill and stamina to listen to and retain the lines of argument in Latin. Luther and his contemporaries attracted freelance stenographers who turned their words into tracts and quickly circulated them. Luther himself made able use of the new medium both for his polemics and for the dissemination of serious theological works and of the Bible itself, which he translated into German.

This mass medium represented the biggest change in religious communication since the invention of writing itself, when the alphabet first had made it possible for a message to exist apart from a speaker and an audience. Now the press let such messages be distributed to increasing numbers of literate individuals. The new medium made the Bible into a message which anyone might own. This radically affected the balance among the three traditional media of gospel communication: the word ministries, the ministries of care, and the ministries of sacramental celebration.

REFORM IN ALLOCATION OF RESOURCES

Even before the printing press began to revolutionize the communication of the gospel, the three channels of word, care, and celebration already had undergone many modifications since the time of Jesus. We have seen how social conditions in early medieval times hindered the ministry of the word so that celebration, the dimension of the church's sacramental cult, was made to carry the burden of the gospel's transforming action. The social and educational recovery of the twelfth and thirteenth centuries later occasioned an effort to revitalize the word ministries and to renew the church's care for those in need. But that attempt to restore the balance and complementarity among word, care, and celebration was not entirely successful. Care and cult had become seriously confused, and it remained for the sixteenth century reformers to sort out the confusion. The accumulation and mismanagement of wealth by the clergy was at the heart of the problem.

From the very first decades of its existence, the church had received and administered goods for the relief of widows and other needy people. Congregations were fulfilling this duty even before it became customary for a church to erect a building to house its own assemblies, or to sponsor a school for training Christian leaders. Bishops controlled church funds in their role as the overseers of the ministry of care for the poor. With the decline of the Roman Empire, Europe reverted to a feudal agrarian society. Dioceses and monasteries became landowners, since wealth now came only from the soil. But the subsequent revival of trade, the growth of cities, and the development of a class of urban craft workers again brought both a real economic change and a shift in the vision of why the church held property. Bishops came to be regarded as nobility, with a right to the "income" from their dioceses just as secular landowners lived off of the taxes collected on their estates. Monks and common priests came to be regarded as craftsmen, using their sacramental skills to produce spiritual goods for which they were entitled to a just fee.

The ministry of celebration thus was submerged into a kind of commodity market. Prayers and the liturgy were regarded as "good works," (and often substituted for them). At the same time, the human and financial resources that should have gone to the *real* good works of caring for the needy were instead diverted to support a socially useless class of leisured clerics and, more insidiously, were siphoned off to purchase political power through corrupt schemes. Luther's breakthrough vision into the fact that salvation is freely given, "by faith alone," must be understood in this context. The Protestant objection to "works righteousness" expresses two distinct strands of criticism. First, liturgical "works" had crowded out the work of caring service to human need. Second, there was both a thriving market and financial corruption connected with actions and things that were meant to celebrate God's intimate and freely given relationship with humanity. These actions and things ranged from the Mass to relics to indulgences to the income-producing real estate of monasteries and cathedrals.

For centuries before the sixteenth, as we have seen, pious lay men and women as well as clerics repeatedly had called for reform in the administration of church wealth. The ideal of Christian poverty sometimes had been condemned as heresy, and other times became enshrined in the lifestyles of saints and the religious orders which they founded. But the issue itself refused to die, and economic developments in the fifteenth and sixteenth centuries brought it to the fore once again. The revival of trade and the growth of cities with their craft workers encouraged the displacement of the barter system with a money economy. Population growth during the sixteenth century brought steady inflation. To gain more currency, in many places the landed classes increased taxes on their estates, revived old varieties of taxation that had fallen into disuse hundreds of years since, or set their sights upon the revenues of ecclesiastical lands. Peasants, the people on the land, were caught in a crunch, with more mouths to feed and higher rents to pay.

Under these conditions, a whiff of the Protestant teachings on freedom was enough to set in motion a movement among peasants to demand economic reforms. The rights they sought included permission to cut firewood, the return of common fields expropriated by nobles, and free access to fish and game. In 1525 the peasants armed themselves and began a revolt, and as many as 100,000 were slaughtered when the revolt was crushed by both Protestant and Catholic nobility.[5] The support of the theological theorists upon which the people had counted never came. This is for us as telling a sign as any of the extent to which Christianity had lost its ability to communicate the message of God's parental love through its care for human need.

The abuse of material goods was a problem which the young Protestant churches were largely spared, inasmuch as they had so few of them. In fact, the decision to sever oneself from the Roman ecclesiastical structure usually meant a sharp decrease in one's standard of living, especially for clerics who took on the added responsibilities of supporting families. Luther was bitterly disappointed to find that towns were unwilling to provide financial support for clerics and their families even after the church properties which previously had supported the clerics were taken over by municipal officials. For Catholicism, the Council of Trent, meeting intermittently from 1545 through 1563, legislated reforms to reduce corrupt financial practices. These reforms were put into effect by a series of reforming popes in the latter half of the sixteenth and early seventeenth centuries.

But a genuine revival of the ministry of care could not be legislated. The Catholic reformation was driven by charismatic individuals like Ignatius of Loyola, Teresa of Avila, and many others who founded or revived religious orders and other kinds of pious associations. These communities engaged in traditional works of charity and, as the cities grew and social conditions changed, devised innovative responses to the needs of God's people. At both the institutional and the personal level, the church was recovering its ability to see Christ in the least of his sisters and brothers. The saintly young Jesuit Aloysius Gonzaga was one of many who died of the plague after nursing sick people during an epidemic. Reforming bishops, too, allocated resources for the care of the poor in their dioceses. Of Bishop Charles Borromeo of Milan it has been written that he:

> sought to relieve the poor, provided advocates to help them in their lawsuits, set himself against usury, established homes for beggars, worked for conciliation in labor disputes, and in a great epidemic reduced his own table, sold his plate to aid in the relief of the sufferers, and had his tapestries made into clothing for the destitute.[6]

Among the communities founded in the sixteenth century which were active in caring for human needs were the Somaschi, the Brothers Hospitallers of St. John of God, the Capuchins, and the Jesuits. The wave of reform continued in France into the seventeenth century with the founding of the Institute of the Visitation, originally intended for women who would do social work in the homes of the poor, and the Daughters of Charity, women from the countryside who nursed and cared for people in the poorest neighborhoods of Paris.[7] These new forms of religious life dissolved the traditional boundaries between cloister and world. Many worked in partnership with diocesan clergy and with lay associations.

Lay sponsorship of charitable institutions continued a trend already evident in the fourteenth century, when the Council of Vienne had provided that competent lay people be appointed to direct hospitals and hospices, answering directly to the bishop. As city governments became stronger in the sixteenth century, often they took over the administration of the hospitals, which were transformed from ecclesiastical to municipal institutions.

It was religious men, however, who carried the ministry of care overseas. Some of the new men's communities, like the Jesuits, and some of the older orders of the church, like the Franciscans, sent representatives to accompany the European explorers who traveled to the Americas and to the Far East. Their work of evangelization in those exotic places included caring for the hungers and hurts of the people whom they met there. Francis Xavier, the Jesuit "Apostle of the Indies," is remembered as a great preacher, but he also personally took care of the sick and prisoners. Franciscan missionaries in the American Southwest built settlements modeled after the monastic establishments that had civilized barbarian Europe in early medieval times. Feudal in character, these missions nevertheless provided the Indians with health care, agricultural

training, and protection from enemy bands and from whites who sought
to exploit them.

Enthusiasm for mission work has remained a characteristic of Christianity from the time of the sixteenth century reformations until our own
day, with Protestants also joining in as Protestant nations became active
in world exploration and conquest. Missionaries have found that care is
one language that is always effective for evangelization, because it is
understood everywhere in the world.

CRYING FOR INTIMACY WITH GOD

While abuses within the church's caring ministries undoubtedly were
great, it is the cultic or sacramental ministries which underwent the most
tragic distortions of all. Sacramental celebration stems from Jesus' own experience of intimacy with God, his "Abba," and from his personal stance
of welcoming all people into that relationship as God's daughters and sons.
To be so welcomed is cause for surprise, joy, and gratitude. There were
no preconditions set in Jesus' invitation to enjoy the Abba relationship
with God—unless we regard as conditions the necessity of desiring the
relationship enough to abandon whatever might hinder it, and the necessity of accepting the invitation from and through the one who made it, Jesus.

It was in regard to the latter condition, paradoxically, that distortions
began to grow. Jesus is the one through whom relationship with God as
Abba is opened to everyone else. Before his death Jesus was personally
available; but the Resurrection changes his availability to a "presence in
absence," a presence in the Holy Spirit in the church. The church becomes the place where the invitation to be God's sons and daughters is
made and accepted. But the church also is an institution, even a bureaucracy. We have seen how aspects of the church came to be understood and
modeled after contemporary social institutions; for example, with bishops
acting like nobility, and monasteries changing hands like feudal estates.
The sacramental cult itself came to be regarded as the church's possession
rather than God's gift of Jesus' continuing availability. "Grace," or the free
gift of relationship with God, seemed to be a kind of currency, with the
church as its treasury. Clergy could write checks against the fund of grace,
as it were. The checks were the sacraments, along with other things and
actions called sacramentals.

To the concrete understanding of simple believers, the comparison of
grace to money deposited in an infinite treasury might actually prove to
be a good way of explaining how the possibility of relationship with God

is reliably opened through the church and particularly through participation in its sacramental worship. The explanation is a good one as long as emphasis is placed upon the dependability of the relationship and the free generosity with which it is given. However, the money-market model of sacramental efficacy was interpreted in a different way by some whose main concern was not to assist the understanding of the simple people, but to secure political and economic power. Ecclesiastical bureaucrats viewed themselves as bankers of God's grace, with the means to hold it back or to trade it for other commodities. The sacramental system had become the basis for a power structure and a caste system within the church.

The sale of indulgences was big business, requiring the services of multinational financial firms to handle the huge flow of cash. These banking houses took their cut of the profits as well. Complicated deals were devised when, for example, Rome wished to sell a bishopric in a large city with all its income-producing properties—what today we might call a "franchise." To help the buyer come up with the purchase price, Rome would also authorize him to sell a particular kind of indulgence—something like a bond issue. That would enable the prospective bishop to borrow the purchase price from a banking house, with assurance that he could repay through the future income from the indulgence sale.

Such arrangements hurt the common people in three ways, at least. The prospect of sure remission of punishment for sin coaxed money out of the pockets of those who could least afford it. The wheeling and dealing with grace scandalized and disillusioned the middle classes who understood something of what was going on. And everyone suffered from the lack of bishops who were truly pastors among the people, rather than successful entrepreneurs. It was just such a situation that prompted Martin Luther's campaign of reform.

Related to this economic use of sacramental power was a more overtly political one, the refusal of the sacraments to a secular leader who persisted in policies annoying to bishop or pope. But the attempt to punish through interdict, excommunication, or inquisition had lost much of its effectiveness by the sixteenth century. Sometimes these measures backfired and fueled nationalistic opposition to central church authority.

The abuses opened up both doctrinal and pastoral questions. They spurred a critical examination of whether sacraments, as ritual actions, really had it in themselves to "save," to "deliver grace," or to begin or strengthen relationship with God. The Council of Trent held for sacramental realism, and embraced the term "transubstantiation" as a description of what happened to the material elements in the Eucharist.

But the pastoral issues perhaps cut more deeply. At the opening of the sixteenth century, it was not uncommon to find that even the most pious people felt desperation and despair over the possibility of having a relationship with God. Fear about "saving one's soul" and anxiety to avoid hell were characteristic of the spirituality of the day. It was the sacrament of Penance, rather than the Eucharist, which afforded people some subjective sense of relief. Many who entered monasteries did so not to celebrate God's saving word, but to assure for themselves a good death through a life of penitential practices. As a pastoral response to this state of mind, the church emphasized that one could indeed find assurance of forgiveness in sacraments properly celebrated. Yet the "automatic" grace of the sacraments seemed paltry indeed when indulgences, too, were said to bring remission of punishment automatically, upon payment of money and/or accomplishment of some ritual. Underneath the doctrinal disputes which come down to us in the history books, we must perceive human hearts longing for some subjective experience of acceptance as God's sons and daughters, over and above mere juridical assurance that such acceptance was indeed an objective fact.

Protestant Christianity answered this need with its joyful rediscovery of the ancient truth that faith saves and faith is God's free gift. This insight would lead to the eventual revisioning of what worship and the sacraments themselves might mean in the churches that are heirs to the Protestant Reformation. Within both Protestantism and Catholicism, mystics opened up a wellspring of spirituality that was practical and psychological in its insight into how to live a religiously rewarding life. The mystics, both Protestant and Catholic, shared an optimism about the value of the human that was as much the legacy of Erasmus and humanism as it was the legacy of the New Testament. But the Catholic mystics generally found viable channels for their devotion and zeal within the established religious communities and within the sacramental system of the church. Both the rediscovery of the sufficiency of faith, and the surge of mystical experience and vision within Protestant and Catholic communities, signal a turn from external forms to internal feeling, from the objective to the subjective, and, in many instances, from conventional to critical understanding.

Yet popular devotions thrived as well. Those which stressed some doctrine challenged by Protestants—for example, the Eucharistic devotions like the Corpus Christi processions—were particularly encouraged by the Roman Church. The Forty Hours Prayer was introduced in Milan by Charles Borromeo in 1577. Gradually, churches began to keep the Blessed Sacrament in a tabernacle placed prominently upon the altar instead of in a simple receptacle to the side. Marian devotions increased as well, and the Rosary took on its modern form.

By contrast, sacramental celebration was foundering. Confirmation and the Anointing of the Sick had ceased altogether in many dioceses.[8] The sacramental life of the common people in Europe at the opening of the sixteenth century centered around Penance rather than the weekly celebration of Mass. At Mass, most people felt like spectators, for the language was unintelligible. Lay men and women received communion once a year, or, if members of pious confraternities, three or four times annually. At Penance, however, each person could understand what was going on and enjoyed the individual attention of the priest. This focus on Penance led to the development of a particular kind of catechesis: moral catechesis aimed at a proper examination of conscience and the elimination of faults. Materials printed to facilitate this kind of teaching became the precursors of the catechism. By the beginning of the seventeenth century, the focus on penance led to an architectural innovation in Catholic Europe, the three-part stationary confessional.

Liturgical innovations of a different sort characterized the young churches of the Far East. Portuguese missionaries like Matteo Ricci studied the culture and the philosophy of the highly civilized Chinese people whom they had been sent to evangelize in the late sixteenth century. They concluded that Confucian rituals of honoring forebears were not incompatible with Christian worship of one God. Indigenous Chinese practices and language therefore were tolerated and even incorporated into the prayers of the new Christians. The Chinese church numbered 38,200 in 1636. But by then, Spanish missionaries also had come on the scene and were denouncing the Chinese liturgy as tainted with paganism and ancestor worship. Eventually the Latin form of the liturgy was imposed on China.

TECHNOLOGICAL AND GEOGRAPHICAL EXPLOSIONS OF THE WORD

The sixteenth century is the era of the church's rediscovery of the Bible. Reform within the ministries of care and celebration cleared the way for reform of the ministry of the word, while advances in technology and world trade opened the possibility of carrying God's word into every home in Europe and into many far-off countries as well. The printing press and a prosperous domestic economy provided generally favorable conditions for lively scholarly discussion. This was the classic era for Protestant theological writings. On the Catholic side, this was the age of the Council of Trent, the council which produced a doctrinal synthesis clearly demarcating Rome's differences with the Protestant Reformers and setting the agenda for the next four centuries of theological discussion within Catholicism.

One can hardly overestimate the impact of print technology, and of the medium of the mass-produced book which it spawned. The peculiar characteristics of the medium of the printed book do not all result directly from the technology of printing itself; and certainly the sixteenth-century form of this medium was different from its modern-day counterpart. For example, there were no copyrights, and authors had no editorial control over the printing of their works. Ideas circulated much more rapidly than ever before, and did so in a form necessarily detached from their source and context. This tended to polarize issues and precipitate hasty reactions, inasmuch as the people had had no time to acquire the sort of media sophistication which we take for granted.

Nevertheless, the very existence of the technology itself precipitated a change in the meaning of the term, "word of God." God's word came to be equated with a book which one could own, transport, and read at one's own convenience. Before the printing press, to get such easy access to God's word one would have had to join a monastery where the scriptures were read aloud several times a day. For the first time, it now became possible for an ordinary person to own a copy of the Bible. There had been a hundred printings of the Vulgate by 1500, but demand was growing for vernacular versions which the owners might easily understand. Between 1461 and 1522, fourteen High German and four Low German complete translations of the Bible were printed. Luther himself translated the Bible, and his work helped to shape the German language into its modern-day form.

Even before this media explosion got underway in Europe, world exploration was altering the political and economic realities of the globe. European nations along the Atlantic coast, geographically disadvantaged in overland trade with the East, sought access to Oriental markets and materials by sea. Voyages of exploration by Portugal, Spain, France, England, and the Netherlands resulted in Europe's discovery of the continents of North and South America along with sub-Saharan Africa and many islands. Where merchants saw new markets, and monarchs saw new realms, Christian leaders saw populations who needed to hear the message of Jesus. As is well known, the Europeans did not manage to keep these visions distinct. Priests accompanied conquistadores, and missionary intentions were espoused to cloak the ambition for political and economic empires.

Perhaps by historical accident, the nations most successful in exploration and conquest of these newly discovered worlds happened to be Catholic nations. The form of Christian faith which they propagated was Roman Catholicism. Moreover, these were nations which still could mobilize religious orders for missionary work: both medieval orders like the

Franciscans, and more recently founded orders like the Jesuits. Women and lay men did not join the Catholic missionary campaign until later. Over vast areas of the globe, therefore, the prevalent style of Christianity today is both Roman Catholic and clerical—and, to some extent, also medieval. This fact is crucial to understanding the religious heritage of South and Central America, Mexico and the Southwestern portion of the United States, along with parts of Canada and the North Central United States formerly settled as New France.

(By contrast, the Christianity of the dominant English-speaking component of the U.S. population was not rooted in missionary work at all, but was transplanted to America by colonials. Onto it were grafted other immigrant varieties as each generation brought its distinctive mix of new settlers. The task of incorporating them into the dominant culture and its religiosity was viewed as an educational one, not an evangelistic one.)

Where missionary Catholic Christianity encountered older cultures and complex political situations, however, it failed to build lasting churches. There is little trace today of the labors of the Jesuits in China and Japan, although in their day their accomplishments were impressive. Nevertheless, this outreach abroad served to revitalize the church's zeal for its teaching ministry at home. The Jesuits and many other communities formulated policies to provide for the education of their own members and, increasingly, lay men and women for a world that now called itself modern. The Protestants, too, gave high priority to the education of common people in their programs of reform.

This educational renewal took shape in a polemical atmosphere in the wake of the Council of Trent, which reformed the Catholic Church and compiled new doctrinal definitions to answer the Protestant challenges. The shadow of that council falls across subsequent developments in the ministry of the word: its personnel, institutions, methods, media, and content.

Personnel. Lay people, in their roles of parents and godparents, bore the greatest responsibility for the education of European Christians in the sixteenth century. The Fathers of the Council of Trent first learned the mysteries of faith at their mothers' knees, and religious visionaries like Luther and Xavier also owed their first religious instruction to their parents. Because of their crucial importance to the church's teaching ministry, parents had to be equipped with knowledge and the tools to teach their children. The foundation of the Confraternity of Christian Doctrine in 1536 provided a new means for lay people to conduct more formal religious education for youth. Although the Council of Trent would legislate Sunday instruction for children, ordinarily the clergy did not directly catechize youth but sought instead to form parents as teachers.

Parish priests fulfilled their responsibility for teaching parents particularly through liturgical homilies and catechetical lectures. Priests of the established religious orders, and of new orders like the Jesuits, augmented what the parish clergy were able to accomplish. The Council of Trent inaugurated reforms designed to rehabilitate parish clergy, particularly through seminary education. The Protestant Reformers also sought to equip both clerics and parents for effective religious training of the rising generations.

But in the American and Asian missions, lay people played a different role. The first European explorers of these regions were lay men who were after adventure and economic and political gains, though most were not enemies of the church. They transported the missionaries and sometimes financed them; they introduced them to indigenous leaders, customs, languages, and geography. However, the evangelization and catechesis of American and Asian peoples was undertaken not by laymen but by the friars and by priests and brothers of new religious foundations. In 1534 Ignatius Loyola organized the Jesuits, who were to make great educational contributions both on the missions and in Europe. Early in the sixteenth century, both third-order sisters and cloistered Franciscan women came to Mexico.[9] Records indicate that some religious women were sent to teach Indian girls. But Tridentine reforms inhibited the educational work of nuns by cloistering them more strictly. However, in the seventeenth century women's communities like the Ursulines and the Visitandines undertook to educate girls in Europe, and eventually in mission territories as well. The first Ursulines came to Canada in 1639. By the late seventeenth century, the young churches of the Americas gave rise to their own indigenous communities of teaching sisters. Marguerite Bourgeoys founded the Congregation of Notre Dame in Montreal in 1670.[10]

As the new churches matured, lay men and women rose in them to undertake the ministry of catechesis. African and Asian men were also ordained to the priesthood in the sixteenth century, but ecclesiastical policy prevented the development of a native clergy in the Americas. In 1555, at the First Council of Mexico, the European clergy barred Indians, mestizos, and mulattoes from the priesthood. This ruling remained in force until the seventeenth century, and it continued to affect attitudes and ecclesial identity thereafter.

Institutions. The sixteenth century contributed four new institutional forms to the ministry of the word: the Confraternity of Christian Doctrine, the missionary village, the theological seminary, and the teaching order. Traditional institutions which continued to develop included the preaching orders, the university, and the college or boarding school, while in comparison the monasteries faded in importance.

The Confraternity of Christian Doctrine, or CCD, had its beginnings in Milan in 1536, when lay men and women gathered under the direction of a parish priest to organize "schools of Christian doctrine for children, youth, and unlettered adults."[11] It is said that Milan, like many of the European cities, had a tradition of lay catechesis, and the organization of the "Company of Christian Doctrine" was not untypical of the period. What gave the Milan schools their place in history was the fact that Charles Borromeo became Cardinal Archbishop of Milan in 1565 and wrote a guide for them entitled *A Constitution and Rules of the Confraternity and School of Christian Doctrine*. Its principles of pedagogy, formation, and organization became enormously influential.

By 1584, when Borromeo died, there were 3,000 teachers and administrators in his archdiocese's Confraternity, with 40,000 children and adults enrolled as students. Several Milanese catechists went to Rome to establish the CCD there in 1560, and shortly afterwards Pope Pius V recommended its worldwide establishment. That was easier said than done, and the CCD saw both fruitful years and lean over the next four centuries.

The situation in the missionary territories of the Americas presented quite different challenges to the ministry of the word. The Indian peoples whom the Spanish and Portuguese explorers encountered had a variety of styles of life—as, indeed, did the Europeans themselves. The Franciscans in Mexico, including territory later taken into the southwestern United States, set up missions which resembled feudal estates. They sought to keep migratory peoples in one place in order to evangelize them. The fact that each mission was staffed not just by priests but also by European soldiers speaks to the question whether the Indians welcomed the change to a sedentary lifestyle. Under Spanish law, such a settlement might be an *encomienda:* a royal feif given to European colonists along with rights to exploit the labor of the people living on the land. Further north, in Texas and along the California coast, the missions seem to have had more the character of nonprofit undertakings. The missions became self-supporting and completely transformed the economic and social structure of the region.[12] It is said that by 1600 Mexico had become a Catholic country and "the stage of direct missionary work was over."[13]

Another noteworthy form of missionary organization was the so-called Jesuit Reductions of Paraguay of the seventeenth century, in which the Fathers "reduced" wandering peoples to sedentary villages completely segregated and protected from European colonists who had previously exploited them. This form of evangelization succeeded in regions where others had failed. From its beginning in 1610, the Christian Indian state had grown by 1641 to thirty reductions with 150,000 Indian Christians.[14] Although removed from the scandalous influences of the morally corrupt soldiers and settlers of the sort that constantly brought setbacks to the Francscan missions, the Indians of the reductions had to arm themselves against repeated raids by Brazilian slave traders.

After and even during the period of evangelization, the young churches of the Americas began to provide secondary education in the form of trade schools and preparatory schools, under the sponsorship of bishops and of the missionary orders. The bishop of Mexico City began a college there in 1536. Several European religious orders of men and of women stemming from the sixteenth and seventeenth centuries either were founded for, or soon embraced, the work of education. These included the Barnabites (1530), the Somaschi (1532), the Jesuits (1534), the Ursulines (1535), the Visitandines (1610), the Daughters of Charity (1633), and the Christian Brothers (1680).

Other religious orders labored to educate and to reform the diocesan priesthood. The Congregation of the Oratory (1575) and the Congregation of the Mission (1625), among others, worked to establish the diocesan and regional seminaries mandated for clerical education by the Council of Trent. In addition, secondary schools were set up expressly to prepare boys for studies at the new theological seminaries. Also influential in the religious formation of both laity and priests was the Oratory movement. Members of religious societies called Oratories sought mutual support in their pursuit of authentically Christian lay spirituality. Their ideas led in turn to the foundation or the reform of several male religious orders.

Methods. The procedures for evangelization and religious instruction devised in the sixteenth century cover a very broad spectrum. The formal protocols of the Jesuits and of Melanchthon were adapted to organized classroom settings. Practical techniques evolved in European parishes to implement the new media of the catechisms, and CCD programs burgeoned; while overseas, contact with diverse political and cultural situations led to developments as different as the American mission system and the cultural syntheses of the Far East.

In parishes on the continent of Europe, lay people received continuing formation in faith through Sunday homilies by their own parish clergy, as they had done since time immemorial. The exhortations of the Protestant Reform leaders and Tridentine legislation alike promoted frequent catechetical homilies. In addition, visiting preachers who were members of religious orders might deliver apologetical or revivalistic sermons. Some of these eloquently moved the people to a renewal of their faith; others failed through excessive bombast.

As printing made it possible to produce and distribute small summaries of Christian belief, both Protestants and Catholics developed instructional methods based on these little books. The loose pages of the catechism were posted in churches and other institutions. As literacy was on the rise, people who saw them there could read and memorize their simple moral advice, doctrinal formulations, and prayers. The catechisms went through many printings and became widely available to parents, who were supposed to use the booklets to instruct their households after the evening meal. Luther advised that a lesson be taught always in the same words so that it might be more easily remembered. Larger, more complex catechisms served as reference works for teachers and preachers.

Borromeo's *Constitution* for the CCD in Milan reflects the method of instruction developed there. Teachers were advised to take the abilities and personal differences of their students into account. One writer has summarized the document's provisions in this way:

> Classes in the schools of Christian doctrine , . . were not permitted to exceed eight or ten participants. Each session was forty-five minutes in length; then followed what was called a *disputa* or quiz-discussion for the same length of time. It consisted of a kind of public debate by the students; since the structure was flexible, students carried on their own discussions. Common prayers led by the pupils brought the session to a close.[15]

CCD teachers were carefully selected not only for their knowledge, but also for attitudes and temperament supportive of such a learner-centered method of instruction. About 150 years after Borromeo wrote the CCD Constitution, Jean Baptiste de la Salle set forth instructions for the interaction between teachers and pupils in the formal classroom setting in "The Conduct of the Christian Schools."[16] It is informative to compare the two. No such event as a "public debate by the students" is envisioned by la Salle.

Missionary catechesis presents quite a diverse picture in the sixteenth century. There are many instances of the gospel's becoming acculturated to the ways of native peoples; but there are other cases in which the people were made to conform to European ways. The work of learning native languages and translating the gospel was the first task facing missionaries. Francis Xavier sought to use Japanese Buddhist religious terminology in his first attempt at a Japanese catechism; later, however, some of this vocabulary was replaced by Latin terms. Catechisms also were written in American Indian languages.

The enforced settlement of American Indian peoples into mission villages involved both persuasive speech and coercion. Having recently completed a successful military campaign to unseat the Muslim administration of the Iberian peninsula, the Spanish saw no contradiction between the gospel and war. One historian writes: "From its mission mandate Spain deduced the right of conquest and annexation. The *conquista* became a war against paganism, as the *reconquista* had been a war against Islam— it was waged for the faith."[17] The friar missionaries generally had benevolent intentions toward the peoples whom they, with soldiers' help, settled into villages. They taught these hunter-gatherer tribes the skills of agriculture and the trades. They taught the people the arts of European music, painting, and architecture. They also taught, by word and deed, that the people's traditional way of life was not a worthy vessel of the gospel.

The missionaries sought to protect the Indians from the worse forms of exploitation by European colonists. However, the missionaries worked so closely with the conquering military administrators that it is difficult to discern today the extent of their complicity in the cultural annihilation of the Indian peoples. A revisioning of early American Christian history according to late twentieth-century insights produces a more critical verdict upon the missionaries' efforts than was common even a generation ago. If we had as many written records and cultural traces of the evangelization of Celtic, Germanic, and Slavic tribal peoples in the seventh through eleventh centuries as we have for the native Americans of the sixteenth century, we could determine the extent to which Mediterranean Christians used similar methods in both cases. Certainly the inculcation of a settled agricultural lifestyle, whether through monastery or through mission, was used both with the "barbarians" and with the "savages."

In the Far East, military conquest was not an option for the European Christians. China was a strong empire while Japan, though not politically unified, was governed by powerful local princes. Francis Xavier adapted his evangelization efforts to the Japanese taste for pomp and ceremonial, and he advised missionaries to learn the rules of Japanese etiquette. People of the lower social classes first were touched by Christianity; the nobility followed later. In China, Matteo Ricci adopted the lifestyle and clothing of a scholar after he failed to attract a following when attired as a Buddhist monk. It must be said that Ricci deserved the respect due a scholar, for he authored several important philosophical and theological works. Missionaries in the Americas, too, contributed numerous scholarly works that help us to understand both the native cultures which they destroyed and the new Christian culture which they helped to establish.

In Europe, the Protestant and Catholic reform movements produced educational innovations that deeply affected the ministry of the word. Luther believed that education was primarily the responsibility of the state. He called upon the towns to establish schools for boys and girls, and he endorsed language study as essential to learning the scriptures. However,

Melanchthon's formal proposal for primary schools in Saxony envisioned instruction in Latin, not German, and there was no mention of Hebrew or Greek. In Melanchthon's curriculum there were three stages of instruction: primary training in reading and writing, then instruction in grammar, and finally training in compositional skills including prosody, dialectics, and rhetoric. Only one day a week, either Wednesday or Saturday, was to be given to "Christian instruction," which was to include prayers, articles of faith, the commandments, some psalms, and Matthew's Gospel. "Difficult" books like John's Gospel and Romans were left for older youth.[18]

This plan was intended for town children. There was also provision for the religious instruction of rural youth on Sunday afternoon, after they had come into town for the morning services. Luther, like many conscientious order priests, long had preached catechetical sermons. Thanks to the voracious printing press, some of these were recorded and have come down to us. Material developed for popular preaching seems to have been the basis of much of what Luther included in his catechisms.

In the Catholic world, the Jesuits also devised a formal plan of studies for youth in their schools. When it was implemented in 1599, the *Ratio Studiorum* emphasized mastery of written and spoken Latin and some Greek, to be followed by philosophical and then theological studies. Pupils were motivated by competitions, by example, and by the opportunity to present recitations and dramas to their parents and to the community at large. One historian writes that "the 372 colleges which the Society maintained in 1616 were training an ecclesiastical and secular elite which shaped church and world more effectively than any other factor."[19]

Other orders and Catholic lay movements of the late sixteenth and seventeenth centuries evolved their own distinctive methods for teaching not only the elite, but all classes of Catholic children and adults. Where both Melanchthon's plan and the *Ratio Studiorum* called for instruction in Latin, later methods turned to the vernacular, and stressed also personal contact, understanding, and affection between teacher and learner. Jean Baptiste de la Salle founded a teacher-training college in 1684 and "developed an educational method which earned him the title of 'father of modern pedagogy.' "

Media. Two technological advances of the fifteenth century drastically altered the "media mix" through which the gospel could be communicated. Movable metal type, along with a process for cheaply manufacturing paper, transformed the book from a handcrafted treasure into a mass-produced commodity. Ideas and information could spread more quickly and more widely than ever before in human history. One scholar estimates that by the end of the fifteenth century, "six million books had been printed and half of the thirty thousand titles were on religious subjects."[20] It became physically impossible to censor vernacular Bibles or other works disturbing to ecclesiastical authority. As we have seen, the prolific printing industry magnified the religious controversies of the sixteenth century.

Yet oral communication of the gospel message remained important. Sermons continued to provide the principal means for the religious formation of townspeople and agricultural workers in Europe, and the peoples of Asia, Africa, and the Americas to whom the Catholic missionaries preached. The liturgy continued to tell the mystery of what God had done in Jesus. Luther's revision of the Eucharistic liturgy, known as the German Mass, was designed to give instruction by representing the events of scriptural history. Luther and many others composed hymns which gave memorable poetic expression to faith and which formed devout believers as they worshiped. A new genre of musical composition developed to meet the needs of the Oratories, which gathered for prayer, informal lectures, and sacred music. The "oratorio" evolved as a meditation upon a scriptural scene, set to music.

Deeds and written words came together in a new kind of synthesis in the Modern Devotion of the late fourteenth and fifteenth centuries, a movement of lay spirituality propagated by the Brothers and Sisters of the Common Life. They revived ideals of simplicity, charity, and poverty, and emphasized uncomplicated piety over institutional forms. While the Brothers and Sisters wrote popular religious tracts, they were perhaps more influential through their charitable care for students and others whom they housed, and through their example to the established religious orders in need of reform.[21]

Of printed media, two genres which came into their own in the sixteenth century deserve attention: the catechism, and the vernacular Bible. Both of these were produced by scholars for the use and benefit of the common people. Luther advocated language study for both the clergy and educated lay people. He is quoted as saying that "languages are the scabbard in which the word of God is sheathed"[22] and "they are the chest in which this jewel is carried."[23] But, in Europe at least, it proved impractical to educate the masses in the biblical languages, and so scripture was translated into people's common tongues. In the missions, the task was enormous, especially in the Americas where many of the dialects had no written form. The missionary confrontation between European and Indian cultures was also a confrontation between literate and oral modes of communication. The Europeans viewed literacy training as a great help to the Christianization of the Indians, if not absolutely necessary for it. Some also viewed European languages themselves as essential to the gospel. This prejudice is apparent in the view that it proved very difficult to teach the tenets of the Christian faith in native tongues. Since the pagans lacked the concepts of the faith, there were naturally no terms in their languages in which the missionaries could clothe those concepts. Further obstacles in some areas were the numerous dialects which made it impossible for the missionary to learn all the tongues. These circumstances brought it about that the Spanish language was commonly used, especially in instructing children.[24]

The American experience indicates that missionaries alone can never successfully translate the gospel to a culture that is foreign to them. The enculturated gospel must rise from the experience of the evangelized people themselves.

Efforts to translate the Bible into European and then into Asian and American languages helped to spur philological studies of the sacred texts already set in motion by the intellectual currents of the Renaissance and humanism. To facilitate this careful study, a Parisian scholar named Robert Estienne introduced the verse arrangement that is familiar to us in a 1551 edition of the Greek New Testament. The numbering of the verses made textual comparison easier, and gave teachers and writers easier access to the texts as well.

The catechism was not invented outright, but evolved from earlier instructional pamphlets and booklets from the early fourteenth century onward. Noteworthy among the predecessors of the catechism was Dietrich Kolde's *A Fruitful Mirror or Small Handbook for Christians*, first printed in 1470. It explains the articles of faith and goes into great detail concerning the Decalogue, sins and vices to be avoided, and virtues and pious practices to be cultivated. This format was useful in preparing for the sacrament of Penance, which was the focus of fifteenth-century religious instruction. Later, the question-and-answer format was adopted in works like Baltasar Hubmaier's *A Christian Catechism*, printed in 1527.[25] In 1529 Luther published his *Small Catechism* for uneducated people in dialogue format, along with a *Large Catechism* for the clergy, which is noteworthy for making practical applications for the rural lifestyle of the peasants.

The *Roman Catechism*, drawn up by mandate of the Council of Trent and published in 1566, was not itself an instructional tool but rather a summary of doctrine for the use of pastors. Catholic popular catechisms, like those of Canisius and Bellarmine, were influenced less by the *Roman Catechism* than by the established conventions of the catechism genre.

Printing, the technology which caused catechisms to proliferate in the hands of ordinary believers, also made possible the growth of libraries, theological and otherwise. For the first time, sustained systematic theological research became possible on a very wide scale. The flood of books and tracts put unsettling ideas into circulation, and the Roman church authorities sought to combat or control these in a concrete way. In the mid sixteenth century the Spanish Inquisition adopted a list of forbidden books, and in 1559 the first Papal Index of Forbidden Books was published. As one historian notes,

> In addition to the writings of the Reformers, all the works of Erasmus, whatever their content, were forbidden; all works on occult sciences . . . all publications issued in the preceding forty years without the name of the author or publisher, and finally, regardless of content, all products of sixty-one printers specified by name, fourteen of whom were from Basel alone. The great majority of editions of the Bible and of the Fathers fell under the prohibition, and many scholars saw themselves deprived of their scientific tools.[26]

The Index failed to achieve its purpose, of course. That such measures were undertaken out of pastoral concern for the ministry of the word at least shows the importance accorded to the link between right knowing and right doing. Only gradually would the church learn again to fight ideas with better ideas, to persuade rather than to coerce.

Content. Both in Europe and abroad, the ancient thematization of the Christian message into creed, commandments, and prayers continued to structure Christian teaching, but the emphasis upon the moral or practical dimension of the Christian life was most pronounced. In the American missions, instruction in lifestyle preceded doctrinal instruction. Once the Spanish friars had decided that the Indians could not be catechized until they were settled into villages, they set about teaching them the customs of village life and the occupational skills of farming and the trades, along with religious doctrine.

In Europe, moral instruction was emphasized in conjunction with the reception of the sacrament of Penance. The cultural obsession with achieving a good death heightened the people's interest in how to make a good and thorough sacramental confession and, to a lesser extent, how to live a good life. Inasmuch as the sixteenth century saw the beginnings of the slave trade and of exploitative structures of a world economy, one wonders about the effectiveness of such preoccupation with moral instruction.

At the level of theological development, the sixteenth century produced unparalleled polemics between Protestant Reformers and Catholics. The old medieval scholastic synthesis had gone to seed, and out of its exploding pods came vital questions about the nature and authority of the church, the capacities of the human mind, and the sources and reliability of guidance for human thought and endeavor. Luther's works alone fill 55 volumes in English. For the first time in history, such questions and the debates they sparked could not be confined to an academic elite. The prosperous and increasingly well educated merchant classes were avidly interested in them, and constituted an eager market for theological theses in published form. Ideas traveled across national borders when university students and merchants' sons returned home after training in the cities of Germany, France, or Italy.

The Council of Trent condensed and codified Catholic positions in several areas of doctrine, particularly those connected with church authority and the sacraments. Moreover, the Council commissioned a compendium of doctrines, the *Roman Catechism*, as a handbook for the guidance of pastors. The conciliar decrees and catechism, like contemporary oral instruction, reflect the controversial atmosphere of the times. They place emphasis upon points which were contested by the Protestants, while neglecting more central issues because they happened not to be in dispute. The *Roman Catechism* had four parts: the creed and faith, the sacraments, moral laws, and prayer. At 400-plus pages, it was little used except as a reference book by the better educated of the homilists. Earlier and simpler Catholic and Protestant catechisms were much more popular and effective with the common people. Most followed an outline based on the "creed, code, cult" format of the catecheses of antiquity.

More significant than the particular contents of the catechisms is the way in which the medium itself became the message. With their abstractly logical outlines and their question-and-answer format, the catechisms promote a fracturing of scriptural narrative into discrete facts and exhortations. Moreover, they convey the impression that religion is a matter of questioning and answering—with a finite number of questions permitted and tidily correct answers provided. Ironically, the pre-answered question may be quite alien to the honest wondering experienced by believers who dare also to think. The catechism book largely determined both the practice and the theory of religious education for four centuries for the majority of Christians on earth. As we take up the story of catechesis in the United States in the next chapter, the catechisms are center stage.

LEGACY OF THE SIXTEENTH-CENTURY CHURCH

- worldwide missionary outreach
- racist policies for ordination to priesthood in the Americas

- theological seminaries
- universities in the Americas
- catechisms
- versified text of the Bible
- Confraternity of Christian Doctrine: CCD
- Forty Hours devotion for Catholics
- tabernacle centrally placed on altar in Catholic churches
- Protestantism: reform of worship, laws, and teaching of many churches
- affordable vernacular Bibles
- Catholic teaching orders
- the mission system of evangelizing in Spanish America
- the Society of Jesus: Jesuits
- denominations among Christians
- Sunday instruction mandated for Catholic children

Notes for Chapter Nine

1. For a discussion of alternate terms, see Erwin Iserloh *et al.*, *Reformation and Counter Reformation*, History of the Church, volume 5, edited by Hubert Jedin and John Dolan, translated by Anselm Biggs and Peter W. Becker (New York: Seabury Press, Crossroad, 1980), pp. 431–32.

2. See Steven Ozment's discussion in *The Age of Reform 1250–1550* (New Haven: Yale University Press, 1980), pp. 219–20. This chapter's portrayal of the sixteenth-century church is based on that work and on: Hans-Georg Beck *et al.*, *From the High Middle Ages to the Eve of the Reformation*, Handbook of Church History, volume 4, edited by Hubert Jedin and John Dolan, translated by Anselm Biggs (New York: Herder and Herder, 1970); Erwin Iserloh *et al.*, *Reformation and Counter Reformation;* Roland H. Bainton, *The Reformation of the Sixteenth Century* (Boston: Beacon Press, 1952); Kenneth Scott Latourette, *A History of Christianity*, volume 2 (San Francisco: Harper & Row, 1975); Rosemary Radford Ruether and Rosemary Skinner Keller, editors, *Women and Religion in America*, volume 2: The Colonial and Revolutionary Periods (San Francisco: Harper & Row, 1983); Michael Warren, editor, *Sourcebook for Modern Catechetics* (Winona, Minn.: Saint Mary's Press, 1983); Mary Stanislaus Van Well, *The Educational Aspects of the Missions in the Southwest* (Milwaukee: Marquette University Press, 1942); Kendig Brubaker Cully, editor, *Basic Writings in Christian Education* (Philadelphia: Westminster Press, 1960).

3. Rosemary Radford Ruether points out that many of these were

spiritualities of women, suppressed by men. See *Women-Church: Theology and Practice of Feminist Liturgical Communities* (San Francisco: Harper & Row, 1985), pp. 11–23.

4. See Roland H. Bainton, *The Reformation*, p. 16.

5. See Ozment, *Age of Reform*, pp. 272–89 for an account of the Peasants' Revolt and Luther's positions on social justice.

6. Kenneth Scott Latourette, *History of Christianity*, volume 2, p. 895.

7. Hubert Jedin remarks that the Daughters "blazed the trail for the grand-scale development of the modern congregations of women, without which the church's social work in the nineteenth century could not be imagined." See *Reformation and Counter Reformation*, pp. 573–74.

8. See Hubert Jedin, *Reformation and Counter Reformation*, pp. 562–63.

9. See Asuncion Lavrin, "Women and Religion in Spanish America, in *Women and Religion in America* volume 2: The Colonial and Revolutionary Periods, pp. 42–78.

10. See Christine Allen, "Women in Colonial French America," in *Women and Religion in America*, volume 2, pp. 79–131. In Mexico, convents of cloistered white nuns proliferated in the seventeenth century, and in the eighteenth century several were founded which admitted Indian women.

11. See Joseph B. Collins, "The Beginnings of the CCD in Europe and Its Modern Revival," pp. 146–57 in *Sourcebook for Modern Catechetics*, p. 147. (Reprinted from *American Ecclesiastical Review* 168:695–706.)

12. Mary Stanislaus Van Well, *The Educational Aspects of the Missions in the Southwest* (Milwaukee: Marquette University Press, 1942), pp. 10–22. Van Well shares the assumption of the sixteenth century that Indians were "immature beings in practically every respect save that of their bodily growth" (p. 5). This prejudice underlies her assertion that the "*encomienda* created a social unit which was not greatly different from that of the ancient European manorial system of serfdom, but in fact became another social institution because of the *vast difference in the two races* concerned" (pp. 11–2, emphasis added). A disinterested comparison of the immigrant tribal peoples among whom the European monasteries were founded, and the American Indian peoples, shows many points of similarity but gives no basis for asserting superiority of either race over the other.

13. See Josef Glazik, *Reformation and Counter Reformation*, p. 581.

14. See Josef Glazik, *Reformation and Counter Reformation*, p. 586.

15. Collins, "The Beginnings of the CCD," p. 148.

16. Excerpted in *Basic Writings in Christian Education*, edited by Kendig Brubaker Cully (Philadelphia: Westminster Press, 1960), pp. 218–23.

17. See Glazik, *Reformation and Counter Reformation*, p. 577.

18. See Erwin Iserloh, *Reformation and Counter Reformation*, p. 234.

19. See Hubert Jedin, *Reformation and Counter Reformation*, p. 568.

20. Ozment, *Age of Reform*, p. 199.

21. Ozment, *Age of Reform*, pp. 96–7. Ozment points out that "[m]ajor humanists and reformers, both Protestant and Catholic, came under the influence of the Brothers during their student years; Rudolf Agricola, Erasmus, and Luther are three prominent examples."

22. Quoted by Robert Ulich, *A History of Religious Education: Documents and Interpretations from the Judeo-Christian Tradition* (New York: New York University Press, 1968), p. 109.

23. Quoted by Erwin Iserloh, *Reformation and Counter Reformation*, p. 234.

24. Van Well, *Educational Aspects of the Missions*, pp. 24–5.

25. See translations and discussions of these works in Denis Janz, *Three Reformation Catechisms: Catholic, Anabaptist, Lutheran*, Texts and Studies in Religion, volume 13 (New York: Edwin Mellen Press, 1982).

26. Hubert Jedin, *Reformation and Counter Reformation*, pp. 486–87.

Chapter Ten

Nineteenth Century:
Evangelizing a New Nation

American Catholics look to the nineteenth century for the Baltimore Catechism and the beginnings of the parish school system, while Protestants discover there the evolution of the Sunday school. These two religious communities viewed each other with hostile suspicion throughout the last century. Within each community, moreover, factions struggled. Methodists, Baptists, and Disciples competed for converts in missionary territory on the American frontier, while Irish and German Catholics vied for diocesan power and services in the growing urban immigrant enclaves. These rivalries were one among many factors shaping the way in which the gospel was communicated. Yet the nineteenth century saw growing cooperation of Protestants with Protestants, and Catholics with Catholics, although not between the two groups. As the new nation strove both to invent and to understand itself after 1789, religious people and their ideas played a major part.

It could easily be argued that the activities of word, care, and celebration transmuted themselves into a secular religion and became incorporated into the governmental structures of the emerging United States of America. To be sure, Christian values are reflected in many aspects of the national life. But for the first time in our story of the gospel, the nineteenth century now shows us an era and a society in which most people were making a distinction between the "religious" sphere and the "worldly" sphere of politics, economics, culture, and science. That distinction began as a theory within the eighteenth-century Enlightenment. However, by the end of the nineteenth century it had proved itself in practice to be the only principle under which people of widely diverging faiths could participate together in a common public life.

Our concern in telling the gospel's story is with the transformation of human society, and with church as a way of being human together. Colonial America knew several experiments which sought to identify state

257

with church. The Puritans had come to New England as "pilgrims" to establish a theocracy. They linked the rights of citizenship to one's covenant with the religious community, but they could not make that arrangement work beyond the first fervent generation. The biblical theme of a promised land for a chosen people became national policy from the seventeenth century throughout the nineteenth as white settlers displaced Native American families. Yet eventually religion was consigned to its place as one—or, more correctly, several—of many special interests cooperating in the democratic process.

On that secular view, religion is the smaller part and society is the larger whole. But our conceptualization is different. We are seeking to tell the ongoing story of the gospel even as particular political organizations come and go. While the gospel has indeed affected governmental structures, nevertheless its activity must be studied on a much wider scale than the political. In this book, we have been observing centuries in which church came into being through the interaction of the three evangelizing activities of proclamation, care, and sacramental celebration. "Church" is the term for the transformed human intersubjective existence which results from the communication of the gospel. This reality of church is not coextensive with any of the individual churches which one encounters in experience, although it can be discerned in them. Much less, to be sure, is this reality captured in the political institutions of the United States itself. Therefore, the scope of our investigation even in nineteenth century America remains deliberately focused upon ecclesial activities.

The term "activity" itself can serve as a keynote for this era. It is a period of lively expansion, growth, and argument. It must have seemed an exciting, overwhelming time to be alive. The United States acquired new territories on its western frontier, new cities where farms or wilderness had predominated, new means of communication and transportation, and new peoples arriving especially from western and then eastern Europe, and from Africa.

It was also a century of wars. The war of 1812 insured the independence from Great Britain first won in the American Revolution. Through skirmishes and an outright war with Mexico, the United States acquired extensive southwestern territories. The War Between the States set brother against brother in an agonizing conflict of ideology and economics whose bitterness had not yet been healed by the end of the century. The Indian wars systematically wiped out most of the original residents of the continent and appropriated their lands. The Spanish-American War asserted U.S. dominance in the Caribbean and gained a Pacific outpost.

Moreover, in this era seeds were sown for nonmilitary social struggles that would mar not only nineteenth- but twentieth-century American society: racial conflicts, economic and social conflicts between women and men, and economic conflicts between workers and those who controlled the wealth which they produced.

The activity of the mind was equally pronounced in this era. With unquestioned reliance on the power of reason and unchallenged trust in the inevitability of progress (both inherited from the Enlightenment) people of the nineteenth century submitted the physical and social world to systematic analysis. Technological inventions brought on the industrialization of America at an exponentially increasing rate. Darwin proposed that animal and plant life arose and differentiated through the mechanism of selective survival of the fittest. As Feuerbach had identified the process of theological alienation whereby the best human characteristics are projected upon the divinity, so Marx described an insidious economic alienation whereby the value of human labor is displaced from worker to capitalist. Freud postulated the existence of the unconscious mind, and at the turn of the twentieth century was defending his theories linking neurosis and psychosexual development. In the early 1900's, John Dewey drew upon the nascent science of psychology in developing a philosophy that would revolutionize pedagogy.

From religious people, there would come both criticisms of these ideas and appropriations of them; but this would not happen until the twentieth century was well along. Nineteenth-century religious life was influenced more powerfully by the Second Great Awakening and by revivalism, on the frontier as well as in the Eastern cities. Revivals set the pace and the tone of much of religious life in America. These evangelical manifestations of religious fervor transcended denominational lines; in fact, they even led to the organization of new denominations and coalitions. In its beginnings the Sunday-school movement, too, though Protestant and evangelical, was nondenominational and unaffiliated with established churches. But later the churches domesticated it, adapting it as a chief means of their own institutional survival. Survival was an important concern for Catholics as well, and the parochial or parish school system evolved as the principal means to build and protect a distinctive Catholic identity in a predominantly Protestant land. The Sunday school laid the groundwork for the development of public schools in this country, and the struggle among different religious constituencies to control funding and curricula of the public schools helped to shape those schools into the independent state-administered institutions which we have today.

THE SITUATION IN NINETEENTH-CENTURY AMERICA

The establishment of the United States of America between two oceans was a communications phenomenon as much as a political one. Networks of various kinds branched out from the east westward, linking centers of population, commerce, and industry with sources of raw materials. Roads were built, then a system of canals, then railroads. The postal system grew, and cheap rates made possible the wide circulation of journals and magazines. The first intercity telegraph line, between Baltimore and Washington in 1844, immediately was put to work to transmit news dispatches about congressional action for a Baltimore newspaper. Transcontinental telegraph service began in 1861. The first telephone message was transmitted in 1876, and at the turn of the century there were nearly a million telephones in operation. Business, political, and personal communication came to depend upon these new networks, and they provided important new means for communicating the gospel.

The gospel had to go into new situations as the country expanded. Churches had been established in the settled Eastern cities and towns. But as pioneers crossed the Appalachian mountains to start farms along the inland river basins, their home denominations for the most part did not accompany them. Generations of unchurched backwoods and mountain families needed a new approach from Christianity. Itinerant Baptist preachers and Methodist circuit riders developed innovative methods for carrying the gospel to remote settlements. In addition, isolated families could be brought together for a revival meeting, which would provide the rare opportunity for meeting other people as well as a chance to hear preaching. A revival meeting at Cane Ridge, Kentucky in the summer of 1801 assembled at least ten thousand people.[1]

The Enlightenment, a philosophical and political movement in eighteenth-century Europe, had inspired the learned leaders of the American Revolution. Transplanted to American soil were Enlightenment values like reliance on the powers of the human mind, individualism, distrust of organized religion and social conventions, faith in progress, and esteem for nature. Over several generations, these values combined with native pragmatism, enthusiasm for political and economic independence, and the challenge of an open frontier to form the pioneer spirit. While especially characteristic of westward-moving Americans, these qualities also could be found among the people who remained in the Eastern towns, cities, and farms.

But the promise of America was not for everyone, despite these egalitarian ideals. Native Americans and black slaves were to have no share in it, even after the abolition of slavery during the War Between the States.

The Indians' resources and the slaves' labor were exploited to make the promise come true for others. Women, too, contributed economically to the building of America but were largely excluded from political participation during the nineteenth century.

The exploitation of these groups did not go unnoticed. Movements in favor of women's suffrage and the abolition of slavery eventually piqued the conscience of the nation. The Protestant churches produced social reformers whose compassion extended abroad to mission lands as well. Geopolitical factors were hampering Roman Catholic mission work, for Portugal and Spain had declined in power, while Napoleon prevented missionaries and funds from going overseas from Europe for about a generation. In the late 1700's and 1800's, foreign missionary societies were organized by American and English Protestants. Their work was both evangelical and humanitarian.

Descendants of the pioneers who had settled the Ohio and Mississippi valleys pushed on further west after gold was discovered in California at mid-century, and especially after the economic and social upheavals of the Civil War. At the same time, European immigrants entered Eastern cities and the Great Lakes region at an increasing rate. America needed their labor for building its transportation systems and for the factories which, since the early 1800's, had been multiplying especially in the Northeast. But their ethnic ways and foreign tongues disturbed the native Anglo population. Particularly alarming to Protestant America was the fact that a growing proportion of the immigrants were Catholics.

That fact concerned American Catholics no less than Protestants, for it meant that the tiny community of "Yankee Catholics," aided by a few exiled French priests, now had to undertake the pastoral care of thousands of starving Irish along with Germans, Slavs, Italians, and others whom they could understand little better than the Protestants could. The problems of assimilating the new Americans were enormous. They strained the social systems of cities, where industrialization already was annihilating traditional family structures. Throughout the nineteenth century, the national economy went through recurring cycles of boom and bust, creating misery for the urban poor and for farmers alike. These tensions erupted in urban violence both in race riots and in nativist attacks against immigrants and Catholics.

A SOCIAL PROGRAM FROM THE CHURCHES

Both the evils of the cities and the evil of slavery in the agricultural South evoked the compassion of Christians who in the nineteenth century sought to imitate Jesus' own compassion toward all forms of human suffering. The first factories were begun before 1820 in the New England textile industry, and soon many kinds of goods were being produced by large-scale manufacture. This represented a radical change in working conditions from the previous system of small shops with craft workers trained through apprenticeship and living nearby. Now fathers, mothers, and children as young as seven or eight years of age all reported to the mill for long hours of work, because a single male worker's pay was not sufficient to cover living expenses for a family.

Home life became all but nonexistent among the urban working class. Parents had to leave small children without adult supervision for the ten- and twelve-hour workdays. The first "schools" for poor children in the early 1800's really were more like what we would term day-care centers, and often they were established as works of charity by churches or by individual Christian people. The dismal conditions of urban life encouraged alcoholism, and that further stressed the finances and the climate of the home. Some sought to remedy this condition by banning liquor altogether. The Women's Christian Temperance Union was founded in 1874 for this purpose, and the movement succeeded in legislating prohibition for a time in the next century. Settlement houses were established in the urban slums. In these shelters, children could learn domestic skills that their parents were too tired to teach them. Settlement houses often were organized and staffed by Protestant deaconesses, who also managed schools, hospitals, and even churches for the poor.[2]

The problems of the typical factory worker were compounded for anyone who did not yet know English or the customs of the new country to which ne or she had come. Protestant agencies mobilized to answer the needs of urban immigrants, and hopefully to win them away from their European Catholicism. The religious awakening experienced by Protestants on the frontier and in the cities also spurred famine relief efforts, hospitals for the sick, and charitable works on behalf of orphans.[3] Not only in America, but in mission lands as well, was this care manifest. In far-off places like Hawaii, the missionaries tried to defend native peoples from exploitation by merchant seamen, much as the Spanish and Portuguese missionaries had sought to do in the Americas several centuries before.

Just as the woes of the poor in Northern cities were largely owing to economic exploitation in the factory system, so in the South the economy of the plantation system fed upon the misery of slavery. Many of the ancestors of white Americans had come to this country as indentured servants, bound to work for a number of years to pay off the expense of their passage. But black Americans had been brought here involuntarily, and could expect no end to their time of service. Some Christians misread the Bible in their attempt to justify slavery or, after slavery was no more, the inferior social position of black men and women. More in the tradition of Jesus and the Hebrew prophets were those who denounced slavery and racism, and worked to do away with these evils.

Catholic charitable works focused on the needs of the European immigrants in the Eastern cities, then along the inland rivers and Great Lakes as Catholic populations expanded quickly in places like Chicago and Cincinnati. (In California, the Mexican government took control of the missions away from the priests in 1835, and a centuries-old tradition of providing for the well-being of the Indian peoples came to an end. California itself was ceded to the United States in 1848.) In 1790, only 35,000 Americans were Catholics, amounting to 1.1% of the population. By 1830, the percentage had risen to 3.0%, and by 1880 to 14.4%, thanks largely to increasing immigration.[4] Three-quarters of the Irish immigrants in the nineteenth century were Catholic, and one-third of the Germans.

The Irish spoke English and blended into the existing poorer neighborhoods. But German-speaking Catholics built ethnic enclaves in Eastern and Midwest cities, where they sought to preserve their language and culture along with their religion. This set a pattern for later-arriving groups like the Italians and Poles, who often maintained their own parishes, schools, social clubs, and fraternal insurance societies. A crucial policy decision was facing the Catholic church. If it opted to shelter faith by encouraging this separatism and keeping the ethnic masses together, it would condemn them to exist indefinitely in disadvantaged urban areas. If it encouraged assimilation into American society and movement westward where a better life could be built on the land, people's faith would be exposed to a heterogeneous society unlike any encountered in Europe.

While the choice was debated in Catholic ecclesiastical circles, anti-Catholic feeling was building in American society. Literary attacks against Catholicism in the 1830's led to anti-Catholic violence. The Ursuline convent and school in Charlestown, Massachusetts was burned in 1834 with loss of life. Riots in the fall of 1842 forced the Archbishop of Philadelphia to close all Catholic churches. Archbishop Hughes answered riots in his city of New York with different tactics: he armed parishioners, and eventually turned to political action. By the 1850's, anti-Catholicism too had become politically organized in the Know-Nothing party, which achieved considerable power in some local elections. These developments made it certain that Catholicism would choose a social life apart from that of mainstream America, at least for several generations. Yet one crucial decision prevented the complete ghettoization of Catholicism. As Irish-American bishops took over power from the French émigré clergy in the 1850's and '60's, they organized American Catholicism as one, English-speaking church. While local concessions might be made to ethnic parishes, with their Polish, Italian, German, or bilingual schools and preaching, nevertheless the ties with the mother countries were severed and a distinctively American church was fostered. Such a church was in a position to communicate easily with other American churches when the social climate would permit.

The nineteenth century was an era of major philanthropic initiatives. Hospitals, asylums, schools for disadvantaged groups, orphanages, old-age homes, and other such institutions were established by cities and counties, by wealthy individuals, and by Protestant and Catholic associations. For every Baptist hospital, there would be a Catholic one; for every Catholic home for wayward youth, a Methodist one as well. The denominations vied with one another to provide services needed by their own constituencies, and they did not discriminate in offering their care to others outside the fold. America benefitted from competition.

Chief among the providers of care were sisterhoods of religious women. Protestant deaconesses trained for service as physicians, as teachers, and in settlement work in the more than 140 deaconess homes that opened in the United States between 1870 and 1900.[5] They used their skills for the poor in American cities and in missionary lands. Several Catholic nursing orders were established in America or transplanted from Europe. It is said that the nursing sisters who cared for wounded soldiers on both sides of the Civil War helped to extinguish the fires of anti-Catholicism in this country.[6]

Great as were the physical misfortunes of war and sickness, the nineteenth century recognized something much worse, a whole new dimension of human misery unknown to previous ages. We call it systemic or structural evil: a wrongness built into the structure of society that is too pervasive for any individual to overcome. Slavery was such an evil. Capitalism in its ruthless early forms was another. Not until the nineteenth century did people become aware of such forces, and recognize that charity while effective on an individual basis was futile in overcoming systemic evil. From a Protestant religious base, social movements like abolitionism, pacifism, and women's suffrage addressed evils on the social scale, seeking to sway opinion and pass legislation in order to relieve injustice and human suffering. From Catholicism, another social initiative arose in response to the exploitation of labor by unfettered capitalism. Pope Leo XIII wrote the first of a series of social encyclicals, *Rerum Novarum*, in 1891, defending the rights of workers to a decent wage and supporting labor unions. Henceforth, "care" for people's needs would extend beyond individual needs to societal ones.

THE STRANGE AND THE FAMILIAR IN WORSHIP

Like their ancestors in every age, people of the nineteenth century yearned for intimacy with the divine in terms that they could understand. America, the land in which so much was new, had to discover ways of experiencing the traditional inheritance of all those baptized in Jesus' name: relationship with God as "Abba." The pluralistic and, eventually, tolerant society being forged in the new nation would become a crazy quilt of liturgical expressions. Two contrasting settings for worship that were characteristic of nineteenth-century America were the revivalistic camp meeting and the ethnic parish. One featured strange and shocking behaviors; the other offered a reassuringly traditional style of prayer and fellowship.

The religious awakening that quickened the frontier and some Eastern cities at the very beginning of the century was numbered the Second Great Awakening, after an earlier one in pre-Revolutionary New England. Thousands experienced the action of the Holy Spirit in their hearts and minds, moving them to repentance and conversion as they listened to evangelical preaching. The Spirit apparently took hold of their bodies as well, and marvelous manifestations were reported. These seem to have been more pronounced at frontier camp meetings than in New England congregations. Barton W. Stone, who preached the revival at Cane Ridge in 1801, called these manifestations "exercises" and described their many varieties:

> The falling exercise was very common among all classes, the saints and sinners of every age and every grade, from the philosopher to the clown. The subject of this exercise would, generally, with a piercing scream, fall like a log on the floor, earth, or mud, and appear as dead. . . .

> The jerks cannot be so easily described. Sometimes the subject of the jerks would be affected in some one member of the body, and sometimes the whole system. When the head alone was affected, it would be jerked backward and forward, or from side to side, so quickly that the features of the face could not be distinguished. When the whole system was affected, I have seen a person stand in one place, and jerk backward and forward in quick succession, their head nearly touching the floor behind and before. . . .

The laughing exercise was frequent, confined solely with the religious. It was a loud, hearty laughter, but one *sui generis;* it excited laughter in none else. The subject appeared rapturously
solemn, and his laughter excited solemnity in saints and sinners.
It is truly indescribable.[7]

If these manifestations bordered on the hysterical, that may be because of the unaccustomed situation in which the people found themselves. Most were isolated farm families who had little chance for social
intercourse, much less exposure to trained speakers whose purpose it was
to excite their emotions. Having set aside the monotonous chores of farm
life for a week or two, they found themselves in close proximity to more
people than they could ever have imagined in one place. Staying up late,
singing and praying by the light of campfires and torches, they were vulnerable to suggestion and ripe for conversion. What in hindsight seems
more amazing than the grace of their bizarre "exercises" is the fact of the
endurance of many of the conversions experienced on those nights. Moreover, among us today are vigorous Christian churches which came to birth
among the people who attended revivals.

Most American Protestants did not go in for such demonstrative worship, but that is not to say that their worship was without feeling. Preachers inspired by John Wesley's Methodism were leaving "hearts strangely
warmed" along the backwoods circuits which they served, and Charles
Wesley's hymns gave people the words with which to express and evoke
such religious sentiments. The great variety of expressions of Christianity
in nineteenth-century America was taken by most to be evidence that God
was at work in the young country. The only worship which most citizens
deemed altogether *too* strange was that of Roman Catholics, although most
outside the Catholic community had never even witnessed it.[8]

Indeed, some Catholic worship was regarded as strange even by
Catholics, because Catholics were strangers to one another. Catholic immigrants from many nations entered this country in increasing numbers.
They spoke different languages, came from different social and geographical circumstances, had different levels of employable skills, and harbored
contrasting and sometimes contradictory expectations of their church. The
Irish, arriving relatively early in the century, spoke English and could fit
into the parishes already organized by "Yankee Catholic" bishops like John
Carroll of Baltimore. When the generation of French émigré priests who
had fled Napoleon began to take over as bishops, they spoke English too.
But in cities like Cleveland, they found themselves having to contend with
newer arrivals from Germany who wanted preaching and prayers in Ger-

man. The fact that the liturgy itself always was Latin helped somewhat to defuse the problem. But people still wanted something familiar to facilitate the divine-human intimacy in their parish church: a pastor who could speak, think, administrate, counsel, and pray like the one back home in the old country.

Ethnic parishes were established, not only for the Germans but for Poles, Italians, Lithuanians, and several other groups. Competition for control of key diocesan offices and resources made relations among the ethnic groups quite tense at times. About mid-century, the Irish themselves began rising into episcopal ranks, as did a few Germans and very few Poles. In some cities they supported the ethnic parishes, with their traditional styles of worship, which helped to ease the cultural transition for two or three generations of immigrant families. Eventually, as happened so often in America, after strangers got to know one another they found one another's worship not so strange after all.

The Orthodox community perhaps remains as one exception to this rule. Orthodox immigrants, like Catholics, seemed suspiciously "foreign" to Protestant Americans; but unlike the Catholics with their Irish, the Orthodox had no English-speaking branch to mediate in the process of gradual understanding. The Russian Orthodox diocese of Alaska was created in 1799, and it had a resident bishop from 1840 until the see was moved to San Francisco in 1872. There were 12,000 communicants in the diocese at that time, most of them Indians.[9] In the late nineteenth and early twentieth centuries, several smaller eastern-rite churches affiliated with this diocese, some because their local Roman dioceses failed to accommodate their special cultural needs. The first Greek Orthodox parish in New York was organized in 1891, and the Greeks have become the largest single Orthodox community in the United States. Both the Slavic- and the Greek-American worship communities maintain seminaries in this country.

Catholics established English-speaking theological seminaries as their norm by the early twentieth century. Seminarians of different ethnicity studied together, and the path was set toward homogenization of worship styles in American Catholicism. Distinctive styles would re-emerge again after the Second Vatican Council in the mid-twentieth century; however, those styles would be musical, regional, or age-related rather than ethnic. The one exception would be the distinctive ethnic style of preaching and song in black American Catholic churches.

Nineteenth-century Catholic liturgy itself was not only Latin but Tridentine, that is, set into exact forms prescribed by the sixteenth-century Council of Trent. A liturgical renewal was already afoot in Germany and France, on the two fronts of historical research and musical restoration;

however, no echoes of that renewal were yet heard on this side of the Atlantic. The rigid liturgical forms failed to capture popular piety, especially the exuberance and feeling characteristic of American religion. Popular devotions like the wearing of scapulars or medals in honor of the Virgin Mary helped to express the people's feeling that they needed special protection in this land. Reports that the Virgin had appeared to several young women in France in the 1830's through 1850's were eagerly received here, but no comparable phenomenon occurred among American Catholic women. The visions of religious sisters in the United States had to do with the future. They dreamed the hospitals, schools and colleges, and other earthly institutions that became the mainstay of American Catholicism. Then they built them.

The hopes and dreams of another group of Americans also found expression in religious terms. Black slaves heard the gospel on the plantations, but they heard the part of it to which the proprietors were deaf. The gospel gave black people images of dignity, struggle, rescue, freedom, and a better future beyond present suffering. These images nurtured the hope which welled up from within the deep spirituality which was their African heritage. Having neither power nor materials to incarnate their hopes in any other form, the slaves sang them. The Negro Spiritual is the first distinctive religious form—and arguably the first indigenous artistic form—to emerge in the United States. With melodies shaped by African speech patterns and traditional tunes and chants, and with motifs drawn from the biblical stories told to them, black people sang to God of their experiences of sorrow and hope. The Spirituals are a treasure from a people with very special insight into the fatherhood of God.

In the short run, the gospel may have accomplished what the whites under whose control it fell undoubtedly intended: the cultivation of docility and cooperation among the slaves. In the long run, it helped black people to survive with integrity and inspired their long and continuing struggle for freedom. The black American experience has been a journey into relationships of justice, as befits the sons and daughters of the Father of Jesus. America could not find its way into justice without black leadership.

Like other ethnic Americans, black people were able to establish churches with their own distinctive style of worship, once the restrictions of slave laws were removed. Powerful rhetorical and poetic skills in preaching, a responsive manner of listening, warm interpersonal relationships, prayerful concern for the everyday difficulties of the congregation, and choral singing in "gospel" style, all remain characteristic of black worship today, even across denominational lines.

COMMUNICATING THE GOSPEL TO A DIVERSE POPULATION

The United States was a new idea: "one nation under God" but with a government in which nothing was ordained by God. Unlike the European monarchies which held themselves to be divinely sanctioned, this country would be governed by the consent of the governed alone. Church would not do government the favor of legitimizing it, and government would not do church the favor of funding it. In practice, this meant that many contrasting religious views could flourish, to the extent that they won popular support on their own merits and ability to persuade. The result was less melting pot than mosaic. Orthodoxy, and even monolithic Catholicism, became colorful ethnic collages in their development as pluralistic American churches; while Protestantism was a riot of wildflowers.

Nothing remotely like this had ever happened to the gospel before. So rich and diverse were the forms of proclamation in nineteenth-century America that it is possible to offer only the most summary introduction of them here. We may begin by noting that, for the first time since the fourth century, becoming a Christian was once again a matter of choice, not birth. Moreover, and for the first time ever, the choice was not only *whether* to join a church, but *which* of many Christian churches to join. While Catholicism and Protestantism were old adversaries, Protestants now found themselves competing with Protestants of other denominations, and Catholics with other Catholics of different ethnicity. Yet Americans felt more inclined toward cooperation than conflict, in the face of the challenge of the frontier and the political and economic challenges in the Eastern cities and farmlands.

The building of a new nation and a new way of life offered opportunities for incorporating religious values into nascent institutions such as the public schools. Here was one situation in which compromise had to be forged in deciding exactly which of the many religious views (if any) rightly should shape the institution.

Europe flooded America not only with people, but with new questions, ideas, sciences, opinions. The American literacy rate was relatively high. Soon the United States was developing its own philosophies and theologies as well, its own inventors and scientists. Where seventeenth- and eighteenth-century Americans had written sermons, essays, and tracts, nineteenth-century thinkers wrote social theory and critical history. Horace Bushnell's term "Christian nurture" reconceptualized the process of becoming a Christian, and Henry Clay Trumbull composed the first history of religious education (though he anachronistically titled it a history of the Sunday school).[10] The theory of voluntarism in religious affiliation arose as a corollary derived from the political voluntarism of American democracy. In return, the church lent the nation the religious theory of salvation history in the form of "manifest destiny." As pious Protestants, Americans were answering the call to revival, conversion, and the churching of America. As intrepid citizens, they were answering the call to "go west" and build a continental empire. It was easy to confuse the two calls.

On the Catholic side, too, the churching of America was a process of organizing to proclaim and reflect the gospel. Still considered a missionary enterprise by Rome in the nineteenth century, the American Catholic church took up its self-administration through a series of councils held in the provincial see of Baltimore, the first archdiocese. (The last three national councils at Baltimore were termed "plenary" after the establishment of other archdioceses, which held their own provincial councils.) From the provincial and plenary councils of Baltimore came the legislation which gave structure to the ministry of the word for Catholics in this country. In addition, Catholic bishops from around the world met in 1869–1870 at the First Vatican Council, where the dogma of papal infallibility was defined. Soon afterwards, in the face of an increasingly centralized administration in Rome, the national councils ceased and no concerted action was attempted again until the time of the First World War. The American Catholic bishops did not again legislate as a body until after the Second Vatican Council.

If the optimism engendered by success in political projects sometimes spilled over into plans made for ecclesial endeavors, nevertheless there were also many who could tell the two apart. A black minister named M.C.B. Mason bravely addressed the following remarks to an overwhelmingly white audience at the Eleventh International Sunday-School Convention in 1905:

> Whence came you? What is the source of your greatness and the secret of your power? In Africa men were talking about the fact that the sum of the squares of the two sides of a right-angled triangle is equal to the square of the hypotenuse before your race was born. Ability? Ability to solve problems? Material problems? No, no! What is it? I will tell you. One night a man, engaged in the work you are engaged in, heard a voice in the midst of his dreams, saying, "Paul, come over into Macedonia and help us." And he went over into Europe, and found your race there; and you know that they were living in the wilderness, and eating the roots of trees, clothing their nakedness with the skins of beasts, and drinking from the skulls of their enemies. And I declare in all earnestness, if the gospel could do so much for such an un-

promising set as it did for your ancestors surely it can do much for my people.[11]

What the gospel did for nineteenth-century Americans becomes apparent as we consider now the personnel, institutions, methods, media, and content through which it reached them.

Personnel. Lay people came into their own again as ministers of the word in nineteenth-century America. The size of the country and the variety of its urban, rural, and frontier challenges were much more than clergy alone could handle—though, to be sure, pioneering clergy played their parts as well. Sunday-school workers traveled through rural districts drumming up students for their schools on weekdays, then teaching them on Sunday. At first the pay for teachers was about 33 cents a day a day; later, they worked for expenses or as volunteers. In the cities, the superintendent of the Sunday school might be a person of social standing. John Wanamaker, founder of a chain of retail stores which still bear his name, was superintendent of Philadelphia's Bethany Presbyterian Church Sunday School for half a century, during which time it became "the largest Sunday-school in America, and with one exception the largest in the world."[12]

Most Protestant communities in the nineteenth century excluded women from ordination and from preaching. While working-class women were employed in homes and in factories to do strenuous labor, women of the bourgeoisie were discouraged from physical and mental exertion. Despite this stricture, ladies organized the first Sunday schools in East-coast cities, and later formed many other associations to support evangelical work. Deaconesses and other women evangelists and teachers in the United States and abroad received their help. This religious "work of women for women," as it was called, had the unforeseen effect of helping women to develop organizational skills that they would use in their struggle for the vote and for other political causes.

Catholic women also were excluded from the pulpit. But in the religious sisterhoods transplanted from Europe or founded fresh on American soil, they had the means of relatively independent action and thought on behalf of the gospel. The Catholic school system depended on the teaching nuns. In the ethnic parishes, sisters from the old country were expected to pass on the language and culture, along with the faith, to children born on this side of the Atlantic. The difficulties they faced in understanding the new ethnic Americans are apparent in the following excerpt from a letter of Theresa Gerhardinger, a very homesick German sister working in Baltimore, to a priest back home just before Christmas of 1847:

Schools will not become large, for there are too many of them, and attendence is voluntary, which is bad. Children attend one school today, another tomorrow, just as they please. If they are corrected they do not come back; learning they often consider recreation. All they want to do is eat cookies, taffy and molasses candy, a cheap sweet. . . .

At the slightest punishment the parents say, "In this country one may not treat children so severely; they, too, must be given freedom." They do not listen to anyone, and even strike their parents if they do not give in to them.

They will not write one letter of the alphabet at home. "I go to school for that," is their answer. Homework cannot be introduced here; the parents do not want it either. Therefore, everything must be studied with them in school. They do not manifest the slightest eagerness to learn German. English, however, they want to learn to read and write. They hate German. All one hears is English. If they want to insult each other they say, "You German!"

They comprehend little or nothing if one tries to convey ideas to them, because they do not know enough German to understand what we mean. They will never learn spelling, for they neither speak German correctly, nor do they understand it. . . . What is most to their liking is jumping, running, dancing, tagging, singing, and fighting. They are like wild animals, and try out all their naughtiness in school.[13]

Not all the sisters were immigrants, of course. Native-born Catholic women were attracted to the new sorts of religious life developing in the cities of the new nation. The first religious community in the United States was begun in 1809 by Elizabeth Anne Bailey Seton, widow of a wealthy Yankee merchant and raised as an Episcopalian. John Carroll, the Archbishop of Baltimore, invited her to begin a school and gave her the rule of life of a French community, the Daughters of Charity, with whom the American community eventually would unite. Mother Seton's sisters branched out from Maryland to other states, often becoming diocesan communities independent from the original community in Emmittsburg. This pattern was typical for Catholic sisters in the nineteenth century as they adapted to the needs of pioneer dioceses. The flexibility and generosity of American religious women made possible the institutional growth of the Catholic church in this country.

Institutions. The Catholic parochial school system, of which the sisters were so integral a part, did not evolve until the latter part of the nineteenth century. In the colonial and revolutionary periods, up through the early 1800's, schools were a luxury for the upper classes. The Jesuits had several male secondary schools in Maryland in the 1600's, and founded a long-lasting one at Bohemia Manor in 1745 or 1746.[14] The Visitation and Ursuline nuns had elite academies in or near several eastern cities. In addition there were residential schools for poor girls and blacks, where they learned to work as domestic servants.

Records of the First through the Fifth Provincial Councils of Baltimore, meeting at intervals from 1829 through 1843, give no hint of a vision of a separate Catholic parish school system.[15] The assumption is that bishops expected Catholic children to attend public schools, for they exhorted parents to assert their civil rights as taxpayers and oppose Protestantism in schools that were supported by public funds. Not until 1852 did the First Plenary Council of Baltimore urge the establishment of Catholic schools as an important apostolic work. A provincial council in Cincinnati in 1862 was the first to legislate that Catholic parents must send their children to Catholic school under penalty of sin. At that time, about half of Cincinnati's Catholic schools were German.

In the meantime Pius IX, who had become pope in 1846, was working to strengthen the central authority of Roman church administration. He made known his opposition to the theory that civil authorities should have control over any school system. (In fact, he condemned this and certain other progressive ideas as heresy in his 1864 *Syllabus of Errors.*) While in some European countries a partnership between Catholic bishops and secular educators might be a possibility, in nineteenth-century America it was inconceivable. When the First Vatican Council declared the pope infallible five years later, the American bishops began to get the picture of what Rome expected. In 1875, after some behind-the-scenes maneuvering by an American layman[16] who favored parochial schools, Rome instructed the American bishops to establish a Catholic school system parallel to the public schools, and to enforce attendance under penalty of withholding the sacraments.

Yet the bishops did not immediately implement this order. Archbishop James Gibbons of Baltimore was summoned to Rome and instructed to convoke the Third Plenary Council of Baltimore in order to carry out the 1875 instruction. Meeting in 1884, Baltimore III laid the penalty of excommunication on any parents who failed to send their children to Catholic schools without seeking an exception from their bishop. Every parish was to build a school near its church within two years. Central diocesan administration was to be set up for these schools. And a commission was to be appointed to draw up a catechism for nationwide use.

The Third Plenary Council of Baltimore was the last. It insured that "every child in a Catholic school" would become the policy, if not the reality, of the ministry of the word for children. The strain on the economic and personnel resources of the poverty-striken immigrant church would be enormous, and initiatives in adult education would have to be postponed indefinitely. The Catholic Church entered the twentieth century as a child-centered, school-centered, introverted ecclesial community. Not until 1905 did a reemphasis on the Confraternity of Christian Doctrine in Rome make possible the broadening of the institutional base of Catholic instruction in America.

In higher education, the Catholic University of America was chartered as a graduate institution in 1887 in the nation's capital, and its first rector was appointed in 1889. The nineteenth century saw the establishment of numerous denominational colleges, both Catholic and Protestant. These became centers for training not only clergy but lay women and men as well for missionary and educational work in this country and overseas.

For nineteenth-century Protestantism the big institutional story is, of course, the development of the Sunday school. It began as a missionary and philanthropic outreach among unchurched people in the cities and on the frontier, supported by voluntary societies rather than by established congregations. Not until 1859, at the Third National Sunday School Convention in Philadelphia, was the Sunday school recognized as an official part of the church. In rural America to this day, the administration of the Sunday school often is entirely separate from other congregational concerns and is considered to lie outside the pastor's sphere of responsibility. By the 1880's, Sunday schools began to include classes for adults as well as children.

The magnitude of the Sunday school's influence can be gauged from statistics cited at the 1905 International Convention. Harkening back to the First National Convention held in New York in 1832, a speaker told the delegates:

> How glad those tough-fibered forefathers of ours would have been could they have looked down the years to an international convention of 1905, and have read the general secretary's report, with its record of Sunday-school organization in fifty-eight states and provinces, in more than 2,000 counties, and in 10,000 townships; and of an army of 120,000 people taking active part in the

campaign of organizing the continent for Bible study and character-training!

The estimated number of Sunday-school pupils in the United States in 1826 was 180,000; in the world, 1,080,000. In 1905 the number of Sunday-school pupils in the United States is reported as 11,251,009; in the world, as 22,648,428. Comparing these figures with the population of the United States then and now, we find that in 1826, 1.8 per cent of its 9,638,453 souls were pupils in the Sunday-school; and in 1905, 14.7 per cent of its 76,303,387 souls are pupils in the Sunday-school. There is advance of a most substantial character, the proportion of Sunday-school pupils to the population of the United States to-day being eight times what it was eighty years ago.[17]

Besides the obvious growth in numbers, the Sunday school underwent institutional development as well during those years. Two general kinds of Sunday schools, with different purposes, can be distinguished by the 1850's. Mission schools represented congregational or denominational outreach toward the poor, immigrants, and other disadvantaged people who were not church members. Besides educational programs on Sundays and even weekdays, missions provided recreational opportunities, entertainment, and a safe haven in the tradition of the settlement house. In another kind of Sunday school, church members provided training for their own children.[18] The latter kind of school has survived into our own times; the former has all but disappeared.

On the frontier and in the towns of the early nineteenth century, the mission or philanthropic Sunday school often had provided the only schooling children received, and they had learned to read there in half-day or all-day sessions. This schooling, along with some formal or informal apprenticeship, constituted an education for most American children up through at least the 1830's. By that time, a system of public schools was taking shape, so that training in literacy and computational skills became more widely available. In fact, Sunday schools themselves had helped to foster an idea which led to the American public schools, the idea that all children had a right to learn. The common public school came to be seen as a necessary institution for a democracy, in order that citizens might have the knowledge needed for effective self-government. It also was viewed as a powerful agent for socializing immigrants into the American mainstream and leveling their ethnic distinctions.

As the early Sunday schools had done what we would view as the "secular" work of teaching literacy skills, so the early public schools of the mid-

and late-nineteenth century did the "religious" work of teaching values, principles, and knowledge of the Bible. In Protestant America, the religious curriculum of the public schools was decidedly Protestant. Although Catholics, Jews, Orthodox Christians and other taxpayers found this objectionable, from about 1850 to the 1930's and even 1940's America's public schools imparted to their students a basic familiarity with Protestant Christianity. One historian writes, "The public school in fact was an evangelical Protestant parochial school."[19]

The widening availability of such public instruction brought further changes in the institution of the Sunday school. The mission schools and settlement houses seemed less necessary now that public schools undertook the tasks of making Americans out of foreigners and teaching them to read. On the other hand, the children of church members now needed to learn only the fine points of their own denominational and congregational life in their Sunday schools, because the public schools were giving them the basics of Christian belief and lifestyle. The Sunday school shrank back to an hour or two of devotional and instruction.

At the same time, Protestant Americans were organizing missionary efforts to carry the gospel overseas. Their concern for others was genuine, but they understood foreign cultures even less than they understood the immigrants arriving daily in America's own port cities. The 1905 International Sunday-School Convention heard an appeal on behalf of Japan which opened with these words:

> It is only a little country, filled with forty millions of little brown people, but it is the cynosure of the eyes of all nations. In 1854 Commodore Perry opened it, a veritable box of curios for the western world, whose curiosity for its contents has seemed insatiable.[20]

The same convention also heard about Egypt, the Arabs, the West Indies, "the Negro problem," and Mexico, where:

> Mexican children are lovable and teachable and easily interested. Bible stories are new to many and easily understood, because the country and customs are so like Palestine—the low, square houses, with the center patio or courtyard, the scarcity of fuel and water in some sections, the plain food of the common people, the slow methods of preparing the meal, plowing, etc., the great number of weary and heavy laden, the unfortunate beggar by the wayside, the lack of appreciation of the value of time, etc.[21]

To support the Sunday schools financially both at home and abroad, a network of aid societies developed. Through these, men and especially women who did not directly engage in the ministry of the word felt that they had some share in it. Such societies introduced Protestant America to the idea that both the poor in their midst and the people of other nations had some claim on the concern of Christians in the United States.

But Sunday schools and missions were not the only Protestant institutions promoting the ministry of the word. Adult education was fostered by movements like Chautauqua, named after a summer assembly on Lake Chautauqua in New York in 1874, and Baraca, a kind of men's Bible study and social organization begun in the 1890's. The Young Men's and Young Women's Christian Associations also did educational work. Denominational colleges and theological seminaries were being organized, first in the East, then across the nation from the early nineteenth century onward. Thanks to training received in these institutions, Sunday school workers and missionaries were emerging as professionals by the turn of the twentieth century. The founding of the Religious Education Association in 1903 marked the beginning of a new era of professionalism.

Methods. The institutionalization and professionalization of religious education at this period were new developments, but the older means of proclaiming and teaching God's word did not cease. Preaching, personal exhortation, and home instruction remained important means of passing on the gospel message. We have seen that word ministries and caring ministries went forward side by side in settlement work among the immigrants and other urban poor. But within intentional educational settings, the nineteenth century brought distinct methodological developments that were to have important effects upon twentieth-century educational practice. These are sometimes characterized as a movement away from "indoctrination" and toward "instruction."

To indoctrinate is to equip human minds and hearts with the truths of Christian faith and knowledge of the events of salvation history, so that people may live in righteousness and obedience to God. Indoctrination becomes manipulation when it is done so authoritatively that people assent to the truth of faith because of fear or the teacher's personal force rather than because of the intrinsic persuasiveness of the truths themselves. Manipulative indoctrination defeats the purpose of the ministry of the word, because it makes free response impossible.

This distinction was less clear to people at the beginning of the nineteenth century than it is to us today. To them the objective success of implanting information in minds seemed to imply the subjective success of winning the free assent of the minds to the truth of the knowledge. Memorization was the method of choice for indoctrination in the early 1800's.

Long passages of scripture (or of the catechism) were committed to memory, just as in medieval times, without much attempt at explanation. Beginning in the 1820's, various plans began to be proposed for limiting the amount of text to be absorbed at one time.

The Uniform Lesson Plan was adopted at the national Sunday school convention of 1872, and remains in use to the present day. A committee of scholars was appointed to choose a Bible text for study on each Sunday of the year, with the objective of covering the whole Bible in six or seven years. Every Sunday-school class everywhere on earth was to study the same text on the same day. No adaptation was made for age or location; moreover, selections were studied out of sequence and context.[22]

By the end of the century, the Uniform Lessons and the method of memorization were attracting criticism on several scores. Because use of the Lessons mandated episodic reading of the scripture, it fostered the beliefs that meaning is independent of context and that every part of the canon has value equal to that of any other part. But these beliefs were being seriously challenged by European and American theological scholars, whose works were being studied in the colleges and seminaries where the future leaders of the Sunday-school movement were being trained.

Their professional training embraced not only theology, but modern studies in psychology and pedagogy as well. Following the American philosopher of education John Dewey, religious education theorists asserted that experience was more important than memorization and could even be impeded by it. Emphasis on the child and his or her needs as the organizing principle of the curriculum led in 1908 to the adoption of a graded Sunday school system at the Twelfth National Convention. The child-centered and experience-centered methodology of the early twentieth century came to be known as "progressive religious education." Alongside that modern instructional practice, the traditional Bible study through memorization and indoctrination also continued in more conservative congregations and denominations.

Progressive educational principles had direct influence on Catholic catechetical practice at the turn of the century because of one crucial fact: religion was taught along with other subjects by the same teachers in the Catholic parish schools. Diocesan superintendents expected religion to be taught with the same attention to scientific principles of pedagogy that was demanded in mathematics or history, and in those subjects the parish schools had to meet the same standards of instruction that the states set up for public schools. Moreover, oftentimes the sisters who taught in the weekday parish school also taught Sunday school for Catholic children who attended public school; or, at least, helped to train others to do so. Therefore, Catholics experienced little dissonance between secular and religious teaching methods. Catholic children might memorize catechism answers, but those would be answers adapted to their level of understanding and accompanied by numerous applications to their own life experience.

Media. Institutional and methodological developments led to developments in the media of instruction. Schoolbooks published for use in the earliest public schools had unabashedly religious content. But as the teaching of religion increasingly was consigned to the Sunday schools, special materials were designed for them. One genre was the edifying story of a good boy or girl who died happily after a short life of suffering and virtue. Books of these stories were given as prizes to encourage attendance and good behavior in the Sunday school.

After the adoption of the Uniform Lesson Plan, publishers used the weekly texts to build curricular materials for the Sunday schools. The Uniform Lesson ㄴㄴ ㄴ 나나나 were sent to newspapers, and many papers featured weekly commentaries on the appointed lesson. The availability of innovative graded curricular materials helped promote the 1908 endorsement of graded instruction, which in turn led to publication of more graded materials.

Catholics had inherited both methods and media of instruction from Europe. The elite secondary schools of the early nineteenth century used pedagogical techniques little changed from those developed in the seventeenth century within teaching orders like the Jesuits, the Christian brothers, and the Visitation nuns. As the ethnic parishes developed their schools, they imported classic catechisms like those of Canisius and Bellarmine. German-language catechisms were printed in this country at mid-century.

When an official English-language catechism appeared after the Third Plenary Council of Baltimore in 1885, it was not well received. The German Catholic press found a lot to criticize in the manual, which had been produced hurriedly and without consultation with the bishops of the council. Summarizing arguments against the Baltimore Catechism appearing in the German-language magazine *Pastoral Blatt* in 1885 and 1886, one historian writes:

> The work was pedagogically unsuitable for children . . . because of its incomprehensible language, its small size (children are more comfortable with a larger volume), the disproportionate number of yes-no questions (91 of 421), the stunting of thought processes involved in questions that contain complete answers, and finally, the monotony of the entire text which gave equal treatment to all matters.

> More importantly . . . the catechism was theologically weak on several scores: the brevity of its treatment of God and the angels, the absence of any consideration of divine providence, only one question about the resurrection . . . and insufficient attention to the Holy Spirit.[23]

Numerous other Catholic catechisms were printed in the late nineteenth century, a fact which further emphasizes the community's dissatisfaction with the official one. A movement to revise the Baltimore Catechism stalled when word came that Roman authorities were planning to issue a catechism of their own. Although such a document failed to materialize, the Baltimore Catechism was not revised until 1941. By that time, over one hundred other American Catholic catechisms and manuals had been printed. Most of those appearing in the twentieth century offered graded series of books, but the catechism format remained dominant in Catholic instructional materials until the Second Vatican Council.

The catechism controversy highlights the importance of the press in nineteenth-century American religious communities. The ethnic Catholic press was a vital link for language groups whose members were dispersed on farms or in several cities. Had the American bishops been able to continue to administer the Catholic Church at the national level after Baltimore III, the ethnic press could have mobilized language-group constituencies spread out across many dioceses. However, the imposition of the decentralized diocesan form of administration in the late nineteenth century divided Chicago's Germans from Cincinnati's, and Baltimore's Poles from New York's, making it futile to build coalitions for the advancement of German or Polish interests nationwide. Diocesan papers, printed in English, emerged as organs of communication for the dioceses. A few nationally circulating English-language Catholic journals and newspapers were independent forums for exchange of ideas; others promoted the interests of the sponsoring agency or religious order.

Among Protestants, religious journals were a major means of proposing and arguing theological opinions. Especially on the frontier, they became voices of the evangelistic revivals sweeping through the river towns and the backcountry. Like-minded people who might have no other contact with one another nevertheless felt that they were members of one community by virtue of the religious journals which they received. The Disciples of Christ liked to point out that God gave them editors instead of bishops.

Content. With denominations multiplying and opinions proliferating in nineteenth-century America, it is difficult to define any characteristic content of the ministry of the word. Perhaps its most distinctive features were a separation of the realm of religion from the realm of everyday business, along with, paradoxically, an almost religious faith in the goodness and progress of the secular American society. American civil religion was born as the belief that Americans were the biblical chosen people inheriting the promise of favors from God.

Protestants agreed to make the Bible the dominant source and content of their teaching. Catholics favored the catechism. If religious education stressed character formation, the character traits promoted were the very ones which insured survival on the frontier: self-reliance, courage, neighborliness, honesty, and hard work. Protestants confused the kingdom of God with the United States; but Catholics confused it with the parish. Striving, against nativist bigotry, to become even more American than the Anglo Protestants, Catholics designed their teaching to produce good citizens, obedient both to Washington and to Rome. Critical thought was not encouraged.

Official Catholic teaching had been cemented at the sixteenth-century Council of Trent. In the nineteenth century Rome added the dogmas of the Immaculate Conception and papal infallibility, condemned "Americanism," and set the church's teaching authority against a variety of liberal or progressive ideas. Yet some influential American Catholics, like Isaac Hecker, continued to work for a wedding of the American frontier spirit and the traditions of Catholicism. With Leo XIII's pro-labor encyclical came a turning point after which Catholic American citizens increasingly participated in public life and policy-making in this country.

Social issues such as fair housing, equal opportunity in employment, human rights, international justice, hunger, and peace have become areas in which the Christian witness of Catholics and Protestants once again can speak with one voice. If Christians in America still deem themselves a chosen people, nevertheless they have discovered that they are chosen not for divine favors but for responsibilities, not for conquest but for service. They carry the gospel into a future which needs its care and its celebration, not just its words.

LEGACY OF THE NINETEENTH-CENTURY CHURCH

- Sunday schools
- parochial schools
- religious communities of women committed to ministries of word and care
- political action by women

- the YMCA and the YWCA
- many denominational colleges and universities
- the Baltimore Catechism
- the Uniform Lesson Plan
- ethnic parishes
- religious journalism, and many religious journals
- revival meetings
- Protestant overseas missions
- denominationally sponsored hospitals and other charitable institutions
- Christian witness against recognized social evils
- several indigenous American Protestant denominations
- theological seminaries
- Negro Spirituals
- papal infallability and the dogma of the Immaculate Conception

Notes for Chapter Ten

1. See Sydney E. Ahlstrom, *A Religious History of the American People,* volume 1, (Garden City, N.Y.: Doubleday, Image Books, 1975), p. 525. The depiction of the nineteenth-century American churches in this chapter is drawn from this work, along with its second volume, and from: Kenneth Scott Latourette, *A History of Christianity,* volume 2 (San Francisco: Harper & Row, 1953, 1975); Rosemary Radford Ruether and Rosemary Skinner Keller, editors, *Women and Religion in America: A Documentary History,* volumes 1 and 2 (San Francisco: Harper & Row, 1981, 1983); Martin E. Marty, *Pilgrims in Their Own Land: 500 Years of Religion in America* (Boston: Little, Brown, 1984); *The Development of the Sunday School, 1780–1905,* The Official Report of the Eleventh International Sunday-School Convention, Toronto, Canada, June 23–27, 1905 (Boston: International Sunday-School Association, 1905); Jack L. Seymour, *From Sunday School to Church School: Continuities in Protestant Church Education in the United States, 1860–1929* (Lanham, Md.: University Press of America, 1982); Michael Warren, editor, *Sourcebook for Modern Catechetics* (Winona, Minnesota: Christian Brothers Publications, 1983); Jack L. Seymour, Robert T. O'Gorman, and Charles R. Foster, *The Church in the Education of the Public: Refocusing the Task of Religious Education* (Nashville: Abingdon Press, 1984).

2. See Rosemary Skinner Keller, "Lay Women in the Protestant Tradition," *Women and Religion in America,* volume 1, pp. 242–93.

3. K.S. Latourette, *History of Christianity,* p. 1019.

4. See J. L. Seymour, R. T. O'Gorman, and C. R. Foster, *The Church in the Education of the Public*, pp. 69–70.

5. R. S. Keller, "Lay Women in the Protestant Tradition," p. 247.

6. For a survey of the sisters' contributions, see Mary Ewens, "The Leadership of Nuns in American Catholicism," *Women and Religion in America*, volume 1, pp. 101–49. The Battle of Gettysburg was fought almost on the doorstep of the first American community of Catholic sisters in Emmitsburg, Maryland, and ninety-one of those sisters worked as nurses in the military hospital near the battlefield.

7. Quoted in S. E. Ahlstrom, *Religious History*, pp. 526–27.

8. Martin E. Marty recounts that the death of a French diplomat in 1780 at George Washington's headquarters obliged members of Congress to attend a memorial mass for him. Though some could not bring themselves to do it, [m]any prominent people did attend and lived to report how different the service was from what they had been taught to expect. See *Pilgrims In Their Own Land*, p. 143.

9. See Sydney Ahlstrom, *Religious History*, volume 2, pp. 493–95.

10. See Horace Bushnell, *Christian Nurture* (New York: Charles Scribner, 1861; Grand Rapids, Michigan: Baker Book House, 1979), and Henry Clay Trumbull, *The Sunday School: Its Origin, Mission, Methods, and Auxiliaries* (Philadelphia: John D. Wattles, 1888).

11. "The Problem of the Negro," in *The Development of the Sunday School, 1780–1905*, pp. 291–93. M. C. B. Mason was corresponding secretary of the Freedmen's Aid Society of the Methodist Episcopal Church.

12. *The Development of the Sunday School, 1780–1905*, p. 308.

13. Mother Theresa Gerhardinger became foundress of the School Sisters of Notre Dame. The portions of her letter appear on p. 126 of *Women and Religion in America*, volume 1.

14. See Sidney Ahlstrom, *Religious History*, p. 413.

15. The First Provincial Council of Baltimore called for establishment of schools, but the wording of the decree (number 34) shows that charitable institutions for the poor are meant. It would be anachronistic to project the parochial school system back into this 1829 decree.

16. James McMaster, editor of the *Freeman's Journal*. See J. L. Seymour, R. T. O'Gorman, and C. R. Foster, *The Church in the Education of the Public*, pp. 85–6.

17. Charles Gallaudet Trumbull, "The Nineteenth Century Sunday-school," *The Development of the Sunday School*, pp. 16–7.

18. Jack Seymour presents the case for making this distinction on pp. 29–34 of *From Sunday School to Church School*.

19. Jack Seymour, *From Sunday School to Church School*, p. 36.

20. See James A.B. Scherer, "The Duty of Young America to Young Japan," *The Development of the Sunday School*, p. 367.

21. See Mary Foster Bryner, "Our Neighbor—Mexico," *The Development of the Sunday School*, pp. 484–85.

22. This can be observed in the list of lessons from 1872 to 1906 given on pp. 49–81 of *The Development of the Sunday School*. The work of the lesson committee is described by H.M. Hamill in "The Uniform Lesson: The Genesis of the International Sunday-school Lesson," pp. 37–48.

23. See Mary Charles Bryce, "The Baltimore Catechism—Origin and Reception," *Sourcebook for Modern Catechetics*, p. 140.

Chapter Eleven

Conclusion

This portrait of the teaching church now comes to a pause. The gospel continues to become what it will be, but we must break off its story at this point. In telling the story of the gospel, we have reconstructed eight versions of it from the public Jesus' own image that God is taking over, the apostles' proclamation that God has raised Jesus, and then the teachings of the churches of the fourth, seventh, tenth, thirteenth, sixteenth, and nineteenth centuries. Each of these reconstructions, or cross-sections of church history, has been a portrait of the church in the act of delivering the gospel message. The first two of them, the ones represented in the New Testament, have been regarded as definitive models for all subsequent proclamation. Nevertheless, the later versions are not simply equivalent to the biblical model. Time is such that, paradoxically, to be "the same" those messages also had to be "different."

Were there no differences, the gospel would not be true, for as we have seen, the gospel is a message signifying and accomplishing the transformation of human being. It changes the world into which it comes, and it changes the media which deliver it. A static gospel would be a counterfeit gospel—a contradiction in terms. To draw a portrait of the teaching church, then, is not to try to show that the message and its institutional bearer have somehow been preserved untouched like a fossil or a mummy. Rather, it is to detect and account for continuities persisting throughout the time when gospel transformation has been happening. We have discerned three of these enduring structures of ecclesial life: activities of care for human need, celebration of intimacy with the "Abba" of Jesus, and reflective proclamation in words of what God has done in Jesus. Our portrait has been drawn to show that these activities, working together, constitute the ecclesial link between Jesus and the church. The persistence of these activities, along with their power to transform human life, count toward certifying the truth of the gospel message. The circumstances of the common life of Christians tend to verify and validate the gospel symbols which draw Christians together. The church, as medium, not only *is* the message but also guarantees the reliability of the message that it is.

Yet a portrait is not a proof. The church may very well assert and proclaim that God, the Father of Jesus who raised him from the dead, is taking over the governance of human affairs from the inside out. But that claim cannot be proven, in the logical and scientific sense of the word. Nevertheless the claim is meaningful. What portraiture gives us are the unfolding meanings, implications, and plausibility of that claim.

Nor has this book "proved" that the three activities of word, care, and celebration are necessary and sufficient for the effective proclamation of the gospel in every age.[1] We have merely described *how* they work *when* they work. Those three activities were proposed at the outset as a heuristic model to guide our investigation. Our use of this model has been fruitful, and our findings may warrant certain decisions about the future of ministry. However, the story we have told by no means supports anything like a formal deduction of the essential nature of the church. (Indeed, whether such a logical tour de force remains possible in our century is debatable.)

What, then, are the implications of the portrait we have drawn? What is now understood about the church and the gospel that was unclear at the outset? First, many facts have been set forth: names, dates, events, and so on. Second, intelligible patterns of relation among those facts have been proposed. These two contributions constitute the making of any history. But our story has also been a portrait, and in portraying the being of the church it has attempted to do something more: to discern the distinctive lifelines of the church's existence, and, within these, to discern the symbolic efficacy of ecclesial transformation as it supports faith. Those lifelines, as we have seen, are lines of communication: the evangelizing activities of care, celebration, and word. Mutual reflective interdependence among these three is what supports and secures faith.

In other words, if faith is a kind of knowing or grasp of reality, the mind continually checks to see that its grasp is secure.[2] In the first place, it checks to see whether its beliefs lead to actions that are worthy, good, and productive. It evaluates other people's beliefs according to the practical applications to which they lead. People collectively submit their beliefs to critical review in terms of the benefits which they bring in furthering the wellbeing of other people. Works of care for human need tend to warrant the beliefs which inspire them. Therefore, inasmuch as our portrait has disclosed the numerous caring ministries brought forth out of the proclamation of the gospel, it reassures the mind that the gospel's grasp of reality is viable and that Christian faith is warranted.

Yet because illusions, too, sometimes lead to beneficial actions, the mind needs something more. So the mind also checks into the logical status and coherence of its beliefs. The mind examines its own nature as a knowing subject, the nature of objective reality as something supposedly available to the mind, and the plausibility of the assumption that subject can grasp object at all. The mind comes to terms with the fact that to know is to create as well as to grasp, for subjects contribute to the very reality of the realities in which they participate. Through such critical reflection the mind clarifies the factors at play in the act of knowing. We see that we know through symbols, which are grasped in ever more complex ways as the mind matures. Concrete and conventional intelligence emerge as two ways of grasping symbol (or rather, grasping the world *through* symbol). Critical understanding attends to the dynamics of this grasping itself (as we are attending to it in this very paragraph), and conjunctive intelligence appreciates that the mind itself is grasped by and arises out of certain central symbols. It becomes clear to conjunctive understanding that when religious symbol embraces the human mind, powerful effects may emerge in the dimensions of personal presence and political power. The mind is partnered with intelligibility that dwells beyond the mind yet also within its own depths. This intimacy, established and celebrated through symbol, becomes empowerment. People collectively submit their beliefs to critical review in terms of the viability of the intimacy which these symbols establish between God and humankind, and the transubstantiation of humankind thereby effected. Our portrait has supplied theoretical underpinnings for the efficacy of the gospel by reporting the efficacy of the worshipful celebrations of divine-human intimacy that have accompanied it. The basic Christian symbols are symbols of change, and they affect human existence no less than bread, wine, and water.

Yet these two validations—that through evaluation of actions and that through enjoyment of the realized intimacy—still do not satisfy the mind, for illusions can also be illusions of intimacy and transformation. The mind goes further and checks into the facticity of what is; that is, it looks into the mirror of the past. Knowing that reality is both fact and artifact, the critical mind fails in its attempt to find any nugget of certitude, any founding event that might prove the validity of all subsequent claims. The past is simply not available to us in the form of discrete events identifiable apart from the narratives bearing them. The past, the real, comes to us only through layers of receptions, that is, through the traditioning of people who handed on what they received *along with* their own interpretations of it. Even the texts of the New Testament are accounts of activities of God to which we have no direct access. Where the critical mind is frustrated by what it takes to be the unavailability of founding events, the conjunctive mind rejoices in the partnering of human reception with divine initiative, and gratefully receives the tradition *through* the tradition—knowing that this is the only plausible way for it to reach us. The meaning of the gospel is not only what it could have meant to Jesus and to Paul, but also what their meanings meant to Augustine, Boniface, Hroswitha, Cyril and Methodius, Bonaventure, the Beguines, Luther, and Seton. Our portrait of the teaching church declines to distill from their receptions of the gospel any such thing as a body of unchanging truths. We have sought instead to discern something even more precious: the reliability of the good news in the hands, heads, and hearts of those who have incarnated it. Truths, like all brittle things, are fragile and require elaborate protections; but the process of truth itself is tough, organic, resilient, and trustworthy.

As the mind checks to make sure that its beliefs grasp reality securely, therefore, it checks into: 1) the actions supported by the beliefs, 2) theories of reality or realization implied in the beliefs, and 3) concordance between the beliefs and those held by other people in the tradition. No one, and no two, of these inquiries alone would be sufficient to secure faith. But when all three are conducted together in a coordinated campaign of reflection, we have a method for ascertaining whether the beliefs are justified. They may be justified only provisionally, for the inquiries which validate them are ongoing, just as the gospel's story goes on. I assert this not as something "proved" by this book, but rather as something reliably discerned through our investigations. Faith is always a thinking, checking, questioning faith, and thinking is one of the motors moving the church into its future.

The teaching church needs to be taught to think effectively, wisely, and faithfully as it faces the challenges of the oncoming centuries. It needs to think about its experiences of care, word, and celebration in the past, and to draw out their implications. Were we to compile a list headed "legacy of the twentieth-century church," it would have to contain a good many questions. We hand on a legacy of unresolved issues like the following, but we also hand on the means of addressing them.

■ What role will magisterial authority play in the churches of the future? The magisterium, or teaching authority, is a ministry of the word. In the past, it has functioned according to whatever theories of knowledge were culturally and intellectually accepted. First-century Christians exercised magisterial authority when they wrote down definitive versions of what God had done in Jesus, the Gospel narratives. Magisterium was the ability to tell a story. Fourth- and fifth-century Christians experienced the magisterium in dogmatic definitions by ecumenical councils. Magisterium was the ability to interpret the story in philosophical categories. Early medieval Christians experienced the magisterium as a missionary outreach among Germanic and Slavic nations. Magisterium was the ability to chop down a sacred oak, evict its god, and carve it into a statue of Jesus. Christians in nineteenth-century America experienced the magisterium in the organization of institutions of learning: Sunday schools, parish schools, denominational colleges and universities. Magisterium was the ability to nurture the life of the mind as it engaged with the Christian tradition in building the new nation. How, then, will Christians experience the magisterium in our future? Will magisterium be the ability to support the institutions of learning already brought forth? Will it nurture and affirm the inquiries that take place within them, as these reflect upon the interplay of care, word, and celebration in the churches?

■ Whom will the teaching church teach in the future? Will the church be "catholic," that is, universal, in its outreach to all peoples? Will it speak to women and to ethnic minorities? Will it find ways to incarnate the gospel in terms available to the diverse cultures of the third world? Will it find ways to shake the complacency of powerful peoples who consider themselves already Christian? Will it address a message of individual salvation to individuals, or will it be brave enough to teach governments and corporations? In the American political system, will the teaching church use its voice to influence the making of public policy in favor of families and other disadvantaged groups? Will it model justice and compassion in its ministries of care? Will it model intimacy and fellowship in its ministries of celebration? Can the churches develop innovative ways to support academic instruction in religious traditions at secular colleges and universities? To whom will the teaching church listen as it prepares to teach?

■ Who will do the teaching of the teaching church in our future? How are men and women being recruited today to take up this important ministry? How are they being supported during their training, and how are they being professionally trained? Will these teachers be thinkers? Will they be able to dialogue with the scientists, poets, farmers, technicians, artists, laborers, managers, care-givers, and writers of the twenty-first century? Will the church's teachers understand the basic assumptions of their contemporaries about what makes truth, what makes reality, what makes credibility? Do the churches intend to pay their teachers a just salary and provide for their continuing professional development? Are the personal and financial resources of the church distributed wisely among the three ministries of word, of care, and of sacrament?

■ Where do lay people fit into the teaching church? How will their experiences enrich the versions of the gospel that are even now taking shape? On what grounds do we designate some Christians as "lay"? Does "lay" mean "lame," in the sense that one has received a deficient form of baptism and therefore is unable to teach? Exactly how many "lame" men and women can the churches of our future afford to have?

What will the churches do to empower lay people to think in faith—not only the professionally trained teachers, but also the rank and file from whom volunteer teachers are called forth?

■ What administrative structures does the teaching church of our future need? At the diocesan or judicatory level, what resource personnel, materials, and programs will we provide? What staff relationships must be fostered between those who oversee teaching and those who oversee the ministries of care and of sacramental celebration? At the parish or congregational level, who bosses whom? Does the sacramental minister exercise one-way authority over ministers of care and word? If all three roles are invested in one person, do they all get equal portions of his or her time and energy? How will churches with international membership harmonize their allegiance to their overseas brothers and sisters with their concerns for the little ones here at home? How long, and how effectively, can an oligarchy administer the religious lives of people who live the rest of their lives in democratic or merit-based organizations? How will the churches of our future adjust their own internal administration to make their teaching more believeable?

■ What will the teaching churches look like? What kind of buildings will be constructed or remodeled to house the teaching ministry of the church? Should they look just like public school buildings? Will congregations dedicate building space to education at all? The church's teaching refers to the integrity of its present ecclesial life as well as to the heritage of its past. Will church buildings therefore provide space for ministries of care as well as for celebration of sacramental worship? Will those attending church school be able to see that the church also houses facilities to feed the hungry, clothe the naked, and counsel the troubled, as well as to celebrate the liturgy? Can the churches find ways to continue building denominational colleges and universities, when these are becoming so expensive and there are so many other demands on the church's resources? Will the church teach by sponsoring the construction of housing for the economically disadvantaged and the elderly? Will it open its doors for latchkey and daycare programs for the children of working mothers, and for senior daycare? Will denominationally sponsored hospitals be run for profit or for service? And what truths will these decisions teach?

■ Will the churches teach together, or against one another? Can facilities and resources be pooled for interdenominational programs of Bible study, youth activities, lectures on current events, and so forth? Will the Sunday school be organized primarily to insure the continuation and growth of the sponsoring congregation, or will it broadcast the gospel to the world at large? Will the parish grade school be permitted to drain the congregation's resources, undercutting its ability to teach all its members and all its neighbors? How long, and how creditably, can churches teach that the table of the Lord is not to be open to all Christians?

■ Where will the church of our future find its artists, poets, and composers? Will there be opportunities for aesthetic experience in connection with our worship, teaching, and care? Will the churches teach the gospel as something beautiful as well as something true and good? Will we devote time and funding to design congregational space in ways conducive to aesthetic vision? Who is teaching the future church's writers to write, its singers to sing? Where are tomorrow's Christian journalists, novelists, and musicians learning their crafts today? Who will there be to dream our dreams for us when the twentieth century's dreamers have fallen asleep?

■ What will the teaching church do when people cease to read? Already our society is called "post-literate" because so many people prefer electronic media over printed ones. The last time Western culture experienced a shift in media use of this magnitude was the sixteenth century, when printed materials first became widely available. Largely because the churches of that era failed to understand the great difference this change would make in the communication of the gospel, Christianity at that time split into Protestant and Catholic factions. That was not quite five hundred years ago, roughly twenty generations. First Protestant, then Catholic Christians have become accustomed to reading the Bible for themselves. Christian education and most curricular materials depend upon that fact. Yet ours may be the last literate generation, the last who are able to read easily. What media will carry the gospel message to the post-literate people of our future? How are the churches learning to communicate in the media of videotape and audiotape? Are they investigating the use of electronic bulletin boards and access to cable systems? Will the churches also recover the skills of teaching through traditional nonverbal media such as artworks, architecture, music, and the sacramental liturgy? In projecting the image of Jesus as symbol of God's love, can the churches overcome the growing resistance to symbolic communication among people increasingly jaded by television commercials?

These are tough and perhaps daunting questions. However the endurance of the gospel through almost twenty centuries of teaching gives us cause to hope. Ultimately our hope is in the promise of Jesus that a rather foolishly parental God is even now taking over on this planet and straightening things out. Our survey of these centuries persuades me that it is so.

Notes for Chapter Eleven

1. In my opinion, the necessity of precisely these three activities has been demonstrated by Edward Farley in *Ecclesial Reflection* (Philadelphia: Fortress Press, 1982), by means of an *eidetic* analysis of the being of the church. Farley's eidetics supplied the outline for the *empirical* (i.e., historical) analysis attempted in this book. See above, chapter two.

2. The threefold checking of the validity of beliefs which I will suggest here is a simplified version of Francis Schüssler Fiorenza's foundational theology, which employs a method of seeking "reflective equilibrium" among three interdependent inquiries. When one checks into the practices supported by a belief, one is seeking "retroductive warrants" for the belief, in Fiorenza's terminology. When one checks out the logical coherence of a belief, one is investigating its "background theories," and when one checks out a belief's conformity with tradition and history, one is engaging in "hermeneutical reconstruction" of the belief. See *Foundational Theology: Jesus and the Church* (New York: Crossroad, 1984), especially the summary on pp. 301–11.

Index